A

FRAMEWORK

FOR

SURVIVAL

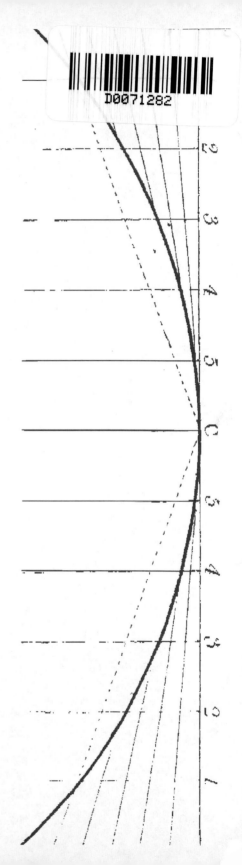

A

FRAMEWORK

FOR

SURVIVAL

*Health, Human Rights
and Humanitarian Assistance
in Conflicts and Disasters*

REVISED AND UPDATED

Edited by

KEVIN M. CAHILL, M.D.

Foreword by Kofi Annan

A joint publication of Routledge and
the Center for International Health and Cooperation

ROUTLEDGE
New York   London

Published in 1999 by
Routledge
29 West 35th Street
New York, NY 10001

Published in Great Britain in 1999 by
Routledge
11 New Fetter Lane
London EC4P 4EE

Printed in the United States of America on acid-free paper.
Design and composition: Jack Donner

A framework for survival : health, human rights, and humanitarian assistance
    in conflicts and disasters / edited by Kevin M. Cahill—Rev. and updated.
        p.   cm.
"A joint publication of Routledge and the Center for International Health
    and Cooperation."
ISBN 0–415–92234–8 (cloth). — ISBN 0–415–92235–6 (pbk.)
1. Disaster medicine—Congresses.   2. Medical assistance—Congresses.
    3. Human rights—Congresses.   4. Humanitarian assistance—Congresses.
    I. Cahill, Kevin M.
RA645.5.F73   1999
363.34'8—dc21   99–20511
                                                            CIP

For Joan Durcan

*and all those who devote their
lives to the service of others*

CONTENTS

ACKNOWLEDGMENTS

The first edition of this book was graciously reviewed and the text was widely used in universities around the world. But there have been new crises and new academic analyses since the first edition, and this volume reflects those experiences and lessons. There are four new chapters, and all the other chapters in this edition have been completely rewritten and updated. I express my gratitude to each of the remarkable list of contributors—all have field experience and hold senior positions, and yet they generously gave their time to contribute to this text that will, hopefully, serve a new generation of students and international-assistance, human-rights and foreign-policy workers as well as people around the world who are searching for a new framework to sustain us as we begin a new millennium.

The Directors of the Center for International Health and Cooperations (CIHC) offered their wisdom, support and in some instances (Vance, Owen, Farah, Eliasson) chapters for this book. The Executive Secretary of the CIHC, Mrs. Renée Cahill, made pleasant and possible the difficult task of pursuing delinquent authors and helping to edit and collate the chapters into a coherent text.

Finally, I wish to thank Ms. Amy Shipper and her colleagues at Routledge for their commitment to this series (to also include *Clearing the Fields: Solutions to the Global Landmine Crisis* and *Preventive Diplomacy: Stopping Wars before They Start*), for their editorial comments, and for a rare flexibility that I had come to expect only in the midst of humanitarian crises.

LIST OF ACRONYMS

ACC	Administrative Committee on Coordination
AIDS	Acquired Immune Deficiency Syndrome
AMA	American Medical Association
ASEAN	Association of Southeast Asian Nations
BRAC	Bangladesh Rural Advancement Committee
BWI	Bosnian Women's Initiative
CAP	Consolidated Appeals Process
CARE	Cooperative for Assistance and Relief Everywhere
CD	Conference on Disarmament
CDC	Centers for Disease Control
CERF	Central Emergency Revolving Fund
CFCs	chlorofluorocarbons
CIHC	Center for International Health and Cooperation
CIS	Commonwealth of Independent States
CMCA	Commission for Mediation, Conciliation and Arbitration (OAU)
CMR	crude mortality rate
CNN	Cable News Network
COPC	community-oriented primary care
CRC	Convention on the Rights of the Child
CSCE	Conference on Security and Cooperation in Europe
DHA	Department of Humanitarian Affairs
DPA	Department of Political Affairs
DPKO	Department of Peace-Keeping Operations
ECHO	European Community Humanitarian Office
ECOSOC	Economic and Social Council
ECOWAS	Economic Community of Western African States
EPIET	European Programme for Intervention Epidemiology
ERC	Emergency Relief Coordinator
EU	European Union
FFW	Food for Work projects
GATT	General Agreement on Tarriffs and Trade
GDP	gross domestic product
GNP	gross national product
HEWS	Humanitarian Early-Warning System
HIV	Human Immunodeficiency Virus
IASC	Inter-Agency Standing Committee
ICC	International Criminal Court
ICJ	International Court of Justice
ICRC	International Committee of the Red Cross
IDHA	International Diploma in Humanitarian Assistance
IFOR	NATO Implementation Force
IFRC	International Federation of the Red Cross

IGADD	Inter-Governmental Authority against Drought and Desertification
IHL	International Humanitarian Law
IHMEC	International Health Medical Education Consortium
ILO	International Labor Organization
IMF	International Monetary Fund
IOM	International Organization for Migration
IRC	International Rescue Committee
MCPMR	Mechanism for Conflict Prevention, Management and Resolution (OAU)
MIA	missing in action
MINURSO	UN Mission for the Organization of a Referendum in Western Sahara
MSF	Médecins Sans Frontières (Doctors Without Borders)
NATO	North Atlantic Treaty Organization
NGO	nongovernmental organization
NMOG	Neutral Military Observer Group
OAS	Organization of African States
OAU	Organization of African Unity
OCHA	Office for the Coordination of Humanitarian Affairs
ODA	Official Development Assistance
OECD	Organization for Economic Cooperation
OLS	Operation Somali Lifeline
ORS	oral rehydration salt
ORT	oral rehydration therapy
ORW	oral rehydration worker
OSCE	Organization for Security and Cooperation in Europe
PHR	Physicians for Human Rights
POP	people-oriented planning
POW	prisoner of war
RUF	Revolutionary United Front
SAM	Sanctions Assistance Mission
SFOR	Stabilization Force (in Yugoslavia)
SNM	Somali National Movement
STD	sexually transmitted disease
TBA	traditional birth attendants
UCI	universal child immunization
UNAMIR	UN Assistance Mission in Rwanda
UNASOG	UN Aouzou Strip Observer Group
UNAVEM	UN Angola Verification Mission
UNCTAD	UN Conference on Trade and Development
UNDP	UN Development Program
UNEF	UN Emergency Fund
UNHCR	UN High Commissioner for Refugees
UNICEF	UN Children's Fund
UNITAF	Unified Task Force (Somalia)
UNOMUR	UN Observer Mission into Uganda and Rwanda
UNOSOM	UN Operations in Somalia
UNPROFOR	UN Protection Force (Yugoslavia)
UNSCOM	UN Special Committee
UNTAC	UN International Transitional Authority in Cambodia
UNTAG	UN Transition Assistance Group (Namibia)
USAID	United States Agency for International Development
WEU	Western European Union
WFP	World Food Program
WHO	World Health Organization

FOREWORD

H.E. Mr. Kofi Annan
Secretary-General of the United Nations

From the Balkans to the Sudan, from Afghanistan to Central Africa, the world is confronted with humanitarian emergencies that seem only to grow in horror and pain. Wars and natural disasters, often joined in a terrible combination, are causing massive loss of life, tremendous suffering and great dislocations of peoples and groups. The need for effective humanitarian assistance has never been greater.

In all these situations, we in the humanitarian community must ask ourselves: Are we doing enough? Are we helping those most in need or just those most immediately in reach? Is our aid the right aid for the emergency in question? Is it affecting a conflict in a way that may perpetuate it rather than end it? These are the questions that we must keep asking to ensure that we not only do good, but do right as well.

This underlines the importance of one lesson of our humanitarian experience. That is that humanitarian aid does not exist in a vacuum. Only rarely are we confronted with a "natural" disaster in which man-made disasters of war and tyranny do not also play a part. From the Great Lakes of Central Africa to Bosnia, we have learned that while the humanitarian imperative is sacred, there is also a humanitarian dilemma.

This is the dilemma that too often has forced us to provide food and clothing to the victims of conflict as well as to its architects. It is the dilemma that too often allows combatants to use humanitarian aid and its recipients as tools in war. It is the dilemma that too often has made camps created for the needy and vulnerable havens for extremists and bases from which they could continue their acts of hatred. It is the dilemma, finally, that makes humanitarian assistance only a poor substitute for preventive political action.

One thing is clear, however: the humanitarian dilemma has made the global humanitarian mission more important, not less. I hope, therefore, that students of humanitarian assistance will find renewed inspiration in the essays in *A Framework for Survival* and join the United Nations' struggle to alleviate human suffering.

INTRODUCTION

Kevin M. Cahill, M.D.

We live in an era when the very foundations of civilized society are shifting or collapsing. National sovereignty is no longer accepted as an absolute right or as a shield from enquiry into local oppression. Rather than being protected in times of conflict, women and children have now become primary targets in avenging ancient hatreds and the victims of violence that is justified by grossly misreading the lessons of religion and history. Instant communications make human-rights violations and widespread physical suffering matters of personal concern; they can never again be relegated to the shadows of our minds, for now willful inaction makes us participants in crimes against humanity. The speed of travel has irrevocably altered the efficacy of standard quarantine protection—Ebola, plague and bioterrorism are very real threats to people all over the world.

Many recent crises demonstrate why humanitarian issues should be absolutely central in America's foreign policy. These issues are usually considered—if they are considered at all—as peripheral concerns by those who formulate and implement our overseas agendas. Yet I offer the following examples:

1. When Ebola breaks out in the Congo or plague erupts in India, the old logic of quarantine is now irrelevant. The speed of travel and the mass movement of people have destroyed any assurance of isolation of, or protection against the spread of, deadly diseases. Epidemics can threaten our basic security as surely as nuclear weapons, yet the imbalance in government spending is appalling. In the 1997 Foreign Aid Bill, 20 times more dollars are allocated for military aid to other nations than are set aside for all foreign disaster assistance.
2. Consider the impact of HIV infection and AIDS in Africa. Are these

purely medical concerns? The *Washington Post* wrote an editorial about a preliminary study on my desk documenting that more than 50 percent of the armed forces in seven African nations are HIV-positive. This is not a surprising figure when you consider that soldiers are young, relatively wealthy, mobile, and have a tradition of imposing their will along the highways and chaotic areas that characterize so much of turbulent Africa. But if you simultaneously consider that the very stability of most African states is predicated, for better or worse, on the military, then you must conclude that the foundation of these nations is fragile indeed, resting on a group of very sick people with a predictable and very short life expectancy who hold power in areas where the diagnosis and medications for AIDS are simply not available. The average annual health budget in many poor African countries is between $5 and $10 per capita, while the cost for antiviral drugs alone exceeds $10,000 per person per year.

3. To further complicate the African AIDS disaster and to emphasize the diplomatic implications of health issues, it should be noted that there are no preemployment HIV tests when the United Nations deploys armed divisions from endemic zones to be part of their Blue Beret forces. Therefore, troops dedicated to peacekeeping are undoubtedly simultaneously contributing to the dissemination of fatal infections.

We must devise innovative methods and better diagnostic, therapeutic and preventive techniques to deal with challenges. If we fail, already existent problems will multiply just as surely as a microbe flourishes in fertile ground. We no longer have the luxury of ignoring humanitarian crises for, even viewed selfishly, we know they have the potential to destroy our own and our children's lives. One would have to be blind or arrogant or very foolish to ignore so many obvious disasters-in-waiting.

The number and severity of humanitarian crises is rapidly escalating in our post-Cold-War era, where the perverse stability of East-West superpower politics can sometimes seem preferable to the chaos that now prevails in "failed states" that dot the world. Civil wars have largely replaced formal conflicts between nations. In World War I, 90 percent of those injured or killed were military combatants, while now civilians account for over 90 percent of the victims.

International humanitarian laws, which were established to provide rules of war, are rarely recognized and are certainly not observed in civil wars. International laws and the Geneva Convention were composed for an earlier era when state governments officially represented combatants. Now childhood warriors with AK-47s rule the roads, and clans use ethnic cleansing as a solution to borders that, according to one's own peculiar view, had been artificially imposed by a historical process they would never forget nor forgive. Today there are more internally displaced persons than international refugees.

In noncomplex emergencies such as floods or earthquakes, where a stable government exists, it is responsible for—and understandably expects to—handle all relief activities. International-assistance workers must accept the traditions and rules of functioning sovereign nations or invite confrontation and painful rejection. Aid offered without respect for the rights of an independent people will almost always result in counterproductive misunderstanding, damaging both donor and recipient.

But in complex humanitarian emergencies, security concerns and political decisions are an intimate part of any relief response. Complex humanitarian emergencies are characterized by the total disruption or destruction of the existing public infrastructure, leading to a situation where there is simply no accepted government and no functioning health, transportation, police or welfare system. There is, therefore, no recourse for those caught in the cross fires of war or chaos, nor for international humanitarian workers willing but often unable to help. There is usually nowhere to hide, and those who must stay are the most vulnerable— women, children and the elderly. Humanitarian-assistance workers are no longer seen by hostile communities as respected and protected neutral healers; increasingly they become the hostages and victims of an anarchy they cannot control.

So we enter an era where humanitarian assistance—whether by international agencies such as the United Nations or the Red Cross, or by governments, or by local and international voluntary agencies—can no longer be delivered using accepted ground rules by which earlier generations could play. The foundations of many societies are eroding, and the bases for a new structure of nations have yet to emerge. Furthermore, the aid community and donors have also lost their innocence and realize that they must carefully assess and question what good humanitarian projects do.

Everyone who tries to offer help in the midst of conflicts and disasters is now painfully aware of the dangers of external aid, of staying too long, and of feeding societies, even hungry societies. The surplus foods may seriously damage the traditional farming and herding patterns that had sustained indigenous populations through all their previous calamities of drought and conflict. The world has learned the horrifying lesson that inappropriate humanitarian aid often becomes a tool of destruction.

Humanitarian assistance, particularly in the midst of conflicts and disasters, is not a field for amateurs. Good intentions are a common but tragically inadequate substitute for well-planned, efficiently implemented operations that, like a good sentence, must have a beginning, a middle and an end. Compassion and charity are only elements in humanitarian-assistance programs; alone they are self-indulgent emotions that, for a short time, may satisfy the donor, but rarely deceive and will always disappoint victims in desperate need.

International humanitarian assistance has never been a simple undertaking. I recall my first experiences in Somalia in 1961—a newly independent nation was being decimated by an unknown disease. In some towns over 10 percent of the population had died from a fulminant diarrhea, and bodies littered the countryside. Even then—almost 40 years ago—and despite all the enthusiasm of youth, one quickly came to understand how artificial it was to think that if we identified the biological cause and defined the appropriate therapy, the epidemic would be solved. It was also difficult to pretend that our efforts were purely impartial and altruistic; I was directing an American military research group and reporting to the local U.S. ambassador. Even if I didn't fully fathom the relationships, I knew politics played a role in our assignment. And one quickly learned that foreign interventions were not always selfless or even beneficial.

Obviously there was great satisfaction in alleviating suffering in a nation of nomads with no doctors, fewer than 20 miles of paved roads and minimal government structures. Flexibility and adaptation were essential, and humility came quickly. Those first experiences in large-scale humanitarian relief projects introduced me to the politics of aid and the necessity for logistics and other disciplines that were not taught in medical school. I quickly became acutely aware of the impact of new foods and medicines and money in a traditional society that, to our dismay, quickly learned to abuse them all.

I kept a research team in Somalia for the next 35 years, shared in their good days and bad, and directed refugee programs during the early 1980s when $1\frac{1}{2}$ million starving victims of drought required aid. And yet when most of the modern world thinks of Somalia today, one conjures up images of only the bloated bellies and cachectic faces seen on TV during the famine in the early 1990s, of civil war, peacekeepers killed and aid organizations fleeing to the safety of neighboring countries. The lessons of previous aid efforts seemed to be utterly forgotten in a $4-billion, unfocused extravaganza that soon matched the surrounding chaos and wastefulness.

As the basic structures of government and society on the Horn of Africa fell under the weight of corruption and greed, humanitarian workers faced fundamental challenges and had to make radical changes. Even the best-intentioned and most-experienced aid organizations modified their principles in order to survive. They hired armed thugs to protect themselves against other armed thugs. Unwittingly they had become, because of their food and vehicles and money, major actors in the tragedy that is still unraveling in Somalia.

By the early 1990s, international aid was the largest portion of the Somali national budget, and propped up a corrupt and repressive regime. When Siad Barre's government finally fled, and national starvation reached critical proportions, many humanitarian organizations did not acquit themselves with great honor. United Nations agencies worked from the safety of Kenya, and voluntary organizations overtly used the crisis to raise their own fund-raising profile. Nations such as the United States found an easy way to unload enormous amounts of surplus food and create a tragic cycle of dependence.

The same tale can be told in the Great Lakes region of Central Africa. With the benefit of hindsight, everyone now recognizes that maintaining the camps of Hutu refugees after the Rwanda genocide merely perpetuated the hold of killers and prolonged the agony of the innocent. In Bosnia, humanitarian and human-rights workers were caught in the unenviable position of knowing that pursuing their principles and maintaining relief efforts were helping—not hindering—the pace of ethnic cleansing.

Yet out of these disasters much good has come, for the international humanitarian community began to assess honestly its approach and to question openly its methods as well as its motives. To paraphrase the Irish poet, Yeats, the world had changed utterly, a terrible beauty was born in the rubble of Mogadishu. The innocence of the sixties and seventies had vanished.

The foreign policy of any nation reflects its fears and dreams as well as its own particular political and economic interests. In the Cold-War era, convinced that our national security was under constant mortal threat, the United States allowed the element of fear to become dominant. Our overseas agenda failed to take into account that the growing disparities between rich and poor, hungry and nourished, free and oppressed had become the driving forces in conflicts around the world.

Now, as the only remaining superpower and finally freed from our Cold-War fears, we can afford to be compassionate as well as strong, and by emphasizing health and humanitarian assistance we could fashion a foreign policy capable of rekindling an American spirit that is now being strangled at home and abroad.

The relationship of health, human rights and humanitarian assistance to foreign policy is not a theoretical exercise. Today, most foreign interventions by the United States are predicated, or at least defended, on humanitarian bases—starving Somalis, homeless Kurds, dead Rwandans. Yet, in my experience, few political or diplomatic leaders understand the health and humanitarian issues they so readily invoke, and they rarely involve health and humanitarian workers in developing or implementing the policies that guide our national actions overseas.

By building on common objectives and universally accepted values, by defining the core needs of all human beings and proposing ways to satisfy those needs, we may be able to create a better framework for survival in a new century. Focusing on health, human rights and humanitarian assistance offers an innovative approach to foreign policy that may be more effective in many cases than the conventional military, economic and geopolitical "solutions" that have so often been so flawed. Time is not on the side of those who believe we can maintain the status quo, that we can continue to confront reality with old rhetoric and allow the past to happen over and over again.

I have had the good fortune to work as a physician for more than three decades in troubled areas of Africa, Latin America and Asia. I have shared in the human catastrophes that are an inevitable part of conflicts, and in the individual and communal tragedies that follow earthquakes and famines, droughts and floods. While undertaking relief and research programs, I have been caught in the cross fires of revolution and experienced the dangers and fears of battle in the Sudan, Somalia, Lebanon, Nicaragua, Vietnam and Libya. I have learned the humbling lessons of Third-World medicine, that politics and prejudice, racism and religion, weather and witchcraft, corruption and incompetence were as much a part of most nations' health problems as the easily definable diseases we were taught in medical school. I also saw firsthand that economic embargoes are not abstractions, the antiseptic instruments of power politics. They are anesthesia supplies that do not come, respirators that cannot be repaired and people who needlessly die. Yet during these long periods overseas, I also became aware of the unique role humanitarian workers may have, especially in societies where there are multiple reasons for suspicion or cynicism or even hatred.

These experiences convinced me that those humanitarian workers who have intimate contact with the suffering masses as well as unusual access to, and the respect and trust of, foreign leaders could contribute to the solution of crises and conflicts in ways impossible for politicians, soldiers and even diplomats. Humanitarian actions can open doors to negotiated settlements; even in the midst of violence, they can create corridors of understanding that eventually become permanent bridges to peace.

But one can open doors or establish corridors and still have little or no impact on the prevention or resolution of conflicts. To change the perceptions of responsibility, the traditional prerogatives of actors in a political process, is not easy and comes slowly. Politicians usually consider humanitarian workers as do-gooders who are presumed to be too innocent to understand the harsh realities of diplomatic decision-making. Health, human-rights and humanitarian-assistance concerns are usually invoked to justify interventions, and relief workers are praised, particularly if the media can record a nation's compassion, and then they are dismissed. In the past, relief workers accepted as an adequate reward the instant and enormous gratification that comes in healing the wounds of war without demanding any further involvement, without, in most circumstances, even staying long enough to assess critically their own efforts.

For example, humanitarian workers have long embraced the comforting concept of neutrality without carefully weighing its political implications. In World War II, few seemed seriously to question whether the Red Cross was morally right to distribute biscuits and food parcels in Auschwitz or Buchenwald but never criticize or publicly condemn Nazi extermination methods. Do today's humanitarian workers have the courage to question whether the aid they deliver is used to foster oppression or as a tool for ethnic cleansing? Do we merely prolong the agonies of war when we contribute supplies without weighing whether our help may simultaneously perpetuate the genocidal power of evil leaders, as happened in the Goma refugee camps? Is it ever possible to stay professionally aloof from such practical, political and deeply moral questions, especially ones that are both predictable and inevitable?

Humanitarian assistance in international conflicts always has a political dimension. This should not be a source for embarrassment—it is a simple fact of life. Politics affects everyone in the chain—from the donors, to the distributors, to the recipients. One has only to look at the funding of large voluntary agencies in the United States to appreciate the political dimension. The Cooperation for Assistance and Relief (CARE), for example, seen as the compassionate voluntary effort of concerned American individuals, receives the vast amount of its budget from the United States Agency for International Development (USAID) and other government sources—and the person who pays the piper can surely call the tune. Who gets food, when and for how long, are based on political factors.

America's multimillion-dollar effort to assist oppressed Kurds in Northern Iraq—code named Operation Provide Comfort—was canceled within a week when our favored Kurdish faction decided they were safer with local Iraqi rather than our preferred Iranian protection. The cover of humanitarian concern was blown away by the cold winds of political reality. I was in Somalia when President Bush sent in 28,000 troops to help the starving masses. TV cameras and reporters were flown to Mogadishu in advance so they could record the troop landings for the evening television news/entertainment. One year and $4 billion later, we left a country in chaos.

One can seriously argue what good, if any, came from the whole sad experience. Anarchy still reigns in Somalia, but the attention of a fickle world, overwhelmed by other tragedies, has moved on. Somalia is no longer newsworthy. Political judgments dictated our arrival and departure schedules. The knowledge or insights of academics and health workers who knew the people and the customs of the Somalis seemed to matter very little to those who defined our "national interest."

The United States had entered Somalia because of a putative concern about the health of a starving populace. The foreign-policy results of a noble gesture gone awry were far more profound than the scenes of famine we were supposed to eliminate. As with Vietnam, a great tragedy flowed from our failed involvement in Somalia. America's relationship with the United Nations unraveled, with catastrophic implications for future international humanitarian missions.

When civil unrest in Rwanda erupted in 1994, UN Secretary-General Boutros Boutros-Ghali literally begged the Security Council to send an expanded peacekeeping force. The United States led the opposition to this appeal because we did not wish to cross what was now called the "Mogadishu line," the commitment of American forces under a UN flag in a foreign country. Within the next two months, 800,000 Rwandans were hacked to death with machetes, and the churches and lakes were clogged with the corpses of innocent victims of neglect. We knew what was happening and we watched but did little except debate procedures, arguing over the methods of payment that had to be assured surplus transport before we would become involved.

Fifty years after the Holocaust, after our nation joined in the chorus of "never again," we silently observed the most intense months of genocide in the history of mankind. Then the most massive movement of refugees in world history began; in a single day more than a million people poured into the small town of Goma in eastern Zaire (Congo). Very late in the course of the disaster, the same donor governments that had refused to help months before now poured $2 billion into an uncoordinated relief effort that resulted in sustaining the very murderers we had failed to stop when the genocide began.

So the question "How can we help?" is usually asked too late, and those who wish to respond are often inadequately prepared for the tasks they must face. Many well-intentioned individuals and organizations who want to help lack the requisite skills to intervene and the expertise to know which interventions are likely to be effective. There is an urgent need for an internationally recognized basic minimum standard of training for personnel involved in humanitarian assistance, and the International Diploma in Humanitarian Assistance course (see Chapter 18) addresses that need.

In *Preventive Diplomacy*, former U.S. Secretary of State Cyrus Vance noted both the strengths and weaknesses of the humanitarian triad: only *governments* have the necessary finances for large-scale emergencies—in fact almost nine out of every ten dollars for emergency humanitarian assistance comes from governments. However, governments protect, first and foremost, their own national interests and, therefore, they are selective as to how and to whom their largess is dispensed.

Only the *United Nations* possesses international legal authority to intervene when crises threaten the stability of regions. The UN Charter provides the broadest mandate to serve the world's refugees and feed its hungry. Unfortunately, the United Nations is an organization of 185 competing nations and often reflects their parochial agendas. Only rarely do all states agree on a common approach, even in the face of certain disaster. The Security Council actually reduced the UN presence in Rwanda as signs of the genocide grew.

In the *nongovernmental* part of the triad, thousands of voluntary agencies may represent the best intentions of societies all around the world, but they often fail to coordinate their efforts, and most of the large organizations are increasingly dependent on government funds, a reality that compromises their impartiality. Voluntary agencies sometimes have their own vested interests and may actually profit by prolonging their role in crises.

In all levels of the triad, there is a temptation to isolate humanitarian interventions from broader conflict-prevention efforts. Both donors and recipients know that ancient alliances, ethnic bonds and mutual interests are perfectly appropriate factors in devising aid projects for traumatized lands, but it is often impolitic to follow logic publicly. We must learn to utilize these realities as tools of reconciliation rather than mere signs of division. We must take advantage of openings when peace and so many lives are at stake.

Humanitarian projects can offer the common ground necessary to initiate dialogue between combatants who might agree on little else. Vaccination programs have allowed "corridors of tranquility," de facto cease-fire zones, to be established in the midst of bitter wars. As I have witnessed in Nicaragua and Lebanon, humanitarian projects can sometimes serve as the only acceptable bridges to peace; they offer an opening wedge, and we must learn to utilize and develop this untapped resource. Focusing on health, human rights and humanitarian assistance offers an innovative approach that can lead to a more effective foreign policy than the conventional military, economic and geopolitical "solutions" that have so often been so flawed. Time is not on the side of those who believe we can maintain the status quo, that we can continue to confront reality with old rhetoric and allow the past to happen over and over again.

With today's instant communication, it is impossible to hide from distant catastrophes. Bloated bellies and destroyed societies are no longer only sad stories to be debated by statesmen far removed in time and space from the carnage. Now the images are on our television screens; they are a major force in our own and our children's continuing education. The magnitude and nature of a nation's response to a humanitarian crisis is dictated largely by the extent of media interest and influence. Unless we intend—rightly or wrongly—to give up being human, we can no longer feel warm and secure in our homes while disasters swirl through the cold world outside.

The fact that we know, instantly and vividly, that terrible wrongs are occurring creates a moral and legal burden that did not weigh on previous generations. No amount of sophistry can ever again humanize the horrors of war or the waste of innocent lives into dull statistics that soften the harsh fact that it is real people who suffer and die. We cannot simply talk about problems, deceiving ourselves that words—even heartfelt concerns—can substitute for corrective actions and compassionate deeds. Compassion has never been worth a damn unless it manifested itself in concrete acts of love.

Complex humanitarian crises have, sadly, become a common interface between the developed and developing nations, between the rich and the poor, the haves and the have-nots. Those of us privileged to participate in great humanitarian dramas have the opportunity adversity offers to build a new framework, using, and sometimes rediscovering, the best of the old structures, but realizing that a new spirit and innovative methods are necessary for international discourse in a new millennium. Our success—or failure—will, to a large extent, define the chances for the very survival of the world.

Part I

REALITY

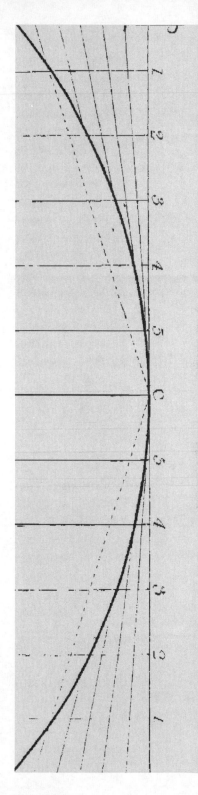

In trying to understand and in attempting to devise a proper response to international humanitarian crises, especially those that flow from civil conflict or follow national disasters, facts can be elusive. In the face of enormous human suffering, especially among protagonists, raw emotions—panic, fear, hatred and revenge—often prevail and usually prolong the agony. Humanitarian workers bring an important dimension to horrific problems, a caring but professional and unbiased approach. They must develop the skills to measure, define, document and assess a disaster so that an adequate and appropriate response can be offered.

Chapters 1 to 6 deal with health issues. Four physicians with extensive field experience in conflict situations (Michael J. Toole, Kevin M. Cahill, Jennifer Leaning, and H. Jack Geiger) describe the scope and clinical patterns of trauma, disease and death as seen during these crises. Mary F. Diaz and Nigel Fisher then focus on the most vulnerable and most affected—women and children.

To contrast, Chapters 7 to 9 focus on legal and economic issues. Michel Veuthey and Richard Falk consider society's efforts to distill the almost unspeakable experience of war and disaster into acceptable international humanitarian rules of law, codes of conduct and basic human-rights conventions. Continuing the emphasis on ground relief efforts in reality, Partha Dasgupta's chapter on the economics of neglect provides an introduction to critical financial and statistical parameters.

Finally, in Chapters 10 and 11, Lord David Owen and Abdulrahim Abby Farah detail the different but often surprisingly mutual concerns of donor and recipient nations.

THE PUBLIC-HEALTH CONSEQUENCES OF INACTION

Lessons Learned in Responding to
Sudden Population Displacements

Michael J. Toole, M.D.

During the past two decades, the world has witnessed a demographic epidemic of unprecedented proportions—an epidemic of forced migrations that has had grave public-health consequences. These mass migrations have in large part resulted from wars, civil strife and violence that have plagued so many parts of the developing world. Now, in the 1990s, the same phenomena have returned to Europe; ethnic-based wars have generated millions of refugees and internally displaced persons in the former Yugoslavia, Chechnya, Armenia, Azerbaijan and Georgia. In this paper, I will summarize our knowledge of the public-health impact of mass population displacement; look at the essential elements of an effective public health response to emergencies involving refugee and displaced populations; and attempt to analyze the reasons for the relative failure of the international community to act decisively and consistently to prevent the most serious adverse consequences of these crises for the affected populations.

In 1980, refugees dependent on international assistance numbered only about five million; by 1992, this number had reached more than seventeen million, increasing to an all-time peak of 27 million in 1995. Since 1995, there has been a steady decline to an estimated 22 million, which still represents one in every 255 people on the planet (Figure 1.1).[1,2] By definition, a refugee is an individual who has crossed from one country to another; in addition, there may be more than 20 million people who have been abruptly displaced from their homes and have fled to other, more secure regions within their own countries. These "internally displaced" persons do not automatically qualify for international assistance. With limited access to relief and without legal rights to the protection accorded refugees by international law, the internally displaced are frequently in a particularly desperate situation.

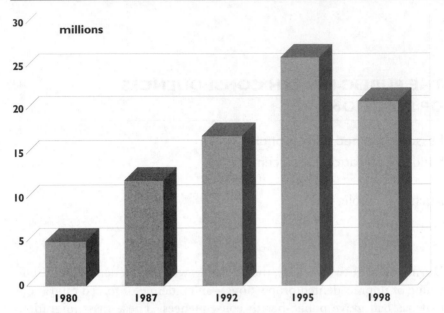

Figure 1.1: Number of Refugees Worldwide, Selected Years, 1980–1998

Most refugees and internally displaced persons have suddenly fled the violence that has engulfed their homes, leaving most of their belongings behind. They risk further violence, starvation and exposure during their sometimes-protracted flight to safety. Most refugees have fled poor, developing countries for safe haven in equally impoverished neighboring countries that struggle to support their indigenous populations. Refugees who cross borders often arrive in a remote, harsh environment where access to food and clean water is limited. They are often placed in crowded, unsanitary camps where their inability to earn an income, their total dependency on the generosity of others and their unhealthy living conditions can lead to loss of dignity, helplessness and despair. When the response to these emergencies by the international community is slow, inadequate or inappropriate, the human cost can be exceedingly high; it is this cost that I shall attempt to describe in epidemiologic terms.

The public-health consequences of mass population displacement have been extensively documented since the late 1970s. On some occasions, these migrations have resulted in extremely high rates of mortality, morbidity and malnutrition. The most severe consequences of population displacement have occurred during the acute emergency phase, in the early stage of relief efforts, and have been characterized by extremely high mortality rates. Although the quality of the international community's disaster response efforts has steadily improved, death rates associated with forced migration remain high, as demonstrated by several recent emergencies. For example, the exodus of almost one million Rwandan refugees into eastern Zaire in 1994 resulted in mortality rates that were more than 30 times the rates experienced prior to the conflict in Rwanda.

Crude mortality rates (CMR) have been estimated from burial site surveillance, hospital and burial records, community-based reporting systems and population surveys. The many problems in estimating mortality under emergency conditions include: (a) poorly representative population sample surveys; (b) failure of families to report all deaths for fear of losing food ration entitlements; (c) inaccurate estimates of affected populations for the purpose of calculating mortality rates; and (d) lack of standard reporting procedures. In general, however, mortality rates have tended to be underestimated because deaths are usually underreported or undercounted and population size is often exaggerated.[3] Early in an emergency, when mortality rates are elevated, it is useful to express the CMR as deaths per 10,000 population per day. In most developing countries, the baseline annual CMR in nonrefugee populations has been reported as between 12 and 20 per 1000, corresponding to a daily rate of approximately 0.3 to 0.6 per 10,000.[4] A threshold of one per 10,000 per day has been used commonly to define an elevated CMR and to characterize a situation as an emergency.[4] The CMR among Rwandan refugees during the first month after their arrival in eastern Zaire was between 27 and 50 per 10,000 per day.[5]

Since the early 1960s, the international community's response to the health needs of refugee and displaced populations has at times been inappropriate, relying on teams of foreign medical personnel, often with little or no training or experience in the developing world. Hospitals, clinics and feeding centers have sometimes been set up without any preliminary needs assessment, and essential prevention programs have sometimes been neglected. More recent relief programs, however, have emphasized a primary health care approach, focusing on preventive programs such as immunization and oral rehydration, involvement by the refugee community in the provision of health services and more effective coordination and information-gathering.

Monthly CMRs in refugee camps during the emergency phase are presented in Table 1.1; these rates are up to 30 times the death rates in the countries of origin of the refugees. Table 1.2 lists CMRs reported from various internally displaced populations; in these situations, death rates have been as high as 45 times the local baseline rates. If we look at trends in death rates over time (Figure 1.2), the rate of improvement has varied. For example, even though death rates among Rwandan refugees in

Table 1.1: Estimated Crude Mortality Rates (Deaths per 1,000 per Month)
in Selected Refugee Populations, 1990–1994

Date	Country of Asylum	Country of Origin	Crude Mortality Rate
July 1990	Ethiopia	Sudan	6.9
June 1991	Ethiopia	Somalia	14.0
March–May 1991	Turkey	Iraq	12.6
March–May 1991	Iran	Iraq	6.0
March 1992	Kenya	Somalia	22.2
March 1992	Nepal	Bhutan	9.0
June 1992	Bangladesh	Myanmar	4.8
June 1992	Malawi	Mozambique	3.5
August 1992	Zimbabwe	Mozambique	10.5
December 1993	Rwanda	Burundi	9.0
August 1994	Tanzania	Rwanda	9.0
July 1994	Zaire	Rwanda	59–94

eastern Zaire were extremely high initially, improvement occurred relatively quickly because an assistance program was mounted promptly by the international community with extensive logistical support by the military. In Sudan (1985), death rates were still well above baseline rates six to nine months after the influx of refugees occurred.[3] In the case of 170,000 Somali refugees in Ethiopia in 1988 and 1989, death rates actually increased significantly six months after the influx. This increase was

Table 1.2: Estimated Monthly Crude Mortality Rates (Deaths per 1,000 per Month)
among Internally Displaced Persons, 1990–1996.

Date	Country	Crude Mortality Rate
January–December 1990	Liberia	7.1
April 1991–March 1992	Somalia (Merca)	13.8
April–November 1992	Somalia (Baidoa)	50.7
April–December 1992	Somalia (Afgoi)	16.5
April 1992–March 1993	Sudan (Ayod)	23.0
April 1992–March 1993	Sudan (Akon)	13.7
April 1992–March 1993	Bosnia (Zepa)	3.0
April 1993	Bosnia (Sarajevo)	2.9
May 1995	Angola (Cafunfo)	24.9
February 1996	Liberia (Bong)	16.5

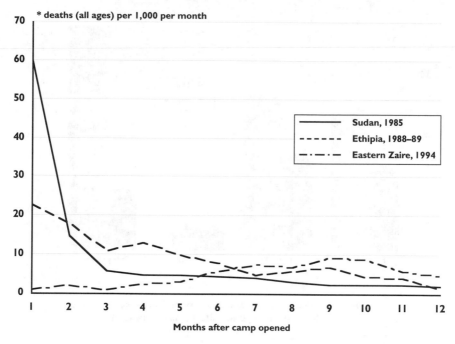

Figure 1.2: CMR* by Month after Arrival of Refugee Population

associated with elevated malnutrition prevalence rates, inadequate food rations and high incidence rates of certain communicable diseases.

Most deaths in refugee camps have occurred in children under five years of age. For example, a population survey of Kurdish refugees estimated that 64 percent of deaths in this population during April and May 1991 occurred in children less than five years of age, who composed only 18 percent of the population.[6] An exception to this trend was documented in the Rwandan refugee camps of eastern Zaire where under-five death rates were no higher than CMRs during the first four weeks after the influx—probably because most deaths in this population were caused by cholera, which has high attack rates and high case-fatality rates among all age groups.[7] In most reports from refugee camps, mortality rates have not been stratified by gender; however, the surveillance system for Burmese refugees in Bangladesh did estimate sex-specific death rates, demonstrating considerably higher death rates in females (Figure 1.3).[8] This might be explained by the fact that female children and women were not brought to clinics for medical attention until their condition was grave.

The main causes of death among refugees and internally displaced persons have been those same diseases that cause most deaths among non-refugee children in developing countries: measles, diarrheal diseases,

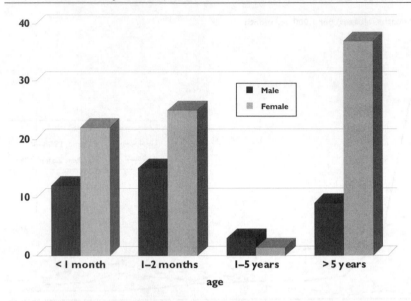

Figure 1.3: Deaths by Age and Sex among Burmese Refugees, Gundhum II Camp, Bangladesh, May–June 1992

acute respiratory infections and malaria.[4] In some settings most deaths have been caused by only two or three diseases, as demonstrated by the data from Somalia in 1992 and eastern Zaire in 1994 (Figure 1.4). Cause-specific mortality data from most other refugee populations show the same basic pattern, although in recent years major outbreaks of measles have been successfully prevented by immunization in most refugee emer-

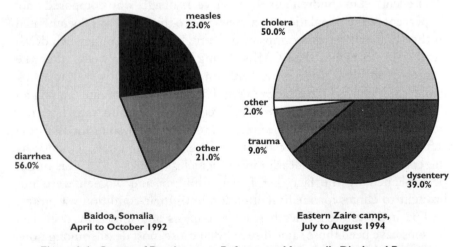

Figure 1.4: Causes of Death among Refugees and Internally Displaced Persons

gencies. Nevertheless, measles—although easily preventable—has been a major cause of death in some instances. For example, in 1985, more than 2,000 children died of measles during a three-month period among the 85,000 refugees in the Wad Kowli camp of eastern Sudan.[9]

Refugees and displaced persons living in crowded and unsanitary camps have been at high risk of epidemics of communicable diseases, including cholera, dysentery, meningitis, hepatitis, typhoid fever and typhus. Cholera has occurred in refugee camps in the Horn of Africa, central and southern Africa, Asia and the Middle East. In Malawi, there were at least twelve separate cholera outbreaks among Mozambican refugees since 1988.[4] Cholera occurred within the first week after the movement of Rwandan refugees into eastern Zaire, resulting in more than 20,000 deaths.[5] In addition, epidemics of bacillary dysentery have occurred among refugees, especially in central and southern Africa. The bacteria responsible for this deadly disease have developed resistance to common affordable antibiotics, making this disease one of the greatest risks associated with population displacement in Africa.

The extent to which AIDS is a problem among refugees and displaced populations is largely undocumented; however, it is likely that HIV transmission is a significant problem in some populations, such as displaced Rwandans, Liberians, Ethiopians and Burundians. An assessment of Sudanese refugees in Ethiopia in 1992 found high prevalence rates of several sexually transmitted diseases (STDs), including infection with the human immunodeficiency virus (HIV) (CDC, unpublished data). Increasingly, STD and HIV prevention should be a component of refugee relief programs; however, during the emergency phase this activity is probably limited to the provision of condoms.

An important underlying risk factor for high death rates in most of these situations has been energy-protein malnutrition. Table 1.3 shows the prevalence of acute malnutrition in children under five years of age during the emergency phase of relief operations in various refugee populations;[10] data are derived from cluster sample population surveys. In refugee camps, prevalence rates between 15 percent and 50 percent have been common. By comparison, the prevalence of acute malnutrition in nonrefugee populations in developing countries is usually between 5 percent and 8 percent. In many internally displaced populations, the rate of acute malnutrition has been even higher than in refugee populations.

In addition to energy-protein malnutrition, severe outbreaks of various rare micronutrient deficiency diseases such as scurvy (vitamin A deficiency), pellagra (niacin deficiency) and beriberi (thiamine deficiency) have also affected tens of thousands of refugees, especially in Africa.[11]

Table 1.3: Prevalence of Acute Malnutrition among Children
Less than Five Years of Age in Selected Refugee Populations

Date	Country (Camps)	Origin of Refugees	Prevalence
1985	Sudan (Kassala)	Ethiopia	50%
1990	Ethiopia (west)	Sudan	45%
1991	Kenya	Somalia	29%
1991	Turkey (east)	Iraq	13%
1992	Zimbabwe	Mozambique	48%
1994	Eastern Zaire (Mugunga)	Rwanda	23%

Experience to date, therefore, indicates that the high incidence of childhood communicable diseases and the high prevalence of malnutrition are the major characteristics of displaced and refugee populations that have led to high excess death rates on many occasions. Part of their vulnerability may also be explained by the high rate of relatively rare micronutrient deficiencies.

Consequently, the interventions that will prevent most excess mortality caused by population displacement are as follows: sufficient food rations, providing at least 2,000 kilocalories of energy per person per day as well as other essential nutrients, especially vitamins A and C;[12] sufficient quantities of clean water (UNHCR recommends between 15 and 20 liters per person per day for consumption, cooking, washing and cleaning);[13] and adequate shelter and sanitation facilities. Other essential components of a public health program include a simple, flexible and accurate health information system; measles immunization for all children between six months and five years of age; a diarrheal disease control program focusing on the treatment of dehydration with oral rehydration salts; epidemic preparedness plans; and appropriate curative care focusing on standard case-management protocols, essential drugs, a referral system and community health worker training, and targeted particularly at malaria and acute respiratory infections. In some cases, selective feeding programs are also indicated.

Unfortunately, several international relief programs during this decade have failed to provide the basic elements described here. The international relief operation on the Turkey-Iraq border in 1991 provides an example of both the achievements and the problems associated with refugee assistance programs. When an estimated 400,000 Kurdish refugees fled northern Iraq into the mountains on the Turkish border, they ended up in several large camps where barbed-wire fences and armed soldiers prevented most of them from entering Turkish territory.

Although the international response was not immediate, airdrops of food that were organized after several days' delay by the military forces of several countries (including the U.S.) probably saved many lives. This impressive use of military power to address a major humanitarian crisis offered an exciting glimpse of the potential role of the military in future relief operations. We need to realize, however, that the military resources of most countries will always be under partisan political control and cannot be consistently relied upon to respond to humanitarian emergencies. The failure of Western military forces to ensure an adequate humanitarian response to crises in Liberia, Somalia, Sudan and Rwanda and their relatively slow response to events in Bosnia illustrate this point.

Back to the Turkish border in April 1991. Apart from food deliveries, very few of the priority programs listed earlier in this paper were established on the ground within the first four to six weeks. The only water sources available to refugees rapidly became polluted; sanitation facilities were either absent or inappropriate; and adequate supplies of oral rehydration salt (ORS) did not arrive until four weeks after the influx. In addition, the rate of breast-feeding among the Kurds was quite low, and many infants were given milk powder or infant formula mixed with unclean water. Not surprisingly, diarrhea was the most common health problem affecting all ages, especially children. Supplies of measles vaccine sufficient to launch a mass vaccination campaign were not obtained until six weeks after the influx; however, epidemics of measles did not occur, probably because immunization coverage rates in Iraq had been relatively high. In addition, medical kits sent from Europe did not contain certain essential items, such as vitamin A.

Mortality rates among the Kurds during their period of displacement were estimated later by a population survey conducted in May 1991 (Figure 1.5). Crude mortality rates (expressed as mean deaths per 10,000 per day) for four two-week periods are shown by the upper bars; under-five death rates are shown by the lower bars.[6] Death rates increased dramatically during the second two-week period (April 13 to 26), the time when the incidence of diarrheal diseases was highest and when relief efforts were still rudimentary. Although some nongovernmental organizations (NGOs) and U.S. Special Forces teams did eventually provide appropriate community-based health care, other agencies set up field hospitals and provided inappropriate inpatient treatment while neglecting to implement basic public-health programs. The overall lack of focus on the most critical public-health problems was due to the lack of central coordination and poor technical leadership. Since Turkey did not offer asylum to most of the Kurdish refugees, the Office of the United Nations High

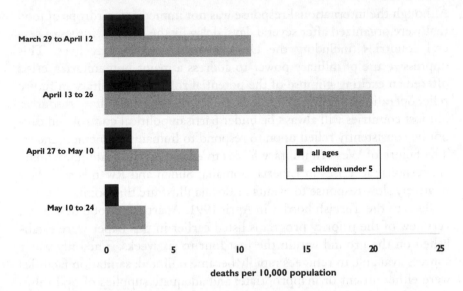

Figure 1.5: Daily Crude and Under-Five Mortality Rates among Kurdish Refugees, Northern Iraq, March–May 1991

Commissioner for Refugees (UNHCR) was not invited to implement its traditional mandate of protection and assistance.

The complexities—and limitations—of the international response to humanitarian emergencies, highlighted by the experience with Kurdish refugees, led to some changes in the system. For example, a UN Department of Humanitarian Affairs was created to help coordinate the response of different UN agencies. Nevertheless, the next big test of the system— the crisis in the Great Lakes region of Central Africa—failed to reveal significant improvements. In the Goma area of eastern Zaire, an explosive cholera outbreak occurred within the first week of the arrival of refugees. This outbreak was associated with rapid fecal contamination of the alkaline water of Lake Kivu, which was the primary source of drinking water for the refugees. As the cholera outbreak subsided, an equally lethal epidemic of dysentery occurred. Consequently, more than 90 percent of deaths in the first month after the influx were attributed to diarrheal disease.

The inability of the world to address promptly the explosive epidemic of cholera among Rwandan refugees in eastern Zaire in July 1994 underscored the lack of emergency preparedness planning at a global level. This epidemic highlighted the inadequate reserves of essential medical supplies and equipment for establishing and distributing safe water, as well as revealing a lack of technical consensus on the most appropriate interventions. Agencies that did have the appropriate skills and experience, such as

Oxfam and Médecins Sans Frontières (MSF), lacked the necessary resources, and those agencies with the resources and logistics, such as the U.S. military, lacked the technical experience in emergency relief.

In general, the constraints to mounting an adequate international response to refugee emergencies can be categorized as political, organizational and technical. In my experience, the technical constraints are the least problematic. The remaining challenges to improving technical knowledge include the refinement of rapid assessment and surveillance techniques; development of effective strategies to prevent micronutrient deficiencies (although a good diet would be sufficient); evaluation of the impact of various water systems on morbidity and mortality; and the adaptation of diagnostic techniques and cold chain equipment (used to refrigerate medicines and vaccines) to field conditions. In addition, further research on the effective prevention of certain diseases that commonly affect refugees (for instance, cholera, dysentery, hepatitis E and malaria) would be beneficial.

More critical is the challenge to improve the management of public-health programs. Experienced technical personnel should be given a greater role in decision-making early in emergency programs. During both the Kurdish and Rwandan relief operations, it was apparent that certain basic skills were lacking among many relief workers; for example, in the management of diarrhea and dehydration and of maternal and child nutritional problems. NGOs need to invest more heavily in the training and technical orientation of their personnel. International rosters of experienced personnel need to be developed and perhaps shared between agencies and nations. In the United States, progress has been made in developing a standard curriculum for training relief workers in relevant public-health practice. In Europe, there are several health courses available through the International Committee of the Red Cross, MSF and other NGOs.

Recent conflict-associated emergencies in well-nourished and relatively affluent populations, such as those in the former Yugoslavia, Chechnya, Armenia and Azerbaijan, have demonstrated somewhat different patterns of health problems. Malnutrition has been a greater problem among the elderly than among children. The collapse or destruction of health services has led to increased morbidity and mortality due to chronic, noncommunicable diseases and to increased perinatal mortality, low birthweight rates and abortions. Nevertheless, the majority of deaths among civilians during the war in Bosnia have been due to injuries associated with the violence.[14]

It is critical that the international community respond to each emergency in a systematic and consistent manner irrespective of the political implications of the particular crisis. To implement the essential programs outlined earlier, the United Nations and its technical agencies must be empowered to gain access to all populations in urgent need of humanitarian assistance, even in areas of contested sovereignty. This is critical in current conflicts such as in Southern Sudan, Angola, Afghanistan, Liberia and Sierra Leone. The role of military logistics support should be seriously examined; however, it will be useful only if the military response is depoliticized and consistently mounted for each emergency. Furthermore, deployment of military forces for humanitarian relief is very expensive and should be subject to cost-effectiveness analyses.

Once access to affected populations is achieved, however, international relief agencies should be held more accountable for the impact of their interventions. In the past, relief operations were often evaluated according to the quantities of relief supplies and personnel deployed. However, the quality of relief supplies, the effectiveness of relief personnel, the adequacy of coordination and the effect of relief programs on reducing morbidity and mortality are more important indicators of achievements. Standardized information systems should be put in place early in each emergency to ensure effective monitoring and evaluation of relief programs. Monitoring should not focus merely on the process of relief assistance (for example, tons of food delivered, numbers of vaccine provided and so on); impact indicators, such as malnutrition and mortality rates, should also be routine components of such information systems. Relief managers, therefore, need to be adequately trained in both the implementation of technically sound relief programs and the accurate monitoring of their impact.

No single agency or government can be held responsible for the continuing vulnerability of conflict-affected populations. Collective international action is urgently needed to ensure that civilian populations worldwide are promptly and effectively protected from both the direct and indirect public-health consequences of organized violence. The idea of *protection* of refugees should be extended to include protection from *preventable* diseases and death. Primary prevention is the basic strategy of public health, and epidemiology is one of its essential tools. In situations of armed conflict, however, epidemiology can be practiced safely and reliably in very few areas. Hence, the traditional documentation, monitoring and evaluation elements of disease prevention may be ineffective in this situation. The provision of adequate food, shelter, potable water, sanitation and immunization has proved problematic in countries disrupted by war. Primary prevention in such circumstances, therefore, means stopping the violence. More effective diplomatic and political mechanisms need to be developed that might resolve conflicts early in their evolution, prior to the stage when food shortages occur, health services collapse, populations migrate and significant adverse public-health outcomes emerge.

Secondary prevention involves the early detection of evolving conflict-related food scarcity and population movements, preparedness for interventions that mitigate their public-health impact and the development of appropriate public-health skills to enable relief workers to work effectively in emergency settings.

Tertiary prevention involves prevention of excess mortality and morbidity once a disaster has occurred. The health problems that consistently cause most deaths and severe morbidity as well as those demographic groups most at risk have been identified. Most deaths in refugee and displaced populations are preventable using currently available and affordable technology. Relief programs, therefore, must channel all available resources toward addressing measles, diarrheal diseases, malnutrition, acute respiratory infections and, in some cases, malaria, especially among women and young children.

Recent emergencies have followed a predictable pattern of political unrest, civil war, human-rights abuses, food shortages and, finally, mass population displacement. There has been almost no preparedness for these emergencies within the public-health community. Agencies involved in health development projects need to be aware of political realities in certain regions of the world and should integrate preparedness planning into all aspects of public-health programs. Health information systems should incorporate plans to simplify and focus on major health problems in the event of emergencies. Immunization, diarrheal disease control and community health worker training programs should likewise incorporate emergency contingency plans. Finally, increased attention needs to be given to the challenges of rehabilitation of national health services following the cessation of armed conflict and the repatriation of large numbers of refugees to their country of origin.

ACKNOWLEDGMENTS

I thank the following organizations for having shared information gathered in the various displaced and refugee emergencies referred to in this paper: UNHCR, Epicentre, Médecins Sans Frontières, Save the Children Fund (U.K.), International Rescue Committee, UNICEF, the governments of Bangladesh, Ethiopia, Guinea, Kenya, Malawi, Nepal, Somalia, Sudan and Thailand; and colleagues at the Centers for Disease Control and Prevention.

2   CLINICAL ASPECTS OF FAMINE

Kevin M. Cahill, M.D.

The majority of the world's population survives with hunger and infections as constant companions and lives in "accident-prone" nations where famine and epidemic diseases often complicate the civil conflicts and natural disasters that are, unfortunately, regular events. Television pictures of the skeletal starving are the tragic, terminal images in a complex cycle of progressive malnutrition, especially in victims already burdened by an incredible array of dangerous parasitic, bacterial and viral organisms. Since widespread hunger and the existence—or even threat—of contagions are the most common reasons offered to justify international humanitarian interventions, it is important that all involved in determining and effecting foreign policy be familiar with the evolving clinical face of famine.

Famines have occurred in all ares of the globe and in every period of recorded history, but our era has the odious distinction of being the period when more people will die of famine than in any previous century. To fully appreciate this indictment it is necessary to realize that today mass death by starvation is rarely due to the vagaries of nature alone but reflects, rather, human decisions. Today's famines are man-made, for we have the ability to control short-term food deficits.[1]

Many factors can cause a local crop failure—droughts, floods, locusts, the spread of the desert, toxins, the erosion or exhaustion of soil—but in our modern world of instant communications and rapid transport there must be an almost calculated effort for famine to flourish. Political decisions—or indecision—ignorance, neglect, and economic and cultural conflicts cause famines today. During periods of peace, corruption and mismanagement may lead to famine. The need for foreign exchange may force food-rich nations to export essential nutrients, leaving the indigenous populations to waste away. Wars, however, are the major man-made cause of famines, disrupting populations and the patterns of planting and harvesting essential for fruitful agriculture. Food stores are looted and hoarded, and supply lines are cut.

The developed nations of the world control the critical surplus of food supplies and have the capacity to both make and resolve or, as is too often the case, simply ignore famines. Throughout the developing world, famines develop on a fragile nutritional foundation where dietary intake is usually woefully inadequate and parasites, such as blood-sucking hook-worms, drain their human hosts of protein, vitamin and iron stores. The physical effects of malnutrition can be readily measured; low weight, stunted growth, frail bone structure, high infant and child morbidity and mortality rates, and decreased work capacity and intellectual performance. Acute prolonged malnutrition also impairs mental development, leading to tragedies that last for generations. The ultimate irony is that the vulnerable poor who are most often affected are the ones who need both the maximum physical and mental health to survive with their meager resources and harsh environmental challenges.

Although I had managed isolated outbreaks of acute malnutrition in Somalia for over a decade, the Sahel famine in the mid-1970s was my introduction to the chaos that stalks large-scale starvation. The traditional supportive nomad society seemed to disintegrate as more than a million refugees overwhelmed the land. Confusion reigned as neither the government nor clan structures could sustain the flood of utterly dependent persons. Most families had become separated, and the individual daily search for food and water dominated the escalating desperation. Infants, children, pregnant women and the elderly died in disproportionate numbers, while the stronger adults prevailed. The apathy and lethargy of a refugee camp contribute to the impression of imminent disaster.[2]

Those people most severely affected can present a clinical picture of great variety. At one end of the spectrum are the walking ghosts with marasmus, the victims of rapid, extensive caloric deficiency or, in a single word, starvation. At the opposite end are those suffering from chronic protein deficiency, or kwashiorkor. As in most disease states, the majority fall between these classic poles; the clinical picture is further complicated by almost universal infection with multiple parasites.

The child with marasmus leaves the impression of an old man's face on an infant's body. There is obvious wasting of muscles with total loss of subcutaneous fat. The buttocks disappear and the skin is loose and wrinkled. Scrawny limbs seem incapable of supporting the typical swollen body. The bony skull appears disproportionately large, and the knees stand out as awkward knobs. Eye lesions and skin rashes, with infected "tropical ulcers," are frequent. Diarrhea is the rule, and complete rectal prolapse from weakness of the anal orifice is not uncommon. A simple measurement of height and weight on a growth chart will document marked stunting. Nevertheless, the marasmic child is almost surprisingly alert, showing constant indications of hunger such as sucking and grasping movements. They are, however, patently weak and they rapidly tire, becoming short of breath after the slightest exertion.

Kwashiorkor is the other major protein deficiency disease. It was almost unknown to the Somali nomads because their customary diet of camel's milk and occasional goat meat is very rich in protein. I cannot recall seeing a single case of kwashiorkor in Somalia before the Sahelian drought of 1976, and there is surely nothing subtle about the striking features of kwashiorkor in the black African.[3]

The hairs turns a soft red or white and becomes straight and limp. The moon faces and swollen bodies do not have the texture of a healthy, cherubic child, but rather are pitted with edematous fluid. These children are apathetic or constantly whining. Skin rashes range from dry, scaly, dark, "crazy pavement" pattern to almost total desquamation and severe ulcerations. The skin is often cold, and many children die of hypothermia when they are moved from the warmth of the mother's body. Obvious heart failure is the usual terminal event.

Micronutrient deficiencies also contribute to the clinical spectrum of famine. Ancient scourges such as scurvy, pellagra and beriberi—due to lack of vitamin C, niacin and thiamine, respectively—are common problems in the severely malnourished. Inadequate vitamin A is recognized as a frequent cause of serious eye problems in refugee camps. Iron-deficient diets can produce profound anemias, especially in the most vulnerable groups—pregnant women and young children.

There were no laboratories in the Somali refugee camps I directed. Fortunately, there was little need for scientific confirmation to permit a working diagnosis for either marasmus or kwashiorkor. Therapy can be extremely challenging, and deaths can be caused by inappropriate actions as well as neglect. Forced feeding can precipitate both diarrhea and aspiration pneumonia. Washing a child can exacerbate hypothermia, and it is better to have a dirty child than a dead one. The careful replacement of fluids, calories and specific nutrients must be coordinated with the therapy for concurrent infections. The clinical picture is rarely due solely to starvation but reflects the added burden of multiple parasitic infestations and respiratory infections. Malaria is extremely common, and measles and tuberculosis are rife.

Tuberculosis is a rampant problem, and establishing isolation tents must be a priority since dissemination of contagious diseases among the immunocompromised malnourished is a lethal combination. The usual benign course of measles, for example, becomes a deadly scourge in the setting of a refugee camp; the greatest tragedy is to watch children who have managed to survive starvation and long treks to the relative security of a feeding station then succumb in epidemic numbers to an infection such as measles, which could have been prevented by a simple vaccine costing less than ten cents.

There is, however, evidence that the relationship of malnutrition and infection is not always synergistic; an appreciation of this phenomenon is essential for those charged with food relief programs. There have been many documented outbreaks of diseases only *after* food supplies are restored. Malaria, for example, appears to decline among those strong enough to survive starvation and then reaches fatal epidemic levels only after intensive refeeding efforts begin. Relief workers have long been aware that their well-meaning efforts may actually be causing unnecessary deaths, thereby defeating the whole purpose of international humanitarian intervention. Recent scientific studies offer an explanation for the transient protective effect of malnutrition against malaria. As essential nutrients, such as para-aminobenzoic acid (PABA) and vitamin E, decline, the malaria parasite cannot develop in the deficient human red cell.[4] As refeeding programs correct these imbalances, fatal malaria outbreaks occur. PABA and vitamin E are high in grain and low in milk and meat products. The implications for those charged with nutrition planning in famine situations such as in Somalia are obvious. The Hippocratic Oath begins with the phrase *primum non nocere*—the first thing is to do no harm. Poorly conceived refeeding programs after famines can kill; the vast mountains of surplus grain may prove fatal if not integrated with appropriate supplemental antimalarial efforts.

Even in optimal circumstances—which hardly describe a Somali refugee camp—the period of rehabilitation for a patient with marasmus is judged in terms of months rather than days, and the pressure of new problems for an overworked health team frequently results in inadequate attention during recovery, inevitably ending in a rapid deterioration and death.

The role of a physician in managing a catastrophic famine is not limited to the traditional diagnostic and therapeutic approach of the profession. He or she must learn to organize truck convoys, establish basic camps and develop a team that will enable the foods donated or purchased to reach the hungry masses. The physician-leader in this situation must emphasize hope rather than disease, offering a future to those who have lost their past.

Medical-school training rarely prepares one for such challenges. The essential qualities required to serve effectively in such situations are not built on technical details that can be memorized, but must be based rather on the broad traditions that once made medicine a noble and learned profession.

The clinical faces of famine in Somalia are seared in my mind. The picture of marasmus or kwashiorkor tells a tale that few can evade, for it stares into our souls (see Figure 2.1).

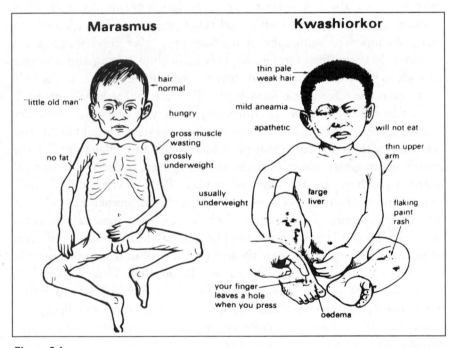

Figure 2.1

Somalia 1992

Jennifer Leaning, M.D.

Humanitarian crises in many parts of the world have marked the years since the end of the Cold War and have forced the international relief system to take stock of its capacities and its limitations. In the years since 1991, when Somalia began its descent into chaos and death, this system has seen equally dramatic failures elsewhere in the world in early warning, preventive diplomacy, mobilization of public concern, galvanization of political will, effective intervention and response. Somalia constitutes the first on the list, however, and in its story lie all the features of failure that lay ahead.

Failure on a scale as grand and miserable as occurred in Somalia was determined by cumulative inadequacies on many fronts. This essay focuses on the role of the international community in attempting to provide relief to a society trapped in a vicious downward spiral of famine and anarchic internal war during the acute phase of the crisis from late 1991 to the end of 1992. Faced with the new intersection of violent disorder and massive food deprivation, the international community recognized only most belatedly and at enormous cost to the Somali people that it was confronting a new kind of challenge: the problem of delivering relief where there is no order; the problem of distributing food and medicine where there is no neutral status protecting those who would help.

EXPECTATIONS FOR SYSTEM PERFORMANCE

In the last 40 years, the international community has increasingly assumed responsibility through its international agencies for providing relief to disaster-stricken areas. This responsibility is pursued through two interrelated main tracks: threat assessment and response. The general theoretical outlines of disaster relief have been hammered out with experience and extended critical evaluation.[1-5]

Threat assessment—the process by which international agencies identify areas of impending crisis in food or vulnerability to natural disaster—is a function of surveillance, a steady-state observational and analytical activity undertaken by experts and officials in local areas, summing up the hierarchy of information and leadership to general levels of evaluation and prediction for given geographical areas. It is also a function of focus, whereby areas that appear problematic as the result of surveys or routine reports become the targets of more in-depth investigations, in an effort to gain knowledge about the true dimensions of risk at hand. The knowledge gained becomes the basis for planning and delivering the needed response. Disaster response, in which the provision of relief to populations is a key element, is supported by informed anticipatory planning efforts and then sustained by a complex process of leadership, coordination and communication—all vigorously directed toward the supply and transport of personnel and goods to the affected areas.

Despite criticism from within agencies and from the public during and after the response phase to particular disasters, years of effort in responding to famine and natural disasters can be said to have honed these aspects of threat assessment and response to commendable levels of effectiveness in many of the UN and nongovernmental organizations (NGOs). The world has come to expect that in any given instance of portending or actual disaster, a set of actions will take place, regardless of political or geographic difficulties: the continual monitoring of threat potential will result in expert assessment of the risk at hand. The threat will be communicated to international agencies and the larger international community. These agencies will engage in timely analysis and decision-making. Needed resources will be identified and mobilized. The strategy and logistics for delivery and distribution of these resources will be defined and agreed upon. The agencies will embark within the appropriate time frame dictated by the disaster on the coordinated implementation of the logistical plan. These agencies will continue the tasks of analysis and communication in order to maintain the required level of international interest and marshaling of resources.

Conduct of Forces during War or Civil Conflict

A minimum level of civil order is an essential prerequisite for this system of disaster relief to be able to function. Local or regional observers and officials must be able to stay on-site to act as sources of information and foci of coordination; medical workers and relief personnel have to be able to reach people in need. Deliveries of people and goods assume relatively safe passage and transport, and the existing relief system has not been linked, conceptually or logistically, to a cadre of armed forces deployed to create or maintain secure corridors or bastions. It is possible to maintain this minimum level of civil order in settings of armed conflict. The codes defined by international humanitarian law permit the transport and delivery of civilian relief in all conditions of war or armed unrest.[6–8] To the extent that the armed combatants understand and observe these codes, the neutral noncombatant status afforded medical and relief workers and their supplies will protect and enable the relief effort. There have been many instances in the last decades when the international community has provided disaster relief in the midst of war, civil strife, armed unrest or rebellion.

The agency charged with responsibility for establishing and monitoring adherence to international humanitarian law is the International Committee of the Red Cross (ICRC). The work of the ICRC is legendary, yet legal experts caution that it takes far more than the specific efforts of the ICRC to ensure the application of the tenets of international humanitarian law. Within the context of war and civil conflict as it has usually played out, two other conditions are essential: a general recognition on the part of the warring factions that this body of law exists and each individual combatant is subject to it; and a more detailed understanding and commitment to enforce these principles on the part of the senior officers on all sides.[9]

The bloody conflicts in Somalia and in Yugoslavia have identified two other, underlying preconditions for the application of international humanitarian law: the warring factions have to adhere to some semblance of a chain of command and communications in order for the senior officers to exert any control; and the warring factions must be constrained in their cost-benefit analysis of war by certain Clauzwitzian notions of means ultimately supporting ends. Chaotic violence fueled by an apparent thirst for mutual annihilation subverts attempts to introduce the principles enshrined in the Fourth Geneva Convention. The fundamental challenge posed by Somalia (and to some extent Yugoslavia) was this: how to provide disaster relief in the setting of savage anarchy.

THE CRISIS IN SOMALIA

Somalia is a nomadic and pastoral society of approximately six million people whose agricultural economy has always been characterized by a precarious balance between rain and food supply. Drought and intermittent famine are chronic scourges.[10] Formed as a republic in 1960 with the merger of the British and Italian colonial territories, Somalia and its native clan structure were held in the oppressive grip of Siad Barre from 1969 until his dictatorship of corruption and intermittently bloody suppression of dissent[11] was violently overthrown in January 1991.

Under Barre, Somalia served as an ideological playground for East-West ambitions in the Horn of Africa and the Middle East and, thanks to this rivalry, became the recipient of large amounts of military aid.[12] Until 1978, Moscow held sway; in the last decade of Barre's rule, the United States was the dominant force. The overthrow of Barre in January 1991 led to months of inconclusive political struggle among the leadership of the several clans that surfaced to claim ascendancy. Much of Somalia was in a state of upheaval, with open armed conflict among clans particularly evident in the north, where a secessionist battle was being waged by the Somali National Movement (SNM) and its Isak clan supporters; and in central Somalia, where several clans were in hot pursuit of the remnants of Barre's clan and supporters.

In January 1991, within days of the overthrow of Barre, Mohammed Ali Mahdi, a businessman and leader of the Abgal, a subclan of the Hawiye clan, declared himself President of Somalia. General Mohammed Aidid, the leader of the Habr Gidir, another subclan of the Hawiye, challenged this declaration. Against a backdrop of simmering conflict and social disruption throughout the countryside, open war erupted between these two subclans in the fall of 1991. This war was waged within and in the environs of Mogadishu, where most members of the Hawiye clan lived.

In early September, during a flare-up in hostilities between these two factions, a UN team consisting of several UN officials and armed Somali guards was held up at gunpoint. The Somali guards were executed in front of the UN officials, who were stripped to their underwear, robbed of all effects, and forced to find their way back to their offices.[13] Within days, the UN, which had just restored a skeleton staff in Mogadishu in July, pulled all personnel out of Mogadishu.

On November 17, 1991, the hostilities between the forces of Aidid and Ali Mahdi exploded across the city, escalating to a massive artillery bombardment of one side of the city against another. For the next six weeks, Aidid's forces pushed Ali Mahdi from the southern sector of the city to a northern stronghold, which Ali Mahdi maintained against all-out assault. As of February 1992, heavy nighttime artillery barrages and more sporadic daytime engagements maintained an ugly stalemate: Aidid controlled the southern two thirds of the city, including the airfield and the deepwater port; Ali Mahdi controlled the northern third of the city, including the hills overlooking the harbor.

The November explosion in hostilities caused consternation in the international community in Mogadishu. Although many in the diplomatic corps (including the U.S. consulate) had left the city in the month after Barre was overthrown, several NGO agencies still maintained offices, their numbers augmented by the several teams of foreign medical workers who had arrived in October 1992 to help the Somali medical establishment cope with the casualties caused by the fighting. The November attack by Aidid against Ali Mahdi turned the entire city into a war zone. Each day for the next several weeks, hospitals reported receiving approximately 100 casualties on average per day per hospital. Any vestige of civil order evaporated.

The latter weeks of November and all of December saw the hostilities reach high levels of carnage. Casualties were produced day and night but, because of difficulties in transport, most (civilian and military) were brought into the hospitals during the day. Many of those who died outright from their wounds were not brought to the hospital, and many who made it to the hospitals died in the casualty area. During periods of most bitter fighting, soldiers would swarm the hospitals, their jeeps screeching into the courtyards and men piling out with wounded companions. They would order physicians and nurses at gunpoint to take immediate care of these victims to the exclusion of those already in the process of evaluation and treatment, regardless of priority of need.

Mogadishu became a place of death, destruction and chaos. Heavily armed bands of men and boys roamed the city. Even with armed guards, travel in the open during the day was hazardous to anyone.

Food scarcity began to surface as a serious issue. After almost a year of civil unrest, agricultural production in the countryside had been reduced to a fraction of pre-1991 levels. Commercial markets no longer existed; food supplies, to the extent they came in from the surrounding regions, were appropriated by the warring factions and distributed to the soldiers in lieu of money. No food had been imported into the country in months. Aidid's forces patrolled the airport and seaport; guns on the hills were controlled by Ali Mahdi's men and aimed at the harbor.

On December 11, 1991, a Belgian worker for the ICRC was shot and fatally injured while engaged in distributing food in a sector of the city that constituted the no-man's-land between the forces of Aidid and Ali Mahdi. Also killed was an elderly Somali clansman who threw himself in the path of the bullet in an attempt to protect the ICRC worker. The circumstances of these deaths underscored the dilemma facing relief workers in Mogadishu: efforts by neutral noncombatants to distribute relief to members of the civilian population were seen by the armed bands of one side or the other only as actions of favoritism in the distribution of most valued commodities. In early January 1992, a Bulgarian physician working for UNICEF was killed in northeastern Somalia.

Word of what was happening in Mogadishu and elsewhere in Somalia trickled out intermittently to the international community. Press coverage depended upon the resourcefulness of journalists in obtaining transport into and out of Mogadishu. The ICRC, the only relief agency with regular flights into and out of the city, did not permit journalists to stay overnight. More official communication depended upon bulletins from the ICRC, since representatives of all other international agencies, with the exception of a few medical and relief teams, had left the city.

MEDICAL NEED AND RESOURCES

In February 1992, Africa Watch and Physicians for Human Rights cooperated in sending two separate missions to Somalia. The intent was to describe and communicate the medical and food relief situation in the country, with particular focus on Mogadishu. Information gained from these missions[14] forms the basis for the following firsthand account of the situation in Mogadishu during this period.

Based on site visits to the hospitals, reviews of medical admission logs, interviews with medical personnel and surveys of hospitalized patients, it is estimated that in the city of Mogadishu between mid-November 1991 and the end of February 1992 approximately 1,200 people per week were killed outright or died of their injuries, and another 2,500 were surviving wounded, with casualties totaling 41,000 for this 11-week period. These estimates attempted to account for systematic underreporting in casualty area logs and the fact that a proportion of those who were injured and who were killed did not reach the hospitals.

As in all traumatic casualties of war waged with high-velocity conventional weapons, the deaths resulted from massive head or abdominal injuries, or from exsanguinating traumatic amputations of limbs. The high proportion of numbers killed to numbers wounded reflected several factors: the lethality of the weapons used; the close range at which they were fired; the absence of emergency field medical response; the absence of emergency transport; and the austere conditions at the hospitals for emergency and follow-up care. The surviving injured were those with superficial wounds, for whom medical care would have only marginal effect on survival, or those who required and received lifesaving medical intervention: amputations, abdominal explorations and repair, fluid resuscitation, transfusions, antibiotics, and splinting and stabilization of limb injuries.

The resources available to manage this burden of traumatic casualties were meager. Three hospitals, variously damaged and looted by the war, provided care for the southern region of the city. These three, Benadir, Digfer and Medina, had a total inpatient capacity of approximately 1,700 beds but a census probably twice that level. Prior to October 1991, none of these hospitals had a specific casualty ward separate from the ambulatory clinics, and none of the staff, Somali or expatriate, were emergency or trauma specialists. In the northern sector of the city, controlled by Ali Mahdi, the November events had forced Somali physicians to contrive a hospital out of a string of 45 private villas. Two large villas facing the ocean, used as operating theaters, and 27 other converted villas constituted what was called the Karaan Hospital. Another 16 villas had been converted for postoperative and convalescent care, permitting a total of 5,000 to 6,000 patients to be hospitalized in these sites at any one time.

The task of caring for the casualties of war prevented any possibility of treating routine or nontraumatic illness. Occasionally people in extremis from untreated diabetes or heart disease would present to the hospitals, but the conditions were sufficiently stressed that most medical conditions went unseen and unattended. To the extent that regular medical care was still delivered at all in the city, it took place out of the homes of those few private physicians who had not either left the country entirely or gone to the hospitals to participate in the emergency effort.

Medical supplies to hospitals on both sides of the divide were brought in by ICRC plane out of Nairobi six days a week. Shortages of tetanus toxoid and antibiotics were acute during February. Blood was obtained from relatives who accompanied the injured; only ABO typing was available. The operating rooms had access to a few hours of electricity from diesel-powered generators; running water was unpredictable and unclean. No gas anesthesia was available in the city; operations were performed on patients under intravenous anesthesia with ketamine. Drapes of any kind were scarce and rarely used; equipment was sterilized at best only once in 24 hours. Elsewhere in the hospitals conditions were grossly unsanitary. Inpatient rooms, corridors and stairways in interior sections of the hospitals (particularly Digfer) were dark and oppressive with stench and debris.

Under these austere conditions, the hospital staff in the casualty and operating areas performed triage, stabilization and, as needed and as could be accomplished, emergency surgery on all arriving casualties. Accuracy and completeness of record-keeping was inversely related to numbers of casualties seen in a given period, as those responsible for maintaining logs were drawn into the medical effort. At Digfer and Benadir there were insufficient staff and resources to provide postoperative rounds or nursing care except intermittently; at Medina, where the staff from Médicins sans Frontières had established their own unit, rounds were afforded those recovering from abdominal and orthopedic operations. For most of the patients at Digfer and Benadir in the south, and at the Karaan hospital in the north, patients depended on their families to provide whatever medical and personal care they required after the first or second day of admission.

Joint review of records with hospital physicians, nurses, and administrators yielded agreement on the following death rates at each site of hospital care: casualty ward, 10 percent; observation ward, 10 percent; operating theater, 5 to 10 percent, inpatient ward, 5 to 10 percent.

Hunger stalked patients and staff alike. The ICRC brought in enough food to afford the Somali staff one meal a day, which was not sufficient to maintain nutritional balance. A slow loss of weight and energy was manifest among the staff and reported by foreign workers, whose own separate sources of food were consumed at their guarded villas, distant from the hospitals and hospital compounds where the Somali staff lived.

No food was available for patients, whose families were the only source of supply. The saying was common: "If you have no family, you die." As the carnage in the city wore on, an increasing number of casualties brought to the hospitals were in this orphaned or abandoned state. Even those with families were in states of moderate to serious malnutrition, impairing wound healing and overall recovery. Based on hospital surveys conducted in February 1992, about 1 to 2 percent of the inpatients in the south were actually dying from starvation. Individual foreign staff workers confided in private that they would try to sneak food to one or more of the Somali workers and occasionally to patients. The stakes were high, however; antagonism from those staff who were not so favored; threats or worse from those patients or their relatives who were not given gifts. In a few cases (an orphaned child on an adult ward), it was possible for foreign staff to provide small amounts of food on a more routine basis. The need so vastly outstripped supply, however, that the risk of creating serious disruption kept acts of generosity to a minimum.

Longer-Term Issues: Medical, Psychological and Public Health

Thousands of the injured survive in Mogadishu as amputees and perhaps hundreds are partially paralyzed. (It is highly unlikely, given the care conditions, that those who initially survived as quadriplegic would have persisted long.) Many more have relatively useless limbs, the result of incomplete knitting of shattered fragments of bone. In 1992 there were no facilities for making prosthetic devices in Mogadishu. It was noted then that rehabilitation of this large population of disabled survivors would require a great investment of time and resources in the postwar setting. The psychological scars of this experience would produce many cases of pathological grief and post-traumatic stress disorder (PTSD). The situation then was too harsh and dangerous to permit much overt expression of psychological issues, since in such situations all available mental energy is focused on surviving, but it was suggested that when the conflict and famine could be eased, the psychological needs of thousands of people would surface and contribute to the complex difficulties of the recovery effort.

Although a coastal city, the relatively arid conditions of Mogadishu made malaria less a problem than elsewhere in the country, where it was prevalent. The lack of food and sanitation, and the widespread disruption in living quarters contributed to epidemic levels of respiratory, enteric and skin diseases, particularly among those hundreds of thousands who had fled to the outskirts of the city, gathering in refugee clusters with virtually no shelter.

VIOLATIONS OF INTERNATIONAL HUMANITARIAN LAW

International humanitarian law, the body of law governing the conduct of combatants toward civilians and neutral personnel in time of war, has developed to a robust and effective net of constraints on military behavior. Although it is still the case that violations of international humanitarian law routinely occur in all wars and civil conflicts, these violations, when observed and reported, usually result in some reimposition of discipline and change in procedure. The ICRC and the international community have become accustomed to some success in requiring warring parties to heed the provisions of the Geneva Conventions and Protocols that prohibit the indiscriminate use of weapons against civilians and guarantee protection of medical personnel, facilities and patients in all settings of armed conflict. Specific violations include all forms of interference in the delivery of medical care, the transport of patients, the supply of medical resources and equipment, and the movement and actions of health care personnel. Firing into hospitals, invasion of hospital premises, interference with medical triage and treatment, and intimidation of health care workers constitute gross violations. Moreover, in settings where food shortages have become acute and the supply of food to civilian populations is considered lifesaving, interference with such delivery is considered a violation of international humanitarian law.

In Mogadishu, violations of international humanitarian law were the norm, rather than the exception. Virtually no one with a weapon had heard of the Geneva Conventions, from the most senior officers down to the lawless bands of heavily armed men and boys who constituted the two armies and myriad subsidiary factions. The sophisticated heavy artillery that had fallen into the hands of both sides came with detailed technical manuals, instructing the user in how to aim the weapon, assess accuracy of hit and readjust settings to ensure more accurate hits on subsequent volleys. The Somali men and boys, many of them unschooled, fired these weapons in the general direction of a target, moved the weapons frequently, and made no systematic effort at accuracy. Their targets, in any case, were private villas and homes in Mogadishu, since the city had become the battleground. Consequently, civilians were inexorably and intimately entrained in the war. Protection of civilians and noncombatants was an absolutely illusory concept.

Violations of medical neutrality took place with regularity in the first two months after the onslaught of fighting in November. In the absence of any knowledge that international conventions existed, and without strong discipline from a centralized command system, individual groups of soldiers carried their hostilities and their concern for their comrades past the gates of the hospitals and into the casualty areas and wards. The most serious violation was that hospital workers were intimidated by heavily armed men into caring for patients out of order of medical triage. No instance of specific deliberate physical injury to a medical worker has been reported, but the presence and threatening demeanor of soldiers with machine guns created a tense and volatile atmosphere in which to take care of casualties.

In January 1992, the Médicins sans Frontières medical staff at Medina organized all medical staff on the south to plead with General Aidid to prohibit armed personnel from entering the hospital compounds in the sectors of the city he controlled. This effort was successful, and large signs in Somali and English were posted at all gates, requiring soldiers and the armed guards of medical personnel to leave their weapons with the hospital guards before permission would be granted to enter the compounds. Although these measures resulted in substantial decrease in the frequency by which armed soldiers invaded the compounds, there were still reports in late January and February of armed men in the heat of battle careening with jeeps of wounded past the guards and into the hospital compounds.

In addition, throughout this five-month period from November to February, there were many reported instances of heavy but apparently indeliberate artillery bombardment of hospitals. These barrages and occasional "sky shots" (random firings into the air, resulting in bullets falling from a height) caused substantial physical damage to hospitals on both sides of the city and deaths and injuries of patients and hospital personnel.

The most dramatic instance of violation of medical neutrality occurred on February 13, 1992, when armed men who claimed allegiance to Ali Mahdi's army entered Keysaney Hospital, the ICRC hospital in the northern sector of Mogadishu, and forced its closure. During the previous two months, at a cost of $200,000, the ICRC had created this hospital on the grounds of an old fort, and it had been up and running for about ten days prior to the armed invasion of the premises. Flying several Red Cross flags from various parapets, staffed with medical personnel who were all clearly wearing Red Cross identification, and filled with approximately 45 patients, there was no possible ambiguity about the status of the building or the mission of its staff. The Somali staff were ordered to disperse at once; the ICRC staff were herded into jeeps and summarily ordered to fly out of the city that evening. Under heavy threat, they were forced to abandon the patients. (It was later learned that these patients were taken to beds in the Karaan Hospital complex.) The incident was not explained, although it appeared from indirect communications that Ali Mahdi disavowed responsibility for this event, stating that the armed men were acting without his authority.

THE PROBLEM OF FAMINE

It was evident to the relief community in Mogadishu in February 1992 that a famine of epic proportions was very likely to hit all of Somalia by late spring or early summer. Local sources of food from agricultural production in Bay and in the Juba and Shebelle river regions had been widely disrupted by civil conflict raging there in spring and summer of 1991. The unrest had also severely limited food imports and virtually halted deliveries of food aid, other important sources in prior times. The drought throughout eastern Africa had also played a role.

Estimates of 1991 food production for Somalia suggested levels of only 30 percent[15] of expected levels. Production issues were only part of the problem, since the normal channels for distribution no longer existed and market forces could not be relied upon. Because of the widespread unrest, it was also impossible to arrive at a comprehensively accurate and updated assessment of need. Local surveys in late 1991 and early 1992, conducted by the ICRC and Save the Children–U.K. in the Gedo region and the displaced persons camps around Mogadishu, suggested very high child malnutrition rates. In March 1992, the ICRC reported "horrifying" levels of

90 percent moderate to severe malnutrition in the populations around Belet Huen and Merca.[16] As in all situations of impending famine, the most vulnerable populations are the displaced; all children, especially those under five years of age; the elderly; and pregnant and lactating women.[17]

The ICRC estimated in March that food needs were approximately 7,000 metric tons per month to feed Greater Mogadishu and 35,000 tons per month for the country as a whole.[18] Nothing approaching that level of delivery was then taking place or in the pipeline. Food supplied by the ICRC, the UN and the NGO community was reaching Mogadishu only by daily flights of the small ICRC plane. The ICRC was also attempting to deliver by sea about 7,000 tons per month to the southern and central regions of the country.

In February 1992, the ICRC updated its food surveys from the summer of 1991. Forecasts for 1992 were grim. Lack of seed and agricultural equipment and ongoing insecurity meant that, even if the spring rains came in abundance, the 1992 harvest would be less than the meager harvest of 1991. The population had already consumed its food and livestock reserves in getting through 1991. Wherever surveys could be attempted throughout the country, high levels of severe malnutrition were found. The February draft document prepared by the ICRC predicted that of the 4.5 million people in Somalia south of the disputed region of Somaliland, one third, or 1.5 million people, were at serious risk of death from starvation over the next six months. In its March 1992 bulletin, the ICRC made this announcement public.

Summary Assessment, February 1992

Medical and food relief workers in Mogadishu shared a common assessment of the situation and what sort of intervention would be necessary to avert the famine that threatened to dwarf the numbers of casualties already incurred in the bitter factional fighting. These relief workers had labored on-site for months, enduring the chronic tension and fear imposed by living in the midst of war. Most of them had known the ICRC relief worker who had been killed; many knew about the other aid worker who had been slain in the north. They had watched and negotiated with the two leaders of the factions and understood to some extent the limits of the agreements these men could and would commit to. They had witnessed and analyzed the politics of food shortage and distribution in the city and the surrounding countryside. They were also in touch with the few relief workers who had made forays by plane into the interior of the country. As the ones delivering medical care and supplying food to the few feeding stations that could be maintained in the insecure setting, they were well informed about the declining nutritional state of the population. In their assessment, the problem was a tightly linked question of food and security. An enormous increase in food aid was needed, logarithmically greater than current influx, if famine were to be avoided during the summer of 1992. The security situation in Mogadishu and throughout the countryside made delivery and distribution of food very dangerous. The shortage of food aggravated the danger in distributing it: the more desperate the need, the greater the value placed on food as a commodity, and the more it would provide the focus for attack.

Consequently, a radically new approach to the distribution of food to famine-affected areas was needed. The strategy usually employed by the international relief community, consisting of incremental and sequential steps of delivery and central storage aimed toward creating and filling a pipeline of distribution, would serve only to escalate the frenzy of violence at those inital delivery and storage sites and do little to alleviate the food crisis. Only a massive food program, delivering thousands of tons a week at many key points in the country, would saturate the markets, fill the trucks of looters and military bandits and, through organized and informal routes, reach the majority of those in need. The need was so severe over such a great geographical area that the old deliberate processes used with moderate success in previous famine settings would not work in a country where violence posed such a barrier to the establishment of formal and sequential chains of supply and distribution.

Many local aid experts in Mogadishu during this period did not feel that the international aid agencies could carry out this massive airlift and ground transport of food without sustained and substantial armed protection, at least during the first several months before the relief efforts began to ease the need and reduce the intrinsic and barter value of food. Men and boys throughout the country were heavily armed and at best only nominally under any kind of local control. The risks of hijack, looting and pillage were so great that aid workers who risked their lives daily in the constrained and moderately well-fathomed threat environment of Mogadishu considered it impossible to expand food relief to other areas without heavy armed guard on the order of 5, 000 to 10,000 armed troops for the entire country.

There was a difference of opinion among local relief workers between those who thought the armed presence—perhaps a police force supplied by the UN—could or should be deployed in advance of negotiating a cease-fire between Aidid and Ali Mahdi, and those who thought such a force would have to await the accomplishment of a cease-fire agreement.

The latter group conceded that a cease-fire was unlikely in the near future, and thus attempts to mount a realistic food aid program were doomed to delay.

Those in the first group believed that since the situation in Somalia required a new approach to food delivery, a new stance on the part of the international community's use of armed force in support of humanitarian relief was also required. Historically and by international agreement, UN forces have been deployed in peacekeeping modes after a negotiated cease-fire agreement has been reached. In the view of people familiar with Somalia in 1992, however, the deployment of UN peacemaking forces authorized to use force to create safe corridors for the transport of humanitarian aid in advance of a cease-fire required an expanded defini-tion of mission that was absolutely essential for the delivery of aid. It was also recognized that even if a cease-fire were accomplished, it was unlikely that relief workers could depend upon armed protection from the forces of Aidid and Ali Mahdi. Cease-fire or not, thousands of UN armed troops would probably be needed to define and support safe corridors.

These views and their attendant controversies were already under active debate in February 1992 among the relief workers familiar with the situation in Somalia. Why did a similar debate not surface at this time in the UN, in the pages of the international press or within and among gov-ernments? Why did it take so long for fragments of this assessment to appear in public declarations? Only at the end of July 1992 did officials of the U.S. Office of Foreign Disaster Assistance conclude, after a five-hour visit to Mogadishu, that "ways had to be found to saturate Somalia with food so that the incentive for the fighting would be reduced."[19] In early September, relief officials moved into rural areas of Somalia and reported that "the country's famine is far worse than previously believed and that present efforts, including an American airlift, are falling far short of what is needed to ease the crisis."[20]

THE RESPONSE OF THE INTERNATIONAL COMMUNITY

The reason for the delay in assessment and response to the disaster in Somalia is complex in detail but simple in outline: only the UN or the United States and the European community had the standing to create an international concensus on these issues, and none, for an unconscionably long period, chose to do so. The challenge was signficant—new ways to deliver food and a new use of force to protect that delivery. To define and meet that challenge required a sense of urgent responsibility, which for months no one wanted to own. In the post-Cold-War era, Somalia was a distant and fractured country whose problems, provided they remained within local borders, did not command high-level attention.

Among the international relief agencies, the ICRC had acquired a deep understanding of the food crisis. For philosophical and political reasons, the ICRC did not endorse the need for a substantial armed UN military presence to support the massive food program that was necessary. Humanitarian aid is best protected, in the view of the ICRC, if it is perceived as absolutely neutral and separate from political considerations. The ICRC position is that an armed force would be perceived as allied with a particular government or with an international institution and thus be treated in local settings as not neutral. Consequently, in the assessment of the ICRC, humanitarian aid efforts protected by this armed force might also be perceived as not neutral and might thus be more endangered, rather than less, by the presence of this outside force.[21, 22] Other agencies with deep understanding of the food crisis had relatively limited resources and were preoccupied with delivering care on the ground. They were not equipped to engage in the debate in the international arena.

The UN, the one agency aside from the ICRC with the authority and resources to shape the international debate, had pulled out of Mogadishu in the early winter of 1991 and maintained a low-profile stance in Nairobi, communicating via relatively junior staff to UN headquarters in New York. Until the appointment in May 1992 of Mohammed Sahnoun as senior UN representative in Somalia, no high-ranking UN staff person out of headquarters had been assigned responsibility for Somalia. Mr. Sahnoun then became one of the UN's harshest critics in regard to its actions in Somalia, charging in early September 1992 that much of the relief failure was due to "an overwhelming United Nations bureaucracy that, in contrast to the Red Cross, is made up of civil servants more interested in careers and perquisites than in the job at hand."[23]

For most of the winter and spring, the efforts of the UN and the United States with regard to Somalia were focused on attempting to arrange a cease-fire in Mogadishu. These efforts resulted in moderate success, in that a shaky agreement negotiated in March succeeded in holding throughout the remainder of 1992. In the same period, however, famine and armed anarchy, unattended-to, secured a stranglehold on the country.

Three factors converged in July and August of 1992 to cause the international community to swing into some form of active response to the deteriorating situation in Somalia. First, the vicious ethnic fighting in Bosnia created such a clamor in Western societies for the UN to intervene—even in a setting where a cease-fire could not be accomplished— that the parallels to Somalia became impossible to ignore. Given the scale of need in Somalia (at least five and perhaps ten times the estimated 200,000 to 300,000 people at risk in Bosnia[24]), if the United States and the UN were seriously compelled to consider sending in 40,000[25] to 120,000[26] armed international peacemaking forces to provide protection to relief convoys and to Sarajevo proper, nestled in the mountains of Bosnia, how could they ignore the relatively simple logistical task of deploying 5,000 to 10,000 UN armed troops in the flat, open terrain of Somalia?

Second, the presence in East Africa of the new UN special ambassador to Somalia, Mr. Mohammed Sahnoun, provided abundant fresh information about the calamity and the occasion for intensified and detailed updates on Somalia in the national and international press.[27,28] Third, UN Secretary-General Boutros Boutros-Ghali began to speak more openly about his own personal sense that the UN had failed to maintain a sense of fairness in weighing relative deployment of resources for relief in areas of former Yugoslavia versus Somalia. His public statement of dissent galvanized a more sustained and informed debate in the press and in the UN about the threat in the Horn of Africa as well as in Europe.[29,30]

In the late summer and fall of 1992, as world attention began to focus on the Somali famine and war, the discussion within governments, the UN and major NGOs revolved around how best to relieve the famine and whether to link the delivery of food aid with the provision of security.[31] By that phase in the crisis, there was very little time left in which to do anything effective, because people were dying at a rate of more than 1,000 per day and those still alive were sinking into a state of inanition where ordinary food aid would have been of no use to stave off terminal decline. It was estimated in late August that unless 60,000 tons of food could be made available within the next month, most of the 1.5 million at risk of death from starvation would be beyond the reach of relief efforts.[32]

Against this background, alarmed reports from United States officials returning from visits to the region prompted President Bush to begin to engage more directly in the crisis. On August 13, 1992, he announced that the U.S. government would transport a UN security force of 500 Pakistani soldiers to Somalia, would begin an immediate military-led emergency food airlift to the region, and would make 145,000 metric tons of food available.[33]

Yet despite these interventions and the intensifying focus of the U.S. Office of Foreign Disaster Assistance (whose head, Andrew Natsios, was designated special coordinator for Somalia relief in mid-August of 1992), the situation in Somalia continued to deteriorate. Military airlifts of food were insufficient to counter the effects of drought, population flight and countrywide violence on food availability and distribution. The small UN security force was unable to restore security even within Mogadishu and was effectively held hostage at the airport by the city's warring factions. Faced with this ongoing dilemma, the United States and the UN reached the decision to have the United States, with UN backing, lead a large-scale military coalition force to intervene in Somalia in order to support the delivery of humanitarian aid. On December 9, 1992, the forward contingent of U.S. Marines landed at Mogadishu beaches and Operation Restore Hope began.

Viewed from the perspective of the fall and winter of 1992, this military intervention constituted a high-risk, controversial, but ultimately reasonable intervention, provided the military leadership maintained a vigorous focus on the delivery of food where it was needed and the provision of security for the humanitarian relief effort. What was hoped by many in the relief community was that a coordinated humanitarian and security strategy would finally succeed in getting large quantities of food to those who desperately needed it.

The events of the next year produced mixed results. During 1993, hundreds of thousands of tons of food were delivered, the security situation throughout much of the country did improve, and yet the military mission became politicized and foundered in bloodshed and disarray. The years thereafter, marked by inconclusive UN military and diplomatic efforts, withdrawal of all international troops in March 1995 and continued clan feuding, have not yet seen a recurrence of the level of human distress reached in 1991 and 1992.[34] Some humanitarian analyses of the 1991 to 1992 crisis period suggest that the famine peaked in the summer of 1992 and that the U.S. military intervention came too late to save the majority of those who died in the famine.[35,36] Other assessments of this crisis period, while conceding that delays were significant and costly, assert that the U.S. response, although late, provided significant human benefit in terms of numbers of lives saved.[37-39] The security impact of the U.S. (and subsequent UN) military roles has received critical assessments from a number of directions.[40-42]

Operation Restore Hope marked a watershed in international politics. For the first time in recent memory, a military force acting on behalf of the UN was deployed to impose security conditions within a nation-state in order to sustain a humanitarian effort on behalf of the inhabitants of that nation-state. This step was perhaps implicit in the doctrine outlined in the UN report *Agenda for Peace*, prepared by Boutros Boutros-Ghali in June 1992, in which he called for specific and dramatic expansion of the UN peacemaking role in ways not currently defined in the UN Charter,[43] but it required a level of creative energy and cooperation rarely seen in the international community. Speaking of Bosnia and the need to move toward a policy in which the UN might have to intervene in violent internal situations, John Steinbruner, defense and foreign policy analyst at the Brookings Institute, was quoted in July 1992 as saying: "Inevitably, we are going to be shaping new doctrine.... Both the principles and the mechanisms are going to have to be invented here."[44]

Somalia from 1991 on has provided the international community with ample opportunity for such invention. With a focus on the years 1991 and 1992, the key unresolved principle was whether the UN or a force acting on behalf of the international community should intervene in settings of violent chaos or oppression in order to uphold humanitarian law and provide relief from extensive human suffering. Key mechanisms in reaching and carrying out that decision include adequate and timely threat assessment and determinations of what kind of force should be used, under whose direction, within what definitions of mandate and rules of engagement. In Somalia, the threat and reality of famine and war during 1991 and 1992 received grossly delayed recognition and response. When international action did result, it arrived late, was deployed clumsily, and blundered into further complex damage.

Of the many lessons that might be drawn from a review of this period, the one emphasized here is that ~~to provide humanitarian relief in areas of widespread violence requires major changes in international arrangements and agreements~~. To pretend that the challenges of the post-Cold-War order can be faced without such changes—including improved and streamlined organizational decision-making, more secure financial arrangments with member states, the creation of a standing and professional international force, an expansion of the UN charter, and revised or expanded membership in the UN Security Council—is to persist in the illusion that institutions do not have to accommodate themselves to events. Somalia and Yugoslavia were desperate tugs on the sleeve of humanity and, unheeded, became harbingers of things to come.

REFUGEE WOMEN

4

Overcoming the Odds

Mary F. Diaz

When one million Rwandan refugees flooded into Zaire in July and August of 1994, many young women crossed the border as war booty. The Rwandan army, running from the rebel advance, captured young women and forced them along, threatening to kill them if they did not join the mass exodus.[1] It was many months before the United Nations and its partner agencies providing relief in the camps realized that so many women had been raped and forced into "marriages" during the Rwandan genocide.

Tens of thousands of Kurds escaped persecution in Iraq in 1991, crossing a mountainous border into Iran and Turkey. International aid workers describe the scene as chaotic as people arrived in camps, cold, tired and hungry from a long journey over mud and ice. An orderly system of food distribution was soon organized, with refugees distributing the rations. In a short time, it became evident that some families were malnourished and suffering—these were families headed by women. Aid workers had appointed only men as food distributors, and admitted they had not realized a particular group of women was at risk.[2]

In the early 1990s, the refugee camps in Kenya became nightmarish for Somali women and girls, but it was several months before humanitarian assistance workers understood what was happening: hundreds of women and girls were raped as they searched for firewood or herded livestock around the perimeter of the camp. Special thorn bushes were planted around the camp sites and antirape committees made up of male and female elders were established in the camps, finally stopping some of the attacks.[3]

Wars, floods and famine wreck thousands of lives in a few hours: everyone is suddenly on the run as families are torn apart. Often women are left to cope on their own. Their husbands and fathers may have been killed or imprisoned; their protection, their legal status and their property rights may have been bound closely to the men in their families. It can all unravel quickly for a widow caring for her children alone. In refugee and displaced settings, women face a different set of problems from men. They are at greater risk of physical attacks and their voices are often drowned out by the tumult of a refugee crisis. It takes deliberate planning to include women in relief efforts, to consider their needs right from the outset, when setting up camps and distributing emergency supplies and medicine, and later, when longer-term assistance programs are set up and funded. While including women may go counter to traditional cultural practices of a community, it can pay off immediately in fairer distribution of help, greater protection for women and children and, later, in more sustained rebuilding and repatriation efforts.

DAY-TO-DAY SURVIVAL PUTS REFUGEE WOMEN AT RISK

The proportion of female-headed households in refugee and war-affected populations is often very high. Immediately after the genocide in Rwanda and the flight of more than one million Rwandan refugees, the Rwandan government found that more than 70 percent of the remaining population was female and more than half the mothers were widows.[4] When refugees returned to Battambang province in Cambodia, more than 64 percent of the adults were women and a third of the households were headed by women.[5] And in Afghanistan, it is estimated that nearly one million men have been killed or disabled in the civil war, leaving more than 50,000 widows in Kabul and tens of thousands of other women who have become primary providers for their families.[6]

In refugee camps, women are often put in particular danger by the very design of the camps. Sometimes women and girls who have been separated from their families are placed in communal housing that provides no privacy. Latrines and water collection points are frequently located at an unsafe distance from where refugee women are housed, while poorly lit camps allow attacks to take place with relative impunity. Land mines are sometimes placed around the perimeters of camps, endangering women and children who are usually responsible for collecting firewood and water.

Even the provision of basic assistance—food, shelter and water—can lower the odds of a woman's survival, making her more vulnerable to exploitation, disease and even death. During the height of the refugee emergency in Goma, Zaire, when thousands of people were dying daily from cholera, women were particularly at risk. Relief workers noted that women were working themselves to death trying to collect wood, water and food rations for their children. To survive meant enduring long walks to ration points (up to seventeen miles without food, water or even shoes) and waiting for hours (including standing in line overnight) for food, water and shelter materials. At distribution points were groups of young men, many dressed in military uniforms, who would erupt in frequent fist fights and riots with machetes.

Decisions about food distribution are generally made by international organizations in consultation with male leaders at the refugee sites. Yet these male leaders may have little understanding of the needs and circumstances of the women who cook the food or feed their families. As a result, the distribution procedures and the food itself may be poorly chosen. In Angola, women reported that the beans that were distributed required soaking overnight and cooking for more than three hours the following day. This forced them to spend most of their time searching for enough firewood and water for boiling and drinking and left little time to plant gardens or work the fields for more sustainable sources of food.

In some circumstances, food distributed through male networks is diverted to resistance forces or sold on the black market, with women and children suffering as a result. In other situations, food is used as a weapon by blocking distribution to civilian populations. Or the men handing out the food may require sexual favors in return, forcing women and girls into prostitution to earn income for supplies on the black market. When women oversee the distribution of assistance items, these types of incidents occur less frequently. A United Nations High Commissioner for Refugees (UNHCR) report notes that in one camp in Malawi, women said they were being deprived of rations and were pressured to give sexual favors or money in exchange for food. When more women were employed at the point of distribution, such abuses were greatly reduced.[7]

Another fundamental need of many refugee women, particularly heads of households, is sufficient income to support their families. Although relief agencies supply some basic needs, refugees need money for many things: to supplement their ration with fresh fruit or vegetables, for clothing and shoes, for soap. The extent to which refugee women are potential earners has usually been underestimated. Without sufficient income or control of household income, refugee women are far more vulnerable to sexual exploitation and may be forced to turn to prostitution.

Women are often overlooked when larger sustainable projects that focus on reforestation, infrastructure development or agricultural activities are put in place. During the war in Sierra Leone, nongovernmental organizations (NGOs) implementing Food for Work (FFW) projects did little to recruit women, although women are responsible for the majority of household food production. Women were not equally represented on the committees that made decisions about the FFW projects. In some cases, a food committee had only one woman, often a relative of the village chief. It turned out that NGOs had recruited male village chiefs to spread word of the project and recruit participants. The male village leaders had recruited mostly men.[8]

In many of the cultures from which refugee women come, women are traditionally involved in food growing and production, but the abrupt changes brought about by crisis may mean they become excluded: sometimes men in their communities push them aside, recognizing that the food ration is a valuable commodity, or relief workers, who do not fully understand women's traditional or potential roles, overlook them.

In recent years, UNHCR and NGOs have had some success in implementing programs to help women generate income. The Bosnian Women's Initiative and Rwandan Women's Initiative provide funds for microcredit and training for women working to rebuild their lives. With initiative funds, women in Bosnian villages are raising cows and opening greenhouses and small cafes. Women in Rwanda are starting brickmaking businesses, producing and selling mushrooms and training each other in sewing and embroidery. The challenge with these types of projects is to avoid the most marginal economic activities, such as handicrafts, for which there may not be a sustainable market. In education, the disparities between males and females is striking: a study of two camps in Somalia showed that of the approximate 4,000 children enrolled in primary school, almost all were boys.[9] Another study found that in a refugee camp in Sierra Leone in 1997, only 26 percent of the students in upper grades (7 to 12) were girls.[10] In Pakistan, UNHCR's education program reached a population that was 92 percent boys. UNHCR staff reported they felt impeded by the huge cultural obstacles to providing education to Afghan girls in the Pakistani camps. They noted that most of the refugees in Pakistan were rural Pushtuns, among the most conservative and tradition bound of all groups in Afghanistan, who often segregated their girls from the rest of their family at the age of eight or nine. Teachers needed to be Pushtun speaking and to travel long distances to remote refugee camps. If women teachers traveled alone, they were sometimes threatened: one received an envelope with bullets in it.[11]

HEALTH RISKS

In the early days of the Goma emergency, women were too weak and too burdened with child care and other responsibilities to seek medical attention. Because they could not walk the long distances to free-standing clinics set up by relief organizations, they were left without medical help. In an attempt to address this, relief workers set up mobile clinics, with medical teams driving or walking from one refugee group to another, in an attempt to identify the most critical cases. Even then, they found that male refugee leaders rarely identified women in need of medical attention, even when the women presented the most acute cases.

Until very recently, the emphasis on health care for women in humanitarian emergencies and refugee camps was almost exclusively on maternal and child health services and the training of traditional birth attendants (TBAs). The most basic requirements of women were routinely overlooked. Refugee women attending the Fourth World Conference on Women in Beijing confronted a senior official from UNHCR, asking why refugee women were not provided with cloth for sanitary napkins. For a week each month, a refugee woman can be severely restricted because she is without a simple piece of cloth. The oversight can force her to spend days confined to her shelter, unable to take her children to the health clinic, or to gather firewood or perform other necessary chores. Where cultural roles demand that women alone take responsibility for these chores, or in female-headed households, the impact of confining a woman to her home for one week each month has severe consequences for her entire family.

Reproductive health care is rarely considered a priority in refugee settings. In the first comprehensive study on the subject, researchers found that fertility rates in some camps were "extraordinarily high," sometimes surpassing those of the country of origin and country of asylum. For example a fertility survey carried out in 1987 among Afghan refugee women estimated 13.6 children per woman. In Cambodian camps along the Thai border, the birth rate was estimated at 55 per 1,000 population.[12]

Only in the past few years have UNHCR and its partner agencies begun providing information about family planning and birth spacing, contraceptives and sex education in refugee settings. In many places where women cannot get family planning services, clandestine or self-induced abortion is not uncommon, despite the risk to women's lives.

Education campaigns about sexually transmitted diseases and HIV/AIDS have been limited in refugee camps and war-affected areas. AIDS is currently ravaging Rwanda, where a guerrilla war keeps the countryside unstable and health workers away. A survey by the government of Rwanda has found that 11 percent of Rwandans are HIV-positive.[13] According to health workers, one of the reasons for the spread of AIDS is that many women who lost their children and husbands during the war are having children out of wedlock, often with men who have wives or other sexual partners.[14]

Often there are few female doctors and health care workers available in refugee settings, making it nearly impossible for women to obtain medical care if they must contend with cultural taboos against talking with men who are not immediate family members. Afghan women in refugee camps in Pakistan face this problem, and with the rise of the Taliban government, which severely restricts women's mobility and access, it has become a serious problem for displaced women in Kabul and other parts of Afghanistan. Often women do not feel comfortable talking with male health care workers and as a result will not seek services.

SEXUAL VIOLENCE

Women and girls face extremely high risk of rape and sexual violence in war and humanitarian emergencies, yet there has been little progress in addressing the problem. Mass rape in former Yugoslavia and Rwanda generated tremendous media attention and inspired human rights groups and feminist organizations to begin campaigning for the prosecution of rape as a war crime. UNHCR and humanitarian assistance groups are beginning to address the problem with preventive measures and some treatment and counseling for survivors, but there is still a long way to go.

Rape, whether part of a massive military campaign, or an individual act of violence in a refugee camp, can result in death, permanent physical injury, sexually transmitted disease and pregnancy as well as post-traumatic stress disorder, depression and suicide.

Women who have been raped may never admit they have been sexually assaulted, but medical staff may document physical signs following rape, such as bruising and lacerations to the genitalia and bruising of the arms and chest.[15] Medical professionals can play an important role in documenting rape and treating survivors.

During the first five years of the civil war in Liberia, nearly half the women and girls interviewed for a study on wartime violence against women reported they were subject to at least one act of physical or sexual violence by soldiers or fighters. The likelihood that a woman or girl would be raped increased if she belonged to an opposing ethnic group or fighting faction or if she was forced to cook for the fighters. [16]

Around the refugee camps for Rwandan refugees in Ngara, Tanzania, hundreds of refugee women and children walked the hills, carrying wood on their heads and in their arms. As the area surrounding the camps became stripped of trees, the refugees had to travel farther and farther from the camp sites. And as they walked greater distances, women and girls were being raped and attacked.[17] An international NGO responded by creating "Crisis Intervention Teams" made up of refugees, including at least one woman per three-person team, to provide safety education and counsel anyone who survived an attack. In one camp for Burundi refugees, a study by the International Rescue Committee (IRC) found that an estimated 26 percent of the women and girls have experienced sexual violence since becoming refugees.[18] The UN and IRC have responded by providing medical care and trama counseling for survivors, as well as referrals to police if the woman seeks to prosecute. In order to prevent further abuse, a community education effort is being put in place, with UNHCR protection offices, camp managers, Tanzanian police and members of the refugee community.[19]

ADDRESSING THE NEEDS OF WOMEN, EMPLOYING THE SKILLS OF WOMEN

The United Nations, governments and humanitarian-assistance organizations have long recognized that people running from war and persecution need protection against forcible repatriation, armed attacks or unjustified and unduly prolonged detention. Finding newer, faster and more efficient ways to get food, health care, shelter and clothing to people in crisis also has been a priority. However, it is only in the last ten years that the special needs and unique roles of refugee and displaced women have been widely recognized and, under pressure from refugee advocates and nongovernmental advocates, steps taken at the international level to address them. Understanding that women, who suffer discrimination and human rights abuses in peacetime, face a different set of problems from men in refugee settings has brought about new ways of developing and implementing programs.

In the mid-1980s, some refugee advocates began to lobby for international action on the needs of refugee women. Following the Third World Conference on Women in Nairobi, Kenya, in 1985, the NGO International Working Group on Refugee Women was formed. Based in Geneva, the working group's mandate was to encourage NGOs, UNHCR and governments to look at the specific needs of refugee women. Four years later, in 1989, the Women's Commission for Refugee Women and Children was created in New York as an NGO that would advocate and provide technical expertise to the United Nations, governments and private voluntary organizations on the unique concerns of uprooted women and children.

UNHCR adopted the Policy on Refugee Women in 1990.[20] A year later it issued Guidelines on the Protection of Refugee Women, which provide information on practical ways to implement the recommendations in the policy.[21] And in 1995, UNHCR issued guidelines on how field workers can prevent and respond to sexual violence in refugee settings.[22]

Written after consultation with UNHCR field workers, government agencies, nongovernmental organizations and refugee women, the Guidelines on the Protection of Refugee Women state that:

> Protection cannot be seen in isolation from the mechanisms that are established to assist refugees. From the initial decisions that are made on camp design and layout to the longer-term programs to assist refugees in finding durable solutions, the choices made in the assistance sectors have profound effects on the protection of refugee women. UNHCR has the responsibility, as part of its protection function, to ensure the non-discriminatory access of all refugees to its assistance.

In addition to laying out the protection needs of refugee women, the guidelines help field staff identify the specific protection issues facing women so that programs can reflect their needs and concerns. The guidelines give concrete recommendations on how to involve refugee women in decisions affecting their security and how to identify particularly risky situations. They stress the importance of collecting statistics, so that demographic data can inform the design of programs. The guidelines suggest mechanisms to improve the reporting of physical and sexual protection problems and programs for improving protection. They propose improvements in camp design and implementation of assistance programs to ensure greater safety.

In an effort to ensure that the guidelines would be incorporated into programs, UNHCR developed a training tool for all staff and implementing partners. This tool, called People-Oriented Planning (POP), encourages field staff to analyze the demographic composition, socioeconomic structure and culture of a refugee population, so that appropriate and effective programs can be established for *all* refugees.[23]

The emergency manuals of UNHCR and most of its implementing partner NGOs stress the importance of managing the overwhelming logistics of massive emergencies, ensuring that the appropriate number of trucks and vehicles are available, that kilos of grains, oil and food supplies are moved quickly into place, and that medicines and medical supplies are prepositioned. POP asks relief workers to consider the *population* being served and its requirements and resources, reminding them that refugee emergencies are not just exercises in logistics. The training offers case studies, which show that analyzing the numbers of men, women, children, adolescents and elderly in the target population and their roles before and after leaving home is critical information in providing relief assistance and benefits all members of the community. For example, when thousands of refugees trekked from Sudan into Kenya, relief organizations were surprised to see that most of the group were adolescent males. The refugees were divided into smaller groups that would live together and share chores, but after a few months health care staff noted many of the young men and boys were malnourished. They eventually realized it was because the boys had never learned how to cook and there were very few women and girls in the population.

POP training emphasizes the importance of establishing direct contact with refugees, and stresses that knowing the profile of the population will help relief staff get to the refugees the correct amounts and rights kind of food, medicine, clothing and shelter materials. It encourages UNHCR and NGO agencies to maximize the participation of women in the administration of camps and the development of assistance programs.

The Fourth World Conference on Women in Beijing, China, further encouraged agencies to address the needs of women in humanitarian emergencies. In preparation for the conference, agencies like the World Food Program (WFP), the food aid organization of the United Nations, issued new policies on women. In its Commitments for Women, WFP stressed that its "commitment to improve the condition of women is based on the fundamental premise that strengthening opportunities and options for women is key to the solutions of the problems of hunger and poverty." WFP has gone on to conduct assessments of its operations in humanitarian emergencies to see how it can begin to implement the new approach and to educate staff about the new policy.

PUTTING POLICY INTO PRACTICE

The success of policies such as the UNHCR guidelines, the WFP commitments and legal instruments to protect women will be proved only when they move from training manuals into the field. In a refugee emergency, when most people are concentrating on the provision of food, shelter, clothing and health care, the special needs and skills of women are often forgotten or ignored. In addition, many field workers, from UN staff to NGOs and local refugee leaders, have little or no knowledge of UNHCR's policy on women or a very limited or distorted understanding of its implications for their work. But progress has been made in the last decade, with a wide range of individuals and organizations pushing the UN and humanitarian organizations to commit themselves to the policies protecting women and girls that are finally in place.

Policies are an important first step in working standards and principles into bureaucracies and into operating procedures, and they can be used by organizations to evaluate programs. When the Women's Commission for Refugee Women and Children visited Bosnia after the Dayton Peace Accords were signed, it asked whether the UNHCR Guidelines on the Protection of Refugee Women were being implemented. It found that few women had been consulted in the design or implementation of projects, even though the UNHCR guidelines and other UN policies call for equal participation of women. Bringing this to the attention of UNHCR and the U.S. government led to a new effort, the Bosnian Women's Initiative (BWI), which promotes greater participation of women in rebuilding Bosnia. This was a first-of-its-kind program of the UNHCR, designed to foster self-reliance through $5 million in small loans, training and assistance directly to widows and women's groups.

UN agencies and governments should make implementation of the Guidelines on the Protection of Refugee Women part of their contracts with implementing agencies and encourage NGOs to accept responsibility for reporting on gender issues. Policies to protect refugee and displaced women will be implemented only if people are held accountable, which is currently not the case. A lack of human and financial resources may compound the problem, but over the long run, giving equal access to women will make programs more effective and efficient.

Some aid workers argue that the policies and programs for women are a form of cultural imperialism, with the West imposing its values onto others. The response to such a challenge is obvious: when customs and practices threaten women's safety and lives, there is nothing to argue. The United Nations and humanitarian organizations have mandates to save lives, and the lives of women and girls are as valuable as those of men and boys. Numerous treaties protect the rights of women and girls, treaties that have been written and approved by most nations of the world.[24]

Given a fresh start, refugee women have proved capable of overcoming the odds, starting anew, and providing leadership even in the most difficult of circumstances. In 1990, when Mangala Sharma fled Bhutan with her husband and young daughter, she encountered a young woman in the refugee camp in Nepal who was crying to be killed. She had been raped by members of the Bhutanese army and had become pregnant. Her husband did not believe her and had taken their two sons and abandoned her in the refugee camp, leaving her desperate and suicidal. Mangala soon discovered dozens of other women who had been raped or sexually abused, many of whom were then turned away by their own families. In response, Mangala created a refugee-run organization, Bhutanese Refugees Aiding Victims of Violence, which trains women in skills such as dressmaking. The money is then used to buy food and other essentials for the women and their families.

Another story of hope from ashes is that of Daphrose. Immediately following the genocide in Rwanda, survivors were often afraid to leave their homes. But as they emerged from hiding, they realized that their experiences of violence and loss were shared. Daphrose, who lost her husband, three daughters and four sons, found that she was not the only widow in her village who needed shelter and food. She helped to organize the first meeting of a widow's group, calling it Duhozanye, which means "let's cheer one another."

"During our first meeting of the widows' association we talked and cried. Mostly we cried," said Daphrose. "Little by little we got used to the situation. We knew crying wasn't the solution. We knew we had a lot of work to do." And work they have done. Together, the association members built 310 houses for themselves and other women who lost family members. "In Rwanda, women are not allowed to go on the roof. That is the man's job. At first we would go out at night to repair our houses, so no one would see us. But then someone found out and gave us pants to wear. Then we decided it did not matter if anyone laughed. We went out during the day." The houses, made of mud brick with tin roofs, sit on small plots where the women grow banana trees, flowers and vegetables. In many yards you will see a goat or small pig, purchased by the association for its members. Some of these efforts are supported by the United Nations High Commissioner for Refugees, which has funds for Quick Impact Projects, and by the United Nations Development Program.

In the sudden ruin of refugee emergencies, women often face the longest odds for survival. Humanitarian assistance groups, with a few vital changes in relief planning, can increase their chances from the beginning. Refugee women and girls, at greater risk when crisis strikes, are perhaps more resilient over the long term. Careful, deliberate efforts to give refugee women a voice will pay off. Fair distribution of food and medicine will save more lives. Providing better protection for women can give them safe space in which to help spur a community's slow recovery from disaster.

5   MEDIATING FOR CHILDREN

Child Protection in Armed Conflicts

Nigel Fisher

Awareness has grown of the dangers of violence to children and of the links between early experience of violence, and violent and other anti-social behavior in childhood and later life. Violence to children is inextricably linked to violence by children, and to manifestations of adult violence.... Reducing violence to children has immense potential for transforming societies for the better.[1]

INTRODUCTION

In situations of armed conflict, children—girls especially—suffer disproportionately. They are the most vulnerable to sickness, exploitation, violence and, all too frequently, death. This chapter examines the intolerable threats faced by children caught in the midst of armed conflict and the new challenges faced by the international community in its efforts to assist such children and their families. The discussion goes beyond the question of humanitarian assistance to examine the collapse, during intrastate conflict, of norms for the well-being and protection of children that are found in every society. It is argued that the increased violence against children in armed conflict is a direct consequence of this collapse of values.

The relevance and applicability of international humanitarian law and human rights law is briefly examined and the argument made for a principled, rather than legalistic, approach to the application of international standards. It is recognized that without concerted advocacy and action for children in the international political arena, it will be difficult to ensure the compliance of warring parties, especially of nonstate actors, with international norms for child protection. The chapter ends with a review of eight areas of advocacy and action that can help to create a climate—ethical, legal and political—in which child protection is more likely to be assured.

A central theme running through the chapter is the premise that armed conflict and children do not mix. Child protection is an absolute right. There is no situation in which it is justifiable to involve children in armed conflict, either as actors or as targets.

IMAGES OF WAR: THE CHILD FRONT AND CENTER

The following statistics on child victims of armed conflict during the period 1985 to 1995 are frequently cited, but familiarity does not lessen their horrific magnitude[2]:

Figure 5.1: Child Victims of Armed Conflict, 1985–1995

- 2 million killed

- 4–5 million disabled

- 12 million left homeless

- More than 1 million orphaned or separated from their parents

- Some 10 million psychologically traumatized

- Up to a quarter of a million children under the age of eighteen serving as combatants in regular and irregular armed forces (as fighters, cooks, messengers, porters, human mine clearers, spies, suicide bombers, sex slaves).

The child is at the center of today's images of war: boy soldiers who wield their automatic rifles with deadly ease; small children separated from their families in vast numbers; the eyes of the traumatized child who has witnessed the violent death of parents and siblings at the hands of marauding militiamen; young girls abducted as sex slaves by armed fighters; children—and women—the targets of mass rape and violence; hundreds of thousands women and children intentionally displaced from their gutted homes and communities, the entire fabric of their lives destroyed.

This is war in which children are not "collateral damage," accidental victims of armed conflict. This is war waged directly against children, and intentionally so. In three short months in 1994, the Rwandan genocide saw the death of between 800,000 and one million Tutsis and moderate Hutus. All, barring a few thousand, were civilians. Some 300,000 were children. An estimated 120,000 children were orphaned or separated from their families. Widespread population displacement accompanied the conflict, while well over two million Hutus, including tens of thousands of extremist *génocidaires*, fled as refugees to neighboring Tanzania and Zaire (now Democratic Congo).

Several thousand kilometers to the north, the protracted civil conflict in Sierra Leone has been a prime example of war waged against children. It has been dubbed "the children's war."[3] Most of the combatants, on all sides, have been children. Tens of thousands of girls have been abducted into sexual slavery by fighters. In the period 1991 to 1997, more than half of the estimated 10,000 deaths and most of the 360,000 people who have been deliberately maimed—frequently though the chopping off of hands—have been children. Of an estimated 1.8 million displaced Sierra Leonians, 700,000 or more—40 percent—have been children. Countless tens of thousands of other children were driven into hiding in the bush as villages were ravaged repeatedly. "The degree of suffering of Sierra Leone's children and adolescents, as targets in the war and usually the primary victims of violence, has been uncommonly high."[4]

There have always been civilian casualties in war. But in today's intrastate conflicts, 90 percent or more of casualties are civilian; and the majority of these are women and children. Fifty percent of the 23 million refugees worldwide, and an equivalent number of internally displaced persons, are children.[5]

What kinds of wars are these, and what channels are open to those who want to ensure child protection in the midst of such conflicts?

Armed Conflict in a Post-Cold-War World

The period following the end of the Cold War in 1989 and 1990 has been predominantly one of intrastate rather than interstate conflict. Gone is the global East-West polarization that tended to define and to some extent contain warfare, whether international or intrastate. With increasing frequency after 1990, simmering tensions between groups within states have erupted into chronic civil conflict, characterized by extreme violence.

A significant number of these civil conflicts are fought in failed states, characterized by the collapse of governments and other political institutions, economic infrastructure and legal systems; by the destruction of the entire social fabric—households and communities torn apart, civil society institutions weakened or destroyed, schooling and other essential services severely eroded; and by deadly conflict pitting neighbor against neighbor. In such "nonstructured ... identity-based" conflicts,[6] distinctions between combatant and noncombatant disappear. Fighting takes place in homes and schools, in city streets and rural communities, in farms, fields, mountains and jungle. The whole social fabric of life is destroyed. Combatants have little or no discipline and banditry is widespread. The collapse and fragmentation of social and economic infrastructure has led to what some have called the "privatization of violence"[7] as armed bands, loyal to distinct warlords, fight for booty rather than for any clear political objective or ideology.

When conflict is labeled as ethnic, when opposing leaders demonize all members of the opposing camp, there is no hiding place for civilians. Traditional refuges such as churches, mosques, schools and hospitals are attacked with impunity. It is insufficient that adults kill each other. Children, as the future of the other side, are dehumanized and targeted also. "To kill the big rats, you have to kill the little rats," proclaimed the Rwandan Hutu extremist Radio Mille Collines in early 1994, as it exhorted its listeners to kill Tutsi *inyenzi* (the Kinyarwanda for "cockroaches").

Today, terrorization and displacement of civilian populations are commonly employed strategies of war. The practice of collective punishment holds sway in many civil conflicts, a form of terror warfare intended to inflict civilian casualties on whole populations because they constitute the base for the opposing force or because, ethnically or nationally, they represent the enemy in their entirety.[8] In such total war, terror against civilians is deliberate, an essential part of a strategy of ethnic cleansing.

The predominance of civil conflict and consequent breakdown in social order, as well as the proliferation of light weapons and small arms, have dramatically heightened the vulnerability of children caught in the midst of zones of armed conflict. In increasing numbers of societies affected by turbulence, violence and outright armed conflict, children are both actors in and victims of violence. As cited above, among civilian victims of armed conflict, children suffer disproportionately. They are least able to defend themselves and are most vulnerable to disease, abuse and exploitation. Their world collapses around them; family, community and school collapse, friends disappear; any sense of normality is destroyed; they are repeatedly exposed to horrific violence and loss. Thus those concerned with child welfare in the midst and aftermath of civil conflict confront a daunting range of challenges in situations in which almost all children are suffering the traumatic effects of exposure to extreme violence and loss.

WHO has estimated that in situations of armed conflict, the death rate of children is up to 24 times greater than in times of peace. While the incidence of death and injury due to violence directly targeted against children has increased markedly in recent civil conflicts, this is only part of the picture of how armed conflict impacts on children's health. In peacetime, communicable diseases are the major cause of death among children. But in wartime, damage to safe water supplies and sanitation systems, disruption of primary health care services, nonavailability of essential drugs or displacement all serve to increase the risk of these diseases.

Children are the first to suffer and die. Morbidity and mortality due to diarrhea, dehydration, dysentery and cholera increase markedly. Acute respiratory infections and pneumonia, malaria and measles increase exponentially and are often fatal. WHO estimates that in certain areas in Somalia during the civil war, more than half the deaths were caused by measles. Under-fives account for the largest proportion of suffering and death from malnutrition. Continued breast-feeding of infants, who are at especially high risk, is important, but mothers are often malnourished too. When food is scarce, it is quickly evidenced in wasting among children, while the contamination of food and water sets in motion the disastrous interaction of infection and malnutrition. This is the foundation upon which the impact of direct, targeted violence against children is built.[9]

CHILDREN AT HIGHEST RISK

While all children are vulnerable in the midst of armed conflict, children of poor, marginalized populations are at higher risk. The most disadvantaged families (economically, socially, educationally) are least able to assure adequate food and health care for their children or to protect them from violence. But at highest risk are children without families, displaced children, and girls.

The Family: The First Line of Protection

The family remains the children's primary protective unit and assurance of survival and development.[10] Separation from the family, especially in the midst of armed conflict, is traumatic in itself, but such separation also exposes the child to heightened risk of abuse, sexual exploitation, forced conscription, physical abuse and impairment, and educational deprivation. This is why any strategy centered on child welfare and protection in the midst of conflict or its aftermath must address the importance of maintaining family cohesion and not only address the needs of the child in isolation from the family and community context. High priority must be given to prevention of family separation or abandonment or, where these take place, to family tracing and rapid reunification of the child with his or her own family or with a foster family, ideally from the child's own community or cultural group.

Building on the long experience of the International Committee of the Red Cross (ICRC), the identification, care, family tracing and reunification of children with families is becoming increasingly systematized and effective in times of acute crisis. In the years following the 1994 Rwanda genocide, more than 60,000 children have been reunified with families or settled with new ones, either through spontaneous adoption directly by Rwandans themselves, or through the family reunification efforts of international humanitarian organizations. Subsequently, ICRC, UNHCR, UNICEF and the Save the Children Alliance have established agreed-upon standards and training guidelines for the care and family reunification of unaccompanied children.

In any society, children of economically marginalized families are most vulnerable to high-risk factors—illness, poor nutrition, family stress, low education levels, inadequate social service support or nonstimulating social environments. When development strategies fail and lead to the onset of violence, the combination of poverty and social disintegration leads to extraordinary physical and psychological suffering for children. As previously noted, the physical impact of organized violence on children in terms of mortality, disease, injury, disability and malnutrition is dramatic and demands immediate action. However, while urgent and critical, the response to physical and survival needs alone is insufficient. The psychosocial, emotional and developmental vulnerabilities of the child must be equally addressed.

Increasingly, children face a total onslaught on the fabric of life and continuity around them: the loss of family members; breakup of families, kinship networks and communities, peer groups and schools; exploitation, physical and sexual abuse, disruption of gender and authority roles. In the broader environment, traditional leadership, political and administrative structures collapse in unison with societal values and mores. Displacement resulting from organized violence is particularly threatening to the child's survival, health and well-being. The additional threat of separation from the family adds to the high risk of abuse, exploitation, physical impairment, educational deprivation and psychological trauma.

The family remains the primary social unit for supporting the survival, growth and development of children. In the midst of crisis, the best interests of the child are served in the context of a family that is cohesive and, if possible, stable. The resilient child—able to achieve good developmental outcomes despite high risk and to cope successfully with adversity—benefits from a range of familial protective factors, beginning with the critical early bonding and interaction with the mother (or substitute caregiver in the family). Separation from the family is traumatic for the child; prevention of abandonment and separation or, where these take place, the rapid reunification with the child's own family or a foster family is critical. For most traumatized children, the best route to recovery is the consistent care and attention of a loving adult.

In the midst of crisis, parents—often the mother as sole head of household—require special support and access to key social services if they are to acquire and use the skills, knowledge and material resources necessary to assure the child of a basic level of nutrition, health, shelter, care and attention, and to filter stressors on the child from outside the family. Even in the midst of armed violence, access to critical information necessary for survival and protection is vital to the capacity of parents and families to provide child care, food security and a healthy environment or to make adequate use of available health services. Families need external material assistance as a last resort and only when their own resources and coping mechanisms are insufficient.

Children abandoned by or separated from the family and the protection and support that it provides are extremely vulnerable to hunger, disease and perhaps death. They are also highly vulnerable to physical, sexual and psychological exploitation and abuse; girls may be raped and prostituted, boys recruited as armed combatants. Special community and family support initiatives, core social services and protective measures are required to aid children's rehabilitation and return to even a rudimentary semblance of normalcy. This usually means providing support to the women—mothers, older sisters—who are often the heads of household. The immediate need for provision of relief does not preclude the need for humanitarian actors to address these wider support requirements.

The normative and political contexts of child rights advocacy and child protection in armed conflict are discussed subsequently. However, as previously stated, it is important to emphasize that, at their most fundamental, child survival, protection and development are best assured within the context of a caring, capable family. The child without a family in wartime is the most vulnerable of all to violence, exploitation, abuse, sickness, malnutrition and death. Unfortunately, few international humanitarian interventions specifically include strategies for promoting family resilience or for reinforcing the family's own coping strategies. The importance of the family environment has thus been given special emphasis in this discussion, prior to a review of the normative and political contexts of child protection. All three contexts are central to a strategy to promote child protection in the midst of armed conflict.

Displaced Children

Displacement resulting from organized violence is particularly threatening to the child's survival, health and well-being.[11] "Studies of refugees and displaced persons show that, during the early stages of displacement, death rates among children under five years of age are far higher than among older children and adults."[12] Displaced persons crowded into camps with polluted water sources, inadequate environmental sanitation and poor hygiene are highly vulnerable to deadly outbreaks of dysentery and cholera. Basic health services are poor or nonexistent, shelter is often inadequate, and children are the first to suffer the consequences. In Goma (Zaire/Democratic Congo), one third of the children who died in six refugee centers in 1994 to 1995 were killed by pneumonia.

While refugees in third countries are afforded international legal protections and can frequently be reached by international humanitarian agencies, populations displaced within the borders of their own country do not have the equal assurance of legal protection and access to emergency relief services. Internal displacement is often unplanned, chaotic and on a massive scale. The internally displaced are frequently harassed by government or factional forces in control of the territory in which they find themselves. Children in such groups are highly vulnerable to conscription and abduction, as well as to psychological, physical and sexual abuse both from marauding forces as well as from adults from among the displaced population itself.

As a result of large-scale displacement, refugees often congregate in camps in third countries, where they can gain access to protection and relief. The nature and consequences of internal displacement are even more diverse; such displacement may be massive in times of acute crisis, or repeated, as the displaced flee from sanctuary to sanctuary in response to threat. The stress of such constant and chronic instability on children is acute and confronts humanitarians with the enormous challenge of ensuring flexible, rapid and sustained service provision. Frequently, displacement is not just a by-product of conflict, but the direct result of a military decision to attack and displace entire communities. In such circumstances, the intercession of humanitarian actors with combatant leaders is necessary to negotiate access to displaced children or, ideally, to negotiate protected zones or humanitarian corridors for such populations. In other cases, it is difficult to locate and identify the internally displaced when they move to periurban locations, relocate with relatives, scatter or go into hiding among the general population.

Addressing the rights and needs of the internally displaced—and especially of children—remains one of the major challenges facing humanitarian actors today and requires a multiple response strategy involving advocacy, assessment, care and protection. At the political level, national authorities—whether the government in power or those aspiring to power—are responsible for the well-being of displaced populations, even though population displacement might be a deliberate strategy employed by these same leaders. Yet constant intercession with authorities to address the conditions of the displaced, prevent child abuse, allow access and return to communities of origin is a vitally important function of humanitarian actors. Recognizing that governments do not always have effective control of areas where the internally displaced are located, "early, impartial and above-board liaison with opposition groups, including military commanders, may be critical to accessing groups of displaced children and ensuring their protection."[13]

A frequently overlooked aspect of protection is the documentation of identity and registration of births. These are significant factors in ensuring future recognition of citizenship, access to schooling, employment and a range of other legal rights.

The design and conduct of assessments among internally displaced populations is particularly difficult, costly and time-consuming, and demands coordinated action between humanitarian actors. Such assessment must involve the displaced, including children, and, given the extreme vulnerability of displaced children to many forms of exploitation and abuse, data on physical safety, psychosocial well-being and a range of child rights violations must be collected in addition to standard nutrition and health status information.

As this chapter is written, coordination of international humanitarian action for the the internally displaced remains the subject of considerable ongoing discussion. Agreement on appropriate coordination arrangements remains elusive. For those concerned with the well-being of the child, it is essential that in discussions of coordination or in direct advocacy and action, "displaced children must never become invisible, must never "fall through the cracks.'"[14]

Sexual Violence: The Particular Vulnerability of Girls and Women

In the midst of armed conflict, girls and women are the main actors in endeavoring to assure family cohesion, protection, food and health security. Simultaneously, they are prone to the most egregious forms of violence. While gender violence is not unique to girls and women, they are targeted extensively and disproportionately. Their health needs are also quite distinct. Several issues are of particular significance: the targeting of girls for rape and other forms of sexual abuse, the resulting risks of HIV/AIDS infection or of other sexually transmitted diseases and the lack of reproductive health services available to women and girls caught in the midst of armed conflict. Furthermore, additional stresses are placed on traditional family roles of girls and women as care-givers and providers.

Increasingly, rape is organized, systematic and brutal.[15] In Rwanda, rape was practiced methodically in all areas where the *Interahamwe* militia were massacring civilians. In Bosnia, rape was used as a means of destroying the very essence of the Moslem community, to break down family ties and community cohesion. From Bosnia to Guatemala, from northern Uganda to Liberia, girls have been abducted by combatants and repeatedly raped or turned into concubines—sex slaves. In many of the camps of combatants in the Sierra Leonean civil conflict, girls outnumbered boys and young men.[16] In the Lord's Resistance Army in Northern Uganda/Southern Sudan, the rank of male combatants determines the number of "wives' to which they are entitled. Girls not wishing to submit are beaten—and sometimes disfigured—until they do. Sexually transmitted diseases, HIV infection and unwanted pregnancies increase exponentially. The traumatic consequences of rape are considered by psychologists to be singularly intrusive, long-lasting and especially difficult to overcome. A study in Colombia points to higher rates of suicide among girls than boys, because of displacement, insecurity and exposure to violence.

Even without subjection to such physical and psychological abuse, lack of access to health services is a special problem for girls and women. The frequent absence of reproductive health services and pre- and postnatal care increases their vulnerability and contributes to an increased incidence of severe gynecological complications and infant and maternal mortality rates. Even the lack of feminine hygiene products for use during menstruation is an assault on health and dignity.

In civil conflict situations, especially among displaced populations, significant proportions of households are headed by females. Not only is physical insecurity for the entire family an increased risk, but the workload of women is increased. Female children are called upon to assist in assuming family support duties them much more than boys are—caring for younger siblings, fetching firewood and water, cooking and cleaning.[17]

The impact of added burdens or responsibilities is not always negative. For example, World Vision International points to the increased role of women in Somalia as heads of local NGOs and women's groups, women and girls in the forefront of movements for peace in Burundi, and the assertiveness of women and girls who have become family breadwinners in Rwanda. But too often, insufficient information is available about gendered roles, strengths and vulnerabilities as the basis for appropriate protection strategies or for activities designed to support the family leadership roles that women—and girls—perform during and after armed conflict.

Lastly, there is an evident requirement for gender-specific analysis that distinguishes the special roles, needs and vulnerabilities of women and girls in armed conflict and that would facilitate the identification of appropriate humanitarian responses and recovery strategies.

APPLYING STANDARDS FOR THE PROTECTION OF CHILDREN IN CONFLICT ZONES

The issue of how to protect civilians in conflicts which not only deliberately target civilians, but use them as hostages and human shields, is ... of the essence in the current humanitarian environment.[18]

Hammarberg[19] notes that total war and terror against civilians flout two important aspects of customary humanitarian law: the principles of *differentiation* (that military targets should be determined with such precision that civilian populations and property are not unnecessarily damaged) and *proportionality* (that there must be a reasonable proportion between the damage inflicted on the civilian population and property and the military value of the operation). Such principles hold little sway when humanitarian relief to large civilian populations is obstructed, when children are targeted or conscripted as killers. The evolution of international humanitarian law has sought to place limits on the conduct of warfare. But in intrastate civil conflict especially, such limits are ignored with impunity; any vestige of respect for social values and international standards is rapidly eroded.[20]

The Universality of Cultural Norms for Child Protection

Yet in every society and culture, there do exist norms and values regarding the care and protection of children, standards upheld by tradition and long-standing practice, as illustrated in Figure 5.2 below.[21]

Violence against children—especially the killing of children—should be abhorrent to most people, as it violates these fundamental cultural norms and and social values. Yet children are increasingly targeted, exploited and forced into active, violent roles. Violence against children is expressed not only individually but collectively. When social cohesion breaks down, the means of expressing prochild values breaks down too.

Sudanese respondents, for example, were asked to explain why they thought values (Figure 5.2) had changed so much for the worse, as children and women are killed in acts of wanton violence against villages and kinship support structures break down. To list but a few of the many reasons given: they identified the breakdown of traditional authority and its marginalization by political movements; the disruption of transmission of traditional values because of family separation; the brutalization and pervasive insecurity caused by war; poor discipline of the military; the availability of light weapons; and the pervasiveness of poverty.

During civil conflict, habitual systems break down but are not replaced by constructive alternatives. Particularly where ethnicity is a factor in conflict, there is a significant failure to universalize social rules and cultural norms that value the well-being of the child beyond the family or kinship group. This creates space for a collective schizophrenia that enables the combatant to love his own children while simultaneously attacking the children of another group, as groups travel the common road from self-excuse through blame to hatred of other groups. Through normal social interaction and observation, children learn to be concerned for others, to care, help or console. But such a "social script"[22] is not

---

Figure 5.2: Southern Sudanese Traditional Values and Practices Relating to the Protection of Children and Civilians in Conflict

PROTECTING CHILDREN

- Children were prohibited from going to fight until after initiation into adulthood.
- Children were protected by society in general, because they belonged to the entire community.
- Children were provided with food first before anyone else in the family.
- Children of the vanquished were not killed by the victor if left behind.
- Traditionally, children were taken away from areas of conflict.
- Children were protected through proper upbringing, by caring for them when sick, hungry, dirty and by teaching them traditional ways to look after cattle, cook and clean.
- Children could not be killed according to tribal law; if a child was killed, his life had to be compensated for with one hundred cows.
- Children who had lost their parents were cared for by relatives, friends or others in the community.

PROTECTING CIVILIANS IN CONFLICT

- Women, children and the elderly were not killed in battle or when captured.
- Women and children were free to move in any location without being killed.
- Civilians were kept in the background and never allowed near battle lines or conflict areas; thus, only combatants used to die in war.
- Traditionally, a woman could throw herself on her husband if he had been injured, to prevent him from being killed.
- Battles were fought on neutral ground, away from population areas.
- Before fighting began, the chiefs had to agree that the issue was worth the shedding of blood.

necessarily inclusive in nature. It can be exclusive, that is, confined to one's own group while excluding others. Pioneers in the education field have built upon the value of what is variously called peace education, global education, or futures education, which is designed to help children learn tolerance, to learn that "different" is not "bad," to expose children of different groups to each other, to encourage inclusivity rather than exclusivity. Religion, to the extent that it is inclusive and universalist, is also a powerful means of transcending lesser divisions and promoting healing.

A Definition of Child Protection in Armed Conflict

If children are to be safeguarded when norms break down, what does child protection in the midst of intrastate conflict mean?[23] In operational terms, such protection might be defined as:

(a) the protection of children from harm inflicted by others (including, for example: exploitation, abuse, neglect, cruel and degrading treatment or recruitment); (b) the protection of the humanitarian imperative or, in other words, seeking to guarantee the right to humanitarian assistance in the face of efforts of combatants to deny access to civilians and children in need and to abuse that assistance. This demands a clear normative position backed up by reference to relevant legal instruments and supported by advocacy, dissemination, training, monitoring and reporting.

Such protection of children means ensuring respect—by governments, persons in authority and others with influence or control over children's lives—for the rights of children, whether enshrined in indigenous norms or in international standards, such as in the Convention on the Rights of the Child, in other international human rights treaties and conventions and international humanitarian law, particularly as they relate to the prevention of all forms of violence, exploitation, abuse and neglect of children. Protection, so defined, involves the practical implementation of human rights and humanitarian law on behalf of children.

In complex emergencies, the promotion of certain fundamental humanitarian principles is essential to ensure that children's rights are protected. Such principles include the primacy of the humanitarian imperative, prohibition of denial of access to humanitarian assistance for children, neutrality, impartiality, accountability, transparency and respect for the safety of humanitarian workers. As discussed below, not all of these principles are enshrined in international law, but they are increasingly recognized and accepted—at least within the community of humanitarian actors—as minimum international standards. However, some legal commentators on international humanitarian law and certainly most parties to internal conflict would dispute this assertion of principled universality.

THE ADEQUACY OF INTERNATIONAL STANDARDS

There is indeed considerable current debate over the relevance and applicability of international humanitarian law and human-rights laws in internal armed conflicts, total wars in which there are no rules and in which terror against women and children is a conscious and deliberate strategy.[24] It is tragic that these conflicts, which are the source of the majority of today's humanitarian crises, are on the increase despite the growth of a considerable body of international humanitarian and human-rights law in recent decades. Today, the international community has at its disposal an impressive array of humanitarian standards and principles—the cornerstones of which are the Four Geneva Conventions of 1949 and the two Additional Protocols of 1977—and of human-rights law, which includes the Convention on the Rights of the Child.

International Humanitarian Law

The Four Geneva Conventions and the two Additional Protocols govern the conduct of military operations and require belligerents to spare those not participating in hostilities. For example, the Fourth Geneva Convention Relative to the Protection of Civilian Persons in Time of War prohibits measures of brutality against civilians, whether applied by civilian or state actors. While the conventions are considered to apply primarily to interstate conflict, Common Article 3 applies to internal conflicts, enumerating the fundamental rights and protections of persons not actively participating in hostilities[25] Common Article 3 has effectively entered the domain of customary law and is considered to be universally applicable to international or intrastate conflict, to states and to nonstates parties.

Of the Additional Protocols, Protocol I governs the conduct of hostilities, requiring that fighting parties distinguish between combatants and civilians at all times and attack only military targets. Articles 77 and 78 specifically refer to children. Article 77 stipulates that "children shall be the object of special respect and shall be protected against any form of indecent assault." Protocol II addresses conflicts within states, supplementing Common Article 3 through the provision that "children be provided with the care and aid they require, including education and family reunion."

It is apparent that collectively these constituent elements of International Humanitarian Law (IHL) stipulate a wide range of protections of civilians in armed conflict, including children. However, two competing ideologies are at work in IHL:

- That of compassion for suffering victims; and
- The discourse of military necessity, namely that war is a necessary evil within which parties should endeavor to do their best—what is feasible—to protect civilians from unnecessary suffering.

By definition, IHL represents a compromise between humanitarian and military objectives and thus leaves loopholes in the standards that are set. An examination of IHL instruments reveals differences in the definition of the age of childhood within and between instruments; in their applicability to internal conflicts as against conflicts between states; in their applicability to nonstates parties, that is, fighting factions or groups that are not governmental. Protection is sometimes open to interpretation, dependant on circumstances, politics and personalities. Certain terms are left vague and open to a variety of interpretations. For example:

- Who decides what is "excessive" loss of civilian life?
- What are "feasible" measures for ensuring protection?
- What is an "indiscriminate" attack or threat of violence?
- What does it mean exactly to say that the child is the object of "special respect"?

It is inevitable that there would be considerable difference in interpretation of these terms between humanitarian actors on the one side and armed groups—governmental or factional—on the other.

The Fourth Geneva Convention has been ratified by 186 countries, but the protocols have lower ratification rates (144 and 136 states respectively). In addition, if one takes as an example the applicability of Protocol II to conflicts within states, a series of legal problems present themselves. Strictly interpreted, its application to internal conflict is limited to situations in which the forces of a High Contracting Party (state) are in conflict with dissident armed forces or other organized armed groups. This would exclude the many current internal armed conflicts between factions in failed states.

Even where countries have ratified, they may argue that IHL does not apply to their internal situation. Again, taking Protocol II as the example: government protagonists might argue that the level of intensity of conflict has not reached the stipulated threshold that would bring Protocol II into force. Even where it may appear that the threshold has been reached, governments may resist application of Protocol II, citing the rights of sovereignty and noninterference in internal affairs.

In conclusion, even this cursory overview of IHL illustrates that a strictly legal analysis will reveal a range of compromises and loopholes that circumscribe IHL applicability, especially to internal armed conflicts.

Human Rights Law

Unlike humanitarian law, human rights laws—and the protections and rights guaranteed in them—are not restricted to particular situations or circumstances, or by the nature of conflict. The principles and legal obligations contained within the normative framework of human rights instruments are fundamental to the protection of children at all times, including in the midst of armed conflict.

Within human rights law, two instruments are of particular concern to children in armed conflict: the Convention Relating to the Status of Refugees of 1951 and its Protocol of 1967, which provide basic standards for the protection of refugees in countries of asylum; and the Convention on the Rights of the Child (CRC) of 1989, which recognizes a comprehensive list of rights that apply during times of both peace and war. The CRC is a powerful instrument, given its near-universal ratification (it has been ratified by every state except Somalia and the U.S.A.). The CRC allows for no derogation of its provisions, even in times of armed conflict; it provides a comprehensive definition of standards for the treatment of all children and demands that the best interests of the child be the primary consideration in all actions concerning children (Article 3).

While the entire convention is applicable to all children in all circumstances, Articles 38 and 39 specifically relate to the protection of children in armed conflict. They address child soldiers, the provision of humanitarian assistance and relief and the rehabilitation and social integration of child victims of armed conflict. Article 38 is important in that it brings together humanitarian and human rights law. Its first paragraph specifically requires States Parties "to respect and ensure respect for rules of international humanitarian law applicable to them in armed conflicts which are relevant to the child." The fourth paragraph of the same article states: "in accordance with their obligations under international humanitarian law to protect the civilian population in armed conflict, States Parties shall take all feasible measures to ensure protection and care of children who are affected by an armed conflict.[26]

However, careful reading of Article 38 reveals compromises on two critical issues. The first is on the age for involvement of children in hostilities: this age is set at fifteen years, despite the definition, in Article 1 of the CRC, of the child as a human being below the age of eighteen years.

Thus in a precise situation of extreme risk to the child, the convention weakens the provisions for protection. Secondly, states are left with the loophole of feasibility: they are required only to take "all feasible measures' to ensure that children below fifteen do not take direct part in hostilities. Once again, what is "feasible" and who decides?

It is worth noting that before the CRC, human rights instruments generally considered children as vulnerable persons in need of special assistance and protection and as objects of rights exercised through their parents or adult guardians. However, the convention establishes a legal framework in which children are specifically recognized as subjects of rights and as having a distinct legal personalty. The convention reflects the perspective, consistently reinforced by the Committee on the Rights of the Child in its monitoring activities, that the rights of the child are interdependent, indivisible and nonderogable. The near-universal ratification of the convention, as noted above, gives it a particular weight and importance.

The CRC is a powerful tool for advocacy, but one has to recognize that despite virtual worldwide acceptance of the CRC, the prevailing reality is still one in which children are consistently subjected to the full brutality of war. As with IHL, human rights treaties and conventions can be formally ratified only by states. But this does not stop child rights advocates from making the case for the universality—and thus for the universal applicability—of the normative frameworks provided by both human rights and IHL.

Graça Machel, formerly the UN Secretary-General's appointed expert on the impact of armed conflict on children, stated in her landmark study presented to the General Assembly in 1996:

> that we seek to have protection framed by the standards and norms embodied in international law, national legislation and local custom and practice.... Any purported mitigating circumstances through which Governments or their opponents seek to justify infringements of children's rights in times of armed conflict must be seen by the international community for what they are: reprehensible and intolerable.[27]

Ms. Machel's argument that humanitarian principles and standards, embodied both in human rights law and international humanitarian law, are universal and must be universally applied is one endorsed by humanitarian actors worldwide. They argue that nonstate parties, not just sovereign governments, should uphold obligations and responsibilities to citizens of a country. Certainly, with the growing trend toward the targeting and exploitation of children in armed civil conflicts, it is vital that standards relevant to children be respected by all actors in such conflicts, including nonstate actors.

Advocates of humanitarian action also argue that a principled approach should involve the advocacy, adoption and enforcement of legal norms and the assurance of respect for the fundamental principles reflected by those norms, "even in places where there is no formal legal system to enforce them."[28] From a humanitarian perspective, no abuse of children is ever justifiable. There can be no argument against adherence to universal principles that assure child rights and protection or against the fundamental thesis that it is intolerable to wage war on children.

Many human rights advocates consider that the legal frameworks provided by international human rights treaties and conventions—best epitomized in the Convention on the Rights of the Child—are generally adequate and applicable to the protection of children at all times, in periods of armed conflict and during postconflict reconstruction, and in situations of conflict both within and between states. While there is room for improvement in these legal regimes—human rights standards continue to develop progressively to address particular issues or groups, such as children—the argument is advanced that the most critical challenge is to improve monitoring, reporting on and compliance with these international standards. Likewise, although IHL originated in the regulation of armed conflicts between states and in the protection of victims of international hostilities, it is cited with increasing frequency with regard to the regulation of the behavior of warring parties in situations of armed conflict within states.

It is acknowledged that addressing the involvement and exploitation of children in armed conflict is a difficult and complex matter. But simply stated, humanitarian advocates argue that "the most significant limitations to corrective action ... have been inadequate public, private, national and international objection to the abuse of children and inadequate efforts to find constructive ways by which they can be protected and assisted when abused."[29]

The argument for adopting a principled position on the rights and protection of children in armed conflict, rather than a strictly legal interpretation of the applicability of IHL and human-rights law, has considerable merit. Yet, despite the universality of such standards, despite the growing number of international conventions and treaties, children are increasingly vulnerable to violence and abuse when trapped in armed conflicts with national boundaries.

Unfortunately, few combatants in armed conflict within states are aware of, or influenced by, assertions of the applicability of international humanitarian law and human rights laws. Civilians—children and women in particular—are targeted, exploited and killed with impunity. From Somalia to Chechnya, from Tadjikistan to Northern Iraq to Sudan, in Rwanda and Democratic Congo, ICRC officials and workers of international humanitarian organizations are held hostage, abused or killed without compunction. In growing numbers of conflicts, the symbol of the Red Cross or Red Crescent provides little protection. At best, there is widespread ignorance among combatants and, at worst, willful disregard of the humanitarian imperative, namely that humanitarian assistance should be provided to all civilians in need, independent of political or military considerations.

While this author concludes that advocacy of a principled approach to the application of international humanitarian and human-rights standards should be encouraged over a strictly legal interpretation, this discussion of the adequacy of international standards has pointed to a number of significant difficulties that impede the application of such a principled approach, especially if attempted in isolation. Thus the following section outlines a range of measures that, if implemented, could promote more consistent and rigorous compliance with international standards, thus leading to greater assurance of protection of children in the midst of armed conflict.

CREATING A CLIMATE FOR BETTER CHILD PROTECTION

When combatants remain unmoved by moral suasion or international condemnation, such strategies have to be complemented by other forms of persuasion in the political and economic domains. If international humanitarian law is as yet unable to provide adequate protection to children caught up in armed conflict, if there is a dichotomy between rhetoric and practice in the application of the Convention on the Rights of the Child, then what steps can be taken to ensure better protection for children? How are the parties to conflict to be taken to task for disregarding humanitarian law and human rights for children?

It is clear that the protection of children—and of civilians in general—is not automatically guaranteed by the existence of international humanitarian law and human-rights laws. The challenge is to ensure compliance, yet in many situations, conflicting parties will argue that such laws do not even apply. This should not lead to the conclusion that such international standards are irrelevant, for their evolution has irrefutably provided a growing legal framework and normative umbrella for concrete measures that have facilitated the protection of civilian populations in the midst of many armed conflicts. But IHL and human-rights standards cannot be applied in a vacuum. They must form part—an important part—of a complex of advocacy and action that emphasizes that application of humanitarian law and human rights is not only a legal issue but also a normative one, based on principles that are universal in nature. Concerning children, this means starting from the fundamental principle that children and armed conflict do not mix—violence against children is abhorrent and not to be countenanced.

The ability of the international community to advance in addressing the problem of rights abuses and of the lack of application of international norms to the situation of children in internal conflicts may hinge on its capacity to marry advocacy and action in the legal, moral and political dimensions. First, this is to combine, in a credible way, a legal interpretation of the relevance and application of international standards with the broader normative position that such standards convey universal principles and behavioral norms regarding children that apply to all people in all situations. This latter principled approach posits that violence against children is abhorrent and unjustifiable without exception.

Such a perspective rejects totally the loopholes of feasibility and expediency in any discussion of protection of children and their rights. But it also recognizes that progress is unlikely without the existence of international political will to promote and enforce such protection consistently and impartially. Whether through their own volition or through the application of international persuasion, pressure or the credible threat of sanctions or other punitive measures, parties to conflict must stop targeting children.

This section considers a range of mutually supportive areas of advocacy and action grounded in both law and principle that, if implemented together, could lead to more assured protection for children in the midst of armed conflict. Particular emphasis is given to initiatives in political arenas, in which the cause of children is habitually overlooked.

I. Extend the Reach of International Humanitarian Law and Human Rights Law

As noted previously, much can be done to widen the applicability and interpretation of international standards and to reduce existing conditionalities regarding their application. This is especially important given the likely acceleration in the twentieth century's trend toward "the increasing international regulation of more and more issues once typically seen as part of state domestic jurisdiction"[30] and if IHL is to become more broadly accepted as applicable to nonstates parties in internal conflicts (see also subsection 2 below).

Wider, more comprehensive ratification of existing instruments could also be the focus of social mobilization activities—for example, to extend ratification of Additional Protocols I and II of 1977 to the Geneva Conventions. This applies equally to regional conventions, such as the African Charter on the Rights and Welfare of the Child. The African Charter stipulates, without exception, the age of maturity as eighteen years, including the age of recruitment and deployment into armed forces. Thus at present, using the criterion of age, the African Charter provides better protection to children in armed conflict than does Article 38 of the Convention on the Rights of the Child. However, by mid-1998, the charter had been ratified by some dozen African states only; fifteen such ratifications are required for the charter to enter into force. Africa's children would be well served by a political leader prepared to spearhead an initiative for continent-wide ratification of the charter.

There is space for development of higher standards of protection within existing laws and conventions. For example, the international Coalition to Stop the Use of Child Soldiers, created in May 1998 to call for an optional protocol to the Convention on the Rights of the Child, is specifically intended to plug the loophole provided by Article 38. Advocates of the protocol demand a prohibition on the military recruitment and use in hostilities of all young people under eighteen years of age. While this does not present a legislative problem for many countries in which the legal age of conscription is eighteen years, it finds more resistance among countries—including a significant number in Europe and North America—which have no conscription policy, but which have voluntary enlistment applicable to young people below eighteen years of age.

There are many reasons why children under the age of eighteen should be excluded from the armed forces. Generally, international human rights law defines a child as anyone under eighteen. Eighteen is the legal voting age set by the laws of a great many countries, marking "the formal transition from childhood to adulthood."[31] The recruitment and deployment of child soldiers should also be considered as unlawful child labor, because of the hazardous nature of the work involved. The ILO Convention No. 138 on Minimum Age, adopted in 1973, establishes the minimum age for hazardous work at eighteen years.

From both an ethical and a logical perspective, it makes little sense to define a child as anyone under eighteen, then to disregard this definition for expediency's sake, especially in situations of highest potential harm to the child. Even those (frequently northern) states who argue that they are not part of the problem when it comes to the deployment of underage children in armed conflict might recognize that it makes absolute sense to subscribe to the highest possible standards for the well-being and protection of children, without exception. As the Coalition to Stop the Use of Child Soldiers has stated:

> A principled stand in defense of children is not an empty gesture. As has been seen in the international campaign against landmines, for the ban to be effective it is essential that, ultimately, the entire world community renounces the use of the weapon, and not merely those of its members who have deployed it indiscriminately or irresponsibly in the recent past.[32]

A very recent example of the possibility of continuous movement toward higher standards of conduct and protection is the creation of the International Criminal Court (ICC) in July 1998, which will try cases of genocide, war crimes and crimes against humanity. The world's first permanent war-crimes tribunal will obviate the need for future creation of ad hoc tribunals, such as those set up in recent years to deal with atrocities committed in the former Yugoslavia and Rwanda. Crimes against humanity are set out for the first time in an international treaty. Of particular relevance for children is the designation as war crimes of: (a) enforced pregnancy (the crime of raping a woman with the expressed intention of making her pregnant), which was inflicted on countless girls during the mass rapes in Bosnia-Herzegovina between 1992 and 1995, and which was the outcome of the genocide and mass rapes inflicted in Rwanda from April to June 1994; (b) the use and recruitment of children under the age of fifteen years in armed forces, in both internal and international conflicts.

2. Ensure Application of International Norms in the Context of Civil Conflict

An important part of the strategy to ensure compliance with international humanitarian law and human-rights law in situations of internal armed conflict, especially by nonstate parties and factions, is to press for written commitments to established international standards by such actors. Graça Machel is of the conviction that "it is well worth encouraging nonstate entities to make a formal commitment to abide fully by the relevant standards" since:

> human rights and humanitarian standards reflect fundamental human values which exist in all societies. . . . Just as the international community has insisted that all States have a legitimate concern that human rights be respected by others, so too it is clear that all groups in society, no matter what their relationship to the State concerned, must respect human

rights.... non-state entities should, for all practical purposes, be treated as though they are bound by relevant human rights standards ... [and] the channels for (their) accountability must be established more clearly.[33]

The example of the Sudan People's Liberation Movement/Operation Lifeline Sudan (SPLM/OLS) Agreement on Groundrules, signed in July 1995, is a precedent-setting milestone toward establishing the applicability of international norms to nonstate actors in situations of armed conflict. UNICEF, as the lead agency for the amalgam of United Nations and nongovernmental organizations that constitute OLS, negotiated the agreement with the Southern Sudanese armed opposition movements. The agreement explicitly expresses its support for the UN Convention on the Rights of the Child, the Geneva Conventions of 1949 and the 1977 Protocols Additional to the Geneva Conventions, as well as specifying a commitment to the protection of civilians. The agreement underscores the importance of neutrality and impartiality in the provision of humanitarian assistance, stating that the "right to receive humanitarian assistance and to offer it is a fundamental humanitarian principle" (Article A1).

Why did a nonstate party sign the agreement? What were the benefits to the SPLM? There were several. It brought together disparate factions under the umbrella of a common commitment. Secondly, "the movements were keen to improve their international credibility and recognized quickly that commitment to humanitarian principles and to the two conventions would further it."[34] Lastly, such action brought with it recognition and an infusion of international aid to southern Sudan.

3. Create Greater Awareness of Humanitarian Law and the Human Rights of Children

Operation Lifeline Sudan also laid important groundwork in the emphasis that it gave to awareness-raising on child rights within its operational area, through a program of dissemination of humanitarian principles to a range of influential parties in southern Sudan—the military, civilian and humanitarian officials, religious leaders and women's leaders, local nongovernmental organizations, traditional chiefs and elders—as well as to international humanitarian workers. It is interesting that the military were integrated into workshops with the rest of the population. Thus, for example, military commanders, civil leaders and parents learned together that the recruitment of children into the military was not allowed under the SPLM's own commitment to the Convention on the Rights of the Child, as expressed in the ground rules agreement.

Ignorance—real or feigned—of child rights and humanitarian principles is a significant impediment to assuring child protection, but it can be
addressed through such dissemination programs. Importantly, the dissemination program emphasized southern Sudanese traditional values and
practices that related to the protection of children and civilians in conflict
and to sharing resources in times of need. This proved a very effective way
of integrating indigenous cultural norms and social values with international standards—the Convention on the Rights of the Child, the Geneva
Conventions and humanitarian principles—for child protection (see Figure 5.2 above).

4. Pursue Better Monitoring of Child Rights Violations

A necessary complement to ensuring more widespread familiarity with
global standards is the development of systematic means of monitoring
compliance with, and violations of, international humanitarian and human
rights law. Systematic documentation of violations of child rights is still in
its infancy. In addition to the work of Amnesty International, Human
Rights Watch and, in some recent cases, the Office of the UN High Commissioner for Human Rights, humanitarian agencies in the field have to
come to grips with the issue of how to collaborate in the monitoring and
documentation of such violations.

There is as yet little comprehensive discussion of how such actors
might ensure that information gathered on abuses of children is channeled—openly or otherwise—to human rights groups, to the Geneva-
based Committee on the Rights of the Child, to the new UN Office of the
Special Representative of the Secretary-General for Children in Armed
Conflict (see subsection 6 below) or to the media, for example. This is
dangerous work in today's conflict situations, where warring parties no
longer see humanitarians as neutral and impartial actors. The issue of how
to undertake such work, how to ensure adequate protection for monitors
and at the same time ensure consistent humanitarian access to children
and other civilians in need, requires urgent and comprehensive review.

5. Advocate Children As a Zone of Peace

There is a Corridor of Peace in our inner being, always, for a child to
run through for protection."[35]

The humanitarian actors who negotiated the OLS agreement built upon
and extended the concept of children as a zone of peace—namely, that
children have a supervening right to protection from the consequences of
any armed conflict—which humanitarian organizations such as the ICRC,

UNICEF, Oxfam and Christian Aid had implicitly acted upon on Biafra in the late 1960s. This concept had persuaded the government of Nigeria to tolerate international humanitarian action in Biafra in the midst of the civil war.

In the early 1980s, Nils Thedin, then a Swedish delegate to the UNICEF Executive Board, called upon UNICEF to turn into reality the ideal of "children as a conflict-free zone in human relations."[36] Shortly thereafter, James Grant, then Executive Director of UNICEF, succeeded in working with Archbishop Arturo Rivero Damas of El Salvador to broker Days of Tranquillity between the Salvadorean government of Napoleon Duarte and guerrilla leaders, to allow vaccination of children throughout El Salvador.

Duarte refused to negotiate a cease-fire with the guerrillas, as this would have given them political recognition, so Grant and the archbishop persuaded both sides to the conflict to unilaterally agree to observe days of tranquillity during the vaccination campaign. Of critical importance was the mediating role of the church, the one institution trusted by most Salvadoreans. Despite deep mutual distrust between government and guerrilla forces, and despite some breaches of the truce, both the military and guerrilla forces honored the cease-fire agreement—an "unlinked bilateral agreement" made by two sides unilaterally.[37]

Immunization rates did decline after the last round of the campaign, but the fact remained that the numbers of children protected against immunizable diseases had increased significantly. Immunization levels remained higher than in pre-Tranquillity times and parents continued to take their children to Days of Tranquillity programs that continued throughout the remaining six years of the Salvadorean civil war. But the concept of "children as a zone of peace" had become a reality and was subsequently applied in a number of armed conflict situations, for example in Uganda in 1986, in Sudan (where Grant's negotiation of eight corridors of peace for relief deliveries led to the creation of Operation Lifeline Sudan in 1988), to Days of Tranquillity in Lebanon in 1987, to a joint UNICEF-WHO medical convoy from Tehran to Baghdad at the height of the Gulf War in February 1991.

Such initiatives have their detractors, who see the zones concept as a vehicle for self-promotion by the external actors involved in their negotiation, but there can be no doubt that vaccination rates rise, that new hope is provided to civilians in the midst of armed conflict, and that the concept that children are above the political divide and outside conflict can gain a footing in the most unlikely environments. Other critics have argued that UNICEF and its partners have settled for the barest minimum entitlements (that is, vaccinations) of children to protection, when their needs were much broader. But again, when humanitarians operate in the political domain, there may be considerable merit in the argument that mediation for children conveys a message far wider than a specific program intervention such as child immunization. The message is that child protection is an absolute right and an absolute imperative and that the involvement of children in armed conflict is abhorrent. There is no situation in which it is justifiable to countenance such involvement.

As this chapter is written (mid-1998), Algeria continues to insist that resolution of the violence taking place in that country, including repeated massacres of scores of innocent civilians (the majority of whom are women and children), is an internal problem that brooks no outside interference. Yet it has quietly asked Norway and Canada to help establish systematic support programs for the tens of thousands of children traumatized by exposure to the extreme violence and terrorism, for which collaboration is now underway. It is conceivable that a concern for children will open doors to dialogue that otherwise remain closed.

The concept of children as zones of peace has appealed to those in authority on two levels—the ethical (humanitarian) and the political—and has illustrated that the two are not mutually exclusive. The political appeal of showing concern for child well-being is attractive to those wishing to gain legitimacy for their claim to power. Yet such a carrot is often insufficient in situations where parties to conflict see little political or military advantage in showing such concern. Other forms of persuasion are required in the political and economic domains, including "credible threats" that will deter them from targeting children. Not enough progress has been made in this domain.

6. Place Children on the Political Agenda

As is obvious, mediation and intervention on behalf of children do not take place in a vacuum. Advocacy for children demands a constant process of interface with political and military actors, as well as with those in the economic domain. Too often, children are invisible to political leaders and decision-makers. It is thus in the political arena that much remains to be done to ensure that the rights of children are taken into account in decision-making processes. The voices of children and of those who speak on behalf of children must be insistent if they are to be heard.

One recent development of significance within the United Nations has been the appointment in 1997 of the Special Representative of the Secretary-General for Children in Armed Conflict. The most important role of Olara Otunnu, the Special Representative, is to speak for children to political leaders, whether in mediating on children's behalf in zones of conflict, or in advocating for consideration of their rights and well-being in regional and global political decision-making forums. It is hoped that the Special Representative will receive the support necessary for his work, especially from governments but also from civil society networks. He can have a strong influence in bringing together child-centered alliances and coalitions drawn from civil society, the media, international organizations, governments, regional and financial institutions and from the world of business, as a means of mobilizing public opinion and political will in favor of the rights of children exposed to armed conflict. In recent years, the power of such coalitions of the like-minded has been illustrated in the successful negotiation of the international treaty to ban antipersonnel land mines and in the creation of the International Criminal Court. Similar multidimensional coalitions are making their political impact felt around the issues of small arms control and of child soldiers.

The Special Representative has the authority to ensure that child rights are consistently considered in the deliberations of the United Nations Security Council and other political organs of the UN. It is only relatively recently that child advocates (such as Graça Machel), humanitarian UN agencies, the ICRC and nongovernmental agencies have been able to present the humanitarian perspective and child protection issues to the Security Council in its debates on crises, civil conflicts included. It is important that the situation of the child be considered as a matter of course whenever such debates take place.

In recent years, the United Nations has imposed economic sanctions on a number of countries—most notably on Iraq—as have other international coalitions against a number of "rogue" states. With the notable exception of South Africa, the imposition of economic sanctions has not proven to be either a rapid or an effective means of forcing rogue regimes to comply with international demands. Whatever the political rationale behind the imposition of sanctions, there is now little doubt that they have a highly adverse impact on vulnerable groups and often very little apparent impact on the targeted national leadership. The suffering and death of thousands of Iraqi children brings into fundamental question the justification for sanctions first imposed against that country in 1991 and still in force in 1998.

It is time that the United Nations—and more especially the Security Council—assumes its share of the responsibility for the impact of its actions upon vulnerable groups within countries upon which sanctions have been imposed. A core list of agreed humanitarian exemptions needs to be defined in advance of the imposition of sanctions, with the express possibility of progressively extending exemptions should it be deemed necessary to continue sanctions from months into years. An example of such progressive exemptions might be the inclusion of school supplies and materials, which would hardly be considered "humanitarian" during an initial period of sanctions, but might be of vital importance to the well-being of children in the longer term.

Systematic and reliable methods of assessing the impact of sanctions on children have to be devised—for example, building on UNICEF's use of multiple-indicator cluster surveys (MICS) in Iraq. If sanctioned regimes take measures to protect vulnerable groups or to specifically ensure a social safety net for children, such steps should be acknowledged appropriately by those imposing sanctions. It is hoped that current initiatives coordinated by the UN Office of the Coordinator for Humanitarian Assistance or under consideration by the Special Representative for Children in Armed Conflict will propose concrete measures to address the humanitarian impact of sanctions on children, the most vulnerable of all vulnerable groups.

The negotiation of peace accords is another field in which the particular needs of children must be considered. Parties often commit themselves to respect human rights or observe humanitarian principles in such agreements—for example in the Guatemalan Comprehensive Agreement on Human Rights or the earlier San José Agreement on Human Rights in El Salvador. Yet in these groundbreaking accords (as specifically stated in relation to Guatemala), "children and children's rights per se have never been raised by either party, neither as a point of contention nor of consensus, in the entire peace process,"[38] even though children had fought as combatants, been raped, tortured, abused, abducted and killed, separated from their families, displaced in large numbers and driven from home, school and community. Concern for the future of the nation demands attention to the particular rehabilitation and recovery needs of children, particularly of those exposed to egregious and sustained acts of violence. Joint commitment of parties to the welfare of children is concrete evidence of commitment to reconstruction and can be an important step on the road to reconciliation.

Demobilization of combatants is an important part of peace processes. In most internal conflicts today, a significant part of any armed group, if not a majority of the fighting force, is composed of child fighters. They have particular needs: for protection at the time of demobilization and decommissioning of weapons; for care; for educational opportunities or to learn a trade; and to earn a living. Not the least is the challenge of their reintegration into families and communities that often view them with fear and hostility. Only sustained, long-term programs have any chance of helping such children to reintegrate successfully. Failure may drive them to resort anew to small arms and criminality as their means of livelihood. It is important to endeavor to control the flow of light weapons, which makes it so easy for children to take up arms; but it is as important to reduce the demand for such weapons by equipping them with the skills that will enable them to have hope for the future.

The definition of peacekeeping mandates has not, as a rule, taken into account the issue of child welfare. United Nations Security Council resolutions covering peacekeeping do not mention children. Sweden has pioneered the inclusion of child rights in the predeployment training of peacekeepers, and others are now beginning to follow its lead. It is important that United Nations peacekeepers be aware that, whatever their country of origin, they are bound to observe international humanitarian and human-rights law during their peacekeeping mission. The growth of child prostitution around UN peacekeeping missions has been catalogued as a problem in a number of countries. Not only is this unacceptable, but the consequences for engaging in child prostitution must be made clear to peacekeepers. Likewise, their accountability, and that of their superiors, for their conduct toward children needs to be clearly specified in the mandate of every peacekeeping mission.

Case studies positing confrontation with child combatants, or examining the particular requirements of child fighters during demobilization and disarmanent can also be included in peacekeeper training. Peacekeepers increasingly play a humanitarian role, from providing logistics support to civilian humanitarian actors, to providing health care to the displaced, or emergency medical care to civilian land mine victims, many of whom are children. Peacekeepers are mobile but are not trained to investigate human-rights abuses or to gather information about abuses of children. The feasibility of including such matters in training and during deployment needs to be addressed.

Finally, some countries that regularly provide peacekeeping forces may wish to discuss with the UN Special Representative for Children in Armed Conflict the possiblity of secondment of experienced military staff to the Office of the Special Representative. When he has to mediate for children in the midst of armed conflict and to negotiate with government forces or other armed groups, the presence of a team member with a military background and peacekeeping experience could be invaluable.

Much of the preceding discussion has been focused on the United Nations but could equally apply to the parallel policy deliberations and actions of regional political organizations. In addition, such organizations could collaborate with the UN Special Representative for Children in Armed Conflict in his intercession for children in conflicts within specific regions. In Africa, the Special Representative and the OAU could combine forces in an initiative to promote ratification of the African Charter on the Rights and Welfare of the Child.

The potential exists for other forms of collaboration—for example, to encourage member states to establish national ombudspersons for children. Building on the experience of the European Network of Ombudsmen for Children, the creation of national ombudspersons for children could provide an invaluable vehicle at national level for independent advocacy for children; to monitor the state of children and the impact of political and economic changes on children; to represent children's rights and interests to national leaders; and to inform the private sector as well as the general public concerning children's rights and measures required to ensure respect for these rights.[39]

7. Tackle the Impunity of Those Who Target Children

Regional bodies can also take the lead in tackling the impunity of those who target and exploit children during armed intrastate conflicts. To date, parties to conflict abuse children with complete impunity. International acquiescence and absence of condemnation or of effective sanction through almost 40 years of terror and extreme ethnic violence by political leaders in Burundi and Rwanda have encouraged those who commit violence to continue along the same path, of which the genocide of 1994 in Rwanda was a horrendous but logical outcome. The cloak of sovereignty thrown around internal conflicts has often muffled the voice of international bodies, and particularly of regional organizations, and has impeded humanitarian intervention efforts. Leaders who, during conflict, have consistently exploited or killed children or recruited them to kill have been welcomed at international negotiating tables. Charles Taylor of Liberia, a consistent violator of children's rights through many years of violent civil war, is now rewarded with the office of president of his country.

No internal conflict is exclusively internal. There are always external economic and political supporters, or arms traders willing to provide weapons. External governments and private companies that channel arms to warring factions, or pay for the right to exploit natural resources under the control of such factions, feed and underwrite conflicts in which children are killed and which place weapons in the hands of child fighters. In return, factional leaders and their external supporters are usually rewarded with international silence or apathy, rarely with condemnation or sanction.

It is time to mount a systematic effort to counter impunity with credible threat. This might include public identification by human-rights organizations of external governmental backers of groups that use and abuse children during armed conflict. This might extend to documentation of external investments, to exposure of private sector backers and to campaigns to boycott their products or adversely affect their share prices. Given the huge power of the international commercial and financial sectors today, it is essential that they be encouraged to adopt socially responsible investment practices and business codes, whether in countries at peace or in zones of conflict.

Leaders of fighting groups that do not protect children could be isolated, made to know that they will not be permitted to travel outside their own country, that their external assets will be frozen, that they would not be welcome at any international forum, including at international negotiations concerning the future of their country, or that they might be subject to investigation by the International Criminal Court. The options for credible action are many. Regional political organizations can lead the way by developing regional codes of conduct that emphasize the obligations of sovereignty and a commitment to international humanitarian law and human rights.

In the area of human-rights enforcement, three regional human-rights commissions and courts have provided pioneering models that Africa is expected to adapt for an African regional human-rights commission in the near future. These are the European Commission and Court of Human Rights; the Inter-American Commission on Human Rights; and the Inter-American Court of Human Rights. These last two have "investigated the killing, torture and disappearance of thousands across Latin America and, in recent years, have successfully urged those states responsible to change their behavior."[40]

The invisibility of children in political forums breeds impunity. Political commitment to child rights in conflict is an essential foundation of the message cited several times in this paper: war against children is morally reprehensible and never justified.

8. Prevent the Onset of Armed Conflict

Given our awareness of the circumstances and conditions which generate marginalization and vulnerability, exploit differences and exacerbate tensions, one need not be an Einstein to determine that tackling root causes is the only answer if we're serious about preventing conflict.[41]

Poverty and lack of development fuel hatred and escalate hostilities. Armed civil conflicts have their roots in structural social, political and economic conditions that generate inequity, discrimination, vulnerability, marginalization and poverty. The victimization of children finds its place in the midst of these. Indeed, "open warfare is only part of a much broader picture of violence against children."[42] Thus it is logical that the implementation of strategies to promote equitable development and social integration is an effective way of reducing the potential for violent social conflict. Within this approach, policies that ensure equitable access for children to adequate preventive health care and other social services, training and employment programs for youth, are significant ways of countering the propensity for violence in society.

The same groups (women and children in poverty, working and street children) who are most vulnerable to rejection and abuse in society (absence of rights under family law, sexual exploitation or exploitative child labor, for example), are also the most vulnerable in civil conflict—to rape, sexual exploitation, abduction or forced conscription as child combatants. Developmental programs for the well-being of the most disadvantaged can help to reduce their vulnerability, can be a factor in reducing recourse to violence, yet may also help to reduce exploitation should conflict erupt and to promote postconflict rehabilitation.

The roots of many so-called ethnic conflicts lie in political exploitation of resource scarcity, high unemployment and poor social service coverage. "Other" groups are blamed by leaders who focus on group demonization rather than on structural problems. Thus development programs that require political leaders to subscribe to certain national poverty-reduction or service-extension goals for all groups in society can have conflict-reduction and peace-building benefits. For example, the international Universal Child Immunization campaign (UCI) of the late 1980s and early 1990s had both social and political benefits. The World Bank[43] has argued for the inclusion of social assessment parameters within development planning that explicitly recognize causes of conflict and social tension, patterns of resource distribution and inclusiveness or exclusiveness of opportunities, and that partnership with social organizations of civil society is important if they are to channel stable development rather than organized violence.

Investment in the universalization of basic education for children—particularly for girls—is an excellent way to promote equitable development and prevent recourse to conflict by the citizens of the future. The challenge is to assure quality. Perhaps the most critical issue is the quality of the teachers. Investment in teachers—especially in the development of many additional women teachers—and in their training is necessary if they are to be able to communicate better with children and to facilitate an interactive teaching-learning process, as against the authoritarian one-way lecture process that prevails in the majority of schools around the world.

The assurance of equitable access to basic education that enables children to think critically, build self-esteem, solve problems cooperatively and in a nonviolent way, and learn positive values, including tolerance and appreciation of differences in others, can be a major contributor to a democratic, participatory society composed of thinking citizens, and thus to peaceful rather than violent resolution of conflict. "The greatest chance we have to prevent violence in society is to raise children who reject violence as a method of problem-solving, who believe in the right of the individual to grow in a safe environment."[44]

On the economic front, when governments face the pressures of economic crisis and structural adjustment, the costs to families and children are immense. Cuts to health services, education and social welfare, including food subsidies, have a disproportionate impact on the poor. Poverty breeds hopelessness, alienation and finally, violence. It is essential that efforts be made to ensure a basic social safety net for the most vulnerable groups, if the downward spiral toward violence is to be halted. Likewise, with the steady globalization of international trade and finance, wealth is created for the few while millions are increasingly marginalized. "Corporate social and environmental responsibility is becoming the business issue of the 21st century."[45] The corporate sector must take upon itself the promotion of investment with greater social responsibility and the development of corporate codes of conduct as its contribution to conflict prevention.

CONCLUSION

Without children, there is no future. To insist on the protection of child rights in the midst of armed conflict is to assert core human values.[46] There can be no inaction when children are mercilessly targeted. Children are no longer accidental victims of war, but they are the victims of a collapse of social and cultural norms, norms that are in turn casualties of war waged without rules and without boundaries.

The international community is struggling to cope with the paradigm shifts that are accompanying these sad developments, in civil conflicts in particular. While traditional emblems of neutrality and concepts of impartiality are brushed aside by combatants, humanitarian actors seek new ways to ensure compliance with international norms and to protect civilians—usually children and women—who are pawns in the game of intrastate war. There is progress, as violent men are brought to account before international tribunals, and as the International Criminal Court comes into being, but progress is slow.

Traditional boundaries between humanitarian and political action are increasingly difficult to maintain. New ways of applying humanitarian and human-rights law in violent contexts are sought. Human-rights advocates must continue to insist upon and advocate for compliance with the highest standards possible when the protection of children's rights is in question. It seems impossible to do this without increased rights-based activism in the international political, economic and even military worlds.

It is urgent not only that children cease to be invisible in these worlds but that they occupy a central place in the consciousness and decision-making of leaders in these domains. It is essential that the predominance of political prerogatives over humanitarian principles and human rights—a tendency seemingly gathering momentum in the United Nations in 1998—be counterbalanced by the emergence of humanitarian and human-rights issues at the core of international political debates.

There is a common thread linking the ethical norms found in every society and the international standards that form the foundation for the achievement of the rights and well-being of the child. This thread is woven into the fundamental purpose of the United Nations Charter: "to save succeeding generations from the scourge of war." The nature of war may be changing, but the goal is not. Children in danger belong to all of us. To insist on the protection of children in the midst of armed conflict is to invest in our own future.

BIBLIOGRAPHY

Bellamy, Carol. *The State of the World's Children 1996*, p. 104. UNICEF/OUP New York, 1996.

Brown, Michael (ed.). *The International Dimensions of Armed Conflict*, p. 653. MIT Press, Cambridge, MA, 1996.

Carnegie Commission on Preventing Deadly Conflict. *Final Report: Preventing Deadly Conflict*, p. 257. Carnegie Corporation of New York, 1997.

Centre for Days of Peace. *Humanitarian Ceasefires: Peacebuilding for Children*, p. 140. Report of a Conference. Centre for Days of Peace, Ottawa, 1991.

Coalition to Stop the Use of Child Soldiers. *Stop Using Child Soldiers!* p. 28. CSUCS and International Save the Children Alliance, London, 1998.

*Cohn, Ilene. *Verification and Protection of Children's Rights by United Nations Human Rights Missions (MINUGUA and ONUSAL)*, p. 11. Guatemala, May 1996.

Colletta, Nat, Markus Kostner and Ingo Wiederhofer . *The Transition from War to Peace in Sub-Saharan Africa*, p. 80. The World Bank, Washington, DC, 1996.

*Hamilton, Carolyn. *Children and War: Humanitarian Law and Children's Rights*, p. 87. University of Essex, May 1996.

Hammarberg, Thomas. "Proportionality between Military Aims and Humanitarian Concerns." Unpublished discussion paper for a meeting of the Technical Advisory Group of the Graça Machel Study on the Impact of Armed Conflict on Children, Stockholm, May 1996.

Hoskins, Eric. *The Impact of Sanctions: A Study of UNICEF's Perspective*, p. 50. Working Paper Series, Office of Emergency Programs, UNICEF, New York, 1998.

Human Rights Watch/Africa and Human Rights Watch Children's Rights Project. *The Scars of Death: Children Abducted by the Lord's Resistance Army in Uganda*, p. 137. Human Rights Watch, New York 1997.

*Kadjar-Hamouda, Eylah. *An End to Silence: A Preliminary Study on Sexual Violence, Abuse and Exploitation of Children Affected by Armed Conflict*, p. 35. International Fédération Terre des Hommes, Geneva, July 1996.

Kumar, Krishna (ed.). *Rebuilding Societies after Civil War: Critical Roles for International Assistance*, p. 328. Lynne Riener, Boulder, CO, 1997.

Kunder, James. *The Needs of Internally Displaced Women and Children: Principles and Considerations*, p. 23. Working Paper Series, Office of Emergency Programs, UNICEF, New York, 1998.

Landers, Cassie. *Listen to Me: Protecting the Development of Young Children in Armed Conflict*, p. 44. Working Paper Series, Office of Emergency Programs, UNICEF, New York, 1998.

Levine, Iain. "Promoting Humanitarian Principles: The Southern Sudan Experience," p. 31. Network Paper 21, May 1997. Relief and Rehabilitation Network, Overseas Development Institute, London 1997.

Levine, Iain. *Protecting Children in Emergencies: Ensuring Their Right to Humanitarian Assistance*, p. 15 and annexes. Working Paper Series, Office of Emergency Programs, UNICEF, New York, 1998.

Life and Peace Institute. "Against the Current: New Thinking on War and Conflict, p. 28. Special edition of *New Routes Journal of Peace and Action*, Vol. 2, No. 1, 1997. Life and Peace Institute, Uppsala.

Médecins Sans Frontières. *World in Crisis: The Politics of Survival at the End of the Twentieth Century*, p. 213. Routledge, London, 1997.

Nordstrom, Carolyn. "Behind the Lines," pp. 3–9, in *New Routes* Vol. 2, No. 1, 1997, Uppsala.

North-South Institute. *Canadian Corporations and Social Responsibility: Overview*, p. 13, (summary of the Canadian Development Report, 1998). The North-South Institute, Ottawa, 1998.

Ombudsman for Children, The. *The Ombudsman for Children, Norway: Monitoring the Rights of the Child*, p. 18. Oslo, May 1998.

Osofsky, Joy (ed.). *Children in a Violent Society*, p. 338. The Guildford Press, New York, 1997.

Otunnu, Olara. *The Rights of the Child: Interim Report of the Special Representative of the Secretary for Children and Armed Conflict* (draft), p. 11. Commission on Human Rights, Fifty-fourth session, Geneva, 1998.

Ratner, Steven R. "International Law: The Trials of Global Norms," p. 65–80 in *Foreign Policy*, Spring 1998.

Refugee Participation Network. *Children and Youth*. RPN Issue 24, Refugee Studies Programme, Oxford, September 1997 (series of articles).

Ressler, Everett, Joanne Marie Tortorici, and Alex Marcelino. *Children in War: A Guide to the Provision of Services*, p. 288. UNICEF, New York, 1993.

Roberts, Adam. *Humanitarian Action in War: Aid, Protection and Impartiality in a Policy Vacuum*, p. 96. Adelphi Paper 305, the International Institute for Strategic Studies, Oxford University Press, 1996.

Sisk, Timothy. *Power Sharing and International Mediation in Ethnic Conflicts*, p. 143. United States Institute of Peace and Carnegie Commission on Preventing Deadly Conflict, Carnegie Corporation of New York, 1997.

UNHCR. *Refugee Children: Guidelines on Protection and Care*, p. 182. UNHCR, Geneva, 1994.

UNICEF. *First Call for Children: World Declaration and Plan of Action from the World Summit for Children; and the Convention on the Rights of the Child*, p. 75. UNICEF, New York, 1990.

UNICEF International Child Development Centre. *Children and Violence*, p. 24. Innocenti Digest No. 2, ICDC, Florence, 1998.

United Nations General Assembly. *Impact of Armed Conflict on Children: Report of the Expert of the Secretary-General, Ms. Graça Machel*, Document A/51/306, p. 96. United Nations, New York, 1996.

Vittachi, Varindra Tarzie. *Between the Guns: Children As a Zone of Peace*, p. 136. Hodder and Stoughton, London, 1993.

Women's Commission for Refugee Women and Children. *The Children's War: Towards Peace in Sierra Leone*, p. 27. New York, 1997.

World Bank. *A Framework for World Bank Involvement in Post-Conflict Reconstruction*, draft document, p. 37. World Bank, Washington, DC, January 1997.

*World Health Organization. *The Impact of Armed Conflict on Children: A Threat to Public Health*, p. 117. WHO, Geneva, 1996.

*World Vision Staff Working Paper No. 23: *The Effects of Armed Conflict on Girls*, p. 35. World Vision International, Monrovia, CA and Geneva, July 1996.

* Studies undertaken for the United Nations Study on the Impact of Armed Conflict on Children, © UNICEF 1996.

6 THE AMERICAN MEDICAL ESTABLISHMENT

An Absent Partner

H. Jack Geiger, M.D.

This morning's headlines—every day's headlines—announce ongoing disasters: the massive health, human-rights and refugee problems of the new world order in Somalia, Yugoslavia, Haiti, Afghanistan, Indonesia, as well as Armenia, Azerbaijan, Georgia and other warring splinters of the former Soviet Union. Other new world order disasters, less dramatic, receive only intermittent attention. These include such items as the effect of sanctions on medical care, nutrition and infant mortality in Iraq; the daily toll in death and dismemberment of land mines in Cambodia, Angola, Mozambique, Afghanistan and elsewhere; the ongoing effects of radioactive contamination from Chernobyl and Chelyabinsk, and of deadly pollution of air, soil and groundwater by lead, other toxic metals and organic toxins in much of Eastern Europe. Dwarfing all of these is the implacable daily toll of poverty and its health consequences in the Third World; to cite the best-known statistic, the 40,000 children who die each day.

The political configurations have shifted, and some of the suffering locals, in consequence, are new. In most respects, however, from the point of view of international health and human-rights workers, the new world order looks much like the old world order. It presents us with the same agendas, challenges and needs. There is nothing new about civil wars and regional wars, except that now they are less likely to be surrogates in superpower struggles and more likely to have been unleashed by the end of superpower confrontation. There is nothing new about deliberate disruptions of medical care, violations of medical neutrality, torture and other blatant human-rights violations; nothing new about the use of poison gas, cluster and fragmentation bombs, napalm or land mines, and nothing new—since Guernica and certainly since World War II—about the deliberate destruction of civilian populations. Similarly, there is nothing new about famines, earthquakes, floods, hurricanes and volcanic eruptions; nothing new about pandemics, whether of "new" organisms such as HIV or "old" organisms like the tubercle bacillus and *Vibrio cholerae*. Most of all, there is nothing new about poverty, unemployment, staggering population increases, absent or collapsing infrastructures and inequity in resource allocation and trade relationships, except perhaps that they have worsened. Half of the less-developed countries are poorer today than they were a decade ago,[1] in part due to structural adjustments and drastic reductions of investment in social programs, courtesy of the International Monetary Fund and the World Bank.

Americans have long viewed themselves—with considerable justification—as extraordinarily generous, humanitarian and responsive to these miseries. Most U.S. citizens have supported and believe (with less justification) that their government has adequately supported the humanitarian efforts of the United Nations, the World Health Organization (WHO), UNICEF, the UN High Commissioner for Refugees, the International Committee of the Red Cross (ICRC), and many other international mechanisms of response. Almost all are proud of U.S. contributions of food, medical care and other forms of disaster relief in acute overseas emergencies. Many are aware of our substantial role in the eradication of smallpox, the international work of such government agencies as the Agency for International Development (AID), the Centers for Disease Control and the Fogarty Center at the National Institutes of Health and of both research and material contributions to Third World immunization campaigns and to the struggles against AIDS, malaria, schistosomiasis and other plagues.

The most impressive evidence, however, is the extraordinary American creation and support of private voluntary organizations, both church-related and secular. The proliferation and individual donor support of organizations such as CARE, Save the Children, Project HOPE, Project CONCERN, the International Medical Corps, Oxfam America and the like is the dominant mode of U.S. involvement in international health efforts. The National Council for International Health 1992 Director of U.S. International Organizations lists more than 700 of them.[2] They range from large foundations—Rockefeller, Carnegie, Pew and Kellog, investing in institutional organizational development in less-developed countries—to the myriad small service and consulting organizations composing the growth industry of recipients of AID and other government contracts. The largest number, however, are devoted to providing food, medical care and other forms of hands-on assistance and direct material relief to those who are suffering overseas. To these must be added the voices of conscience—the international defense of health and human-rights by such organizations as Physicians for Human Rights, Human

Rights Watch, the Lawyers Committee for Human Rights, the medical network of Amnesty International, the Committee for Health in Southern Africa and others.

There is, however, another side to the ledger of our international contributions, and it provides no cause for national self-congratulations. In relation to the size and depth of our health professional riches and the strength of our medical establishment, our international health contributions are inexcusably limited. Given our resources, it is not an overstatement to describe this as a moral failure. The relative absence of the American medical establishment from international health efforts is at once a cause and a symptom of that failure.

Although the United States has a physician surplus and by the year 2000 will have an estimated 145,000 surplus physicians and one of the highest physician/population ratios in the industrialized world,[3] we have for decades *imported* tens of thousands of physicians from developing countries, the brain drain that has been more aptly described as a hemorrhage from nations that have as few as one physician for 4,500 people— or 45,000 in rural areas.[4] At the same time, almost without restraint, we have *exported* millions of tons of tobacco,[5] tens of millions of potentially dangerous prescription drugs improperly promoted and lacking appropriate warnings,[6] millions of tons of toxic wastes and—more recently— thousands of U.S. manufacturing operations seeking not only low wages but the freedom to create occupational and environmental health hazards without fear of effective regulation or penalty. We have also aggressively sold lethal arms of almost every description to Third-World nations, siphoning billions of dollars away from their most urgent domestic needs for health care, food, housing and social support services. These contributions do not arrive in packages neatly labeled "gift of the American people."

In the postcolonial decades following World War II, with the eager support of American foundations and the best intentions of fostering excellence, we also exported a model of medical education and training: tertiary-care-based, high-technology, bench-research-focused on medical schools and teaching hospitals, which was wildly inappropriate to the needs of developing countries, often did more to deepen their social inequities in health care than to correct them and devastated their health care economies. During those same decades, inexcusably, some Third-World populations were used, without full informed consent, for clinical trials of experimental contraceptive and other pharmaceuticals.

What one observer has call our "rich heritage of past contributions to international health"[7] presents, in fact, a very mixed record. Our international record on human-rights over the past half-century, and particularly during the past two decades, is equally mixed. We can, however, draw some lessons from both sides of the ledger if we are to do more for international survival, health and human-rights in a new world order. We will need at least two things that we do not now have.

The first requirement is a coherent, proactive, integrated and sustained U.S. policy on international health to replace the essentially uncoordinated and often inconsistent mixture of public and private sector efforts that now make our interventions seem so fragmented, spasmodic and reactive. A defined and consistent governmental policy on international health would permit coordination of public and private sectors. It would inform domestic health manpower and agricultural policies and provide a consistent rationale for our relationships with and contributions to WHO and the health-related, refugee and relief agencies of the UN. It would permit intelligent linkage of international health efforts to economic assistance aimed at building infrastructure and reducing poverty—the root cause of so many health problems. It should be expressed in adequately funded long-term programs, free from political biases and right-wing ideological and religious constraints.

The second requirement is a far greater effort and contribution from the American medical establishment, particularly from its academic sector: the institutions training new cohorts of physicians, dentists, nurses, public-health workers, health educators, health administrators and planners—the essential and primary resource for any expanded U.S. efforts in international health and human-rights. Given the dependence of American health professional education on government support, a significant increase is not likely to occur without the development of a consistent international health policy.

U.S. HEALTH PROFESSIONALS IN INTERNATIONAL HEALTH

It is the academic sector—the production of people with a commitment to international health—that is likeliest to initiate real change. What has that sector done? There is little current data on the magnitude and specifics of the current involvement of American physicians and other health professionals in international health work. Even policy-makers lack precise information on the numbers, the types of organizations involved and the kinds of work being done. A 1984 survey[8] by the Johns Hopkins University Department of International Health and the National Council for International Health estimated that some 8,700 U.S. health professionals were thus engaged, including at least 1,488 nurses, 1,417 physicians and nearly 900 health and hospital administrators, managers and planners, and some 2,700 trainers and educators, dentists, environmental health specialists, social workers, nutritionists and technicians.

Those figures represent less than one half of 1 percent of all U.S. physicians and barely more than one tenth of 1 percent of all U.S. nurses. Given the depth and richness of American health resources, that contribution is shamefully low. Contrast the American statistics with the more than 2,000 physicians, 13 percent of its total supply, sent to Third-World nations during the 1970s and 1980s by Cuba, a nation one twentieth the size of the United States.[9] More to the point, the U.S. figures compare poorly with those of other Western industrialized nations—France, for example—that encourage and reward international health service as a matter of government policy.

Nevertheless, the 1984 survey showed a 63 percent increase over figures assembled in 1969, and the numbers are probably somewhat higher today. By no means all of the overseas personnel, however, are engaged in humanitarian work. The authors of the 1984 survey noted: "Church-related organizations still employ the largest number of health professionals, but private voluntary organizations, corporations and universities have almost caught up."[10] The importance of corporations reflected the market for U.S. health manpower in oil-rich nations; the rise in NGO employment reflected the rapid increase of small consulting firms working for the U.S. government.

Less than half of the U.S. health professionals, furthermore, were long-term (salaried and working for one year or more); one third of all physicians were volunteers and most were in clinical work with limited long-term impact on health services development: "their service areas are often relatively small, based in hospitals whose levels of technology and staffing increase the cost of care, thereby limiting access and community participation."[11] Compared to the average for all organizations combined, physicians and nurses were overrepresented in church-related organizations; nurses were underrepresented in universities; physicians were underrepresented in governmental agencies; administrators, managers and planners were concentrated in corporations.

The bottom line represented by these 1984 figures is that supply—the recruitment and involvement of U.S. health professionals in international work—fell significantly short of the demand. There were more than 241 budgeted vacancies—that is, those for which secure funding is available—in international health programs for physicians alone, and budgeted positions do not begin to reflect the real unmet need.

U.S. HEALTH PROFESSIONAL SCHOOLS
AND INTERNATIONAL HEALTH

The United States has more than 127 medical schools, close to 30 schools of public health and hundreds of schools of nursing, dentistry, pharmacy and other health-related professional disciplines. A relatively recent survey[12] counted 494 international health programs or projects at these institutions, but they involved only 69 percent of the medical schools and 50 percent of the schools of public health. Most of the projects in developing countries (the People's Republic of China and Mexico had the largest number) were short-term and tenuously funded. In medicine, more than 90 percent of the projects were classified as "training" and "research"—in all probability, representing the assignment of a small number of visiting faculty at overseas medical schools—and only 7 percent were devoted to institutional development. In contrast, while training and research were also major emphases in school of public-health projects, almost half were devoted to institutional development for overseas medical schools, health science centers and universities.

Perhaps the most important figures in this study are those involving American medical students. More than 90 percent of U.S. medical schools permit overseas electives for students, most of them limited to two months or less. However, one study estimated that fewer than 5 percent of American medical students studied abroad, and not all in developing countries.[13]

STUDENTS: THE DRIVING FORCE FOR CHANGE

This relatively poor showing reflects lack of support, not lack of interest. Appeals for international health training and experience, and the practical steps required to facilitate them, have come from American medical students with increasing urgency for more than a decade. In 1985, Dr. Helen Burstin, then the president of the American Medical Student Association (AMSA), argued for a U.S. international health service corps relying on loan forgiveness in exchange for service in less-developed countries to help "young physicians to give of themselves in a needy world."[14] A year earlier, Dr. David Kindig and Dr. George Lythcott called for an international health service corps of:

a carefully selected group of doctors with skills emphasizing public health, prevention, a knowledge of appropriate technology and the organization and management of health services ... there is ample evidence that many American medical students have interests in careers in such international humanitarian service, but the opportunities are limited and fragmented."[15]

Victor Sidel pointed out that American physicians "are among the most isolated from in-depth knowledge of health problems and of health services outside their own country" and argued that U.S. medical schools "should consider international work an indispensable part of a core medical education."[16] J. E. Banta, testifying before a Senate subcommittee in support of one of the several failed congressional efforts[17] to create an international health service corps, noted that: "there has not been an established, clear and coherent pattern for international health workers; efforts have been ad hoc, fragmented, obscure and devoid of the possibility of long-term career planning."[18]

THE AMSA PROGRAMS

No group has responded more vigorously to these challenges than AMSA. Since the early 1980s, AMSA has published "International Health Electives for Medical Students," a listing of faculty contacts and curriculum information on international health at U.S. medical schools and an international health funding guide for U.S. medical students and residents.[19]

From 1986 to 1990, AMSA sponsored an International Fellowship Program in which 26 medical students and residents from 19 U.S. medical schools completed an eight-month rotation in Ghana and Nigeria. They were assigned to five medical schools for clinical rotations and community health assignments together with Ghanaian and Nigerian medical students in both urban and rural settings under the supervision of a faculty preceptor in the Department of Community Health. Then four African medical students participated in a ten-week program of community-oriented primary care activities in the United States. AMSA's stated goals were:

> to prepare medical students and residents for leadership roles among U.S. health professionals working with the medically underserved at home and abroad; to offer opportunities for aspiring young physicians to learn about health problems and delivery systems in developing countries and to enable medical students to examine appropriate roles for U.S. physicians in international health.[20]

More recently, AMSA (with funding from the Pew Charitable Trusts) created an International Health Partnership Program in Community-Based Medical Education, linking the University of Rochester Medical School with the Universidad Autonoma de Chiapas in Mexico; the University of Colorado School of Medicine with the Universidad del Valle in Colombia; and the University of Massachusetts Medical School with the Universidad Autonoma Nacional de Honduras. Two post-third-year medical students from each school—U.S. and Latin American—will work in community health projects in their partner schools for three to four months, and faculty members from each will participate in a two- to three-week exchange.

It is important to note that international health exchanges and rotations are not limited to undergraduate medical students. Since 1982, Yale University School of Medicine has regularly sent residents and fellows to Haiti and Tanzania.[21] The University of North Carolina at Chapel Hill has similar programs,[22] and the University of New Mexico Medical School is deeply involved in bilateral faculty exchanges for curriculum development with Xian Medical University in China—an effort in which the Chinese Ministry of Public Health, Project HOPE and WHO are also involved.[23]

PREPARING STUDENTS FOR INTERNATIONAL HEALTH WORK

Only 9 to 15 percent of the estimated 2,400 U.S. medical students who had done international health work, however, had participated in formal medical school courses covering the clinical aspects of the diseases students were likely to encounter and the social, economic and environmental aspects of the community and health system in which they worked.[24] A national survey of U.S. medical schools identified only 26 schools—22 percent of the U.S. total—that offered training programs in international health. Though the availability of training is increased somewhat by regionalization and by medical school access to appropriate courses in some schools of public health, the authors concluded that "medical schools in general do not appear to train students adequately for their international health care rotations."[25]

The combined effect of appropriate training and the international health experience itself is illustrated by a study at the University of Arizona, which since 1982 has offered an intensive three-week orientation course, a "core curriculum for international health," each year for 24 selected U.S. medical students. Of 154 course graduates surveyed in 1991,

81 percent said they planned some form of international health work as part of their future careers.[26]

These limitations in the appropriate training are likely to improve, however, with the recent formation of the U.S. International Health Medical Education Consortium (IHMEC), with members representing more than 50 American medical schools. IHMEC will promote international health medical education in four program areas—curriculum, clinical training, career development and international health education policy. IHMEC proposes to establish a network of clinical sites overseas and standards for selection of both trainees and sites; develop stronger career tracks for potential certification of students, residents and faculty involved in international health training and programs; and facilitate collaborative training relationships with students and faculty in foreign medical schools.[27]

RELEVANCE AND REWARD: INTERNATIONAL HEALTH AND U.S. PROBLEMS

"For medical students and residents," one study notes, "a two-month elective in a developing country can be a profound experience ... can dramatically alter their perceptions of health, health care and societal and personal responsibility ... [and] can lead to permanent changes in career direction."[28] Almost invariably, students return with fresh eyes for American society and American health care, recognizing the profound similarities between what they have just experienced in developing nations and the problems of underserved and poverty-stricken urban and rural American populations—the Third World in the United States. Not infrequently, they find that they can adapt and use here what they have learned from their international colleagues and mentors. International health experience has become a two-way street—not *for*, but *with* less-developed countries—and its rewards are not merely the growth of a corps of professional international health workers but also the enrichment of American medicine and public health.

Here, I speak from personal and career-determining experience. As a senior medical student in 1957, I was fortunate to spend six months in South Africa's rural homelands and urban townships, working and studying in novel institutions called community health centers practicing community-oriented primary care (COPC). It seemed clear to me then that my life's work would be international health, and I prepared myself accordingly: training in internal medicine, infectious disease, epidemiology and social science. At the completion of that process, in the bitter summer of 1964, I found myself in rural Mississippi, organizing health care for civil-rights workers in a population staggering under the burdens of poverty, racism and inequity and their health consequences. The parallels were inescapable, and it occurred to me that what worked in South Africa—community health centers and community-oriented primary care—might be adapted to our needs. The first Office of Economic Opportunity–funded community health center opened at Boston's Columbia Point housing project—not so different from a township—six months later; the second, a year later in rural Bolivar County, Mississippi. Today there are almost 600 such community health centers across the United States, the primary source of care for some six million low-income Americans. They are a modest but permanent part of the U.S. health care system with an enviable record of effectiveness.[29] There is a wonderful bilateral footnote to this small story: 35 years later, as South Africa prepared for liberation, I have been returning there to describe the U.S. experience and to help reintroduce the community health center/COPC concepts as models for the development of their new health care systems.

In the evolution of international health work, what was once unidirectional (and often, as "technical assistance," openly paternalistic) has become bilateral, and what was bilateral has, in turn, become a network in which institutions of developing countries in Asia, Africa, Latin America and the Caribbean collaborate with each other as well as with schools and programs in the industrialized world.[30] More than 50 institutions from all sectors are now joined in the Network of Community-Oriented Educational Institutions for Health Sciences, with headquarters in the Netherlands; it organizes an international conference every year, with Training Professionals for Future Health Care as the topic for 1999.

At a time when the United States is struggling mightily to emphasize primary care, health care teams, preventive medicine and community-based interventions, we have as much to learn from developing countries as we did almost a century ago when we sent our students, residents and young faculty to Europe to learn the secrets of bacteriology, biochemistry and the electrocardiogram. A significant expansion of international experience for U.S. health professionals is neither a gift nor a drain on our resources; it is, instead, in our own domestic interest and could contribute significantly to our own efforts at health care reform.

SCHOOLS OF PUBLIC HEALTH AND OTHER OMISSIONS

This brief review, of necessity, slights the central role and importance of the U.S. schools of public health, both as trainers, researchers and collaborators in international health and as primary loci of research and training in tropical medicine. (More than one in four of the Arizona course graduates indicated that they planned to obtain an Master of Public Health degree; more than 15 percent of the students at U.S. schools of public health come from overseas; the Ministries of Health in a score of developing nations are headed—and staffed—by our graduates.) Schools of public health are surely not the "absent" sector of our medical establishment.

The details of such programs as Johns Hopkins' Health and Child Survival Fellows, or Harvard's work on diarrheal diseases, though relevant, are also beyond the scope of this discussion. If this omission is justified at all, it is because applicants to schools of public health are those who are already committed, either to international health or to public-health work in the United States. If the field of international health is to grow, the recruits must be found at an earlier stage, in schools of medicine, nursing, dentistry and other professional and technical disciplines.

The medical establishment surely includes the American Medical Association (AMA), but here the record is much more sparse. The AMA helped establish the World Medical Association and supports the work of WHO; it was a contributor to the formation of the National Council for International Health, and it publishes intermittent reports on American physicians in international health work.[31] Its journal reports on international health activities and has spoken out courageously on the U.S. responsibility to export health workers. Beyond that, however, AMA efforts in international health have been limited.

Similarly, the Association of American Medical Colleges has other more urgent priorities. Several decades ago it sponsored the production of a five-volume international health curriculum[32]; more recently, in collaboration with the Educational Commission for Foreign Medical Graduates, it has explored the development of innovative programs in international medical education,[33] and it surveys U.S. medical schools intermittently on their international health activities.

Finally, any complete account of the medical establishment's role in international health would include a detailed report on the work of U.S. philanthropic foundations, great and small, not merely as funders but as catalysts for change and innovation. They most assuredly are not absent partners—particularly the W. K. Kellogg, Henry J. Kaiser, Rockefeller, Carnegie and Pew foundations—and their present importance in support of international health will grow as government support recedes.

HEALTH AND HUMAN RIGHTS

During the past two decades, perhaps the fastest-growing curricular development in undergraduate and graduate medical (and other health professional) education has been the proliferation of courses in medical ethics. Yet there has been almost no effort to teach human rights or to explore the unique roles and responsibilities of medicine in the protection of human rights—including the rights of refugees—and in the documentation of violations and abuses. Perhaps the closest we have come, sadly, is in the development of a new medical specialty—the treatment of torture victims. This development illustrates the blurring of the distinctions between "international" and "domestic" health concerns and the obsolescence of such terms as "tropical medicine." With large and ever-growing immigrant populations of Cambodians, Vietnamese, Haitians, Salvadoreans, Guatemalans and others and the frequency of overseas travel, international health problems and the need for relevant expertise have become domestic concerns.

Two pioneering exceptions to the prevailing medical silence on human rights should be noted. At Columbia College of Physicians and Surgeons, Professors Sheila and David Rothman have created a fellowship program in which carefully selected medical students and residents are offered elective human-rights placements around the world in organizations as varied as the National Medical and Dental Association of South Africa and the Israeli-Palestinian Physicians' Committee for Human Rights. At the postgraduate level, Physicians for Human Rights, in collaboration with Harvard Medical School, recently conducted an intensive three-day continuing medical education course on human rights, the first in a proposed national series.

CONCLUSION

Increasing the U.S. contribution in collaboration with the health institutions of other nations is in our own best interest and certain to yield returns of substantial relevance to our own health problems. The United States needs an international health corps, the equivalent of the National Health Service Corps, with scholarships and loan forgiveness to facilitate overseas work for debt-burdened medical and other health professional graduates. We must establish and reward professional academic career lines in international health, and develop and expand the international health curricula in all health professional schools and residency programs.

Beyond such specifics, we need a coherent international health and human-rights policy, a sustained governmental commitment, without which none of these increased efforts are likely to occur. The American medical establishment can and should contribute to the formulation and implementation of such a policy, from which it would surely benefit. A young American serving as a medical officer in Nigeria put it best a few years ago. She wrote: "We would do better to believe that we are all in it together, that the problem belongs to us all. We must believe that privilege implies responsibility, that education implies the power to change."[34]

THE CONTRIBUTION OF INTERNATIONAL HUMANITARIAN LAW TO THE RESTORATION AND MAINTENANCE OF PEACE

Michel Veuthey

In today's unstable situation, the first purpose of international cooperation is, and should remain, the prevention of armed conflicts: as Article 1 of the United Nations Charter provides, "to maintain international peace and security."[1] The second is to preserve humanity in all circumstances, even during armed conflicts. This is the primary intention of international humanitarian law.

The contribution to peace made by international humanitarian law should not be overlooked. Humanitarian law is a permanent reminder that armed conflict, with enmity between civilians on opposite sides of a conflict, is a temporary, exceptional situation: no enemy is an enemy forever,[2] since civilized life—both within and between communities—is founded on peaceful relations (peace being not the absence of conflict but harmonious management of conflicts).

Furthermore, the very nature of humanitarian law shatters the dangerous illusion of unlimited force[3] or total war, creates areas of peace in the very midst of conflicts, imposes the principle of a common humanity and calls for dialogue. International humanitarian law is increasingly becoming part of global security issues on the national, regional and international levels: security today[4] also means human security, through solidarity in peace and restraints in conflict that safeguard the common humanity.[5] Bringing protection and relief to victims of conflicts can have a strategic value in preserving regional and global stability.[6] The implementation of humanitarian law should form part of a culture of conflict prevention in the twenty-first century.[7]

The opinions expressed in this chapter are those of the author and do not necessarily reflect the official position of the International Committee of the Red Cross.

THE NATURE OF HUMANITARIAN LAW

The simplest and most universal definition of humanitarian law is found in the commandment, "Love thy neighbor as thyself." The great Rabbi Hillel's response to a question on the Torah was "Do not do unto others what you would not want to be done unto you. This is the essence and the rest is commentary."[8] Practically all traditions know this fundamental principle.[9]

The historical sources of humanitarian law are universal and timeless. Throughout the history of humankind, all civilizations have developed rules within the group, tribe, nation or religion to ensure its survival—in Asia, Buddhism,[10] Hinduism,[11] Taoism[12] and Bushido[13]; in the Middle East, Judaism,[14] Christianity[15] and Islam[16]; in Africa,[17] a multitude of customs valid only within a given tribe; in Europe, the mutual restrictions imposed by chivalry, before the condottieri and lace-clad war generals were supplanted by the humanists (Grotius, Hobbes, Kant, Pufendorf, Rousseau, Vattel, Henry Dunant and Francis Lieber)[18]—all aiming to avoid excesses that would turn clashes into anarchy and hence make peace more difficult to achieve.

Thus, in Article 6 of his "Perpetual Peace," Kant wrote: "No State at war with another must allow itself hostilities of a kind which would make reciprocal confidence impossible during future peace."[19]

Humanitarian law may be expressed in the provisions of bilateral agreements,[20] concluded before hostilities begin (cartels), during hostilities (truces, instruments of surrender) or at the end of a conflict (cease-fires, peace treaties), laying down the treatment to be given to civilians, prisoners, sick and wounded and neutral intermediaries. Or it may take shape in multilateral agreements, frequently concluded in reaction to a bloody conflict.

For example, each of the stages of humanitarian law codified in Geneva from 1864 to 1977 followed a war that created a shock wave in public opinion and for governments: the battle of Solferino (1859)[21] between Austrian and French armies was the impetus for the First Convention in 1864; the naval battle of Tsushima (1905) between Japanese and Russian fleets prompted adjustment of the Convention on war at sea in 1907; World War I brought about the two 1929 Conventions, including a much broader protection for prisoners of war; World War II led to the four 1949 Conventions[22] and an extensive regulation of the treatment of civilians in occupied territories and internment; and decolonization and the Vietnam War preceded the two 1977 Additional Protocols,[23] which brought written rules for the protection of civilian persons and objects against hostilities.

The total ban on antipersonnel land mines[24] signed in Ottawa on 4 December 1997 was the result of a worldwide campaign by governments, UN agencies, the Red Cross and Red Crescent Movement and NGOs in a full partnership that stressed the human suffering and socioeconomic costs caused by antipersonnel mines.

Similarly, most of "Hague Law" stems from the Peace Conferences of 1899 and 1907. World War II and regional conflicts prompted the drafting of the United Nations instruments on human rights, disarmament, the prohibition of terrorism and mercenaries, protection of the environment[25] and protection of the rights of children.[26]

The terminology used to refer to these international treaties may vary (humanitarian law,[27] international humanitarian law applicable in armed conflicts,[28] laws of war,[29] law of Geneva,[30] Red Cross Conventions, law of The Hague,[31] human rights in armed conflicts[32]), but all seek the same objective—namely, to limit the use of violence. Some of these instruments, like human-rights treaties, are based on a peacetime approach, while others, such as humanitarian law, are normally applicable during armed conflicts. Yet their scope often overlaps, especially as regards the fundamental guarantees they embody.

The fundamental rules of humanitarian law[33] are closely linked to the survival of human beings, not only individuals but also entire populations, by the safeguarding of cultural objects and places of worship[34] and objects indispensable to the survival of the civilian population[35]; the protection of medical establishments and units (both civilian and military), public works and installations containing dangerous forces (such as dams, dikes and nuclear power plants)[36]; and the preservation of the natural environment.[37] Even beyond these objectives, the need to maintain a minimum of confidence between adversaries (in other words, the prohibition of perfidy) is one of the pillars of humanitarian law, both customary and written.

By its very nature, humanitarian law aims, through acts of humanity, to preserve the survival of humankind,[38] to ensure that "civilized" life is still possible and to maintain the necessary conditions for a return of peace even during a conflict. As one well-known expert on international law, Denise Bindschedler-Robert, writes,

> The law of armed conflicts is certainly not a substitute for peace. Nevertheless, in the last analysis it preserves a certain sense of proportion and human solidarity as well as a sense of human values amid the outburst of unchained violence and passions which threaten these values.[39]

As a psychologist expresses it: "It can save us from dehumanizing our-selves by dehumanizing our enemy."[40]

THE UNIVERSAL APPLICABILITY OF HUMANITARIAN RULES

It is important for the sake of peace that humanitarian rules and principles be respected in all circumstances. The International Court of Justice, in the Nicaragua case, considered Article 3 as "elementary considerations of humanity," binding all individuals.[41] In the case of "collapsed States,"[42] "postmodern wars,"[43] anarchic conflicts,[44] the international community of States Party to the 1949 Geneva Conventions should reaffirm their col-lective responsibilty according to Article 1, common to the four Conven-tions and to Protocol I. According to this provision, "The High Contracting Parties undertake to respect and to ensure respect for this Convention in all circumstances." Should measures be limited to diplo-matic démarches and the adoption of resolutions or rather the use of sanc-tions and peace-enforcement operations in order to stop genocide and arrest war criminals? A number of Security Council resolutions, including those on anarchic conflicts, call upon all parties to respect international humanitarian law and reaffirm that those responsible for breaches thereof should be held individually accountable.[45]

The commencement of the applicability of humanitarian rules is some-times deferred. Perpetuating the illusion of peace, refusing to recognize the state of conflict and ignoring or concealing victims may jeopardize the application of the law or, indeed, the restoration of peace. As the number of victims grows—individuals are taken prisoner, are tortured and exe-cuted, or disappear—and methods and means of warfare degenerate on both sides, it becomes extremely difficult to revert to the legal path. Examples of this are the Algerian War 30 years ago, as well as more recent, even ongoing conflicts. While large-scale military operations are characterized for too long as "operations for the maintenance of order" or even "fraternal assistance," hatred accumulates and sincere but belated efforts to set reciprocal limits run into enormous problems, with an adverse impact on civilians and prisoners. The pacifying value of human-itarian restrictions thus emerges late in the day, accompanied by the bit-terness caused by too many violations. The revolting policy of "ethnic cleansing" is a confirmation of grave breaches of humanitarian law, the very embodiment of hatred and rejection.[46] As for genocide, it should be considered as a threat to international peace and security,[47] as we do not need another century of megadeath.[48]

The period of applicability of humanitarian rules is also subject to change. Often the actual hostilities are brief, and a lightning war gives way to a long period that belongs no longer to war but not yet to peace. During this period, which may last several years, victims remain: thousands of prisoners remain in detention years after the cessation of hostilities (as was the case in the western Sahara, in the Iraq-Iran conflict, even in the conflict between Iraq and Kuwait), and civilian populations come under attack or are continually under military occupation.

At the end of hostilities, the accumulation of unsolved humanitarian questions often constitutes an additional obstacle to successful peace negotiations. Humanitarian questions are mentioned more and more frequently in Security Council resolutions. Such was the case in the Arab-Israeli conflicts, in Lebanon, in Yugoslavia and in Somalia. The question of the repatriation of prisoners of war between Iran and Iraq was referred to on two occasions in Security Council resolutions:

- In Paragraph 4 of Resolution 582 (1986), which, after an appeal for an immediate cease-fire, reads: "Urges that a comprehensive exchange of prisoners of war be completed within a short period after the cessation of hostilities in cooperation with the International Committee of the Red Cross."
- In Paragraph 3 of Resolution 598 (1987), which, after paragraphs demanding that a cease-fire be observed and requesting the Secretary-General of the United Nations to dispatch a team of observers, reads: "Urges that prisoners of war be released and repatriated without delay after the cessation of active hostilities in accordance with the Third Geneva Convention of 12 August 1949."

Many of those prisoners had not been registered, and the International Committee of the Red Cross (ICRC) was unable to visit them under the arrangements provided for by the Third Convention; a persistent obstacle to their repatriation was the insistence of certain parties on prior settlement of other (military and political) points in the negotiations. ICRC nevertheless considered that the conditions for complete repatriation of all these prisoners were fulfilled, pursuant to Article 118 of the Third Convention, the first paragraph of which clearly stipulates: "Prisoners of war shall be repatriated without delay after the cessation of active hostilities."

Pending a full-scale repatriation, humanitarian measures also incumbent on the parties in accordance with their obligations under the Third Geneva Convention—such as the obligation to release the names of prisoners, to authorize ICRC to visit them, to organize the repatriation of

wounded and sick prisoners, or even to take voluntary humanitarian measures in favor of prisoners of war who are minors or who have been
imprisoned for a long time—are gestures of goodwill that can only serve
to promote further gestures of the same kind.

Humanitarian law lies at the heart of peace, focusing as much on maintaining peace as on restoring it. Breaches of humanitarian law aggravate
and prolong conflicts; on the other side of the coin, application of the law
mitigates and shortens conflicts. Let us consider these two observations.

THE CONTRIBUTION OF HUMANITARIAN LAW
TO THE MAINTENANCE OF PEACE

The role of humanitarian law in maintaining peace is clear from the fact
that many conflicts, both internal and international, have been sparked by
serious violations of humanitarian law. Massacres of civilian populations
in the Middle East, Latin America, Indochina and Europe inflamed
hatred and passion rather than imposing fear and submission.[49] Furthermore, breaches of humanitarian law have accounted for the spreading of
conflicts. For example, refugees, victims of persecution in their homeland,
often bring to neighboring or more distant countries the violence to
which they were subjected.

Even during internal armed conflicts, population displacements are
strictly prohibited. Article 3 common to the 1949 Geneva Conventions
and their Additional Protocol II of 1977 contains rules that, if respected,
would have the direct effect of significantly reducing the number of
refugees and internally displaced persons and victims in general.[50] Respect
for international humanitarian law would also imply the separation of
combatants from civilians, disarming camps, careful siting of refugees and
preventing combatants from using refugees for cover or aid supplies.[51]

International humanitarian law is applicable no matter how righteous
the causes are for which the two sides are fighting. Violations of humanitarian law were at the root of Security Council resolutions asking for
international armed interventions in Somalia in 1992, and in Bosnia the
attacks against the "safe areas' and the shelling of Sarajevo led to the
NATO "Operation Deliberate Force" in 1995.[52]

Breaches of Humanitarian Law Leading to Conflicts

"Pacification" as a euphemism for genocide is the most extreme example
of a breach of humanitarian law that leads to conflict, and is not only a
question of terminology. History has demonstrated the illusory nature of
the idea that a conflict may be shortened by resorting to torture or mas-

sacres, bombardments of civilian populations, or terrorist attacks against civilians. From World War II to this day, violations of humanitarian law have served merely to strengthen the adversary's determination to resist. They also have severely undermined the legitimacy of that party to a conflict that condones inhumane practices. As Albert Camus wrote during the Algerian War, one should be watchful "to fight for a truth without destroying it by the very means used to defend it."[53]

Using the fate of prisoners of war as a pawn in peace negotiations, as was done at the end of the October 1973 war between Israel and Syria (the October/Yom Kippur War), is a serious abuse that has proved to be counterproductive in both the short and the long term. As ICRC stated in December 1973:

> The commitments arising out of the Geneva Conventions are of a binding and absolute nature. Under those commitments, each State unilaterally undertakes, vis-à-vis all other States, without any reciprocal return, to respect in all circumstances the rules and principles they have recognized as vital. These do not involve an interchange of benefits but constitute a fundamental charter that proclaims to the world the essential guarantees to which every human being is entitled.[54]

Breaches of humanitarian law leave lasting and often serious aftereffects that hinder the return to civil and international peace, a fact witnessed during the American Civil War,[55] on the Eastern Front in World War II, in the Pacific between American and British on one side and Japanese on the other, between Japanese and Chinese, and in the Middle East.

Humanitarian issues that are not resolved during the conflict often handicap the restoration of peace between former adversaries; only when they are settled can normal political and economic relations be resumed, sometimes many years after the cessation of hostilities. The issues of mistreatment of POWs, MIAs and several thousand Eurasian children, and the case of former "reeducation camp detainees," paralyzed the relations between the United States and Vietnam for some 20 years after the end of the war.

THE CONTRIBUTION OF HUMANITARIAN LAW TO THE RESTORATION OF PEACE

The role of humanitarian law in restoring peace is twofold. It leaves open the possibility of dialogue, thus averting degradation by excessive violence both between international adversaries and among one's own population.

And it aims to solve humanitarian problems (refugees, prisoners, disappeared, missing in action and so forth) that can become serious political issues.

Application of Humanitarian Law to Shorten Conflicts

Well before the first signs of political negotiation, humanitarian gestures help, informally, to institute a minimum of dialogue between adversaries. Such dialogue may result in cease-fires, often tacit, between enemy positions to evacuate the dead and wounded; truces to let civilians out or supply them with food and medicines; or contacts to exchange news of the latest captures or even to exchange prisoners. A humanitarian truce may lead to a complete halt in the fighting. In Santo Domingo in 1965 for instance, the joint efforts of the ICRC delegate, the president of the local Red Cross and representatives of the United Nations and of the Organization of American States succeeded in halting the fighting for 24 hours in order to collect the wounded; during that time negotiations were held that put a final end to the armed clashes.

In the case of the Nigerian civil war, a historian points out:

> For the Federal Government, relief per se was not the issue. Shortly after the war broke out the International Committee of the Red Cross asked for permission to penetrate the federal blockade and fly a plane load of medical supplies into Port Harcourt. General Gowon immediately approved the request and throughout the war remained committed to the principle of allowing food and medical supplies to reach the civilians in Biafra. He supported these endeavors in order to alleviate the human suffering, to promote international good will, and to facilitate what he always believed would be the inevitable transfer of popular allegiance from Biafra to Nigeria once peace was restored.[56]

Humanitarian clauses are the first ones adversaries wish to negotiate. For example, the provisional government of Algeria sought first of all to negotiate a "special agreement" with the French government under Article 3 common to the 1949 Geneva Conventions and then, after Paris refused, initiated the procedure for accession to the four 1949 Geneva Conventions.[57] In 1984 in La Palma, El Salvador, the first item in the negotiations between the government and the guerrillas was "to humanize the war."[58] The first contacts between Soviet representatives and mujahedeen in Afghanistan dealt with the plight of prisoners of war. The first talks between various warring factions in former Yugoslavia, held in Geneva in

1991 under the auspices of ICRC, focused on humanitarian issues (exchanges of prisoners and relief supplies to civilians).

More recently, the release of Nelson Mandela from prison in 1990 paved the way for the negotiation of a peaceful settlement of political issues in South Africa.

The treatment of prisoners plays an important role in the return to peace, as does the treatment of civilian populations. Repatriation of refugees is an essential component in the restoration of peace, but is exceedingly difficult if villages have been razed and roads and fields strewn with mines. The question is highly relevant today for hundreds of thousands of Afghan, Angolan, Burundian, Cambodian, Mozambican and Rwandan civilians.

The scourge of antipersonnel mines continues to kill and to maim indiscriminately thousands of innocent civilians every year and especially refugees and internally displaced persons. Mines are not only a cause of displacement, they also constitute one of the chief obstacles to the return of entire populations once the fighting is over.

Physical suffering is very often accompanied by mental trauma due largely to the separation imposed by captivity. Similarly, the virtual absence of any system of notifying deaths could leave countless families in a state of uncertainty concerning the fate of their relatives. Restoring family ties, providing family messages and reuniting families, according to the provisions of humanitarian law, are an important factor in healing war sufferings.[59]

In noninternational conflicts, amnesty in fact corresponds to an essential feature of prisoner-of-war status—namely, impunity for participation in the hostilities. It may also be a powerful means of relieving antagonism; a measure of national reconciliation following a crisis; or a political solution to a crisis, to encourage partisans of armed struggle to turn (or return) to democratic forms of political struggle.[60] It is, indeed, with this in mind that Article 6, Paragraph 5, of Protocol II of 1977 invites governments "to grant the broadest possible amnesty to persons who have participated in the armed conflict." The object of this provision, according to the ICRC commentary on Protocol II, "is to encourage gestures of reconciliation which can contribute to re-establishing normal relations in the life of a nation which has been divided."[61]

The same question also arises at the international level: Should one prolong hatred and punish criminals (on the losing side), or wipe the slate clean and decree, as in the Treaty of Nimeguen of 1678 an official "act of forgetting"?[62]

Today, the question of whether priority should be given to pardon or to criminal prosecution is still a subject of negotiations. When Bangladesh was created after a war between India and Pakistan, criminal proceedings against 195 Pakistani prisoners of war and civilian detainees held for violations of humanitarian law (accusations of genocide) were curtailed: Pakistan made full repatriation of all prisoners, without exception, a condition for peace negotiations. The matter was brought before the International Court of Justice by Pakistan and later, with the agreement of the parties involved, was struck from the register.[63]

The provisions of the 1949 Geneva Conventions—reaffirmed in 1977—would no doubt be sufficient to punish the violations that still occur in many conflicts. Actual prosecutions have been rare and unilateral events. Nevertheless, governments party to the 1949 Conventions (practically all members of the United Nations) should not too easily escape their responsibility to prosecute violators of humanitarian law: the preventive role of the effective use of the universal jurisdiction provided for in the 1949 Geneva Conventions for all States Parties could contribute not only to justice but also to peace.

The experiences of the International Criminal Tribunals for the former Yugoslavia and for Rwanda have proved constructive in many respects, despite the difficulties encountered,[64] and will undoubtedly be of valuable assistance in the discussions now under way with a view to setting up a permanent international criminal court with universal jurisdiction.[65]

CONCLUSION

Humanitarian Law: A Sum of Experiences

Humanitarian law, both customary and treaty law, is a sum of real-life experiences. It is based on warnings against the destructions of war, and on advice on how to overcome difficult choices and avoid tragedies that have become increasingly deadly as modern means of destruction have become more powerful and the number of protagonists involved has grown.

One should use the dynamic role of humanitarian action to disarm the adversary or, in the words of Sun Tzu, "build a golden bridge to the retreating enemy."[66] The military, political and economic effectiveness of humanitarian behavior—on top of the fact that such behavior is consistent with ethical requirements—should be constantly emphasized, in the hope that we may finally move on from chaos to peace, from internecine strife to dialogue. Octavio Paz writes:

Hölderlin sees history as a dialogue. Yet that dialogue has always been interrupted by the sound of violence or the monologue of chiefs. Violence exacerbates differences and prevents us from talking and listening. Monologue is the negation of others; dialogue does of course maintain differences, but it provides an area within which alterities coexist and become interleaved. To establish such a dialogue, we have to affirm what we are while at the same time recognizing others and their inherent differences. Dialogue prevents us from denying ourselves and from denying the humanity of our adversaries.[67]

This perspective has much in common with the Dalai Lama's declarations and writings on the vital necessity of compassion in order to cope with today's difficult challenges:

A leitmotiv: compassion, compassion, compassion, which enables peace to be achieved, both individual and collective. Altruism is the key to universal peace. It is the only option in today's planetary debacle. It is a matter of life and death for humanity.[68]

The problems we face today—violent conflicts, destruction of nature, poverty, hunger and so on—are mainly problems created by humans. They can be resolved—but only through human effort, understanding and the development of a sense of brotherhood and sisterhood. To do this, we need to cultivate a universal responsibility for one another and for the planet we share, based on good heart and awareness.[69]

The Letter and the Spirit

The letter of humanitarian law is essential. It must, however, be applied in the proper spirit: for the benefit of victims, rather than to serve transient interests.

It is not only legal experts who can understand humanitarian law; every human being is capable of grasping its fundamental principles. Pierre Boissier, founder of the Henry-Dunant Institute, used the following method in training new ICRC delegates in the Geneva Conventions: he gave his students a blank page and asked them to rewrite in their own words the essence of the Four Conventions, placing themselves, in turn, in the position of the wounded (First Convention), the shipwrecked (Second Convention), prisoners of war (Third Convention), civilians in an occupied territory (Fourth Convention) and enemy forces. This powerful maieutic ploy brought out the essential provisions of instruments that seem at first sight extremely complex and difficult but then, as individuals respond to vital requirements, are easily understood.

TOWARD A GLOBAL CONCEPT OF HUMANITARIAN ACTION

Humanitarian law has evolved from a law protecting only certain categories of individuals (from the medieval knights to today's prisoners of war), to a set of provisions ensuring fundamental human rights, guaranteeing the survival of civilian populations in wartime.

Humanitarian instruments in force form part of international law and are interlinked with the system of international security, whether for arms control or for peaceful settlement of conflicts. They have still to be replaced in the general context of the development of cooperative relations at the political and economic levels.

Humanitarian action cannot be confined to exceptional or emergency situations. Different actors (individuals, organizations and governments) will be involved in different situations, each most effective in one particular sphere of activity. According to international humanitarian law, ICRC plays the unique role of neutral intermediary between parties to the conflict: "Through humanity to peace" could be the motto of ICRC in many operations today.

Nevertheless, no one should lose sight of the problem as a whole and, in particular, of how their actions are interrelated with those of others.[70] At the same time, implementing humanitarian law facilitates a return to peace and the reconstruction of a country, and emergency relief organizations (like ICRC) will give way to development organizations (such as the United Nations Development Program, the World Bank, the WHO, the FAO and others, including the other components of the International Red Cross and Red Crescent Movement[71] and the increasing role of nongovernmental organizations, on the national and international level).

The fundamentals of humanitarian law may be thought of as forming part of a wheel of cooperation,[72] responsibility[73] and accountability.[74] The initial stage is the emergency situation, in which survival is paramount; reconstruction and development follow, and then the building and maintaining of a balanced, sustainable economy; the next stage is the pursuit of peace, with efforts such as those of the United Nations and regional and subregional organizations; legal mechanisms follow for the settlement of conflicts in the form of international treaties and national constitutions; the final stage is the attainment of the ideals of humankind.[75] The fundamental principles of the Red Cross, namely humanity, universality, neutrality, independence, service, unity and impartiality, could provide useful guidelines for organizations engaged in humanitarian action, not only for the Red Cross and Red Crescent Movement.

Humanitarian law and its principles thus form part of a chain of solidarity: at the height of a conflict, with the necessary support of other political and economic measures (military peacekeeping and peacemaking measures should normally be kept separate from humanitarian activities— at least humanitarian activities by non-UN organizations, especially from ICRC) and efforts to mobilize public awareness, they often constitute a vital link contributing to the restoration of peace. As President Abraham Lincoln said, "Do I not destroy my enemies when I make them my friends?"[76]

8   HUMAN RIGHTS, HUMANITARIAN ASSISTANCE AND THE SOVEREIGNTY OF STATES

Richard Falk

During the Cold War, the conduct of international relations was focused on the challenge of the "strong state," that is, the state with the capacity and ambition to project its influence beyond its sovereign territory by military means. In such a setting, peace and security concerns dominated the political imagination, and such ideas as "containment" and "deterrence" were the core of global policy. In the post-Cold-War world,[1] the challenge of the "weak state" has become a recurrent center of concern. A weak state is a state that is in the grips of a war of internal fragmentation or that is in any sense ungovernable, as a consequence of civil strife, overwhelming humanitarian crisis and even the collapse of minimal capacity to provide "law and order." Fashioning appropriate responses to the challenges posed by weak states remains controversial and reflects the transitional nature of the post-Cold-War world. Unlike the simplicities of the Cold War, the distinctive nature of each weak state challenge makes issues of interpretation of crucial importance. This chapter discusses international humanitarian diplomacy as the response mode to the challenges posed by various weak state emergences.

A CONCEPTUAL ORIENTATION

In approaching humanitarian diplomacy as a subject of inquiry, it is helpful to distinguish among seven overlapping dimensions:

1. *The Geopolitical:* The shaping of international diplomacy as a result of the initiatives, ambitions, interests and worldviews of a leading state or states.
2. *The Statist:* The formal and functional ideas about territorial supremacy and the equality of states that are embodied in the doctrines and practice of state sovereignty, providing the cardinal principle of

international relations since the Peace of Westphalia (1648) and continuing to be formally acknowledged in the UN Charter and contemporary international law.

3. *The Normative:* The moral and, increasingly, the legal mandate given to the organized international community and, more controversially, to other actors, to protect civilian victims of official abuse, natural disaster, political chaos and strife and circumstances of belligerency without necessarily awaiting the consent of the government that represents territorial sovereignty, thereby to engage in interventionary diplomacy that may even include the use of force under the authority of the United Nations or of a regional institution and possibly even by the action of one or more states.

4. *The Logistical:* The combination of technical and military capabilities, at acceptable financial cost, to complete successfully the humanitarian mission within a finite time period and without a high risk of being drawn into a large-scale guerrilla war.

5. *The Psychopolitical:* The psychological underpinnings of political behavior, although frequently overlooked and notoriously difficult to assess, are of critical relevance. Although many elements could be discussed, matters of *perception, memory* and *identity* will be mentioned here. Perception is the way in which issues of cause and responsibility are perceived by key leaders, by public opinion and by the media. Memory refers to past occurrences that shape interpretations and policy debates. Identity is the relative degree of identification in the wider world community.

6. *The Domestic:* The relevance of ethnic or nationalist solidarity with the victims of a humanitarian emergency in important states with financial, military and diplomatic influence, thereby exerting domestic pressure on a government to take or support action.

7. *The Media or "CNN Factor":* The degree to which the media decides to put a spotlight on particular instances of the humanitarian emergency, or is either unable or unwilling to raise awareness due to its sense of the obstacles to coverage or its assessment of viewer concern.

Recalling the importance of "the lessons of Munich" during the Cold War, it is evident that for the British Foreign Secretary, the experience of the United Kingdom in Northern Ireland over the past 20 years or, for President Bush, the abortive effort by the United States to ensure stability in Lebanon after the 1982 war, made these leaders feel reluctant about intervening to stop bloodshed in Bosnia during the early 1990s. In the United States, the debate on humanitarian intervention included frequent references to "quagmire" in discussions of Yugoslavia—thinly disguised invocations of the long ordeal of the Vietnam War. Whether a particular historical memory serves to discourage the repetition of mistakes or as an unwarranted pretext for irresponsible behavior is a matter of severe controversy. What is evident and beyond question is the relevance of memory, and its prevailing interpretations, to the current debates about what to do in the face of humanitarian crises.

Matters of identity and identification are also important, since the North-South settings of many of today's humanitarian crises also raise issues of race, religion and culture. The stronger the bonds of identification, the greater the pressure to act compassionately and effectively. As a corollary, the weaker these bonds, the greater the temptation to remain disengaged. Such a pattern fosters an impression of racism in relation to humanitarian diplomacy, especially as the most difficult challenges at present are arising in black Africa. Concerns about identity are further complicated by the fears—genuine or feigned—of weak states that their humanitarian crises are being exploited by geopolitical forces of regional or global scope and by their insistence that international responses must under all circumstances respect their sovereign rights.

The inability to disengage the normative and psychopolitical from the geopolitical and the logistical generates much of the controversy about where to draw the line between sovereign rights and human rights. The controversy is partly conceptual and theoretical, attracting academic analysis and prescription, but it is partly political, pitting opposed world order tendencies against one another and placing geopolitical considerations into contention with statist considerations. It is necessary to comprehend all seven dimensions in their contextual specificity if we are to develop a convincing world order approach to the array of agonizing humanitarian challenges being posed in this early post-Cold-War period of world history.

Broad discussion of these underlying issues is also complicated by the urgency of recent and ongoing crises of human rights abuse and humanitarian emergency in Bosnia, Somalia, Sudan, Iraq, Rwanda, Zaire (renamed Congo), former Yugoslavia (in relation to Kosovo) and elsewhere in the world. Some of these crises have been internationalized, with the media dramatizing the commission of atrocities, generating public pressures to act, especially in settings where the citizenry of powerful countries in the West identify ethnically or religiously with the victims. Responses engaging the geopolitical, the statist, the normative, the logistical and the psychopolitical are being organized with a variety of consequences. The human suffering is so acute and the difficulties of effective alleviation are so great that there is an understandable public disposition to suspend discussion of practical or legal constraints on action and to focus only on how to fashion effective and immediate responses. As has been often observed, legal guidelines developed in relation to moderate circumstances tend to be cast aside in crisis situations. Less often noticed is the extent to which logistical constraints distort responses by inducing governments and international institutions to take action more for the sake of doing something than in a manner likely to alleviate human suffering. In fact, under some conditions, doing something is definitely worse for the victim population than doing nothing. Such concerns were voiced in the course of the international debate about whether to resist or facilitate the breakup of two oppressively governed states—former Yugoslavia and Iraq.

The tendency to ignore geopolitics and downplay logistics, while understandable, is unfortunate for several reasons. For one thing, even if not acknowledged, geopolitics is rarely absent from the motivating behavior of leading states. In retrospect, the U.S. government, probably mistakenly, jeopardized democratic prospects in Iraq by failing to set political conditions as the basis for agreeing to a cease-fire in the Gulf War. The largely unacknowledged motive for doing this back in 1990 was a preoccupation with regional stability and moderation. This was understood at the time to mean containing Iran and resisting the further spread of Islamic fundamentalism—that is, factors on the geopolitical level that were consistent with the statist level (thereby respecting traditional notions of Iraqi sovereignty), but that contradicted imperatives on the normative level (ignoring adverse effects on the Kurds and the Shi'ites of leaving Saddam Hussein and the Baath Party in control of a unified Iraqi state; in effect, relinquishing the opportunity to liberate the Iraqi people from brutal oppression either by encouraging separatism by the oppressed groups or by making the democratization of Iraq a war aim of the UN coalition as it had been for the allied powers in relation to Germany and Japan after World War II).

On the contrary, with respect to former Yugoslavia, the U.S. government early on, when large infusions of capital and diplomatic support might still have held the Yugoslav federation together, was insufficiently committed to maintaining the unity of Yugoslavia. This American posture was partly in deference to Germany's regional ambitions and Croatian separatist sympathies and partly out of dislike of the governing communist elite in Belgrade, and especially of Slobodan Milosevic. In both the Iraqi and Yugoslav instances, the normative dimension was subordinated to the geopolitical. In relation to Iraq, however, the problematic aspect of the U.S. approach was the practice of activist geopolitics in the Middle East, whereas in relation to Yugoslavia it was the practice of passive or laissez-faire geopolitics. To understand the policies acted upon, it is necessary to explicate as well as possible the geopolitical motives, which are both more conjectural and more essential because these motives are rarely acknowledged, and if so, only obliquely. Unlike the statist and normative levels of explanation, the geopolitical tends to remain hidden or obscure. The geopolitical is not formally legitimated in a manner comparable to the legitimation of statist practice by way of the doctrine of sovereignty or through normative justifications by way of human rights and international law.

Geopolitical motivation also operates within regional settings in a manner that often imposes heavy additional burdens on human rights and humanitarian assistance. As a regional actor in the Middle East, Turkey has used its positive links with the United States to discourage support for Kurdish separatism elsewhere in the area, especially in Iraq. Similarly, Thailand, still concerned about the spread of Vietnamese influence in Southeast Asia, has for many years pursued a policy of covert military and economic support for the Khmer Rouge that seriously threatens UN efforts to restore peace and human rights to Cambodia. As suggested above, other crucial dimensions affecting the viability of an interventionary approach to major humanitarian emergencies involve the domestic political factor and the degree and nature of media coverage. The American process of commitment is particularly beholden to the mobilizing or inhibiting impacts of public opinion among the citizenry, which itself is both a cause and reflection of media treatment. The greater identification of elites and the media with the ordeals of the Bosnian victims of Serbian atrocities than with the much larger numbers of Rwandans massacred in 1994 was undoubtedly influenced by the European setting of the former events and its greater resonance among the citizenry in America.

Despite these complexities, a more general and coherent orientation seems desirable and possible. This effort is particularly important at this time in the United States, with regard to both public opinion and the policy-making community. The United States, for better and worse, has in the last few years merged its role as geopolitical leader with its championship of a variety of normative causes. This merger reached a climax during the Gulf War, leaving an ambiguous legacy: effectiveness and resolve on one side; insensitivity and inconclusiveness on the other side. One consequence has been to raise suspicions about the capacity of the UN Security Council to act independently of its main geopolitical sponsor. Such a perception of UN independence is extremely important over time in achieving some reconciliation between the statist claims of sovereignty and the normative claims of human rights and humanitarian assistance.

In some respects, the logistical complexities of severe humanitarian crises are equally troubling. Reviewing with hindsight the heated controversies surrounding the feasibility and effectiveness of intervention during the early stages in the war in Bosnia is instructive. There were widely differing assessments about what sort of capabilities would be needed by the intervening side to deter "ethnic cleansing." These differences reflected many factors, including a range of views as to likely Serbian responses to various levels of force used against them. Within the U.S. government, military advice, conservative in light of the recollected experience in Vietnam, tended to insist that a much larger military commitment was necessary than the politicians at the time thought the citizenry or the Congress would support. It was the prevailing view in policy circles that it would require a minimum of 300,000 fully armed troops for an indefinite period to protect the remaining Muslims in Bosnia from Serbian and Croatian attack; the burden of humanitarian intervention seemed too high—especially against the background of such long, unresolved internal struggles as have been experienced in Vietnam, Afghanistan, Northern Ireland and "Palestine."

Regarding Iraq, the media carried reports, probably not read by most readers, that the "intelligence community" was convinced that the no-fly air zone south of the thirty-second parallel in Iraq would not protect the Shi'ites who had taken refuge in the marshlands, as these insurgent forces were primarily under attack by as many as ten Iraqi army divisions. To engage these forces effectively would have required resuming a full ground war against Iraq, with enormous collateral suffering inflicted on the civilian population, or an actual invasion and occupation of Iraq, again an undertaking of great magnitude and uncertain effect. Not only would such an approach have failed to relieve the suffering, it might have accentuated and prolonged it. The same intelligence sources indicated a concern that further encroachments on Iraqi sovereignty would strengthen Saddam Hussein's hold on power both internally and internationally.[2] Of course, responsible international leadership must avoid being pushed into such undertakings, but this may be easier to say than to do. The wavering between action and inaction by both Prime Minister John Major and President George Bush in relation to both crises revealed a tug-of-war, quite literally, between doing something not very helpful and doing nothing while abuse and atrocity persisted. In other words, logistical constraints (which include anxiety both about the consequences and scale of military action and about the financing of large, continuing operations) can be formidable even if normative pressures are acknowledged as providing ample legal and moral grounds for overriding deference to sovereign rights. In this regard, every one of the prominent humanitarian crises during the decade exemplifies this tragic predicament of confronting logistically overwhelming challenges.

THE SHIFTING WEIGHT OF POLITICAL DISCOURSE

In the last several years, increased support has been given to claims associated with the defense of human rights and the protection of humanitarian assistance at the expense of traditional deference to sovereign rights. Such a shift has resulted sotto voce in lowering the barrier on UN involvement in situations where the government in power withheld the consent granted it by Article 2(7) of the UN Charter, which declares off-limits to the UN all matters "essentially within the domestic jurisdiction" of its members. In 1991, Secretary-General Javier Pérez de Cuéllar signaled the new thinking on domestic jurisdiction in his annual report on the work of the UN:

> It is now increasingly felt that the principle of noninterference with the essential domestic jurisdiction of States cannot be regarded as a protective barrier behind which human rights could be massively or systematically violated with impunity.... [T]he case for not impinging on the sovereignty, territorial integrity and political independence of States is by itself indubitably strong. But it would only be weakened if it were to carry the implication that sovereignty ... includes the right of mass slaughter or of launching systematic campaigns of decimation or forced exodus of civilian populations in the name of controlling civil strife or insurrection.[3]

This formulation by the Secretary-General seemed calculated to exert influence and seemed to reflect a trend in the early 1990s toward a more proactive United Nations relationship to humanitarian crises situated within the territory of sovereign states. This orientation reflected an enthusiasm for multilateral efforts to restore governance to "failed states," seen as the most serious threat to world order after the end of the Cold War, and encouraged the initial efforts in Somalia. Again, it was Mr. de Cuéllar who provided the most authoritative statement of this erosion of sovereignty in the context of humanitarian diplomacy in the following passage:

Has not a balance been established between the rights of States, as confirmed by the Charter, and the rights of the individual, as confirmed by the Universal Declaration? We are clearly witnessing what is probably an irresistible shift in public attitudes towards the belief that the defense of the oppressed in the name of morality should probably prevail over frontiers and legal documents.

We must now ponder this issue in a manner that is at once prudent and bold. In a prudent manner, because the principles of sovereignty cannot be radically challenged without international chaos quickly ensuing. In a bold manner, because we have probably reached a stage in the ethical and psychological evolution of Western civilization in which the massive and deliberate violations of human rights will no longer be tolerated.[4]

There are several revealing difficulties with this formulation of an undoubted trend in interpretation and practice. To begin with, the former Secretary-General's reference to the ascendancy of "the rights of the individual" misses a central point that it is group rights that seem most characteristically at issue in the worst humanitarian crises, which arise from ethnic and/or religious struggles as in Bosnia, Sudan, Somalia, Rwanda, Burundi and Iraq. Also, the generality of Mr. de Cuéllar's reference to eroding sovereignty in "defense of the oppressed" is suspect, especially if one contemplates the plight of refugees, most spectacularly, perhaps, in relation to "boat people" from such countries as Vietnam and Haiti. Most surprising of all is his association of this new phase of international relations with "the ethical and psychological evolution of Western civilization." Such a nineteenth-century formulation seems startlingly out of place at the end of the twentieth century!

The most serious oversight in Mr. de Cuéllar's important formulation is its obliviousness to geopolitics. It is correct that if the issues are perceived as sovereign rights versus human rights, then there is a significant shift in favor of human rights both at the level of discourse and practice and both in the settings of international organizations, especially the United Nations, and in relation to leading states. Such a shift is even more pronounced if geopolitical factors fall on the human-rights side of the ledger, as they do in Yugoslavia and to a varying extent in Iraq since the 1991 cease-fire. But what if geopolitical factors fall on the sovereign-rights side of the ledger, as they do in Kuwait, elsewhere in the Gulf and in Indonesia? What if the UN, in conjunction with a state, causes severe humanitarian distress while using force to further a geopolitical ambition? Such certainly appears to be the case with respect to the maintenance of comprehensive sanctions on Iraq more than seven years after the restoration of Kuwaiti sovereignty. This effort that has been backed by the UN Security Council, although with increasing misgivings by several members, has amounted to a punitive peace that has caused the civilian population acute suffering without achieving its alleged political goals of undermining the regime of Saddam Hussein. It creates the strongest impression yet that the UN is dominated by geopolitical priorities when it comes to peace and security policy with important strategic implications.

The basic conclusion seems clear when related to the conceptual framework described earlier: sovereign rights are selectively giving way to human rights (including a wide range of humanitarian concerns about the relief of civilian suffering, especially famine), but not if geopolitical calculations favor deference to sovereignty. One small confirmatory illustration: during the August 1992 crisis in Iraq involving the establishment of a protective zone for the Shi'ites in the southern part of the country, Turkey refused to allow its air bases to be used for such a mission; no questions were raised about Turkey's sovereign right to withhold support, despite the evident humanitarian urgency and the UN mandate.

Should those who espouse humanitarian concerns welcome this course of development? In general, yes, but with a few caveats, already prefigured. We need to appreciate that geopolitics rules the roost when it comes to the enforcement of human rights and decisions relating to humanitarian intervention. This means, among other things, that the overwhelming number of instances will involve the flow of force from North to South and that strong states in North and South are definitely off-limits. (Can anyone imagine a UN humanitarian intervention in the United States to protect Native Americans from alleged ethnocide?) It also means *exclusions* for mixed reasons of motivation and capability (it is difficult to construct a plausible scenario that involves helping Tibet, the Punjab or Kashmir achieve self-determination in the face of China's and India's opposition, regardless of the strength of human rights/humanitarian argument) and *double standards* (it is difficult to conceive of any major UN efforts to protect the East Timorese or West Papuan peoples from Indonesian oppression, which has amounted in some past instances to ethnic cleansing).

There are further grounds for caution. The loudest voices of opposition to this trend come from weak and poor states in the South that continue to regard respect for sovereign rights as integral to the protection of political independence and territorial integrity. Also, many of the champions of this recent expansion of humanitarian claims come from circles in the North that adhere in their writings and diplomacy to "a realist world-view." One of the prime features of realism as applied to world order thinking is to be scornful of normative constraints on the foreign policy of leading states whether derived from international law or morality. The U.S. repudiation of the World Court's 1986 decision regarding Nicaragua is a dramatic illustration of realism in action.[5] If realist thinking embraces the humanitarian agenda, it can be understood in two main, somewhat contradictory, ways—either as a belated acknowledgment, made easier in the aftermath of the Cold War, that normative factors are important even if not all-important,[6] or that in the new world order the humanitarian agenda can provide a useful geopolitical foundation for projecting power by way of reliance on force (the most cynical reading of President Bush's approach to the Gulf crisis in 1990 and 1991, and to President Clinton's efforts to impose the terms of the cease-fire on Iraq since early 1993).

INTERNATIONAL LAW

International law is in a state of flux regarding these issues. The encounter between sovereign and human rights has not been authoritatively resolved either by an international codification of rules or through a series of judicial pronouncements issued by a fairly unified World Court. Early in this decade there seemed to be a definite trend in diplomatic rhetoric, the practices of states and international organizations, and public opinion to brush aside sovereign rights in the face of serious humanitarian emergencies arising from either political circumstances or natural disaster. However, the experience in the mid-1990s raises questions about whether this trend toward the internationalization of response to internal breakdowns has merely faltered or has been halted, if not reversed. Nevertheless, the practice of humanitarian intervention may still have introduced into customary international law rules and principles establishing rights (and according to some, duties) of humanitarian assistance on behalf of the organized global or regional communities and of states acting on their own.

There now appears to be a strong consensus among international law experts that the UN can authorize humanitarian intervention, including the use of force, even absent any internal condition that poses a threat to international peace and security. Whether the same scope of authority exists in relation to individual states that act for alleged humanitarian purposes is open to more doubt, and the diplomatic record is more ambiguous. In the aftermath of the Gulf War, the then British Foreign Secretary, Douglas Hurd, vigorously argued that Britain and its allies could act in Iraq on behalf of the Shi'ites without the benefit of Security Council Resolution

688 because "[r]ecent international law recognises the right to intervene in the affairs of another state in cases of extreme humanitarian need."[7]

But recall the Western reaction to the 1978 Vietnamese intervention in Cambodia to drive the Khmer Rouge from power, thereby saving the Cambodian population from an admittedly genocidal regime, a circumstance of undoubted "extreme humanitarian need." Leading Western states as well as China and Thailand (who for geopolitical reasons were intent on keeping the Khmer Rouge as a force in being) focused on Vietnamese "aggression" and regional ambitions, demanding immediate Vietnamese withdrawal from Cambodia. Undoubtedly, the Cold-War context was an overriding geopolitical factor, as were Vietnam's dubious humanitarian credentials, given its own antidemocratic regime and sometimes suspect human-rights record. International law has not established a "clean hands" requirement as a precondition for humanitarian intervention. Indeed, the history of humanitarian intervention over the past two centuries discloses that dirty hands and suspect motives were more common than not.[8]

The mandate of the UN, or in some settings, a regional actor or even an NGO, is an important legitimizing dimension of humanitarian-assistance operations undertaken in defiance of the will of an internationally recognized government. International law is shaped in the process of responding to such events, which test the collision of such opposed conceptions as territorial sovereignty and the protection of human rights; that is, the manner in which current humanitarian crises are resolved will provide important precedents that are likely to influence the legal posture toward future crises of a similar kind.[9] The humanitarian law of war as embodied in the Geneva Conventions of 1949 (especially Convention IV on the protection of civilians) and the Geneva Protocols of 1977 provides an indispensable foundation for negotiations and diplomacy in the difficult circumstances of unconventional warfare and massive civilian misery and is particularly helpful to representatives of international institutions and NGOs.[10] A further effort to elaborate rights and duties of states, international institutions and nongovernmental relief organizations specifically in relation to humanitarian crises would be of great practical value as a source of guidance in these difficult settings.

REINFORCING HUMANITARIAN CLAIMS

The qualifications addressed previously represent real concerns, but strengthening normative claims relative to sovereign claims is of great historical relevance in this period of heightened ethnic and religious conflict.

To raise confidence and diminish skepticism requires a concerted effort to limit to the extent possible the encroachment of geopolitics upon the dynamics of response on behalf of human rights and humanitarian distress. Such an assertion is easy to make. The challenge is to propose tangible steps.

The former UN Secretary-General Pérez de Cuéllar set forth some useful guidelines intended to address this set of concerns:

> First ... the principle of protection of human rights cannot be invoked in a particular situation and disregarded in a similar one. To apply it selectively is to debase it.
>
> Second, any international action or protecting human rights must be based on a decision taken in accordance with the Charter of the United Nations.
>
> Third ... the consideration of proportionality is of the utmost importance.... Should the scale or manner of international action be out of proportion to the wrong that is reported to have been committed, it is bound to evoke a vehement reaction, which in the long run would jeopardize the very rights that were sought to be defended.[11]

These guidelines are of undoubted importance, but unless interwoven in the political texture of UN operations, they are likely to be of interest only to those scholars and commentators who pay more attention to forms than substance. One need only scrutinize the recent record of the Security Council, especially in relation to the Gulf War and its follow-up, to notice the disregard of such a framework. Secretary-General Boutros Boutros-Ghali made an admirable effort to have similar humanitarian emergencies treated similarly with his plea that the crises in Somalia and Sudan deserve as much attention as the debacle in Yugoslavia, and it seems to have had some effect.

Thus vigilance and autonomy by the Secretariat of the United Nations in relation to these guidelines is one approach. An indispensable step in this direction would be a willingness of geopolitical forces to revalidate the office of Secretary-General by encouraging the election of public figures of moral and political stature who would be expected to operate with the sort of independence associated with the tenure of the most respected and principled former Secretaries-General Dag Hammarskjöld and U Thant.

Another approach, as proposed in a peacekeeping context by the Secretary-General in his June 1992 report, *An Agenda for Peace*, but also applicable to humanitarian claims, is adequate financing and standby capabilities. Without assured logistical capabilities for response, the UN must make a Faustian bargain with its richest and most powerful members, thereby bringing geopolitical factors inevitably, if covertly, to bear on the shape, effectiveness and legitimacy of the UN response. Even limited financial and logistical capabilities would be important both for confidence-raising and to enable more independent, principled action by the UN, at least in small- and medium-range situations.

A third approach is to augment the disposition already present to shift attention from response to prevention. The small UN observation and monitoring force in Macedonia is the clearest illustration of peacekeeping in a preventive or anticipatory mode. The recurrent flare-ups in Kosovo have underscored the importance of this particular effort and its success in avoiding wider zones of political violence in the Balkan region. Surely one area of effort should center upon restraints on arms trade, both by way of agreement and through policies adopted at the state and regional levels. Here, too, the pieties and the politics are not always mutually reinforcing—to restrict arms trade while not curtailing interventionary diplomacy of a geopolitical variety may only aggravate the vulnerability of weak, dissident states in the South.

Such a concern leads naturally to a fourth approach, which may seem utopian to those with a firm realist outlook, but in a formal sense is already legally mandated: namely, to endow citizens with an effective way to challenge foreign policy initiatives in domestic courts as violating international law. Such challenges have been frequently mounted in the United States since the Vietnam War with little success; they are usually brushed aside on procedural grounds, grandly justified by reference to the anachronistic "political questions doctrine." Curtailing geopolitics from below and within is part of an evolving notion of constitutional democracy in an increasingly integrated world. Every person, and certainly every citizen, should be entitled to a determination of whether or not a particular, contested action of the state is consistent with international law. Constitutionalism would be extended to include a commitment to adhere to a lawful foreign policy as determined, when appropriately challenged, by an independent judicial body.

A fifth approach follows from the first four. It summons the world of informal citizens' associations (the NGO dimension of international life) to monitor responses to allegations of human-rights violations and in furtherance of humanitarian assistance as rigorously as the violations themselves occurred. For instance, in responding to the horrifying campaign of ethnic cleansing in Bosnia, such an approach would publicize the failure to condemn Croatian violations as vigorously as Serbian violations. These independent assessments, which emanate from an emergent "global civil society"[12] have proved invaluable in exerting pressure on even the most powerful governments when it comes to uncovering patterns of gross violations of human rights or serious instances of environmental deterioration. Such monitoring could also increase pressure to treat similar situations similarly, thereby minimizing the machinations of geopolitics and helping to implement guidelines advocated in the abstract by Pérez de Cuéllar.

Monitoring is, of course, only the beginning. As it is, many NGOs in the humanitarian context are playing a variety of roles involving the delivery of services and the mitigation of human suffering. There is a useful diversity of NGO perspectives, illustrated by the general insistence of the International Committee of the Red Cross on respecting statist guidelines, as contrasted to the style of Médecins sans Frontières that stresses the priority of humanitarian considerations and casts aside, to the extent possible, statist and geopolitical constraints. It is not a matter of choosing one style over the other; both are needed and with due sensitivity can and do complement one another in specific circumstances.

CONCLUSION

More than ever before, the early 1990s briefly focused attention on the humanitarian agenda. The main cases—Yugoslavia, Somalia, Sudan, Rwanda, Liberia, Zaire (later Republic of Congo) and Iraq—are tragedies of immense proportions for the peoples involved; each strains both the moral imagination and logistical capabilities to, or beyond, the breaking point. Such prominence temporarily shifted the balance of language and law away from sovereign rights and in the direction of humanitarian assistance. To the extent that these tragedies persist and receive diminished attention, there is a definite prospect of political despair and a revival of realist cynicism about humanitarian challenges throughout the United Nations and elsewhere. Such demoralization represents a very serious setback for advocates of more robust efforts in relation to the challenge of humanitarian emergencies of various kinds.

It is important to develop a trustworthy framework of humanitarian response that will alleviate human suffering and victimization in settings in which the logistical challenges are not as overwhelming as they were in many places around the world during the last several years. It may be that we are entering an era of recurrent overwhelming challenge—a type of "new world disorder"—but such pessimism is premature, and it is important to do everything possible to avoid it becoming a self-fulfilling prophesy. Just a short while ago the political atmosphere seemed more favorable than ever before to weighting the balance of international law in favor of humanitarian intervention as authorized by the UN and other international institutions. Although such authorizations were always controversial with several important countries in the South and contained dangers of abuse mentioned above, the earlier indications of a basic shift of normative emphasis were to be welcomed.

There is one further lesson that can already be learned from the downward spiral of events in the mid-1990s. In circumstances of ethnic tension, maintain even defective mechanisms of peaceful coexistence, and if these collapse, seek by all feasible means either their restoration or a negotiated transition to some new, less-than-perfect arrangement that terminates violence and encourages reconciliation and compromise, as well as encourages expanded roles for NGOs as agents of humanitarian diplomacy and explores the possibilities for greater reliance on preventive approaches.

In conclusion, two broad tendencies seem to be emerging from the experience of the decade with humanitarian diplomacy:

- an interventionary impulse to alleviate the suffering associated with humanitarian emergencies regardless of the barriers of national sovereignty;
- a disillusionment on the part of major governments, especially the United States government (particularly evident in relation to the Congress), with the burdens of humanitarian diplomacy.

Partha Dasgupta

The subject of political economy is concerned with the circumstances in which people are born and the manner in which they are able to live and die. Since life involves the use of resources, economics—a somewhat more specialized subject of inquiry—studies the strengths and weaknesses of various methods of allocating those resources.

Of all resource allocation mechanisms, the *market mechanism* has undergone the greatest scrutiny in the literature of economics. Although it is rarely defined in formal terms, its outlines are familiar. A market mechanism is a means of allocating resources in which the state restricts its activities in the socioeconomic sphere to facilitating the operation of private markets by developing and enforcing commercial laws, protecting private property rights and so forth. The *competitive market mechanism* is a special example in which all commodities have markets and all parties are price-takers in these markets.

Even the competitive market mechanism, however, cannot be relied upon to protect and promote human well-being. The reasons are many and varied, including the fact that markets are not a propitious set of institutions for producing public goods (such as immunization, public sanitation and courts) and merit goods (such as primary and secondary education). One obvious—though often overlooked—reason is that for the competitive market mechanism to function efficiently, everyone must have something to bring to the market if he is to take anything back home from it.

One may suggest that even when a person owns no physical assets, he owns one inalienable asset—namely, labor power—but the science of nutrition has shown that this presumption is false.[1] The only thing an assetless person owns is *potential* labor power. Conversion of potential into actual labor power can be realized only if the individual finds the means of making the conversion. Nutrition and health care are a necessary means for conversion, as are primary and secondary education. For this reason these commodities are often called basic needs. The "economics of neglect" deals with the circumstances in which the conversion of potential into actual labor power is not possible because basic needs are not met for a large proportion of the population.

One of the most impressive and pleasing achievements of modern economic analysis has been the demonstration, through both analytical and empirical means, that a central responsibility of governments is to ensure that the basic needs of their populations are met. All too often since World War II, however, governments of developing nations have been encouraged to spend time and resources on matters at which they have proven singularly inept and intrusive (for example, in the production of private goods, such as steel and motor cars), and have not been charged with performing vital functions (the supply of public goods and food security). Shibboleths such as "public ownership of the means of production" have proven enduring even while people have remained uneducated and gone malnourished and diseased. Health education, the gathering and dissemination of knowledge, the establishment and enforcement of laws of property and contracts, the central role of political and civil liberties and, more broadly, the motivational forces necessary for the promotion of well-being have not exactly held sway in most poor countries. Nor have they attained the high ground in development economics, even though they constitute the proper domain of government activity. The market mechanism, as I have defined it, is particularly inept in South Asia, Africa and Latin America, largely because their rural populations have very few resource endowments at their command.

In this chapter I will provide an account of the possible economic consequences of a failure to meet basic needs. Surprisingly, we have little quantitative feel for such an important question and, in particular, about the loss of productivity owing to low nutritional status. The science of nutrition and public health has advanced considerably over the years, but economists have not taken advantage of its findings. I have, for example, been unable to find any good estimates of rates of return on investment in primary health care and nutritional guarantees. For this reason, my account will in the main be qualitative, and I will squeeze out the occasional quantitative estimate only when I am able to. Along the way, I will also provide evidence of the extent to which governments of poor countries have systematically neglected their responsibilities to provide basic needs for their populations. The two basic needs I will address are the commodities required for health and education. Nutrition and primary health care are the two chief inputs in the "production" of health. The role of education in economic life will be addressed, and I will also examine corresponding issues raised by the differences between the two genders. Finally I will argue, by looking at data on expenditure in warfare, that the lack of provision of basic needs in poor countries cannot have been due to a paucity of funds.

HEALTH: MORTALITY INDICES

Table 9.1 presents a list of countries that, in 1995, enjoyed a per capita income of less than US$3,500. The idea is to look at a snapshot of the standard of living in each country by noting four social indices: life expectancy at birth, per capita income, infant mortality rate and adult literacy rate.

Life expectancy at birth is the number of years a random newborn can expect to live, on the assumption that current age-specific mortality rates will persist. In the sample countries in Table 9.1, national *per capita income* is positively and significantly correlated with life expectancy at birth.[2] That the two seem to go together may suggest that growth in income is the sole means of achieving greater life expectancy, but it would be wrong to make this inference.

Differences in life expectancy at birth between rich and poor nations are large. In sub-Saharan Africa life expectancy at birth today is approximately 50 years; in Western industrial democracies, the figure is about 76 years. There are also large gaps in the infant mortality rate and literacy. The *infant mortality rate* is the number of live-born infants out of every 1,000 who die during their first year. In Western industrial democracies, the infant mortality rate is down to something like 10 per 1,000, and primary and secondary education have a universal reach. The infant survival rate is 1,000 minus the infant mortality rate. Plainly, it is not unrelated to life expectancy at birth, but it focuses on something quite different: nutrition and hygiene at the earliest stage of life. It is also related closely to the health of the mother, the duration of lactation and the mother's educational attainment.

Table 9.2 shows the extent of undernourishment among children under five years of age in the three regions where undernourishment is pervasive. For children, the indices shown are anthropometric. Life expectancy at birth tells us something quite different from anthropometric indices. For example, newborns and children under five are less wasted in sub-Saharan Africa than they are in Asia. Within Asia the worst

Table 9.1: Indicators of Living Standards, 1995–1996

	Per Capita Income*	Life Expectancy at Birth (Years)**	Infant Mortality Rate (per 1,000)**	Adult Literacy Rate (%)***
Bangladesh	240	57	83	38
Benin	370	54	84	37
Bolivia	800	61	71	83
Botswana	3,020	52	40	70
Burundi	160	46	106	35
Central African Republic	340	49	103	60
Chad	180	47	92	48
China	620	69	38	82
Ecuador	1,390	70	31	90
Egypt	790	65	57	51
Ethiopia	100	49	113	36
Gambia	320	46	78	39
Haiti	250	54	94	45
Honduras	600	69	29	73
India	340	62	73	52
Indonesia	980	64	47	84
Jordan	1,510	69	21	87
Kenya	280	54	61	78
Lesotho	770	58	96	71
Liberia	490	48	157	38
Madagascar	230	58	100	46
Malawi	170	41	137	56
Mali	250	47	134	31
Mauritania	460	53	124	38
Mauritius	3,380	71	20	83
Morocco	1,110	66	64	44
Nepal	200	56	82	28
Niger	220	48	191	14
Nigeria	260	52	114	57
Pakistan	460	63	95	38
Paraguay	1,690	69	28	92
Philippines	1,050	68	32	95
Rwanda	180	36	105	61
Senegal	600	51	74	33
Sierra Leone	180	37	164	31
Somalia	110	48	125	24
Sri Lanka	700	73	17	90
Sudan	310	54	73	46
Swaziland	1,170	59	68	77
Tanzania	120	51	93	68
Thailand	2,740	69	31	94
Tunisia	1,820	69	28	67
Uganda	240	41	88	62
Yemen	260	57	78	33
Zambia	400	43	112	78
Zimbabwe	540	49	49	85

*   GNP per capita, 1995 US$
**   1996
*** 1995

The data composing Table 9.1 is from UNICEF State of the World's Children 1998 Statistical Tables, Table 1: Basic Indicators, http://www.unicef.org /sowc98/.

Table 9.2: Indicators of Undernourishment in Poor Countries, 1990–1997

	Sub-Saharan Africa	South Asia	Latin America
Under-five Malnutrition (%)	50	69	21
Low Weight for Age (%)	40	70	11
Low Birthweight (%)	16	33	10

The data composing Table 9.2 is from UNICEF State of the World's Children 1998 Statistical Tables, Table 2: Nutrition http://www.unicef.org /sowc98/.

I used "underweight: moderate and severe" to reflect low weight for age, and "wasting" and "stunting" to reflect malnutrition.

figures are in the Indian subcontinent. But life expectancy at birth in the Indian subcontinent is higher than in sub-Saharan Africa: it is 61 years, as compared with 51 years. This illustrates the limitations of the index, which is the expectation of longevity at birth. Ideally we would be interested in longevity at different stages of life, or age-specific mortality rates, which reflect the threats a class or gender faces at various stages of life. Today, across countries the variation in life expectancy at age five is much less than the variation at birth. For example, a five-year-old girl in Western industrial democracies can expect to live another 74 years, whereas her counterpart in sub-Saharan Africa can expect to live an additional 60 years or thereabouts. This is what we would expect. The impact of food, sanitation and health care deprivation is felt dramatically during early childhood. In hostile environments large groups of people get weeded out in the early years of their lives. In fact, some of the weeding gets done at the household level by the parents' practicing differential child care.

Between genders, life expectancy at birth differs in almost all countries. (A current exception is India, where the figure is approximately 62 years for both.) Differences have changed over time because of evolving technological possibilities and altered lifestyles. For example, in the first half of the nineteenth century in England, female life expectancy at birth exceeded that of males, but mortality rates for females in the age range 10 to 39 years were greater than those of males. Today, female mortality rates in Western Europe and the United States are lower than those of males at all age levels.[3]

The first three years of life are crucial; they tend to leave a marked imprint on future capacities. A longitudinal study in Guatemala that controlled for differences in nutrition in early childhood revealed that the absolute difference in the average heights of two poor populations (a control group and a group that was provided with food supplements) remained approximately constant from about the age of three. Moreover, the intellectual performance of the control group in later years was significantly worse. Growth failure in early childhood, according to the data, predicts functional impairment in adults (for example, in stature, strength, intelligence, numeracy, literacy, lean body mass and, for women, obstetric risks).[4] The finding suggests that unless conditions improve for a deprived group, the absolute gap in final heights due to nutritional differences between two populations is reached by age three. The issue, therefore, is not whether one can be a stunted but healthy adult, but whether one becomes a stunted adult because of periodic nutrition, sanitation and health care deprivation during childhood.

We should note as well that a determinant of prenatal and infant mortality rates is the mother's size and health; for example, birthweight is influenced by the mother's condition.[5] It was thought for some time that the condition of the placenta is to a large extent impervious to the mother's health status, but this is not so.[6] This is one way in which the effect of food and health care deprivation in early childhood is passed on to the succeeding generations. But a person is subject to different mixes of risks as she passes through infancy to early childhood. For many purposes, even the first year is too large an interval to work with, since the risks an infant is vulnerable to in the first month are different from those she faces in subsequent months. A good portion of infants who die in the first month (the neonatal period) is composed not only of those suffering from congenital defects, but also of those who were born prematurely or who experienced fetal growth retardation. Therefore, for certain purposes it makes sense to distinguish neonatal mortality rates from postneonatal mortality rates. Such data are not easy to come by in many countries, but as a pithy summary of the earliest set of risks to which a person is vulnerable, the infant mortality rate has much to commend it.[7]

NUTRITION AND INFECTION

Nutrition is not the sole determinant of good health; food adequacy standards depend to an extent upon other factors as well, including potable water, immunization and general medical care, sanitation and personal hygiene. Waterborne diseases (such as cholera, typhoid and hepatitis) and water-based diseases (such as guinea worm) are immediate examples of why nutrition alone is not sufficient for good health. While diarrheal infections (a central cause of infant and child deaths in poor countries) are not usually transmitted by contaminated water, they are spread by contact, and this can be contained by washing in clean water. Unhappily, more than a billion people in Africa, Asia and Latin America have no reliable access to drinking water.[8] Thus, it is not unusual for children in poor countries to suffer from six to eight episodes of diarrhea per year, on average, which adds up to some two months' diarrheal illness each year. This pattern systematically retards growth.

One well-known study compared weight, as a function of an infant's age in weeks, with frequent illness.[9] It showed a direct, negative relationship between the number of days an infant suffers from diarrheal illness and the infant's growth. Airborne diseases (such as influenza, pneumonia and whooping cough) also continue to be prominent causes of infant and child deaths in poor countries, responsible for a quarter to a third of child mortality there. But although infections produce short-term faltering in growth, they cannot explain the long-term deficits in growth observed among the poor in poor countries. A diet has to be very marginal if it cannot cover the relatively modest quantities of additional nutrients required for catching up during childhood and adolescence. This is a prime reason governments should be concerned with food needs when developing notions of nutritional status and the capacity to do work.

There is synergism among diseases, in that reducing deaths from one disease helps reduce deaths due to other forms of illnesses. A wide-ranging empirical study on infant and child mortality rates in poor countries found that there is a threshold level for the under-five mortality rate (about 150 per 1,000), such that progress in reducing the rate is slow when the number is above it, whereas it is fairly rapid when the number falls below it.[10]

There is a similar link between malnutrition and diarrheal infection. A study of data on children in the age group 6 to 36 months in the Matlab Thana experiment in Bangladesh reports on the relative risks of death from diarrhea among the severely malnourished, as compared with the risk among those who were not suffering from severe malnutrition.[11] About 60 percent of all deaths in this age range occurred in the five months following the monsoons, when infections are rampant. Children with no previous diarrhea indicated a positive association between malnutrition and subsequent diarrhea. Furthermore, diarrheal illness in one period was found to increase the likelihood of its occurring in some subsequent period.[12]

The complementary needs of nutrition and freedom from infections are also synergistic in cases of tuberculosis, measles, cholera and most respiratory infections. This means that a person's nutrition requirements up to a point diminish as his environment improves, which in turn implies that there is some possibility of substitution among them. Severe or repeated infections are a common cause of malnutrition, and there are several paths along which this happens, including both supply and demand factors.[13]

On the demand side, infections create an additional need for nutrients by increasing a person's metabolic rate and the rate of breakdown of tissues. They also indirectly reduce the supply of nutrients. This they do for a variety of reasons. First, infections often reduce a person's appetite. Second, they lower a person's ability to absorb nutrients, by affecting the functioning of the gastrointestinal tract. Third, they entail increased loss of major macronutrients, vitamins and minerals through the feces because of the increased speed of transit of the food that is eaten. Finally, infections result in the direct loss of nutrients into the gut. Malnutrition is frequently precipitated by outbreaks of infectious diseases such as gastroenteritis.

The debilitating effects of infectious diseases go beyond undernourishment. Infections can lead to an increase in the excretion of micronutrients; a deficiency in any of these is damaging. For example, in Asia some five million people suffer from noncorneal xerophthalmias, a disease linked to vitamin A deficiency. In sub-Saharan Africa more than 30 million people are estimated to suffer from goiter, caused by iodine deficiency, and half of all children under twelve years are thought to suffer from iron-deficiency anemia.

The relationship between nutrition and infection seems to work the other way, as well. Reviewing an extensive literature, one study concluded that malnutrition predisposes one to diarrhea.[14] Moreover, a person's ability to fight an infection once he has caught it is reduced under conditions of moderate to severe malnutrition; his immune system is affected. There are exceptions, however: nutritional status has negligible impact on morbidity and mortality associated with the plague, smallpox, typhoid, yellow fever, tetanus and AIDS. It is even possible that mildly undernourished hosts enjoy survival advantages over their well-fed counterparts for some of these infectious diseases. For example, someone suffering from iron-deficiency anemia would enjoy this perverse effect were the invading pathogen unable to obtain enough free iron to multiply as rapidly in the bloodstream as it would in a well-nourished person. This remains a matter of speculation, but historically it may have been important. Of the infectious diseases identified as the leading causes of deaths during the eighteenth and nineteenth centuries, those whose relationship with nutritional status could be "perverse" accounted for about one third of deaths. Fortunately, so far as public policy goes, it is not a matter of any great moment that we do not know if such "perverse" effects are at all significant. Today it is possible to have our food and eat it, too: modern public-health measures can prevent the spread of many such life-threatening pathogens.

GROWTH AND DEVELOPMENT

The first three years of life have a pronounced effect on a person's mature body stature. Early nutrition and the extent of freedom from infections leave deep imprints. Failure in growth amounts to wasting (low body weight) and stunting (low height), and there is now much epidemiological evidence that both increase the chance of morbidity and mortality.[15] By the end of the first year, a child's growth rate becomes quite small and physical activities assume great importance. The energy cost of growth has two components: the energy stored and the energy used. One way a child can economize energy expenditure is by reducing physical activities. Mild to moderately wasted preschool children under free-living conditions have been observed to spend more time in sedentary and light activities than their healthy counterparts. They have been found to rest longer and to play more often in a horizontal position.[16] A Jamaican study found stunted children in the age group 12 to 24 months to be significantly less active than their nonstunted counterparts. The energy thus saved was comparable to the energy cost of growth at that age.[17] At an extreme, when we observe little children in poor countries lying expressionless on roadsides and refraining from brushing the flies off their faces, we should infer that they are conserving energy.

Marked differences in activity levels have been reported among a sample of infants from poor households in rural Mexico, between those who received nutritional supplements and a control group.[18] The former made greater contact with the floor, slept less during the day, spent more time outdoors, began playing almost six months earlier and so forth. The thesis here is that low nutritional intake depresses activity, which isolates the child from contact with the environment and from important sources of stimuli to both cognitive and motor development. It is significant that the control group in the study was not clearly undernourished.[19]

Motor development is the process by which a child acquires basic movement patterns and skills, such as walking, running, jumping, hopping, throwing, kicking and holding something in her grip. In normal circumstances, children develop these fundamental motor patterns by the age of six or seven years. It is through such movement patterns and skills that many childhood experiences, especially learning and interpersonal experiences, are mediated. During infancy and early childhood, interactions between the mother and child are of critical importance in this development. This is a hidden cost of anemia and low energy intake on the part of the mothers. Since housework and production activity are mandatory, reductions in discretionary and child-rearing activities offer the mother a way of maintaining her energy balance. To be sure, societies differ in the way people other than the mother are involved in a child's upbringing. Nevertheless, the mother is an important figure in a child's cognitive and motor development in all societies.

Long-term malnutrition would appear to be particularly associated with mental development; the presence or absence of current malnutrition has a less pronounced effect. Under conditions of severe undernourishment (for example, marasmus or marasmic kwashiorkor), retardation of psychomotor development in young children has physiological reasons as well. Some of the damage is extremely difficult to reverse and may indeed be irreversible. In one study, for example, even after six months of nutritional rehabilitation of a sample of infants hospitalized for severe malnutrition, no recovery was observed in their motor development.[20] It may be that severe malnutrition affects development of the brain, whose growth starts rapidly at around ten weeks of pregnancy and continues in spurts to about three or four years of age. (Fetal iodine deficiency is well known to damage the central nervous system.) However, there is evidence that malnutrition has an effect on brain development only when it coincides with a period of rapid growth and differentiation.[21] Equilibrium reactions (otherwise called righting reflexes) are functions of the cerebellum and play an important role in the development of motor control.[22] It is, of course, possible that even such anatomical changes as have been observed are results of retardation rather than permanent injury, but this is not known with any certainty.[23]

Among schoolchildren the matter is somewhat different, in that peer group pressure tends to counter the instinct for reducing physical activities. This is likely to be especially so among the boys. To be sure, even for them decreased activity is a line of defense.[24] However, some studies indicate that in school-aged children the low energy expenditure associated with nutritional deficiency can be traced to low body weight: basal metabolic rates of underweight children are low. The development of lean body mass among undernourished children is retarded. This has a detrimental effect on their capacity to work when adults.

On a wider front, malnutrition and infection have been found to have a pronounced effect among schoolchildren on such processes as attention and concentration. There is abundant evidence that children who suffer from nutritional deficiencies and infections perform badly on aptitude tests.[25] As noted earlier, in extreme cases nutritional deficiencies affect the central nervous system. In less-than-extreme cases the matter is not one of brain function; frequent absence and attrition affect learning, as well.

The studies with which I am familiar did not explore the extent to which it is possible for a person to catch up in height during adolescence if she had suffered from deprivation when young, but it is possible to make up past deficits, although the process is slow.[26] In order to catch up, a stunted adolescent needs more protein and energy than would be required by a normal adolescent. If the person was deprived when young, however, the presumable reason was poverty, in which case she will hardly be in a position to command more than is required for normal growth during adolescence.

PREGNANCY AND LACTATION

Earlier, we observed that maternal malnutrition results in low birthweight and high prenatal and neonatal mortality. During pregnancy, well-nourished women in Western industrial societies acquire something like 7.5 kilograms of extra weight. (The median infant birthweight there is 3.3 kilograms.) This translates into an energy cost of a bit more than 80,000 kilocalories over the nine-month period. The cost is not distributed evenly over the three trimesters of pregnancy. Nevertheless, for practical purposes it makes sense to recommend a uniform addition to energy intake for the duration. It works out to about 285 kilocalories per day.[27]

The energy cost of lactation is the energy content of the milk secreted plus the energy required in converting food intake into milk. For healthy women in Western industrial societies, this additional energy requirement is roughly 700 kilocalories per day. If requirements during pregnancy have been met, a woman will start lactating with about 36,000 kilocalories of additional reserve fat. This is a source of approximately 200 kilocalories per day if the reserve is to be drawn down over six months. It follows that she needs an additional 500 kilocalories per day.[28]

To what extent is the health cost of nutritional deprivation shared between a pregnant woman and her fetus? The evidence is mixed. A Gambian study has shown that it is shared during the lean season: women lose weight during pregnancy and the proportion of low-birthweight babies increases. This is a finding among people who would presumably have adapted to an annual food cycle. Nutritional supplementation programs introduce a new variable. One study found energy supplementation to have no effect on lactation performance. On the other hand, average birthweight in the wet season responded to energy supplementation. (There was no response during the dry season.)[29]

A similar finding has been reported from a field study of nutritional intervention among marginally undernourished women in west-central Taiwan.[30] While a combined energy-protein supplementation had a significant effect on prenatal growth of the offspring, the study did not discover any effect on maternal anthropometry (for example, skin-fold thicknesses). Additional food was usurped by the fetus.

ADULT STATURE AND PHYSICAL PRODUCTIVITY

When nutritionists talk of physical work capacity, they mean the maximum power (that is, maximum work per unit of time) a person is capable of offering. It transpires that the most compelling index of a person's physical work capacity is his maximal oxygen uptake, which is the highest rate of oxygen uptake a person is capable of attaining while engaged in physical work at sea level. The reason maximal oxygen uptake provides us with the measure we need is that it is dependent on the body's capacity for a linked series of oxygen transfers (diffusion through tissues, circulation of hemoglobin, pulmonary ventilation and so on). It also measures cardiorespiratory fitness: the higher its value, the greater the capacity of the body to convert energy in the tissues into work. Broadly speaking, taller and heavier nonobese people have greater work capacity. Unskilled laborers in poor countries are often slight and weak, but they are seldom out of shape; it is sedentary workers who often are. As a very rough approximation we may distinguish people's capacity for physical activities solely by their physical work capacity.

Much international attention has been given to saving lives in times of collective crisis within poor countries. International agencies have also given attention to keeping children alive in normal times through public-health measures such as family planning counseling, immunization and oral rehydration. This is as it should be. That many poor countries fail to do either is not evidence that the problems are especially hard to solve. In fact, these are among the easier social problems: they can be fielded even while no major modification is made to the prevailing resource allocation mechanism. The harder problem, in intellectual design, political commitment and administration, is to ensure that those who remain alive are healthy. It is also a problem whose solution brings no easily visible benefit. But the stunting of both cognitive and motor capacity is a prime hidden cost of energy deficiency and anemia among children and, at one step removed, among mothers. It affects learning and skill formation and thereby future productivity. The price is paid in later years, but it is paid.

EDUCATION AND PRODUCTIVITY

The output of education (knowledge, skills and so forth) is a durable capital asset. A society's formal education system (schools, colleges and other centers of learning) offers the means by which people are able to acquire this asset. Other sources of education are the family, friends and the community at large. In this section I will deal with the instrumental value of education in general, and of numeracy and literacy in particular. I will also address improvements in labor productivity brought about by education.

That primary education has a considerable effect on industrial labor productivity has been widely documented. A study in the state of India showed that primary education is important even for the cultivation of traditional varieties of wheat. Agricultural laborers who had been through primary education made more effective use of labor and made better choice of production inputs. The study also showed that the impact of secondary education increased significantly, suggesting that returns from secondary education increase with the coming of new technology of the kind embodied in the Green Revolution.[31]

There are now a number of cross-country estimates of social rates of return on various levels of education. Table 9.3 provides estimates for three regions: sub-Saharan Africa, Asia and Latin America (including the Caribbean). The aggregation involved is heroic, but the figures are telling. In each region, among different levels of education the primary level has the highest product value (a rate of return of about 26 percent), secondary education much less so (about 15 percent), and higher education least so (about 13 percent). One cannot escape the thought that poor countries have consistently underinvested in primary education relative to education's higher reaches.

Table 9.3: Social Rate of Return on Education, by Level of Schooling (percent per year)

Region	Primary	Secondary	Higher
Sub-Saharan Africa	26	17	13
Asia	27	15	13
Latin America and the Caribbean	26	18	16

Source: G. Psacharopoulos, "Returns to Education: A Further International Update and Implications," *Journal of Human Resources* 20 (1985).

The effect of parents' education on their children has been investigated and has been found to be beneficial. For the most part, the studies have explored the effect of some six to seven years of schooling, but they have differed over the measurement of well-being. Some have looked at household consumption of nutrients and the use of contraceptives; others have looked at child health in general, at infant and child survival rates and at children's height.[32] These studies confirm that education helps mothers to process information more effectively and enables them to use available social and community services more intensively. Education also appears to impart a degree of self-confidence that enables a person to make use of whatever new facilities are available. This is an invaluable asset for rural populations living through changing circumstances. Female education, especially secondary education, also has a pervasive and significant effect on female reproductive behavior.[33] Although the links here are complex,[34] female education as a general rule appears to lead to a reduction in fertility rates.

There is a strong complementarity between social and community services and literacy and numeracy. Among the most important examples of the former are agricultural extension services, trade facilities with the rest of the world, provisions for health care and advice on health care. Remove these services, and rates of return on primary education are likely to decrease. Literacy and numeracy are unlikely to be of much use if they have nothing to act upon. One study used data from Bangladesh to argue that maternal education has little effect on child mortality rates because health services in rural Bangladesh are negligible.[35] By the same token, literacy is of little use to people who remain unemployed and are unable to make use of their literacy.

Calculations of rates of return on primary education are based on highly aggregated data, and they cannot reveal a central reason for recalcitrance on the part of poor families in acquiring education. A fine early empirical study noted the large costs poor families must bear when they send their children to school.[36] Poverty forces parents to send children out to work at an early age. Child labor (employing both girls and boys) in the marketplace, including bonded labor, is common. Children are an early source of income, of much value to impoverished parents. By the age of six, children in poor families in the Indian subcontinent tend cattle, goats and younger siblings, as well as fetch water and collect firewood. Therefore, even when primary education is subsidized, schooling is costly for poor households, as the poor have limited access to credit, and so the benefits flowing from these subsidies are captured disproportionately by well-off families. In the case of rural India, to the extent wealth is correlated with caste hierarchy, education subsidies are captured mostly by the higher castes. There is also a gender bias in educational attainment. In patrilineal societies, the benefits derived from sending a daughter to school are less than those from sending a son. An educated girl may also be perceived as less pliable than an uneducated one and hence will be at a disadvantage in the marriage market.

Across households within a country, poverty and illiteracy usually go hand in hand; each reinforces the other. Across countries, the matter is different, since countries differ in their social ethos and political design. In an earlier work, I showed that among poor countries there was no systematic relationship between real national income per head and improvements in adult literacy during the 1970s.[37] I also discovered that there is a positive correlation between countries with a bad record in political and civil rights and those with a good record in improvements in literacy. I have no compelling explanation for this statistical fact. What is incontrovertible is that it is possible for a poor country to break away quickly from the grip of illiteracy. It requires concerted effort from several parties: the household, local organizations, the village community, religious organizations and the government. It involves government engagement in the form of free primary and secondary education, free midday school meals and so forth. These factors are required to bring private returns on education closer to social returns.

Is female education socially cost-effective in poor countries? A rough calculation based on World Bank data on Pakistan indicates that female education is an excellent form of social investment.[38] In 1990, educating an additional 1,000 girls in Pakistan would have cost $40,000. Each year of schooling there has been estimated to reduce the under-five mortality rate by 10 percent; this translates to a saving of 60 deaths of children under five. Saving 60 lives with health care interventions would have cost around $48,000. But this is not all. Educated women typically have fewer children than average; an extra year of schooling reduces female fertility by 10 percent. Given Pakistan's astonishingly high fertility rate of 6.6 births per woman, a $40,000 investment in educating 1,000 women would avert 660 births. The alternate route of family planning expenditure for achieving the same result would have cost around $43,000.

WARS AND STRIFE AND THE FUNDING OF BASIC NEEDS

No discussion of basic needs is complete without at least a reference to political and civil liberties, but they, too, have been systematically neglected in the economics of development. Space forbids me to enter into these issues in any detail here, but many studies indicate that poor countries with better political and civil-rights records performed, on average, better in terms of growth in national income per head, improvements in life expectancy at birth and the infant survival rate.[39] There is some evidence that civil and political liberties are necessary (though not sufficient) for protection of the environmental resource base of rural communities. What are popularly called human rights not only are of fundamental value, they would appear to have instrumental worth, as well. For me this has been one of the few agreeable findings in what is an unusually depressing field of research.

All too often, human rights have been systematically and strenuously violated in the majority of poor countries.[40] Government violence against citizens is also a commonplace occurrence in most poor countries. Political instability is often allied to such violence. More than 50 of the approximately 115 so-called developing countries are run by military-controlled governments. From 1958 through the end of 1981, there were more than 50 successful coups in 25 sub-Saharan countries, and more than 50 major attempts that proved unsuccessful. The coercive powers of the state are enhanced by the accumulation of machinery for warfare. Among those classified by the World Bank as "developing countries" (having a gross national product of less than $785 per head in 1996), military spending represented about 12 percent of government spending between 1990 and 1996. This should be contrasted with the corresponding figures for health and education, which were 4 percent and 11 percent, respectively (see Table 9.4).

Excessive armaments expenditure is not the monopoly of military dictatorships. The Indian subcontinent is a telling case. Table 9.4 shows the stark contrast between military spending and the sums allocated to health and education—the contrast being particularly stark when we consider the status of developing countries such as India and Pakistan in levels of life expectancy at birth, infant survival and literacy (see Table 9.1). India and

Table 9.4: Government Expenditures on the Military, Health and Education As Percentage of Total Government Expenditures, 1990–1996

	Military	Health	Education
World	10	11	6
Developed Economies	9	12	4
Developing Economies	12	4	11

The data composing Table 9.4 is from UNICEF State of the World's Children 1998 Statistical Tables, Table 6: Economic Indicators http://www.unicef.org /sowc98/.

Table 9.5 Government Expenditures on the Military, Health and Education
As Percentage of Gross National Product

	Military	Health	Education
World	5.0	4.1	4.9
Developed Economies	5.2	4.7	5.2
Developing Economies	4.3	1.6	3.8

Source: R. S. McNamara, "The Post–Cold War World: Implications for Military Expenditures in Developing Countries," Proceedings of the World Bank Annual Conference on Development Economics 1991 (New York: World Bank, 1992).

Pakistan have fought three wars against each other, and each country's military accumulation has been dominated by a display of paranoia about the other. Neither country can afford its armaments expenditures, and yet there are no signs of a breakthrough in this long-drawn-out stalemate: there are no regional trade agreements in the offing, no collaborative ventures and no serious cultural exchanges. That in earlier times each was supported by a rival superpower is on occasion offered as an excuse on their behalf, but it is no excuse. Each is a sovereign nation. If their political and civil leaders had displayed the required courage and vision, the governments of India and Pakistan would have entered into negotiations long ago, and kept the superpowers at bay.

Table 9.5 contrasts military expenditure among poor countries with expenditures in health and education. The bias is self-evident and was not unique to the period after the Cold War. The evidence is incontrovertible: if the allocation of public expenditure had been systematically directed at basic needs, the quality of life in poor countries would have been vastly different from what it is today. It is not low income that keeps the rural populations of poor countries in such wretched shape: the problem lies elsewhere and can be located easily if one cares to look for it.

10 REFLECTIONS FROM THE DONOR

Obligations and Responsibilities of All Nations

Lord David Owen, M.D.

It is important to stress that while there are obligations and responsibilities among donor nations to help provide humanitarian assistance, promote good health, eradicate disease, protect human rights and emphasize humanitarian principles, there are obligations and responsibilities on recipient nations, too. In 1989 we started to see the end of a world polarized since 1945 between communism and democracy, capitalism and the command economies. We are all now, Russians and Chinese included, readier to accept, to a lesser or greater extent, the market economy. Even the distinction between developed and developing nations is diminishing. More nations, like India, have characteristics of both within their own territory.

What should be the ingredients of any new approach to the dilemma of the growing imbalance between the rich, industrialized nations and some of the poorest nations, particularly on the African continent, and also the contrast between nations with a good and bad health record? The Organization for Economic Cooperation and Development (OECD) and the World Bank are the key institutions on economic relations. The Development Assistance Committee of the OECD is the key Western policy institution. There is a case for bringing the UN more into this field, but it must not be done by weakening or reducing the credibility of these proven vehicles. Adjustments are needed in the structure of the world economy, but that can happen only by consent and within the framework of an avowedly market-based structure.

There is no substitute for altruism, concern for others and philanthropy, but new relationships can also be encouraged to develop on the basis of enlightened self-interest. It is not just filling the begging bowl but making an investment with reasonable returns, and often with the private sector fully participating. I do not wish to belabor the point of self-interest, but there is no doubt that in donor countries, it is easier for ministers responsible for overseas development or health funding to persuade their electorate to allocate resources when it is possible to demonstrate some return to them from an investment. There is a need for investment to be properly conducted. Too often in the past, in the hands of weak or corrupt governments, we have seen new investment go disastrously wrong. But it has failed even more frequently when well-intentioned governments have had an inadequate understanding of market economics.

It would be of mutual advantage for any new structuring of the world economy to be based on an open acceptance of different though often complementary commitments from both donor and recipient nations. Thankfully, the world is moving toward such a new contractual approach between nations, based on mutual obligations and responsibilities in many fields.

We have seen contractual relationships develop in their most structured form in the European Community of 15 member states, soon to enlarge to 26 and more. The Association of Southeast Asian Nations (ASEAN) countries have also developed their own distinctive pattern. The North Atlantic Free Trade Agreement among Mexico, Canada and the United States is another powerful example, and others are emerging. We are seeing a recrudescence in the authority of the Organization of American States, and there are many who believe that the massive and often unique problems of the African continent will be helped by an increase in the authority and effectiveness of the Organization of African Unity, after the horrors of Rwanda. The Organization on Security and Cooperation in Europe is a large grouping of nations that essentially links the North Atlantic Treaty Organization and the old Warsaw Pact countries. It was created in the early 1970s. The economic and political development of its member countries has been dramatic in the 1990s as many countries started preparing for membership of the European Union (EU).

Politics and economics are inseparable. Where organizations start by aiming for a common market and dealing predominantly with trade and economics, experience shows, this inexorably leads to wider political activity. But the same is not true when politics is put first and we have experience of market reforms languishing behind. The terms of membership have become more demanding in many groupings, and they are developing the concept of contractual obligations freely undertaken and often legally binding. Nations, however, contribute in different ways and at times unequally, and the best structures are designed to provide for give and take. Bargains are struck in which there are different gains and different losses, but the outcome aims at overall fairness, albeit over time. These relationships are not characterized by the description of recipients or donors. Some nations may be net financial contributors, others net gainers, but the relationship is still that of partners. Under the leadership of Kofi Annan the UN will, I hope, consciously turn away from the very concept of donors and recipients, and fashion instead a relationship of partners. But partnership also means sharing of resources and responsibilities.

It is part of the purpose and principles of the United Nations enshrined in Article I of the Charter to achieve international cooperation in solving problems of a humanitarian character.

Chapter I: Purposes and Principles

Article I. The Purposes of the United Nations are:

1. To maintain international peace and security, and to that end: to take effective collective measures for the prevention and removal of threats to the peace, and for the suppression of acts of aggression or other breaches of the peace, and to bring about by peaceful means, and in conformity with the principles of justice and international law, adjustment or settlement of international disputes or situations which might lead to a breach of the peace;

2. To develop friendly relations among nations based on respect for the principle of equal rights and self-determination of peoples, and to take other appropriate measures to strengthen univeral peace;

3. To achieve international cooperation in solving international problems of an economic, social, cultural, or humanitarian character, and in promoting and encouraging respect for human rights and for fundamental freedoms for all without distinction as to race, sex, language, or religion; and

4. To be a centre for harmonizing the actions of nations in the attainment of these common ends.

Those purposes and principles were challenged and often torn up in the former Yugoslavia and Rwanda in the 1990s. The world saw on television humanitarian abuses of a degree and depth that were scarcely conceivable for those accustomed to living comfortable Westernized lives at the threshold of the twenty-first century. In both countries we saw the urgent need for a rapid-reaction-force capability to act within days at the early stage of ethnic cleansing. A capability to protect and ensure the delivery of food, medicine and other vital supplies was obviously needed. We saw nightly on our television sets the difficulties of linking humanitarian and peacekeeping operations. Yet most of these situations the UN Charter wisely anticipated. The UN, as we saw in Iraq in 1998, with its on-ground inspection teams to destroy Saddam Hussein's capacity to manufacture and deploy weapons of mass destruction, is still an essential mechanism for world peace. Also the power of initiative of the Security Council was shown to be a very useful fallback for even the one super-power, the United States of America. Time and again one hears the UN being criticized by residents, politicians, diplomats and commentators as if it is an organization divorced from its member states, when the vast majority of its actions or inactivity is determined by the decisions in the Security Council and elsewhere by those very same member states.

In the Security Council the Charter has shown itself to be an extremely flexible instrument of policy-making. The absolute doctrine of noninter-ference in the affairs of a member state, itself a product of the old East-West conflict, had by 1998 been replaced by a cautious interventionism. The Charter can be used as a legitimate instrument for dealing with humanitarian abuses in extremis inside a member state. This new inter-ventionist role, however, whether in Somalia, Bosnia, Haiti or Rwanda, has revealed many practical difficulties in its implementation. What starts as a purely humanitarian intervention soon assumes additional tasks.

It is not always possible or even desirable to remain neutral between opposing military forces, but the impartiality of the UN must be main-tained. There are lessons to be learned from these interventions; in the case of Rwanda, the refusal to intervene in April 1994 needs to be absorbed, and future interventions will have to be very carefully judged by what, I hope, will soon be an enlarged and more representative Security Council. Some now call into question the use of the UN militarily, point-ing to the success of NATO in Bosnia. But it is very important to remem-ber that NATO in Bosnia intervened on the ground only when the United States was ready to commit its troops in 1995, and then only to help implement the Dayton Accords.

In many instances it will still be prudent for governments to rely on nongovernmental organizations such as Médecins sans Frontières, Oxfam and Save the Children to cross frontiers when governments fear to tread. The Security Council will not attempt to become the peacemaker of first resort in all cases when internal conflict emerges within member states. Nor can its proven peacekeeping role be expected to easily or always develop into a proactive peacemaking role. Nor is there always going to be a definable exit strategy, as the United States has demanded, for every deployment of UN forces.

The UN has more freedom to develop at the start of the twenty-first century in ways that, in the Cold-War period, would have been inconceiv-able, but it is not capable of policing or providing for every world crisis. The UN has to limit itself to working with the member states in a part-nership; it will never replace the member states as a world government.

What the UN can do is to mobilize its member states to act to uphold the Charter.

I was a member of the Independent Commission on International Humanitarian Issues[1]—which produced, in addition to its final report, many detailed reports on how humanitarian principles should govern our response to famine, indigenous peoples, the encroaching desert, street children, the vanishing forest, refugees, the disappeared and modern wars. I am convinced that humanitarianism embraces more than just human rights. Human rights were rightly moved higher up the world agenda by President Carter in the late 1970s. But inevitably at that time the very words "human rights" became embroiled in the rhetoric of the East-West confrontation. Also, the definition of what were human rights reflected the Judeo-Christian tradition, itself predominantly Western. What our Humanitarian Commission attempted to do was to bring other great traditions, those derived from the Muslim, Buddhist and Hindu faiths, into a broader and more international definition of humanitarianism. It was helped in doing this by having Sadruddin Aga Khan and Crown Prince Hassan as its cochairmen.

If, as I hope, UN activity is to be ever more influenced by humanitarian attitudes, then it is essential that they are universally acceptable attitudes. That means that they cannot always reflect the same order of values that dominate in the Western industrialized democracies. Furthermore, international humanitarian attitudes need to be enforced by the more extensive application of international law. Crimes against humanity must be able to be brought before an international criminal court if there is to be any really new international order. Ad hoc tribunals, such as have been established for the former Yugoslavia and Rwanda, suffer from having to build up their own resources and develop a pattern of working from scratch.

Of all UN humanitarian concerns, health—in the wider World Health Organization (WHO) definition—is the one that provokes the least controversy and receives the maximum cooperation. Within the UN family WHO has a proud and enlightened record of advancing the cause of humanitarianism. In seeking further to promote humanitarianism, the UN would be wise to reassert the preeminence of better health, for it can still do much to lighten the multiple loads of life. The greatest success of the WHO has been the eradication of smallpox. I was involved, albeit very much on the margins, in the Smallpox Eradication Program during my period as U.K. Minister of Health, starting in March 1974, when one of the first papers presented to me dealt with the program, which had started in 1967. In 1973 the number of recorded cases of smallpox in the world had been 135,904. This was the highest for fifteen years. Nevertheless, I was advized that "target zero" was still felt to be on course, and the Ministry of Health and WHO doctors were optimistic.

In 1975 the eradication of smallpox from Asia was achieved, but it was still present in Ethiopia and Somalia. Asian eradication was itself a formidable milestone, since it meant the end of transmitting the variola major virus, which had caused the most severe form of smallpox. However, I well remember officials coming to me around this time, desperately worried about the future effectiveness of the whole eradication program. Smallpox was spreading rapidly among the hundreds of thousands of people displaced by floods and famine in Bangladesh, proving once again that disease is the all-too-frequent accompaniment of natural disaster. The number of smallpox outbreaks in Bangladesh had increased from 78 in October 1974 to 1,280 in mid-May of 1975.

I was told there were no reserves of money left within WHO to cope with this extra demand. Sweden was contributing more money, and I unhesitatingly found extra money from our own hard-pressed U.K. National Health Service budget for WHO. This was a practical example of enlightened self-interest in health policy. We did the same in the United Kingdom the following year, when smallpox, though suspected of being confined to 66 villages in Ethiopia, looked likely to break out across the country as Ethiopia was engulfed by civil war. The WHO health teams faced formidable difficulties dealing with the scattered and mobile population in the Ogaden Desert, and they needed more vehicles and personnel. Despite the increased WHO activity, the smallpox virus did spread to adjoining countries. In Djibouti, Kenya and Somalia some 3,000 cases occurred. Even so, the last case of naturally occurring smallpox was in Somalia in October 1977: 10 years, 9 months and 26 days from the start of the Intensified Smallpox Eradication Program.

A tragedy then occurred when two cases of smallpox, resulting in one death, were caused by a laboratory infection in Birmingham, U.K., in August 1978. Fortunately, this did not spread, and on May 8, 1980, the Thirty-third World Health Assembly made the historic announcement that smallpox had been eradicated from the entire world. That was a magnificent result and one of the great successes of international activity.

Eradication of smallpox could never have been achieved without the existence of WHO, nor without the dedication of WHO staff, with their ability to stimulate the interest and commitment of health staff in individual nations. Eradication was not a centrally imposed program; rather, each national program adapted itself to fit particular circumstances. There was also an active research program running parallel to the fieldwork.

The program gathered momentum from 1967, but even as late as 1976 and 1977 no one could be certain of a successful conclusion. As we now look to future health challenges, we would be wise to learn some of the lessons from that smallpox program, and the 1,460 pages of *Smallpox and Its Eradication*[2] provide a comprehensive source.

In 1988 the global eradication of poliomyelitis was launched. In the World Health Report 1997, 116 countries had already conducted national immunization days, and the number of reported cases in 1996 was down by more than 90 percent since 1988. Eradicating other major diseases—whether cholera, dengue hemorrhagic fever, schistosomiasis, AIDS or malaria—will be harder. Health has no frontiers; nor, unfortunately, has ill health. Hunger and famine still haunt millions of people. Millions survive on far too few calories. Millions barely have access to water and even less access to clean water. It has been estimated that every day, 40,000 children die from illnesses that are made life-threatening because of malnutrition. For many of these diseases, unlike smallpox, there are no vaccines or even curative medicines. Those medicines that are available in developing countries may not be the best, and health care can be rudimentary. Unlike smallpox, many of these diseases are hard to diagnose, to trace and to control. Also, we cannot hope to manage most of these diseases by relying only on health workers, for all aspects of public health are involved—water supply, sanitation, housing, nutrition and a host of other factors—necessitating multidisciplinary activity.

AIDS is the global illness that has captured the world's attention. Even though the number of people who are HIV-positive is relatively smaller in the industrialized world than in the developing world, media attention has ensured that massive resources for research have been allocated. Pharmaceutical firms identified a clear commercial interest, and this provided the funds for the new drugs that are now providing, if not a cure, a way of curbing the illness and improving people's life expectancy and lifestyle. It is estimated that 30.6 million people in the world are HIV-positive, and the latent period means that there are many more who will develop the virus. More than 90 percent of new HIV infections are, however, in developing countries that cannot afford the new expensive drugs.

I would be a happier person if I could see any prospect that a fraction of the effort devoted to AIDS would be devoted to malaria in the coming decade. Today, more than 2.5 billion people are at risk from malaria every year in more than 90 countries. More than 500 million acute clinical cases in any one year are infected by malaria, and it causes or contributes to 3 million deaths, more than any other communicable disease except tuberculosis. Malaria is the most dominant and debilitating disease in the world, particularly among children in the endemic regions. A serious humanitarian strategy for relieving global suffering must give malaria a far higher priority than it has at present. Insufficient financial resources at both the national and international level are reducing the effectiveness of national malarial programs, as are political upheaval and wars.

I was fortunate to be of a generation of medical students in which tropical medicine was an integral part of our study course. Sadly, that can no longer be said for every medical school in the world. When I began as a medical student in 1956, the effort to eradicate malaria was in full swing. Even during the consolidation period of the 1960s, medical opinion was still optimistic that the disease would become a rarity. Unfortunately, a resurgence of malaria took place in the 1970s; even so, when I ceased to be Minister of Health in 1976, most were hopeful that malaria would soon be eradicated. Unfortunately, that optimism was misplaced. Even more worrying is the way the situation has worsened with the spread of resistance to drugs by the parasite and to insecticides by mosquitoes. A ten-year study in Thailand has confirmed that the parasites are mutating to become resistant. Quinine, used for more than 500 years against malaria, is becoming less effective.

Eradication of malaria is no longer a WHO objective, having been replaced by the less-ambitious target of control. It was very appropriate that in October 1992 a conference of all the nations' health ministers specifically discussed the problems of malaria. At present neither our governments nor the pharmaceutical industry devotes anywhere near sufficient funds to research or prevention. Experts are, however, hopeful of developing a specific peptide as a vaccine for malaria. But the world should not wait for the development of a vaccine before taking substantial steps toward eradication. I hope that the eradication of malaria will be restored as a formal objective of the World Health Organization. Yet for such a pledge to be credible, it will require immediately a greatly expanded research effort on both vaccines and new drug therapy. In terms of control, it will need to involve from the outset many other UN agencies in an integrated program. The treatment of bed nets and curtains with insecticides has in recent years produced good results and, where these are introduced, overall childhood mortality can be lowered by 15 to 35 percent. But it also has to be admitted that, with DDT banned, the substitutes are often not as effective; nor has the discipline of dealing with the breeding grounds been maintained, and control has not been helped in countries where wars and poverty have diminished their public-health capacities.

Malaria eradication, starting in the year 2000, could provide the challenge for a new humanitarian effort. It will be far more demanding and include many more scientific disciplines and much greater communal effort than was represented by the challenge of smallpox in the 1960s.

Will the donor countries be ready to find special finances for malaria? One reason they might is that it is possible to see a return at least in part for their own citizens. First, the eradication of malaria would end the necessity for preventive drug therapy and for any vaccination. Second, as tourism becomes ever more global, and travel to sub-Saharan Africa and Asia from the European and North American continents becomes ever more popular, the tourist industry has developed an interest in the success of the program. There is even some indigenous malaria still in the United States of America, which would become more troubling if newspaper stories of tourists' dying from cerebral malaria started to appear in the American press. There is also the future possibility of extensive climatic change making malaria endemic in hitherto unaffected areas.

Sustainable—which means environmentally sound—growth will not be achieved without a complex interplay between former donor and recipient nations. There is a sound economic case for increasing direct aid from the developed to the developing nations. This was the essential message of the 1980 Brandt Commission report, *North-South: A Programme for Survival*, which stated that: "above all, . . . a large scale transfer of resources to the South can make a major impact on growth in both the South and the North and help revive the flagging world economy."[3] The hemisphere divide of North-South is confusing, for there are developing nations within Eastern Europe. Yet it is noticeable that Bosnia-Herzegovina is attracting preferentially far more aid than, for example, Rwanda, the poorest nation in Africa, though both have been devestated by ethnic wars.

One of the great problems for the world economy is the debt overhang and the fact that some of the poorer countries return their whole aid support program in interest charges. A greater readiness on behalf of the rich nations to write off debt to the very poor is essential, and some campaigning is under way to mark the millennium with a quantum leap in debt relief. But if such action is to be undertaken by developed nations, then developing nations, under the new partnership arrangements, will have to be readier to accept responsibilities in fields such as providing more efficient public health, reducing narcotic production and sales, forest management and fire prevention and better pollution controls. They will, inevitably, have to absorb some of these costs and be ready to make that contribution, provided the payback comes through in different forms and with overall more money from the richer nations. One way the rich can contribute is through conservation—for example, funding tropical reforestation schemes.

Another area for reciprocal action involves the rapid population expansion in parts of the developing world. Population growth places enormous stress on developing countries' capacity to provide sufficient food and improve standards of living. It also makes many in the richer countries feel that the problems of the developing world are insoluble. Yet there has been a rapid decline in birthrates in Europe, the United States and China, where 80 percent of women use contraceptives. The world population in 1997 totaled 5.85 billion people; it is expected to reach 11 billion by 2150. We all know that it is not enough just to provide for birth control; the high rate of infant mortality—which makes families have more children as insurance—poor prenatal health care and the lack of education for women have all to be addressed. These programs not only need funding by the richer countries with low birthrates; they need commitment from within the poorer nations with high birthrates. The programs need to be better managed and given the high priority they deserve. Population control is just as important an ingredient for sustainable development as protection of the environment. It has become, unfortunately, emotionally linked with internal political debates about abortion and the right to life, and the U.S. Congress has cut appropriations for international population programs, even though these programs have excluded any support for abortion and steered clear of the fundamentalist debate.

In summary, I do not see the donor nations enlarging foreign aid substantially if there is no obvious sign that the recipients in the developing world will accept responsibilities that contribute to international objectives beyond the confines of their nation-state.

On pollution control, the December 1997 summit at Kyoto agreed that the EU, the United States and Japan would cut their greenhouse gas emissions by 2010 by 8 percent, 7 percent and 6 percent, respectively, below 1990 emission levels. But it left the signatory countries to pursue their own figures rather than tie in all countries to mutually agreed actions. There is little sign that the United States intends to fulfill its promise. If traditional donor nations are to accept such reduced pollution targets, as some traditional recipient nations advocate, then the recipient nations would be wise to make commitments as well, otherwise the donors will be less generous in other areas where they contribute to development in recipient nations. It is little use for campaigners and recipient nations to talk about insufficient "political will" without recognizing that there is a real voter resistance to many of the actions that need to be taken and that such voters need to be convinced that other countries are taking their fair share of unpopular actions.

The reluctance to contribute more money among donor nations is already very marked. With the economic collapse of the Soviet Union, a heavier load is bound to fall on the other G-8 countries—the United States, Germany, Japan, the United Kingdom, France, Italy and Canada. There is abundant evidence that the United States is going to expect the European Union increasingly to match its contribution to international projects—not unreasonable given that there is broad equivalence between their GDPs.

The U.S. Congress is becoming ever more resistant to moral arguments for increasing the foreign aid budget. That budget is now the smallest proportion of GDP since World War II and the smallest proportion among all industrialized countries. In the United Kingdom over the last decade, our aid budget as a proportion of GNP has also been substantially reduced—and, I regret to say, without any obvious political backlash.

The U.S. aid budget is heavily skewed toward Israel and Egypt, where political factors weigh heavier than poverty. The United Kingdom and France traditionally skew their aid programs toward former colonies, and the ability of the Japanese to tie their aid to the purchase of Japanese goods is quietly envied by many other industrialized nations. The old liberal belief that tied aid has a special value has been surreptitiously ditched by many nations, even if they continue to espouse its virtues.

By 1998 the United States had become massively in debt to the UN, despite having a treaty obligation to pay 25 percent of the UN budget and 30 percent of the regular UN peacekeeping budget. There is, however, a strong case for the United States to take a lower share of both budgets, and Japan and the European Union should offer to shoulder at least 5 percent so that the U.S. basic contribution drops to 20 percent. In the future, as the Carnegie Commission on Preventing Deadly Conflict has argued,[4] all nations on the Security Council should fund their own contribution to a UN peacekeeping rapid reaction force as part of the price for being on the council. It is absurd that defense departments all over the world charge their foreign ministries extortionate amounts for peacekeeping operations that then reclaim these amounts from the UN. The public justification for maintaining defense spending in future years in at least the EU will increasingly be that it is making an indirect or direct contribution to UN or NATO/WEU peacekeeping. The concept of "common security,"[5] which we developed in the Palme Commission's Report, *Common Security*, is now becoming accepted wisdom, but the means of financing such a concept are still too narrowly assessed.

When peace came in 1980 to Zimbabwe, it became easier to deal with the tsetse fly and malaria. But the disease then spread again as fighting developed in Mozambique through the 1980s and into the 1990s. Had there been even a small UN force on the Kuwait-Iraq border in the summer of 1990, there could well have been no need for massive military action in Desert Storm in 1991. A preventive UN deployment, as in Macedonia in late 1992, might, if put into Bosnia-Herzegovina in early 1992, have prevented the war. Nations that maintain large defense forces, such as Indonesia, must not get upset if potential donor nations first demand reduced defense expenditure. The promotion and sale of ever more sophisticated defense equipment to poor nations by rich nations is quite simply wrong. It is also dangerous to sell to nations who are not even friends, as many countries did with Iraq. It meant that Saddam Hussein used our arms against our own forces. Politicians, at last, are becoming more sensitive to the anger of their electorates when their own soldiers are shot at by weapons provided by their own country. There is also a growing frustration when voters are asked to increase aid contributions or contribute to peacekeeping operations for countries that spend large sums of money on arms, on grandiose spending on palaces and on government offices and international airports.

Part of a new contractual world order is a more open and honest understanding of mutual obligations and responsibilities. Compassion, concern and altruism, as well as the concept of international citizenship, are far better nurtured in a world order where value for money is not a concept to be ashamed of; where investment can be seen to produce a return; where debt write-off can be expected to benefit the poorest, not those who rule; where peacekeeping and peacemaking are not constantly undermined by arms sales; where national boundaries are not allowed to be changed by force of arms; and where humanitarian principles, attitudes and actions are underpinned by the sanctions of international law.

Abdulrahim Abby Farah

On all sides there were small, fragile shelters made of shrubs, bits of cardboard, bits of plastic. It was clear they wouldn't keep out the rain and you could see through many of them. . . . I felt anger and frustration and a kind of shock at the stark impoverishment of the people. No shelter, no food, no proper clothes, no guarantee even that they would last into next week . . . I remembered the gesture of humiliation by a woman trying to cover her knees, a person who had probably been comfortable in Somali society two years before."[1]

Africa has long been plagued by disaster—natural and man-made. Its history is replete with stories of drought, famine, pestilence, floods and other natural calamities; man-made disasters bring to mind the plague of slavery, internecine strife and the ravages of colonialism. Within the past 50 years to this catalog of human calamities other horrors have been added—civil war, ethnic cleansing, forced displacement of populations, human rights violations and gross misgovernment.

Before the advent of modern government, African tradition required each tribe or community to assume collective responsibility for the welfare of their own in times of disaster. There was no other entity they could turn to for help. If a tribesman fell victim to hunger, disease, impoverishment or threats to his person, that individual could rely on his immediate clan for succor and protection. Each became, in a sense, his brother's keeper. Of course, this system of social insurance entailed rights and obligations and served to cement ties between clan members. Independence saw the advent of party politics and the weakening of traditional ties through the relegation of customary laws and practices. There was a marked shift of power from traditional society to the newly established political bases in the towns. Tribesmen began to look beyond their clans for the satisfaction of their social needs.

The international community has played and continues to play a major role in responding to some of these basic needs in Africa, particularly in the field of development and in the provision of humanitarian assistance during times of emergency. Indeed, since the founding of the United Nations in 1945, there have been profound and positive changes in the attitude of peoples throughout the world toward one another in times of disaster—changes that have affected relationships well beyond national boundaries. The right to international humanitarian assistance is no longer a concept, it is a fact. It is supported by a series of international treaties, covenants and other legal instruments that give tangible expression to our common humanity.

By working together in a series of complex disaster situations, donors and recipient states have developed improved methods of cooperation that have advanced the effectiveness of their activities. However, there are still a number of issues that need to be addressed to facilitate further progress in this field.

This paper will concentrate on some of the concerns of recipient states insofar as they relate to the mobilization of humanitarian assistance, the conditions that accompany such assistance, its impact on local institutions and capacities, questions relating to coordination and accountability and measures that would enhance the overall effectiveness of such assistance.

Let me begin by recounting some of my personal experiences in regard to humanitarian assistance, since they will serve to highlight a number of basic operational concerns at the grassroots level. I was at one stage a war refugee following the invasion and occupation of my homeland (Somaliland) by Italian forces during World War II; a camp administrator for famine refugees in Somaliland during 1951; and, many years later, the UN Secretary-General's representative for African refugee problems. In these contrasting roles I was able to gain an insight into the operations of humanitarian aid programs from the perspective of a beneficiary, a relief official and a donor.

Being a refugee or a displaced person is not an experience that one can easily forget. As other refugees will testify, flight from terror, violence and conflict can happen so swiftly that within a matter of hours, persons in secure circumstance can be swept away by the rapid tide of events and find themselves in a strange and unsavory environment so markedly different from that which they were familiar. In place of the physical and emotional security that with family life provided, they find themselves homeless, destitute and torn from familiar surroundings. In my case, it took days of hectic travel by foot, then by truck and subsequently by warship from Berbera to Aden. By the time I and others arrived at the refugee camp, we were in a state of physical and mental exhaustion.

In later years, during visits to camps for refugees and the displaced, I sensed the same feelings among their inmates. While I would not wish to relive those days, the experience was instructive to the extent that it left me with a deep understanding of the lot of the refugee and the displaced—an understanding that helped me to gain a clearer perspective of some of their concerns.

A primary concern is the demand by refugees and the displaced that their rights be respected and that they not be treated as social flotsam. They are proud of the homes they come from and are sensitive to any slight that they perceive as offensive to their way of life and cultural heritage. They would like those who have come to help them to understand their background and values and the circumstances that brought them to the camps.

My next experience with disaster happened in 1951 while serving as a district administrator in the British Somaliland administration. One of my duties was to administer a refugee camp of 5,000 men, women and children—all nomads. Prolonged drought had taken a heavy toll of their livestock, which provided their only means of livelihood. Hunger eventually drove them to rural centers for help. Many died on the long trek; those who were able to reach the camp were invariably in an extreme state of exhaustion and malnutrition.

Being a colonial territory, Somaliland's only contact with the outside world was with Britain. The people had no knowledge of the existence of any international relief organization except that of the ICRC, which, they were told, confined its operations to war situations. Through a system of indirect rule, the Somalis were largely left to fend for themselves. It was the tradition among clans to take collective responsibility for the welfare of their own in times of emergencies whenever circumstances made this possible. Appeals to the authorities for assistance was the last and not the first resort.

While the Somaliland refugee camp was not without its store of administrative problems, I found that by following two basic principles reflecting local sensitivities, acceptable solutions were invariably found:

1. First, develop a friendly and caring atmosphere in which the relief official is viewed not as some hard-nosed and distant official but as one who has an understanding of the local culture and a genuine interest in the physical and emotional needs of those requiring care. Without such knowledge and interest, well-intentioned words or actions might cause offense where no offense was intended.

2. Second, decentralize the camp's administration so that day-to-day

contact with the camp population is conducted through camp elders, thus retaining traditional mechanisms and channels of communication with which the inmates are familiar. In the same manner, encourage dialogue between the camp elders and those in the area where the camp has been located, so that in the event of disputes arising between the camp inmates and the local population, mediation mechanisms are in place. Disputes are inevitable when large masses of people suddenly descend on a relatively poor and populated area. The indiscriminate destruction of trees and other vegetation for firewood and shelter, and increased pressure on local water and food resources and on community facilities, are issues that often arise with the mass displacement of people.

I have recalled my experience to give some idea of the sociological concerns of recipients at the grassroots level and to recall an important fact that, when people are forced to move in large numbers to unfamiliar surroundings, their coping mechanisms disappear. They find a measure of assurance if a system is instituted that provides for the continuation of their traditional governance.

AFRICAN REALITIES

Few will underestimate the complexity and formidable nature of the social and economic problems facing the African continent. Speaking in the United Nations General Assembly at the height of the great Sahelian drought of 1984 and 1985, President Abdi Diouf of Senegal aptly described the African environment when he said:

For reasons of geography and history, our continent has the sad privilege of holding, according to all economic indicators, a whole array of negative records. It has the greatest concentration of refugees and displaced persons: one half of the land-locked countries; three quarters of the least advanced and most affected countries; the lowest literacy rate; the lowest level of development, with 70 percent of the population near or below the threshold of poverty; and endemic and unremitting drought and desertification.[2]

To this sad litany of problems must be added those brought about by the abuse of political power, inefficient governance and gross mismanagement. The tragic events that subsequently destroyed the state of Somalia constitute a microcosm of what has happened or is happening in many African states south of the Sahara—civil conflict, famine, displacement of

populations and the senseless destruction of life, property and infrastructure. No region on the continent has escaped these disastrous situations.
As others have noted:

> Famine also changes the demographic map; it makes people move. Vast
> numbers of people, mostly illiterate, who have often lived outside the
> reach of government and modern services, are thrown into contact
> with, and dependence on, the outside world. Drought forces them to
> move, forsake old homes, meet new people, and confront new choices.
> Ironically, in their misery, these people may land on the first rung of
> non-subsistence life. At the same time, their economic position, and
> capacity for self sufficiency, become more marginal than ever. This is
> the context into which the relief worker steps.[3]

As if this dismal record of negatives were not enough, Africa has to contend with another list of formidable handicaps such as external indebted-
ness, inadequate infrastructure, aid dependency and policies within some
states that ignore the human rights of their populations. Moreover, where
national constitutional laws are disregarded, leadership is often inexperienced and violently contested and national policies are shaped by factional
rather than by national interests. No one can be comfortable about this
sad state of affairs. While African leaders can do very little against natural
disaster, they do bear a great deal of responsibility for poor governance
and the civil wars that have wrecked their countries.

In recent years there have been few intervals when the international
community has not been confronted with urgent appeals from the African
continent for help to overcome large-scale suffering following natural or
man-made disaster. Without such aid, it is difficult to imagine what would
have happened to those whom it was possible to help. This chapter
focuses attention on some aspects of international humanitarian assistance, not for the purpose of being critical but in the hope that some of
the concerns of African recipient states, together with those of outside
observers, will help to ensure that in terms of aid mobilized and delivered,
the optimum return is obtained for the goodwill expressed, the generous
donations subscribed and the efforts expended.

THE "DONOR" AND THE "RECIPIENT"

Much has been written by relief organizations of their experiences in disaster situations and of their performances. The question many ask is
whether such assessments are too subjective to be convincing, and

whether they would be more persuasive in content if they reflected the candid views of the recipient state. International humanitarian assistance involves a relationship between the giver and the receiver. Their common objective is to collect, deliver and distribute aid speedily, efficiently and with the minimum of costs. This can be understood given the limited funds available and the many competing demands for assistance from disaster-stricken states.

A major concern arises from the inadequate flow of information from donors to recipient states regarding the results of their fund-raising efforts, their planned aid programs, the nature and design of their relief projects, the number and qualifications of their proposed expatriate staff and their proposals for employing to the maximum qualified local staff. As matters stand, recipient states are obliged, in many cases, to rely on the international media for scraps of information about a relief organization's fund-raising activities. This is unsatisfactory and does not help promote a climate of confidence. Often the media will focus on the misdeeds of one or two relief agencies and, in the process, raise doubts about the integrity of their dealings. I will return to this matter later when I discuss concerns relating to the question of accountability, the qualifications of expatriate workers and experts and the involvement of the recipient state in the design, planning and execution of relief programs.

WEIGHING APPEALS

Disaster-stricken states normally launch appeals for assistance after a very careful study of the situation and an assessment of needs. Such studies are carried out jointly by government and United Nations teams.

Recipient states recognize that the quality and credibility of the assessment will determine, to a major degree, the size and nature of the international response. Unfortunately, the problem of convincing the donor community to respond promptly to an emergency situation is a perennial one. Few countries reserve sufficient funds in their national budgets to support international humanitarian-assistance programs. The United Nations system itself is chronically strapped for funds. While it has a small reserve to meet contingencies, it must rely on voluntary contributions from the international community—an arrangement that not only is time-consuming but makes it difficult to predict its outcome.

A number of situations have occurred when countries faced with impending natural disaster have appealed to the international community only to find their appeals ignored or placed low on the donor's list of priorities. When aid was eventually offered, it either came too late or it was inadequate. This is not to suggest that the donor community should respond to appeals on face value, but given the fact that the appeals were largely prepared and fully endorsed by an impartial body—the United Nations—recipient states feel that they deserve to be given the benefit of the doubt. When responses to appeals are unjustifiably delayed, the affected states are given the impression that donors are either unconvinced about the integrity of their appeals or, for political reasons, indifferent to the plight of the disaster-stricken population.

Of course in times of famine, it doesn't help matters when key agencies primarily responsible for the mobilization and supply of food aid allow their internal bickerings over "turf" to interfere with the efficient discharge of their mandated responsibilities. Yet such an impression was gained by the former head of Ethiopia's Relief and Rehabilitation Commission in his dealings with the Food and Agriculture Organization (FAO) and the World Food Program (WFP). At the time of the Ethiopian famine in 1984, he found that the relationship between the two agencies was an unnecessary hindrance to the prosecution of the campaign against famine in his country.

In his memoirs, the commissioner explained that while the two agencies were nominally independent of each other, in some matters the WFP needs the approval of the Director-General of the FAO. Explaining further, he writes:

> My problems were multiplied because of this antagonism. If I came to Rome and saw one without seeing the other, there was great indignation from the slighted party. If I tried to meet with both, I never knew which to see first. Each blamed the other for the kind of assistance I had been granted or the manner in which it was delivered. As a beggar needing the help of both, I was forced to humor them in their petty quarrels.[4]

NEGLECTED APPEALS

There have been instances in several major disaster situations where well-founded appeals for help were ignored by major donors at the cost of countless numbers of lives. Take, for instance, the Ethiopian famine of 1984 and 1985. An expert panel found that:

> explicit information on the deteriorating conditions had been received at donor and UN agency headquarters throughout the summer [of 1984].... Whatever information had been brought before certain donor governments, the response vis-à-vis Ethiopia was based purely on

political considerations until the media [television cameras] drew public attention to what the governments had chosen to ignore.[5]

This finding was confirmed by the government concerned. In his account of the Ethiopian famine, the Ethiopian Commissioner for Relief and Rehabilitation had this to say:

In November 1983, I held another donors' conference in Addis repeating my appeal for food aid. I then flew to New York to inform the UN General Assembly of our need for aid. . . . None of these appeals were heeded. No donor government responded with anything like the urgency the situation warranted. Our socialist friends in Eastern Europe completely ignored us. There was a slight increase in food supplies, medicines, and clothing through the voluntary agencies, but foreign governments either thought we were crying wolf or used their dislike of the Marxist regime as an excuse to turn their backs. Later some governments claimed they had not heard there was a famine until late 1984. If that was so, it was because they chose not to listen.[6]

Another source charged that:

The problem lay with the agencies themselves which simply refused to listen to warnings issued by the Ethiopian Government. This was confirmed by Oxfam in a confidential internal report which stated "virtually no one, including Oxfam, took the request very seriously." The cost of the delay was more than a million lives.[7]

Graham Hancock cites a similar situation that occurred in Somalia in 1987; the Somali government began formally to notify its main partners that it believed an emergency was imminent. It requested food aid so that relief feeding could begin before any deaths occurred. Interagency bickering and stonewalling by donor representatives unjustifiably delayed an adequate response for more than six months, during which time many lives were lost and countless suffered. Commenting on the incident, the author explained that he had "cited this example of delayed and inadequate donor response to Somalia's 1987 emergency . . . because it provides a detailed illustration of the ways in which expatriate aid workers have the power to make arbitrary decisions that may mean the difference between life and death for thousands of poor people."[8]

Perhaps one of the most glaring examples of the tragic consequences that result when appeals for international assistance are neglected is the case of Rwanda. Despite warnings about a probable explosion of ethnic cleansing, countries that had the means to avert the impending tragedy decided to remain indifferent. The resultant disaster, in terms of wanton killings, human misery and displacement of populations, has few parallels in this century.

FUND-RAISING

Another matter bearing on the question of donor response relates to the raising of voluntary donations by international organizations and relief agencies. If there were a free flow of information between the donor and the receiver, speculation on the amount raised or the manner in which it is spent would be obviated. In many cases the media provide the channel by highlighting reports on the shortcomings of a relief agency's activities that do little to improve the climate of confidence. These reports have involved incidents in which aid agencies have grossly mismanaged donations collected from the public for their humanitarian activities. In the circumstances it is natural for the recipient state, in whose name the funds are being mobilized, to expect the agencies concerned to exhibit prudence and probity in the disbursement of funds, share budgetary information and be made accountable to an agreed-upon authority for the budget's financial administration.

ACCOUNTABILITY

The question of accountability is of paramount concern to the recipient state as it is to the donor. As an international expert panel observed:

> There have been many charges that fund raising has become a very profitable business allowing some organizations to exploit emergency situations for their own material interests rather than channeling proceeds to those in whose name the money has been raised. Recipient states feel that donor organizations should level with them on the amounts that have been raised and how that money is being spent. They cannot understand why there should be any difficulty in this procedure since the states themselves are always held accountable for any assistance handed to them by the donor community.

Continuing, the panel observed that:

> Aid agencies are, in many cases, not accountable to any very clear constituency. Their supporters, be they governments or individuals, have

difficulty establishing how well their money is used. Often they have to rely on the agencies' own assessment of their performance. These are anodyne, censored accounts which rarely hint at the catastrophes which may have occurred during a project's life.[9]

FRAGILE LOCAL CAPACITIES

Another concern often expressed by recipient governments is the organizational chaos that initially follows when a full-scale disaster relief operation gets under way. Arriving teams of relief workers seem to display little or no knowledge of the burden they place on the affected country's fragile infrastructures and modest governance. Equally irritating is the "we know best" attitude some display whenever suggestions are made. Ethiopian relief workers experienced this during the 1984 to 1985 famine. As the head of the Ethiopian Relief and Rehabilitation Commission (RRC) observed:

> Most high-level delegations and individuals came to Ethiopia after having been briefed at home about our Marxist government. They came with the preoccupation that every government official, including those of the RRC, would try to deceive them and cover up by not allowing them to visit certain areas. . . . Certain Western visitors and relief workers who had been in Ethiopia a few weeks or even just a few days, exploited this lack of trust. . . . Although they had just arrived in our country, they acted as if they knew more about what was happening than we did; or, even more infuriating, that they cared more about our people than we did. This was certainly not the case. The experience, knowledge, and compassion of the RRC's dedicated staff could be matched by no one. The idea of foreigners coming and telling us our jobs was obnoxious in the extreme.[10]

In a booklet on natural disaster issued by the UN Association of the United States, the authors described the kind of chaos that sometimes occurs when individual aid teams descend, uncoordinated, on a disaster-stricken country without an adequate knowledge of its needs and priorities or of the absorptive capacity of its institutions and infrastructures. The booklet described it as:

> a kind of "mass assault" on a disaster country by a number of governments, intergovernmental and nongovernmental agencies, each one trying to meet a real or supposed need, by sending personnel, equipment

and supplies which do not meet the needs of the disaster victims. The work is done, after a fashion, but at the cost of delays, lack of co-ordination and efficiency with gaps and duplications of effort and at high expense—all of which creates justified criticism.[11]

The same concern was echoed by another international panel, which charged that:

> there is an aid culture in many African capitals. A small African capital can have more than a hundred visiting aid missions to deal with in a year, each adding to the demands of the local embassies for reams of statistical information about the country and projects. The most capable national officials become fully tied-up dealing with the donors. There are projects where the professional man-hours devoted to monitoring and reporting on behalf of the donor exceed those devoted to implementation.[12]

Similar concerns were expressed by the head of the Ethiopian Relief and Rehabilitation Commission during the height of the 1984 to 1985 famine. To quote his words:

> What was most unjust was that, after taking months to make decisions and bring in the supplies, the donors upbraided us for every day's delay at our ports. They seemed to forget the fact that an underdeveloped country is, by definition, a country lacking in infrastructures. The ports of Ethiopia were never meant to handle large amount of supplies—but the western media continued to criticize the Ethiopian government unfairly for slow handling of relief goods, even when the West had in some cases taken five months to deliver them.[13]

PROBLEMS OF COORDINATION

It is generally recognized that international responses to disaster appeals require a clearer and better division of labor among relief agencies. According to one expert:

> Coordination is probably the most overused and least understood term in international parlance. Everyone is for it, but no one wishes to be coordinated. It would be unfair to denigrate the courage and dedication of individuals or agencies. Yet humanitarian action is marred by unnecessary duplication and competition among the bevy of outside helpers

who normally flock to the scene of disasters. A mid-summer 1994 census in Kigali, Rwanda, for instance already registered over 100 NGOs, prima facie evidence that economies of scale and critical mass were absent from calculations.[14]

The World Bank also recognizes the problem faced by recipient states with regard to aid coordination. In one of its most recent publications, the bank was equally concerned by:

> serious shortcomings in the present arrangements for aid coordination in reconstruction, as evidenced by fragmentation of assistance and large administrative burdens. The overlaps and gaps in mandates, and the sheer number of actors (Rwanda attracted seven major UN agencies, at least 200 NGOs and all major donors) can exacerbate confusion and induce delays. The burden on new and inexperienced administration of recipient countries, imposed by separate demands from a multiplicity of donors, weakens its capacity to implement. A key problem is that the international community is often ill equipped to respond quickly on the ground. Pledges are made rapidly, but commitment takes longer, and there is a considerable lag before actual disbursement takes place. The recovery from disaster or from conflict take several years, while there is a tendency for donors to disengage once the disaster or conflict has receded from public attention.[15]

BURDEN-SHARING

There still remains a chronic imbalance in the apportionment of responsibility for the care of African refugees between the international community and the countries of asylum despite the principle of burden-sharing. This imbalance is of great concern to the affected states because of the hidden costs that the refugee presence imposes on their fragile economies and on their development goals. Despite the joint representations made on the matter at the Second International Conference on Assistance to Refugees in Africa (ICARA II), there is the perception that the impact of refugees is not fully understood. Apart from the care and maintenance programs of UNHCR, Africans want donors and relief agencies to include in their aid programs adequate funds to provide for the impact on the host's economy and administrative capacity, for the diversion of scarce resources from development projects, and for the impact on the environment, the local population and the cost of living. There is a general feeling among African states that they receive less refugee assistance on a per capita basis from the international community than countries of asylum in other regions of the world. Moreover, refugee assistance must be additional to and not at the expense of normal development aid given to a host country.

BUILDING LOCAL CAPACITIES

Why cannot international agencies and relief organizations do more to utilize the services of qualified local personnel instead of bypassing them and employing expatriate staff to do jobs that can be performed equally well by local people? This is a perennial question that recipient states often ask and one to which aid and relief agencies do not reply. It is not difficult to imagine the chagrin felt by local professionals when, as part of their humanitarian assistance, relief agencies bring in armies of experts and young, often inexperienced relief workers. The cost would be considerably less, and the experience gained by local personnel would constitute a permanent asset for the country if indigenous workers were employed for relief efforts. As it happens at present, experience and techniques acquired during a relief operation depart with the expatriates when the program ends.

Whether intentional or not, this reluctance to utilize the services of local people to the maximum gives support to the notion that the practice suggests a colonial mentality from a time when the most-qualified local officer was seldom permitted to advance beyond the position of the least-qualified colonial officer.

A study of relief operations in 1984 to 1986 when 35 million people in some 20 drought-stricken countries were at risk, commented:

> that little or no effort is made to increase local capacity to manage disasters. In the Horn of Africa, where continued conflict and drought guarantee the recurrence of famine, it is imperative that local populations be empowered to manage the crisis. Otherwise, a dangerous dependency will set in and the need for external intervention will increase rather than decrease.[16]

These views echo the need expressed by recipient states that operational policies of relief agencies be reviewed and changed where necessary so that qualified nationals from the recipient state are given the opportunity of participating at the higher level in the design, planning and execution of projects. As a visiting journalist to Somalia commented in 1992:

Emergency type organizations are not going to be here forever and, when they go, who will take over? Better to let them do imperfectly what you can do perfectly, for it is their country, their war and your time is short.[17]

The relief operation in Somalia seems to have been no exception. As one journalist observed: "between March and December 1994, Somalis saw the number of UN civilian employees double to nearly 800, even as humanitarian activity ground to a halt." He went on to say that a Somali employee, having worked under five different foreigners at the humanitarian unit, said he had finally figured out that the expatriates were interested only in collecting their subsistence allowance of $100 or more per day beyond their salary and perks.[18]

It is unfortunate that after so much time, effort and sacrifice made by UNOSOM on behalf of Somalia, one of the impressions it left behind was that of an international mission that had become inflated, overpaid and underworked.

Another African specialist has also commented on the negative impact that an overreliance on expatriate staff can have on the development of an indigenous service. As she observes in her book:

> Even when things went well, dealing with donors could place heavy burdens on governments. Too often, when donors brought in expatriate staff, these experts moved into ministries and formed foreign enclaves there that answered not to the host government but to the aid agency back home. Because it was easier than trying to teach African "counterparts" to take over, the expatriates continued to run the project themselves, and when their time was up it is no surprise that the work they were doing did not survive their departure for very long. Confusing and blurring lines of authority, donor enclaves could not help but sap the confidence of host country officials in their ability to take charge of their own affairs.[19]

The alleged practice by donors and international agencies of preferring to employ foreign experts over local ones was assailed by another African specialist. Referring to the charge that many African professionals stay abroad because they can't get good jobs at home, she expressed surprise. "If that is so," she asked, "why were we told about the 80,000 experts who cost US$180,000 a year each? What are they there for? I was told," she said, "that's the fault of the donors who tie aid to the acceptance of their experts."[20]

DIRECTORY OF LOCAL PROFESSIONALS

Some international and voluntary agencies are more sensitive than others about the need to build on local capacities and open up employment opportunities for qualified local people. Others argue that they have no means of knowing "who is who" in the affected country, or where qualified nationals who had fled the country might be found.

This particular problem was tackled by the New York-based Center for International Health and Cooperation (CIHC) during the beginning of the Somalian famine aid operation in 1993. Through contacts with Somali nationals living in the country, in refugee camps in neighboring states and in asylum countries as far abroad as Europe and the Americas, CIHC compiled a directory listing the names, academic qualifications, work experience and current addresses of more than 600 Somali professionals in various fields of expertise. The directory was distributed free of charge to all principal agencies operating in Somalia in the hope that they would be able to utilize the services of some of those named in the agencies' recruitment programs. Unfortunately this effort met with little positive response. It was clear that some international agencies had their own networking arrangements, in which expatriate individuals are able to float from one operation to another with the utmost ease.

Having been involved in the preparation of the directory, you can imagine my surprise to find during my stay in Somaliland in 1994 that one of the international agencies had recruited the services of a veterinary officer from as far afield as Nepal to treat Somali camels and livestock when there were several unemployed but highly qualified Somali veterinary officers available locally.

POLITICAL PITFALLS

In recent years there has been a growing tendency for donor governments to channel a considerable portion of their development aid through international nongovernmental agencies. One of the reasons given is donor dissatisfaction with the ability of recipient governments to deploy resources efficiently or for the purpose intended. Another reason suggested is that by working through NGOs, donors can establish contact with people at the grassroots level.

In situations where this practice is pushed to the limit, reactions are provoked. Charges have been leveled at some NGOs that they are government-run entities, and their activities become suspect. This aspect was touched upon in a report by the Independent Commission on International Humanitarian Issues when it observed that: "international NGOs are subjected to a more subtle form of political pressure through official funding which they accept. When an agency takes money from a government, its independence can be compromised.[21]

The Ethiopian government was confronted by this problem during the 1984 and 1985 famine. Accordingly to Kurt Jansson, who led the UN relief mission, the NGOs' position in Ethiopia was strong because some of the major food donors insisted on distribution by NGOs of their choice.

Over the months in 1984 and 1985 the share of food distribution going through the NGOs continued to grow until it reached a point in November 1985 when only a little more than 30 percent was handled by the RRC. This naturally undermined the RRC's position as the indigenous institution responsible for relief and rehabilitation of drought victims.[22]

In a number of conflicts, some international relief agencies and NGOs have found themselves involved in conflict mitigation despite the terms of their mandate, which is relief or development. Such involvement is rarely accepted by the parties concerned since it invariably results in accusations of partisanship. Moreover, conflicts are not areas where political amateurs should venture—NGOs may have the goodwill but rarely do they have the knowledge about the complexity of local conflicts. Humanitarian assistance requires a climate of confidence and trust for its objectives to be realized. If this assistance is even remotely tainted by political subterfuge, that assistance will fail.

Tragically, the record of humanitarian interventions is replete with cases in which NGOs or their personnel have been declared persona non grata by recipient states mainly for the reason that their activities were seen to amount to interference in the internal affairs of the country. Relief and development agencies should confine themselves to their professional specialties and leave peacemaking to those better qualified to help—local leaders and institutions and the various peacemaking organs that have been established for that purpose within the international community.

EXPERIENCE IS A NECESSITY

Recipient states are by no means indifferent to the quality and experience of international NGOs who volunteer their services in times of emergencies. Even if the exchange of information on a bilateral basis is limited, the field accomplishments of many organizations in other emergency situations are known to many recipient states from studies and reports made by others. Recipient states are aware that inexperience can often lead to blunders.

This was typified during the 1984 and 1985 Ethiopian famine. A team of young, inexperienced NGO workers, many of them just out of college, were recruited and sent to help out in the famine. With little previous experience of Africa and none of Ethiopia, they were clearly out of their depth. Reacting emotionally to any events that they, with their Western standards, did not think appropriate induced some members of the team to talk constantly to French magazine reporters and newspapers hostile to the Ethiopian regime. When the articles appeared, the writers had added their own horror stories to them. The result was an extraordinary version of events that, when investigated, turned out to be highly exaggerated and unreliable in facts.[23]

In other comments on the performance of some NGOs, it was clear that not all the NGOs were experienced in emergency work. Many NGOs had serious management problems. Some took on too much without having the necessary capacity to distribute what they had received from the donors. Poor leadership plagued some of the NGOs, and there were too many changes in personnel and too many absences on leave and business abroad. Competition and jealousy was not uncommon. The home offices needed material for their fund-raising and pressured their field staff to show results.[24]

African recipient states are very much aware of the shortcomings of international agencies and NGOs but, except when matters affecting their relationship are pushed to the extreme, do not voice publicly their criticisms or displeasure. Being countries in need, they maintain a relatively discreet silence and have learned to "bite the bullet." However, misunderstandings would be cleared up and future ones prevented if relief agencies and the countries they wish to help could establish better methods of communication and listen to each other's concerns. In this respect I recall my discussions in 1989 with a senior minister of Mozambique on the question of relief operations during the height of the country's civil war. In the course of our talks, he remarked that there were more than a hundred NGOs in the country and that each had come with its own agenda and was acting as if it alone knew what the country required. Continuing, he said that most of their projects had nothing to do with the government's own list of priorities, but since there was so much need, anything was better than nothing.

COMPLEX EMERGENCIES

While all disaster situations have their mix of challenging and complex problems, none are as intractable to the affected country as those situations that combine underdevelopment with internal conflict, natural disaster or both—situations often referred to as complex emergencies. They can invoke politically sensitive issues, such as sovereignty, interference in internal affairs, human rights and ethnic discrimination.

In Africa alone:

> Sixteen nations are involved in some form of civil conflict, spawning an estimated six to seven million refugees, close to half of the world's total refugee population. An additional 17 million Africans are internally displaced, in most cases because of civil wars. Since the 1960s, the countries of sub-Saharan Africa have suffered from deadly conflict to a greater degree than any other world region except Southeast Asia."[25]

As a report issued by the World Bank observed:

> Conflict has become a major constraint to alleviating poverty; it has halted progress and driven countries backwards. The legacies include widespread population displacement, damaged infrastructure, schools, health facilities, housing and other buildings; reduced productive capacity; a decimated government revenue base; an erosion of human and social capital; greatly reduced security, and an increased proportion of people needing social assistance. Increasingly, landmines prevent access to infrastructure, agricultural lands and productive facilities.[26]

INTERNATIONAL HUMANITARIAN INTERVENTION

People who are displaced within their own country by war and civil conflict are in many cases worse off than those who leave their homeland. Refugees can be granted asylum and can be protected by international humanitarian law. None of these conditions holds true for the displaced. They remain in theory under the jurisdiction of their own government, which in many cases has been responsible for uprooting them. If that government continues to persecute or harass them, the only kind of protection they can seek is that offered by voluntary agencies, churches and international organizations. But such bodies are themselves obliged to work within the parameters set by the government concerned.[27]

The brutal assaults launched by government forces against population centers during the civil wars in Ethiopia, Sudan, Somalia, Rwanda, Angola, Sierra Leone and Liberia made clear to the international community that the principle of state sovereignty virtually allowed governments to act as they pleased within their own borders. In these types of situations two conflicting sets of concerns emanate, one from the displaced people themselves and the other from their governments.

Because displaced people are both voiceless and helpless, great efforts are required to ensure that they are not denied humanitarian aid and that more forceful measures are taken to afford them a measure of protection. Their plea would urge that national sovereignty be adjusted to contemporary "humanitarian needs so that the rights guaranteed to individuals under international human rights conventions are fully respected."[28]

The prime concern of these displaced populations is not sovereignty but food, medicine, shelter and protection. Displaced populations cannot understand why organizations tie themselves with conditions that compel them to channel their food and medical aid through governments with whom intended beneficiaries are at war. To them, the concerns about principles of sovereignty and noninterference in a state's internal affairs—principles often invoked when matters related to unilateral humanitarian intervention are raised—should be seen as legal subterfuges to cover up the misdeeds of the governments concerned.

To many governments, particularly where civil conflict rages within their own borders, the concept of unilateral intervention looked very much like a plot to return colonialism through the back door. Others felt that it struck at the roots of their newly won independent and sovereign status within the family of nations. Even though the United Nations proposals sought permission, in certain situations, to undertake unilateral humanitarian intervention to ensure the safe and swift delivery of humanitarian aid to people in distress, recipient states were convinced that unilateral intervention, whether by the United Nations or any other body, would constitute domestic interference and a violation of the state's territorial integrity. In their view, the principle of consent is an essential attribute of sovereignty, and it would be a mistake to give the UN functions that were neither specifically provided in its Charter nor supported by international law. However, international opinion is moving swiftly in the direction of the distressed populations.

Expressing his views on the matter, former Secretary-General Boutros Boutros-Ghali stated:

> The time of absolute and exclusive sovereignty, however, has passed; its theory was never matched by reality. It is the task of leaders of states to understand this and to find a balance between the needs of good internal governance and the requirements of an ever more interdependent world.[29]

SUSTAINABILITY

This paper has attempted to draw attention to a number of major concerns that trouble recipient states in connection with the provision of international humanitarian assistance. The message they would like to send is that even though they may be classified as disaster-prone states, they want to avoid being mere recipients of international charity each time a disaster occurs. They want the international community to go a step forward—to provide the country with the resources and technology by which they can prevent or at least reduce the destructive effects that drought, famine and pestilence often inflict on their impoverished communities. Recipient governments want donors to continue their aid beyond the immediate disaster period to ensure that conditions return to normal and that they are equipped to resume the development process.

Addressing this concern, the World Bank recently warned that recovery from disaster could take several years, while there is a tendency for donors to disengage once the disaster has receded from public attention. In the bank's view, rapid reaction to countries emerging from conflicts is critical to enable and reinforce an incipient peace process, deter a resurgence of violence, and build a foundation for longer-term reconstruction.[30]

Is there a moral imperative that obliges all of us to do whatever is possible to provide aid to those who are in need? Some years ago, while in charge of a famine refugee camp, it was my practice to accompany the camp doctor during his daily rounds of the settlement. I remember being shocked one day when he told me outside the shelter of a very sick woman that it would be a waste of his time as well of hospital space and medicines if she were admitted for treatment, since she was too far gone and beyond medical help. He explained that he only had the resources to attend to other sick refugees who had a better chance of survival. I found his approach extremely difficult to accept; the sick woman's relatives were outraged. Being fatalists, they believed that only God could determine when or whether a sick person would die. In their view the doctor should treat all equally, and should neither select nor neglect his patients. Yet this was the reality they had to live with. At the time I did not realize that this would be my first encounter with the concept of triage. Although it is a practice accepted on the battlefield, some thought should be given to the concept, since it is being mooted in some quarters as a solution in dealing with increasing appeals for aid from disaster-prone countries.

In the view of some experts, triage could well become a reality in regard to the apportionment of funds for relief and development aid:

Not only are financial pressures in Western Parliaments clashing with burgeoning requests for outside help, but a world organization with a universal mandate and membership as well as a global operational network means there is virtually no crisis not on the UN's agenda. Consequently, as does the surgeon on the battlefield, the international community must increasingly confront stark choices: who needs no help, who cannot be helped, and who can and must be helped.[31]

This leads me to one final concern that disaster-affected states would like to emphasize. They would like to urge the donor community not to allow itself to be diverted from its moral and humanistic obligations because of the seemingly unending number and frequency of appeals for humanitarian assistance. The President of Ireland addressed this matter at the conclusion of her visit to Somalia when she asked:

How can we celebrate human achievement and diversity of culture if we disregard the life chances of men, women and children in their thousands, in their millions? What is needed is a people-to-people approach in which ordinary people in Western societies are engaged. An approach which provides the stimulus of direct response from people's normal human reactions and generosity of spirit, that cuts through the bureaucracies and excuses.[32]

Part II

PLAYERS

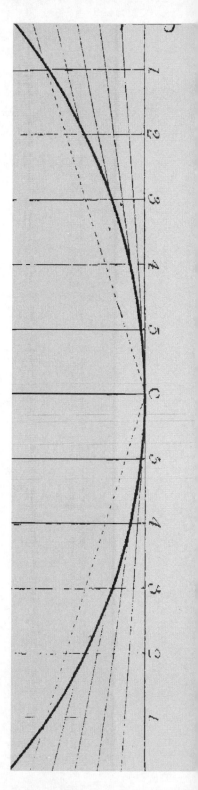

Mankind's efforts to respond to external crises have evolved over the millennia. Society's safety net gradually moved from tribes and clans to nation-states and international organizations. It is, however, a current irony that, in the post-Cold-War era, following the collapse of a bipolar superpower world, there has been a significant weakening of national sovereignty coupled with a resurgence of calamitous ethnicity and religious prejudice.

This situation complicates the possible responses to humanitarian crises, constraining how and by whom aid can be delivered. We have also learned that, despite much rhetoric, humanitarian efforts simply cannot be divorced from political and even military factors.

In Chapters 12 and 13, Jan Eliasson and Sadako Ogata focus on the indispensable role of the United Nations in humanitarian crises, while in Chapters 14 to 17, Philip Johnston, Joelle Tanguy, Aengus Finucane and Fazle H. Abed document the development and unique approach of nongovernmental, voluntary organizations at both local and international levels.

THE CHALLENGES OF HUMANITARIAN ACTION

12

Protecting People and Supporting Peace

Jan Eliasson

From the humanitarian emergency in Northern Iraq in 1991 to the unprecedented genocide in Rwanda in 1994, from the killing of humanitarian workers in Chechnya in 1997 to the kidnapping of humanitarians on duty in Somalia in April 1998, humanitarian action and international humanitarian law have incessantly been exposed to abuse and obstruction in the most difficult circumstances.

In 1991 the major challenge was to muster an effective response to meet people's vital humanitarian needs in a coordinated way. Important lessons have been learned since then. Overall, operational humanitarian capacity for early and effective response in emergencies has improved considerably.

The United Nations has instituted and refined mechanisms to strengthen the delivery of humanitarian assistance by UN agencies and NGOs. One significant development was the establishment by the General Assembly in 1991 of the Department of Humanitarian Affairs (DHA) led by the Emergency Relief Coordinator (ERC). The complex issues to be addressed by this new department ranged from negotiating access for humanitarian workers and supplies, to early warning of emergencies and to mine action programs. The department also improved the coordination of humanitarian action with political and peacekeeping initiatives. The advances made in operational effectiveness, however, have been at least partly offset by generally deteriorating conditions, more flagrant violations of International Humanitarian Law, larger displacements of people, lack of security of humanitarian workers and lack of space for humanitarian development. The roles of these institutions, the progress made in recent years in humanitarian action and the challenges faced are explored in this chapter.

ESTABLISHMENT OF DEPARTMENT OF HUMANITARIAN AFFAIRS (DHA) AND ITS CONVERSION TO THE OFFICE FOR THE COORDINATION OF HUMANITARIAN AFFAIRS (OCHA)

In 1991 member states held a pioneering debate on the capacity of the United Nations to coordinate humanitarian assistance. These deliberations, and a subsequent report of the Secretary-General on the subject, provided the basic elements for resolution 46/182, adopted by the General Assembly on December 19, 1991. This, in turn, led to the establishment by the Secretary-General, in March 1992, of the Department of Humanitarian Affairs.

Resolution 46/182 constituted the "road map" for the new department. In discharging its responsibilities, the department has to bear in mind the balance struck among the guiding principles of the resolution. That is, at all times United Nations humanitarian assistance will be provided in accordance with the principles of humanity, neutrality and impartiality. The sovereignty, territorial integrity and national unity of states will be fully respected. Assistance will be provided with the consent of the affected country and, in principle, on the basis of a request from that country. The guiding principles, however, also stress the responsibility of states to take care of the victims of emergencies occurring on their territory, and the need for access to those requiring humanitarian assistance.

The resolution also emphasized the importance of addressing the root causes of disasters, as well as ensuring the smooth transition from relief to rehabilitation and development.

Over the years, this department was called upon to fill numerous other gaps in humanitarian assistance. These included the running of mine action programs, the Oil-for-Food Program for Iraq, and capacity-building programs in disaster mitigation. In 1997, as part of his reform of the organization, Secretary-General Kofi Annan decided to transform DHA into a smaller Office for the Coordination of Humanitarian Affairs (OCHA). The programs mentioned above were handed over to other parts of the UN system, and OCHA was dedicated to the functions outlined in the original resolution: the coordination of humanitarian assistance, policy development on humanitarian issues and advocacy of humanitarian principles.

The original resolution provided the United Nations with four tools for coordination: the Emergency Relief Coordinator (ERC) and his function, the Central Emergency Revolving Fund (CERF), the Inter-Agency Standing Committee (IASC) and the Consolidated Appeals Process (CAP).

Emergency Relief Coordinator

The Office of the Emergency Relief Coordinator has headquarters in New York and Geneva. I had the privilege of being appointed the first ERC and Under-Secretary-General for Humanitarian Affairs in 1992, a position I held until 1994. Currently, the New York headquarters office focuses on policy development, substantive servicing of the UN's deliberative organs, particularly in advocating humanitarian concerns and requirements vis-à-vis the Security Council, and ensuring an effective interface between the humanitarian, political, peacekeeping, human rights and development dimensions of crisis management. It works closely with the relevant entities to ensure humanitarian access and to address the root causes of emergencies, as well as to facilitate a smooth transition from relief to rehabilitation and development. It also manages the Central Emergency Revolving Fund (CERF).

The Geneva headquarters is the focal point for emergency operational support and relief coordination, as well as for disaster reduction. It leads the interagency process for needs assessment and the preparation of consolidated appeals. Once relief operations are in place, the Geneva office monitors follow-up, identifies unmet needs and prepares updated situation reports in close cooperation with all the partners in a particular program. These include the donors; the United Nations agencies and organizations concerned; and other humanitarian, governmental and nongovernmental organizations. The Geneva office also has primary responsibility for action and issues relating to natural disasters.

Central Emergency Revolving Fund

The second innovation of the resolution was the establishment of the Central Emergency Revolving Fund (CERF) of US$50 million. The CERF was designed to ensure that resources are available to operational organizations for prompt response to emergencies, whether man-made or natural. Guidelines and financial procedures were established to elaborate how agencies could initiate use of the CERF and how it is replenished from resources subsequently collected.

Inter-Agency Standing Committee

The third tool for coordination is the Inter-Agency Standing Committee (IASC), which meets at the executive level twice a year to address policy issues concerning the United Nations' response to emergencies. Its membership comprises the UN agencies involved in humanitarian action. The International Committee of the Red Cross (ICRC), the International Federation of Red Cross and Red Crescent Societies (IFRC), and the

International Organization for Migration (IOM) participate fully in the work of the committee, together with three NGO consortia (InterAction, ICVA, SCHR). The standing committee also meets and consults when a situation calls for urgent action. The IASC is chaired by the Emergency Relief Coordinator.

During the interval between meetings of the standing committee, a working group holds regular consultations at the middle-management level. A small secretariat was established with presence in both New York and Geneva as part of OCHA.

At the field level, the chief United Nations Resident or national is the main channel and instrument for coordination, and has an important role to play in the early warning of emergencies. Once an emergency has occurred, the resident coordinator will normally serve as the Humanitarian Coordinator and head the disaster management team in the affected country. The country teams are also crucial to the preparation of consolidated appeals. In some instances, the IASC, under the leadership of the ERC, may decide to designate one of the UN agencies as lead agency or to appoint a separate Humanitarian Coordinator.

Consolidated Appeals

The consolidated appeal process is used to address emergencies that require collective action. OCHA works closely with the operational agencies and NGO representatives, both in the field and at headquarters, to ensure that an effective and efficient, well-coordinated plan for assistance is prepared. Bearing in mind the importance of strategic planning, OCHA has sought the active participation of the World Bank and the International Monetary Fund at the earliest point in the recovery process, in order to address the transition from relief to rehabilitation and development.

CHALLENGES FACED BY DHA

The months following the adoption of General Assembly resolution 46/182 and the emplacement of the institutions and mechanisms for its implementation allowed some perspective on the dimensions of the UN's humanitarian role. Below are the key issues faced by DHA as we perceived them in 1992.

First, while humanitarian assistance must be provided regardless of whether there is an immediate solution at hand, the United Nations was being increasingly called upon to address simultaneously both the humanitarian and the political dimensions of conflict situations. Somalia, Yugoslavia and Mozambique are examples of these. Humanitarian assistance, delivered impartially, can have a positive impact on peacemaking efforts. Bringing relief to those afflicted can supply new avenues for negotiation. Corridors of peace and zones of tranquillity can help to reinforce peacemaking initiatives. These are parts of a chain that constitute the essence of what one may call humanitarian diplomacy.

Second, the United Nations was required in an increasing number of emergencies to negotiate not only access of personnel and relief supplies but also arrangements to ensure their safety. The situations in Somalia, Sudan, former Yugoslavia and Iraq are tragic reminders of this dilemma. The presence of a relief operation was not always sufficient to deter hostile action and, sadly, sometimes even invited such action. At the same time, humanitarian organizations in several instances preferred not to have armed protection. There was a need for caution but also for imagination and flexibility in addressing each security situation. In finding solutions to the ever more serious safety problems, the Secretary-General needed the full cooperation of all parties concerned.

Third, the serious problem of land mines, millions of which remain scattered in current and former combat zones, had to be urgently addressed. The indiscriminate maiming that mines inflict on innocent people is an affront to the international conscience. In addition, the presence of land mines seriously hampers relief assistance, repatriation and rehabilitation; de-mining had therefore to be vigorously pursued. As pointed out by Secretary-General Boutros Boutros-Ghali in his report *An Agenda for Peace*, de-mining is a crucially important element of building peace.

Fourth, the United Nations system had been developing a valuable network of early-warning systems for environmental threats, natural disasters, mass movements of populations, the threat of famine and the spread of disease. This capacity needed to be systematically mobilized for preventive action. This task required the close cooperation of not only UN organizations but also interested governments and NGOs. The Department of Humanitarian Affairs was entrusted with the responsibility of serving as the focal point for the collection, analysis and dissemination of early-warning information relating to disasters and emergencies.

Fifth, cooperation among operational organizations was essential for effective UN response to disasters and emergencies. There can only be benefits from cooperation and disadvantage from the lack thereof, the biggest loser of all being the innocent victims needing assistance. Moreover, this cooperation must be all-inclusive, applying equally to the relationships among UN organizations and with the ICRC, IFRC, International Organization for Migration and NGOs. Cooperation must also be extended to and strengthened with the relevant regional organizations, such as the Organization of African States (OAS). In addition to putting into place various mechanisms for coordination, we needed to continue to promote a climate, indeed a culture and a natural environment, of cooperation.

Last, while the UN stood ready to meet growing challenges in response to emergencies of increasing number and complexity, it needed to be provided with the necessary resources to do what it was asked to do. This applies not only to the immediate humanitarian requirements but also to rehabilitation and development. Resources needed to be mobilized to prevent emergencies from recurring, forcing societies to cope with the same devastating consequences.

While significant progress has been made on some of the operational issues outlined above, the gains have been partly lost to other emerging challenges.

CURRENT CHALLENGES

The challenge today is not that of being able to react, but rather one of safeguarding the humanitarian space within which humanitarian action takes place.

In many parts of the world, the past decade has been a period of important advances for democracy, human well-being and global integration, replacing the bipolar superpower divide of the Cold-War era. But it has also been a period when an increasing number of people have been marginalized and excluded from mainstream development. State structures have disintegrated, and in numerous places irregular civil wars have provided antagonistic social and ethnic rifts in previously seemingly cohesive national societies.

Since the fall of the Berlin Wall in 1989, the very symbol of a change from one era to another, more than four million people have been killed in armed conflicts and millions have been forced to leave their country as refugees or, failing to cross a border, to seek a safer haven within their own country as internally displaced persons. This latter group, now totaling some 25 million, exceeds the number of refugees.

The most important challenge to humanitarian action in addressing the needs of these and other conflict-affected populations pertains to protecting their lives, protecting their rights and protecting their opportunities to sustain a livelihood resilient against the culture of violence.

International humanitarian and refugee law as well as internationally agreed-upon instruments for human rights constitutes the foundation for humanitarian action. The challenges to peace, as well as to humanitarian action, are rooted in the phenomenon of brutal violations of all these basic principles and norms laid down in international instruments.

In the 1990s we have seen the development of the most destructive forms of wars. They are not fought in defense of national interests. They do not follow the code of conduct of armed forces. They are hardly fought to achieve political aims, and their leaders stop at nothing to exploit national riches for their own gain. These devastating wars constitute the most hideous threat to the civilian population.

The safety, dignity and security of people unwittingly exposed to abuses and violence is an international concern. The notion of security must accommodate both the security of states and the security of people.

Many of today's conflicts demonstrate that violation of the security of citizens within states eventually moves beyond borders and constitutes a threat to regional and international peace and stability. Humanitarian action, therefore, cannot be separated from political commitments. Humanitarianism is based on impartiality, neutrality and integrity. However, humanitarian action takes place in politically charged environments and cannot be expected to meet all the challenges it encounters without political support.

LESSONS FROM EXPERIENCE: INTEGRATED APPROACHES

Multidimensional conflicts need multidimensional responses. The UN has several comparative advantages that make it particularly well suited to provide such responses. It has a unique mandate, legitimacy and wide-ranging capabilities, from security, disarmament and conflict resolution to humanitarian action, human rights and sustainable development.

A major comparative strength of the United Nations is that it is uniquely able to combine politics, law, economics, social and environmental action, human rights and other aspects of international action. War or peace—human misery or prosperity—is determined by all these factors together. The United Nations in this way embodies a modern, broad concept of security.

In the new security context, where threats to human security cannot be held separate from the security of the nation-state, the Security Council is becoming increasingly involved and must keep itself apprised of evolving events. The formal obligation to respect national sovereignty must not be allowed to obstruct international action when parts of the civilian population are being subjected to genocide or other acts of terror. Sovereignty primarily stands for responsibility to protect the citizens of the state.

I envisage a ladder of protection from values and norms to humanitarian law and humanitarian diplomacy, from negotiated safety of humanitarian space to sanctions and other forms of political, nonmilitary enforcement; from civilian police and other guards to a UN-mandated military protection force by consent of the parties and, finally, peace-enforcement measures.

In this, the experience from former Yugoslavia provides important lessons. Gradually, civilian, humanitarian, police and military entities have found a fruitful form of coexistence without which the whole peace edifice may crumble. UNPROFOR, the UN-led peacekeeping operation, had its mission very much linked to the delivery of humanitarian relief in which the UNHCR played a lead role. The successors of UNPROFOR, the NATO-led Implementation Force, IFOR, followed by the Stabilization Force, SFOR, have gradually increased or broadened their engagement in regard to the Dayton Peace Accords and in relation to the civilian international presence on the ground.

Experience from the Great Lakes region of Africa illustrates the difficulty in acute crises of ensuring proper protection, paying due regard to national security concerns when armed elements infiltrate refugee groups and make them shields for political and military aims. The civilian and humanitarian character of refugee camps must be upheld. Otherwise, the whole humanitarian protection regime may be discredited. Unless due respect for international humanitarian law is guaranteed by all parties, states and irregular warring factions alike, the whole humanitarian edifice based on human solidarity will suffer. Greater political commitment is required in this field.

The international community was unable to stop genocide in Rwanda, despite early warning, and was paralyzed in the face of ethnic cleansing in former Yugoslavia. We must learn from these failures. And we must reject impunity for such crimes against humanity.

The experience from Somalia in 1992 made it clear that there is no panacea in complex humanitarian crises that can be labeled military, political, socioeconomic or humanitarian. A creative mix of these and other instruments is needed.

Regrettably, some of the hard lessons learned by the international community, as in the case of Somalia, have weakened the political will to intervene in situations involving serious threats to humanitarian action. Rwanda and eastern Zaire are telling examples. Impulse rather than imperative has seemed to be the pattern: Albania and the former Yugoslavia mobilized forceful political response, whereas Afghanistan and the Great Lakes did not.

Political action must involve humanitarian considerations. Military protection is but one, and not always the ideal, expression of political response to support the safety of humanitarian action. At the same time, humanitarian workers cannot and should not substitute for political conflict resolution. But they need a good grasp of the local realities in order not to be unwittingly perceived as partisans. Such a perception, false or correct, may make humanitarian action the very target of warfare.

There is no guarantee of security in the midst of violent conflict, where resources, including those of humanitarian aid, are the source of combat and where abuse and ethnic cleansing of the civilian population is the cruel tactic of greedy warlords. Almost by definition, humanitarian action is exposed to perils. Some can be reduced by careful design, management and approaches to humanitarian assistance, and dissemination of humanitarian law and norms.

One innovative feature of multidimensional peacekeeping activities is the role played by civilian police. Civilian police are one component holding a potential for an extended role in future peace support activities. The initiative taken by Sweden during its presidency of the UN Security Council July 1997 led to a presidential statement in which the council recognized an increasingly important role for civilian police in contributing to the building of confidence and security in order to prevent conflict, contain conflict or build peace in the aftermath of conflict.

Civilian policing should not be seen as a mere auxiliary to military peacekeeping. It has its own distinct rules, purpose and functions. It should work together with all the elements of modern, peacekeeping military troops and observers, political and human-rights officers, humanitarian personnel and staff from regional and other organizations, often including NGOs.

Civilian policing involves an approach of assistance and service, not of control and coercion. Police officers work close to the people, establishing their authority from the people around them. In this way they are in a privileged position to grasp the hopes and fears of those whom the international community has come to assist.

BEYOND THE CRISES: A PROGRAM FOR PREVENTIVE ACTION

Prevention has been called a good cause in search of a program. The statement highlights the need to move decisively in the direction of early response by developing means of concrete action for prevention. Response to crises, including conflict prevention, will have to emanate from an ever-wider group of actors. There is a growing role for regional organizations and other international actors, including nongovernmental organizations. This may change the role of the United Nations to some extent, but it will become no less crucial.

Effective UN preventive action requires more than organizational improvements to develop methods of collecting information and sounding the alarm bells. It can only come about through a mobilization of the manifold resources of the entire UN system. It requires a flexible utilization of a broad arsenal of diplomatic, political, economic and other instruments. The program outlined here does not deal with UN preventive action in a restricted sense. Many of the measures are also needed for reasons that have little to do with prevention.

A United Nations that is more effective at the core task of preventive diplomacy and conflict prevention will also be a stronger organization moving beyond the present crises. Conversely, without major reform, the UN role will also fail in its tasks in preventive diplomacy. The following aspects must, in my view, be part of a program to strengthen the United Nations by strengthening its capacity for preventive action.

Work Together with NGOs and Civil Society

The last few decades have seen the rapid growth of a vital international civil society. In much the same way as domestic politics the world over is no longer an exclusive domain for politicians and officials, international affairs are today the affairs of everyone. Contemporary diplomacy is largely public; states and multilateral organizations act in a constant interplay with media, international and national nongovernmental organizations (NGOs), trade unions, business and civil society at large.

Civil society is an important factor in preventive diplomacy in at least two ways. It is often a part of the crises that preventive diplomacy aims at de-escalating. It can also be an instrument in finding appropriate solutions. It would be futile to engage in conflict prevention without taking careful account of the effects of various measures not only on governments but on all actors in society. The United Nations and other practitioners of preventive diplomacy must, therefore, have access to the viewpoints and concerns of civil society, through formal or informal channels.

Nongovernmental entities are of course under no formal obligation to be neutral or impartial. In some cases their chosen role is instead to manifest solidarity with the suppressed. It should, however, be recognized that this may considerably limit their ability to take on functions that require the confidence of all parties.

The United Nations should work together with civil society in both the analysis and action phases of preventive diplomacy. It should look at civil society as an important partner also in prevention, as it has recognized it in dealing with human rights, the environment and humanitarian relief.

Address the Root Causes of Conflict

It is possible to identify a number of political, social, economic, environmental and other factors that typically increase the risk for conflicts. To identify such risk factors in concrete situations is the role of any early-warning system designed to trigger a preventive response.

Effective preventive action, however, implies that root causes for conflicts are addressed not only when warning lights are flashed. To promote democracy, respect for human rights, protection of refugees and sustainable economic development worldwide must be part of a comprehensive preventive strategy. The same goes for international cooperation in response to humanitarian emergencies. The United Nations is in a unique position as the only global organization that incorporates all these aspects in its work.

Respect for the rights of persons belonging to national and other minorities is particularly important to conflict prevention. The Declaration on the Rights of Persons Belonging to National or Ethnic, Religious and Linguistic Minorities has set high standards and confirmed that this, in the same way as human rights in general, is a matter of legitimate international concern.

Poverty and underdevelopment are the root cause of many conflicts. Multilateral as well as bilateral development cooperation can, under the right circumstances, be preventive. A distinction should be made at the same time between general conditions that may post long-term risks and should be addressed through an overall policy for sustainable development and specific developments or abuses that may trigger violence and conflict in the short term.

Addressing the root causes of conflict must also involve dealing with weaknesses of the international system as such. The codification of the Law of the Sea, which has been a major endeavor under UN auspices throughout the last two decades, is just once example of how the development of legal norms can help avert future conflicts.

Thus effective preventive action must begin by addressing the root causes of conflict. There is a medical analogy: in order to raise public health, you must begin by looking at living conditions, how people live and work, what they eat and drink, which environmental risks they are exposed to and other such factors. We should recognize that the dietitian is no less important than the surgeon in fighting heart disease.

13 THE PLIGHT OF REFUGEES

Issues and Problems Affecting
Their Humanitarian Needs

Sadako Ogata

Although refugees have existed throughout history, the period of the 1990s has witnessed a rapid trend of large-scale refugee movements due to the changing nature and increasing complexity of conflicts in the post-Cold-War era. As a result, the role of the United Nations High Commissioner for Refugees (UNHCR), established in 1951 to provide international protection to refugees and find lasting solutions to their problems, has also expanded and diversified. As of 1998, the number of refugees and other persons of concern to UNHCR was approximately 22 million, up from some 13 million in 1991.

For the first four decades of UNHCR's existence, the bipolar structure of the Cold War gave a certain degree of clarity and predictability to the international management of refugee affairs. Refugees who fled communist regimes, decolonization conflicts or, later, proxy wars between the superpowers were granted asylum for ideological or strategic reasons. Protection of refugees tended to be uncontentious, being both a political and humanitarian corollary of the ideological divide between the two superpowers, even though lasting solutions were generally difficult. Voluntary repatriation was not a feasible option in the absence of a change of regime, and although some refugees were integrated into the country of asylum, in most cases refugees languished in camps for long periods of time. UNHCR operated, in principle, only in countries of asylum. Refugees crossed international borders that were also ideological boundaries. Because polarization made political solutions difficult to achieve, neutral, uncontroversial humanitarian action was needed to keep the victims alive in exile.

In the post-Cold-War world, the nature of conflicts affecting international peace and security has changed. Internal conflicts have become more common than interstate warfare. These conflicts are increasingly ethnopolitical group confrontations. They invariably result in massive and extremely rapid displacement, both internally and externally, as in the former Yugoslavia, the Great Lakes region of central Africa, the Caucasus and Central Asia, because population displacement is not only the result but also the very objective of the fighting.

These large and politically motivated displacements have created humanitarian tragedies unseen on such a scale before, and have threatened regional security and stability. Countries have become more reluctant to receive refugees because of heightened awareness of the socioeconomic burden they pose, the reduced strategic and political value of granting asylum and fear of threats to their national security, and have pressed for early return of those who have fled.

Concerned about the impact of refugee problems on international peace and security, the international community has also tended to focus increasingly on the situation inside the country from which refugees are fleeing, and to encourage greater humanitarian action within borders. All this has led to the increased involvement of UNHCR in conflict situations, whether in the context of protecting refugees in asylum countries that are themselves unstable or insecure, or in terms of assisting refugees to repatriate to war-affected countries or meeting the protection and assistance needs of the internally displaced who find themselves mixed with refugees or returnees.

The changing nature of refugee problems in the 1990s poses challenges to UNHCR as the organization approaches its half century of existence. This article will, first, review the major humanitarian emergencies in the 1990s; second, analyze issues emerging from these crises; and third, examine the international response to refugee problems in the 1990s.

HUMANITARIAN EMERGENCIES IN THE 1990s

In the early 1990s, the world witnessed large-scale humanitarian catastrophes in northern Iraq, the former Yugoslavia and the Great Lakes region of central Africa. These major humanitarian crises fundamentally altered the response of states and humanitarian organizations, including UNHCR, to massive forced population movements.

The 1991 refugee crisis in northern Iraq proved to be a watershed in international humanitarian action. Within a matter of days, nearly two million Kurds fled to the mountains along the borders with Turkey and Iran. Turkey did not allow most of those fleeing to enter its territory on grounds of national security concerns. Many people subsequently perished in the snow-covered mountains during the initial days of the crisis. The Kurds huddled in areas where access was difficult and assistance costly and, more important, where certain countries viewed their presence as a potential trigger of further conflict. The interest of the international community was not to promote asylum abroad, but to help the people to return home, and to prevent the destabilization of the region.

For the first time, the UN Security Council viewed a refugee flow as a potential threat to regional peace and security and adopted resolution 688 under Chapter VII of the United Nations Charter. This action coincided with the restrictions and limitations imposed upon Iraq following the Gulf War, and made possible an international military intervention to create a "safety zone" that allowed the return of refugees and displaced persons to their homes in northern Iraq. Following an agreement signed between the UN and the Baghdad government, the UN deployed its guards to enhance security. UNHCR established its presence in northern Iraq and was able to successfully to assist refugees and displaced persons to return to their homes by September 1991, only five months after the exodus, marking the fastest rate of return in UNHCR's experience. Northern Iraq was a rare example of the positive interaction between political, military and humanitarian actors to resolve a refugee crisis.

The outbreak of conflict in the former Yugoslavia in late 1991 posed a major challenge to UNHCR, far more complex and certainly more prolonged than northern Iraq. In November 1991, UNHCR was requested by the UN Secretary-General to lead and coordinate the international humanitarian response for refugees and displaced and was later given the responsibility of assisting other affected populations in the former Yugoslavia. Despite the deployment of the UN Protection Force (UNPROFOR) to support humanitarian assistance, ethnic cleansing, massacres, shelling, sniping, denial of access to civilian populations and security threats to staff hampered UNHCR's efforts for nearly three long years until the signing of the Dayton Peace Agreement in December 1995.

Integral to the Dayton Agreement is Annex VII, which allows the return of refugees and displaced persons to their homes. Under the Dayton Agreement, the Stabilization Force (SFOR) provides a security umbrella, the International Police Task Force (IPTF) maintains law and order, while UNHCR helps the refugees and the displaced persons to return home. However, continuous obstruction by political leaders, the opposition to minority returns, and lack of housing and employment opportunities have slowed down returns. Out of a total population of 2.1 million refugees and displaced persons, only some 183,000 refugees and 200,000 displaced persons had returned by late 1998, mainly to areas controlled by their own ethnic groups.

The third major refugee crisis of this decade occurred when, following ethnic conflict and genocide in Rwanda in 1994, 1.7 million Hutus fled to Zaire, Tanzania and Burundi. Simultaneously, ethnic violence in Burundi displaced another 250,000 persons, many of whom also fled to Tanzania and Zaire. The presence of the former Rwandan military and militias mixed among the refugees created serious security problems, endangering the lives of refugees as well as humanitarian workers and contributing substantially to the conflict and fighting that broke out in eastern Zaire in late 1996. At the heart of the problem was the inability or unwillingness of the host country and the international community to separate those deserving international protection from those who did not, to move the camps away from the borders and to ensure their civilian character. The maintenance of security in refugee camps is the responsibility of the country of asylum, and as a humanitarian organization, UNHCR had very little means at its disposal except to draw the attention of the international community to the serious situation and to boost the capacity of the local authorities to the extent possible.

Eventually, the humanitarian consequences became dire. When civil war broke out in eastern Zaire in late 1996, refugees were caught in the fighting and some 600,000 of them were forced to return to Rwanda, which was ill-prepared to receive such large numbers in the space of a few days, particularly as, some weeks later, almost all Rwandans from Tanzania also returned. UNHCR and other humanitarian agencies struggled to rescue the remaining refugees dispersed in the Zairean forests. Some 250,000 of the Rwandans were eventually evacuated and returned to Rwanda. Thousands of others, however, died of exhaustion, hunger and disease or at the hands of the military forces.

In comparison to earlier years of this decade, in the late 1990s large-scale emergencies appear to have been replaced by refugee crises that are smaller in size and scattered in nature, where the human suffering and the need for concerted international response of political as well as humanitarian actors are no less, but which have attracted less international visibility. In some cases, new conflicts have sprung up in the neighborhood of, or been linked to, earlier conflicts, as in Kosovo and the Democratic Republic of Congo. In others, unresolved factional rivalry, lingering insecurity and renewed outbreaks of violence continue to undermine the political process for a solution, as in the case of Cambodia, Afghanistan, Georgia and Angola. In these areas, refugees who had earlier repatriated find themselves displaced once again or forced into exile. Of greatest concern, however, is the situation in West Africa, where the crises in Sierra Leone and Guinea Bissau have uprooted hundreds of thousands of people.

The most brutal and horrendous tactics have been used to force civilians to flee, once again highlighting the nature of modern conflict, where displacement of people is the ultimate goal of the military strategy.

ISSUES AND INTERNATIONAL RESPONSES

The refugee problems of the 1990s, whether in the context of large-scale emergencies or lesser-known crises, raise several important issues, three of which are outlined as follows:

Protection and security of refugees;
Durability of solutions; and
Political and financial support.

Protection and Security of Refugees

While it is true that millions of refugees around the world continue to enjoy asylum, at least on a temporary basis, there is, at the same time, a disturbing trend among states to restrict or refuse asylum. In many developed countries, asylum policies and procedures have become more and more instruments of border control to deter asylum seekers and illegal immigrants alike. In some cases, key provisions of the 1951 Convention Relating to the Status of Refugees and other instruments have been interpreted so restrictively as to destroy their meaning and purpose. In the developing world, several countries have sought to close their borders because they find the political, economic, social and environmental costs of hosting large refugee populations unmanageable, or because they see refugee influxes as a potential threat to their national and regional security.

Respect for the principle of *non-refoulement* (nonreturn), including nonrejection at the frontier, is a fundamental principle of refugee protection. In a world where serious human rights abuses cannot be prevented, it is important to ensure that those who have to flee find safety. Asylum must be upheld as the fundamental instrument of protection and, therefore, access to asylum remains a primary goal of UNHCR's strategy for international protection. Since it is states that accord asylum, UNHCR will continue to work closely with them to promote the admission of refugees while addressing states' concerns to reduce the number of those who need international protection. This will entail a greater focus on preventive strategies to address the causes that force people to flee and on the search for early and lasting solutions to existing refugee problems. The corelation between protection and solutions has never been stronger than now, when asylum is under threat.

Another aspect of the protection concern is the decline in the quality of asylum. The basic purpose of asylum is to protect those whose lives have been threatened in their own country. Unfortunately, in many situations refugees have continued to suffer from insecurity and violence in exile because of the inability or unwillingness of the host state to ensure the safety and civilian nature of refugee camps and refugee-populated areas. As the crisis in the Great Lakes region of Africa has shown, this has implications not only for the protection of refugees but also for the safety of the local population and humanitarian workers, as well as for the security and stability of the home and host countries. Armed attacks and incursions from refugee camps into neighboring countries can destabilize an entire region. Unfortunately, the Great Lakes crisis has not been the only situation where the presence of arms and armed elements in refugee camps and insecurity in refugee-populated areas have threatened the safety of refugees, the local population and humanitarian workers, and jeopardized national and regional security and stability. Not surprisingly, the security concerns related to a refugee problem are a real disincentive for many states to admit refugees into their territory.

Following a recommendation of the UN Secretary-General in his *Report on the Situation in Africa*, UNHCR is working closely with the UN Department of Peacekeeping Operations on proposals to establish standby arrangements to strengthen the security of refugees and host communities, in which civilian, police and military options could be available to respond to a variety of differing or escalating security needs. Measures would include support to the host country, for instance, to build the capacity of the local police and judiciary through training and provision of equipment as well as monitoring by international police contingents.

Durability of Solutions

Refugee exoduses create such formidable and visible challenges that often much less attention is given to the problems that occur in the repatriation phase. Yet, time and again in this decade, the fragility of the peace process and the failure to link reintegration, reconciliation and reconstruction have set back repatriation and led to renewed displacement.

The voluntary repatriation of refugees, along with their successful reintegration in their own country, is not only the best solution to a refugee problem, it is also an essential aspect of peace-building and reconciliation of divided communities. Refugees and displaced persons often return to communities still divided by the conflict. Their situation is fraught with many uncertainties. Bitter memories of violence and forced displacement have to be overcome, and those who return and those who remained must learn to coexist again. Greater attention and support must be given to reintegration and rehabilitation of refugees and displaced persons so that a more firm foundation for peace can be created.

Reintegration and reconstruction are invaluable elements of a reconciliation process. To take Rwanda as an example, a quarter of its population has returned from exile. More than 200,000 returnee students, for example, need to go back to school. People need roofs to be put on their houses so that they can have shelter. Each home built or roof repaired can defuse tensions and contribute to peace.

Humanitarian organizations can play an important part in the reconciliation process in other ways, too, in the context of voluntary repatriation. In Bosnia and Herzegovina, UNHCR runs buses across interentity lines to promote freedom of movement and bring communities together. Likewise, UNHCR's Open Cities initiative rewards communities who encourage minorities to return by providing preferential assistance.

An important link between reintegration and reconciliation is ensuring that the protection and security needs of the returnees, as well as those of the communities to which they return, are properly met. Unfortunately, in the peace-building process adequate attention is not always given to building a national capacity to provide security, reestablish the rule of law and set up an independent judiciary. Such measures would go a long way in reestablishing the confidence of refugees and displaced persons and encouraging them to return in safety and dignity. Indeed, for UNHCR, monitoring the protection of returnees is a fundamental task, because a safe return is the first step toward a sustainable return.

UNHCR's community-based reintegration assistance to returnees and local populations also helps to bring together groups divided by conflict. Such assistance is geared to meet the immediate needs of the returnees and the receiving communities and to encourage them to begin economic and self-supporting activities, bringing them to the point where they can be integrated into the national reconstruction and development process.

Building peace takes time and is multifaceted, requiring humanitarian, development and political actors to work in a concerted manner. Just as the importance of coordinating humanitarian assistance has been recognized through such mechanisms as the UN Office for the Coordination of Humanitarian Affairs (OCHA) and the Inter-Agency Standing Committee (IASC) of the United Nations and other humanitarian organizations, so, too, more attention needs to be given to address the gap between humanitarian aid and development assistance. To this end, UNHCR is an active partner in the dialogue with the World Bank, UNDP, UNICEF, OCHA, the World Food Program and other multilateral and bilateral actors.

Political and Financial Support

Despite the experience of one crisis followed by another, the international humanitarian response remains largely selective, ad hoc and improvised, subject too often to the vicissitudes of the strategic interests—or their absence—of major powers and countries adjacent to the theater of conflict, which determine the level of political and financial support. Post-Dayton Bosnia is a good example of the strategic relationship among political, military and humanitarian action seeking to resolve displacement problems despite difficulties. In contrast, the refugee crisis in the Great Lakes region of central Africa represents the failure of the international community to establish such an integrated approach.

Frequently, humanitarian action in the 1990s has been used as a fig leaf to hide the lack of political will to address the underlying conflict. When refugees and other victims of conflict are in life-threatening situations, humanitarian agencies must stay and continue to work: saving lives is the fundamental obligation of humanitarian action. Ironically, unarmed humanitarian workers are left to face security risks so grave that governments are not prepared to expose their military forces to them. During the period of 1992 to 1998, approximately 140 UN civilian staff were killed in the course of duty, and a similar number taken hostage or imprisoned. But while humanitarian action can help to save lives, concerted political action is needed to address the causes of conflict and end the human suffering.

The major crises of the 1990s have demonstrated in a dramatic manner the limits of humanitarian action without decisive political support. The international community is increasingly reluctant to intervene militarily even for humanitarian purposes. Interventions, when they occur, are usually constrained by limited mandates. The willingness of the international community to intervene in humanitarian crisis suffered a setback after Somalia. In Somalia, the United Nations thought it would rapidly replicate the relative success of northern Iraq. Troops sent in to support humanitarian agencies found themselves gravely unprepared, mired in a civil conflict of unforeseen complexity. Casualties among the soldiers not only made the humanitarian mission unsustainable, but also created resistance in the public opinion of Western states against further military interventions, particularly in the key country, the United States.

It was only the proximity of the former Yugoslavia to the West, and the horrors of Srebenica, which finally convinced Western countries to dispatch troops with a more decisive mandate than UNPROFOR's and to compel the warring parties to discuss peace at Dayton—and this, three years after the conflict started. In Rwanda, United Nations Assistance for

Rwanda (UNAMIR) was withdrawn after the killing of a number of soldiers, at the very time when a multinational force was most needed. The withdrawal of UNAMIR from Rwanda in April 1994 coincided with an explosion of genocidal violence that killed hundreds of thousands of innocent victims. In refugee camps in eastern Zaire, the international community was unwilling to take any decisive action to separate the armed elements and political extremists from genuine refugees. In November 1996, the Security Council resolution supporting the dispatch of troops to help protect refugees in the embattled areas of eastern Zaire was not implemented, with severe humanitarian consequences for refugees and other civilians.

If political support is imperative to find solutions to refugee problems, financial support is necessary to continue responding to humanitarian needs of refugees, returnees and other displaced persons. UNHCR is dependent on voluntary contributions from member states, which reached unprecedented levels in the first half of the 1990s, jumping from around US$563 million in 1990 to US$1.1 billion in 1992, and remained at that level until 1995. More recently however, funding has fallen, forcing UNHCR to reduce its budget dramatically. Regrettably, the worst hit are those crucial activities in countries to which refugees are returning, in the areas of reintegration and reconciliation, which, if not carried out, could create the risk of a relapse back into instability and displacement.

The rise and fall in donor interest emphasize the need to place funding of refugee and other humanitarian assistance on a firmer footing. Funding should be both flexible and predictable: flexibility, to rapidly shift funds from one activity to another as needs emerge or fall, and predictability, so that funding is available in a timely and assured manner. Assured and adequate donor support would go a long way in strengthening the capacity of humanitarian organizations to respond effectively and efficiently to refugee crises.

CONCLUSION: LOOKING AHEAD

The experience of the 1990s has dramatically transformed the nature of humanitarian action and international response to refugee problems. The key factors in this have been the changed perceptions of security and the changing nature of war, which in turn have affected the capacity and willingness of states, the key players in the international refugee regime, to cope with refugee problems. Humanitarian organizations such as UNHCR have been compelled to rethink strategies and policies and to adapt and innovate. This process of change has had important lessons to offer, as refugee problems in the Balkans, central Africa and the Middle East show. The most important lesson of all has been that humanitarian action alone is not enough to stop human suffering.

Humanitarian action without a political framework is an inadequate response to refugee problems that evoke serious security concerns. The international community must focus not only on the humanitarian conse-quences of a crisis but on the political will to address the causes, and the urgency to do this cannot be overstated. Just as the early part of this decade was marked with euphoria at the end of the Cold War, the closing years are shrouded with uncertainties and signs of instability: financial turmoil in Asia, social and economic crisis in Russia, slowing down of the peace process in the Middle East, renewed conflict and tensions in many parts of Africa. Such uncertainties are breeding grounds of potential dis-placement and humanitarian crises.

The last hundred years have seen the development of humanitarian action as an aspect of international solidarity and responsibility. This past decade has seen the limits of humanitarian action without parallel effort to address the conflicts that uproot people. As a new century approaches, the challenge for the United Nations will be to equip itself better to combine political action with humanitarian responses, so that protection of refugees and the prevention and solution of refugee problems can be built more firmly on the foundations of a peacemaking and peace-building strategy.

FURTHER READING

The following bibliography, which is organized on a topic-by-topic basis, identifies some of the most accessible and useful literature on issues relating to the refugee prob-lem, focusing on publications issued in 1996 and 1997.

Defending Refugee Rights

Amnesty International, *Refugees: Human Rights Have No Borders*, London, 1997.

Barutciski, M., "The Reinforcement of Non-Admission Policies and the Subversion of UNHCR: Displacement and Internal Assistance in Bosnia, Herzegovina (1992–94)," *Journal of Refugee Studies*, Vol. 8, No. 1/2, 1996.

Bascom, J., *Losing Place: Refugee Populations and Rural Transformations in East Africa*, Providence: Berghan Books, 1996.

CRISP, J., "Meeting the Needs and Realizing the Rights of Refugee Children and Adolescents: From Policy to Practice," *Refugee Survey Quarterly*, Vol. 15, No. 3, 1996.

Dowty, A. and Loescher, G., "Refugee Flows As Grounds for International Action," *International Security*, Vol. 21, No. 1, 1996.

Frelick, B., "Assistance without Protection," in *World Refugee Survey 1997*, Washing-ton, DC: United States Committee for Refugees, 1997.

Goodwin-Gill, G., *The Refugee in International Law*, Oxford: Oxford University Press, 1996.

Gowlland-Debbas, V., *The Problem of Refugees in the Light of Contemporary International Law*, The Hague: Martinus Nijhoff, 1996.

Human Rights Watch, "Discussion Paper: Protection in the Decade of Voluntary Repatriation," New York, 1996.

Human Rights Watch, "The Rohingya Muslims: Ending a Cycle of Exodus?" Report No. C809, New York, 1996.

Human Rights Watch, "Uncertain Refuge: International Failures to Protect Refugees," Report No. 9/1(G), New York, 1997.

Jacobson, K., "Factors Influencing the Policy Responses of Host Governments to Mass Refugee Influxes," *International Migration Review*, Vol. 30, No. 3, 1996.

Jacobson, K., "Refugees' Environmental Impact: The Effects of Patterns of Settlement," *Journal of Refugee Studies*, Vol. 10, No. 1, 1997.

Journal of Refugee Studies, Special Issue on the Rwanda Emergency: Causes, Responses and Solutions, Vol. 9, No. 3, 1996.

Keely, C., "How Nation-States Create and Respond to Refugee Flows," *International Migration Review*, Vol. 30, No. 4, 1996.

Kibreab, G., *People on the Edge in the Horn: Displacement, Land Use and the Environment in the Gedaref Region, Sudan*, London: James Currey, 1996.

Kibreab, G., "Eritrean and Ethiopian Urban Refugees in Khartoum: What the Eye Refuses to See," *African Studies Review*, Vol. 39, No. 3, 1996.

Kibreab, G., "Environmental Causes and Impact of Refugee Movements: A Critique of the Current Debate," *Disasters*, Vol. 21, No. 1, 1997.

Kuhlman, T., *Asylum or Aid? The Economic Integration of Ethiopian and Eritrean Refugees in the Sudan*, Aldershot: Avebury, 1995.

Lawyers Committee for Human Rights, *African Exodus: Refugee Crsisis, Human Rights and the 1969 OAU Convention*, New York, 1995.

Malkki, L., *Purity and Exile: Violence, Memory and National Cosmology among Hutu Refugees in Tanzania*, Chicago: University of Chicago Press, 1995.

Saulnier, F., "Rwanda: The Human Shield Strategy," *The World Today*, January 1996.

Internal Conflict and Displacement

African Rights, *Sudan's Invisible Citizens: The Policy of Abuse against Displaced People in the North*, London: African Rights, 1995.

Chimni, B., "The Incarceration of Victims: Deconstructing Safety Zones," in: N. Al-Naumi and R. Meese (eds.), *International Legal Issues Arising under the United Nations Decade of International Law*, The Hague: Martinus Nijhoff, 1995.

Cohen, R., "Protecting the Internally Displaced," in: *World Refugee Survey 1996*, Washington, DC: United States Committee for Refugees, 1996.

Cohen, R. and Cuenod, J., *Improving Institutional Arrangements for the Internally Displaced*, Washington, DC: Brookings Institution and Refugee Policy Group, 1995.

Curtis, P., "Urban Household Coping Strategies During War: Bosnia-Hercegovina," *Disasters*, Vol. 19, No. 1, 1995.

Deng, F., "Dealing with the Displaced: A Challenge to the International Community," *Global Governance*, Vol. 1, No. 1, 1995.

Fleck, D., *The Handbook of Humanitarian Law in Armed Conflicts*, Oxford: Oxford University Press, 1996.

Forsythe, D., "The International Committee of the Red Cross and Humanitarian Assistance: A Policy Analysis," *International Review of the Red Cross*, No. 314, 1996.

Franco, L., "An Examination of Safety Zones for Internally Displaced Persons As a Contribution Toward Prevention and Solution of Refugee Problems," in: N. Al-Naumi and R. Meese (eds.), *International Legal Issues Arising under the United Nations Decade of International Law*, The Hague: Martinus Nijhoff, 1995.

Frelick, B., "Unsafe Havens: Reassessing Security in Refugee Crises," *Harvard International Review*, Spring 1997.

Human Rights Watch, "Turkey's Failed Policy to Aid the Forcibly Displaced in the Southeast," Report No. D809, New York, 1996.

Human Rights Watch, *Failing the Internally Displaced: The UNDP Displaced Persons Program in Kenya*, New York, 1997.

Human Rights Watch, "Zaire: 'attacked by all sides.' Civilians and the War in Eastern Zaire," Report No. 9/1(A), New York, 1997.

Kleine-Ahlbrandt, S., *The Protection Gap: The International Protection of Internally Displaced People: The Case of Rwanda*, Geneva: Institut Universitaire de Hautes Etudes Internationales, 1996.

Kumar, R., "The Troubled History of Partition," *Foreign Affairs*, Vol. 76, No. 1, 1997.

Lavoyer, P., "Refugees and Internally Displaced Persons: International Humanitarian Law and the Role of the ICRC," *International Review of the Red Cross*, No. 305, 1995.

Lee, L., "Internally Displaced Persons and Refugees: Toward a Legal Synthesis?" *Journal of Refugee Studies*, Vol. 9, No. 1, 1996.

McDowell, C. (ed.), *Understanding Impoverishment: The Consequences of Development-Induced Displacement*, Providence: Berghan Books, 1996.

Mooney, E., "Internal Displacement and the Conflict in Abkhazia," *International Journal on Minority and Group Rights*, Vol. 3, No. 3, 1996.

Posen, B., "Military Responses to Refugee Disasters," *International Security*, Vol. 21, No. 1, 1996.

Refugee Survey Quarterly, Special Issue and Select Bibliography on Internally Displaced People, Vol. 14, No. 1/2, 1995.

Rieff, D., "Nagorno-Karabakh: Case Study in Ethnic Strife," *Foreign Affairs*, Vol. 76, No. 2, 1997.

Rohde, D., *A Safe Area: Srebrenica: Europe's Worst Massacre Since the Second World War*, New York: Simon and Schuster, 1997.

UNHCR (Office of the United Nations High Commissioner for Refugees), *UNHCR's Operational Experience with Internally Displaced Persons*, Geneva, 1994.

Yett, S., "Masisi, Down the Road from Goma: Ethnic Cleansing and Displacement in Eastern Zaire," Washington, DC: United States Committee for Refugees, 1996.

Return and Reintegration

Allen, T. (ed.), *In Search of Cool Ground: War, Flight and Homecoming in Northeast Africa*, United Nations Research Institute for Social Development, London: Africa World Press and James Currey, 1996.

Amnesty International, "Rwanda: Human Rights Overlooked in Mass Repatriation," Report No. AFR47/02/97, London, 1997.

Amnesty International, "Great Lakes Region: Still in Need of Protection: Repatriation, Refoulement and the Safety of Refugees and the Internally Displaced," Report No. AFR02/07/97, London, 1997.

Amnesty International, "Who's Living in My House? Obstacles to the Safe Return of Refugees and Internally Displaced People," Report No. EUR/ID, London, 1997.

Ball, N., *Making Peace Work: The Role of the International Development Community*, Washington, DC: Overseas Development Council, 1996.

Berdal, M., *Disarmament and Demobilisation After Civil Wars*, Adelphi Paper No. 303, London: International Institute for Strategic Studies, 1996.

Baranyi, S., "The Challenge in Guatemala: Verifying Human Rights, Strengthening National Protection and Enhancing an Integrated Approach to Peace," *Journal of Humanitarian Assistance*, Web site www.jha.sps.cam.ac.uk.

Boutwell, J. et al. (eds.), *Lethal Commerce: The Global Trade in Small Arms and Light Weapons*, Cambridge, MA: American Academy of Arts and Sciences, 1995.

Bush, K., "Towards a Balanced Approach to Rebuilding War-Torn Societies," *Canadian Foreign Policy*, Vol. 3, No. 2, 1995.

Coletta, N. et al., *The Transition from War to Peace in Sub-Saharan Africa*, Washington, DC: World Bank, 1996.

Crisp, J. et al., *Rebuilding a War-Torn Society: A Review of UNHCR's Reintegration Programme for Mozambican Returnees*, Geneva: UNHCR, 1996.

Doyle, M., *UN Peacekeeping in Cambodia: UNTAC's Civil Mandate*, Boulder, CO: Lynne Rienner, 1995.

Ferris, E., "After the Wars Are Over: Reconstruction and Repatriation," Working Paper No. 10, Migration Policy in Global Perspective Series, International Center for Migration, Ethnicity and Citizenship, New York: New School for Social Research, 1997.

Human Rights Watch, "Bosnia-Herzegovina: A Failure in the Making. Human Rights and the Dayton Agreement," Report No. D808, New York, 1996.

Human Rights Watch, "Guatemala: Return to Violence: Refugees, Civil Patrollers and Impunity," Report No. B801, 1996.

Human Rights Watch, "Tajikistan: Tajik Refugees in Northern Afghanistan: Obstacles to Repatriation," Report No. 8.6 (D), New York, 1996.

Kibreab, G., *Ready and Willing But Still Waiting: Eritrean Refugees in Sudan and the Dilemmas of Return*, Uppsala: Life and Peace Institute, 1996.

Koser, K., "Information and Repatriation: The Case of Mozambican Refugees in Malawi," *Journal of Refugee Studies*, Vol. 10, No. 1, 1997.

Kumar, K. (ed), *Rebuilding Societies After Civil War: Critical Roles for International Assistance*, Boulder, CO: Lynne Rienner, 1997.

Meron, T., "Answering for War Crimes: Lessons from the Balkans," *Foreign Affairs*, Vol. 76, No. 1, 1997.

Moore, J., *The UN and Complex Emergencies: Rehabilitation in Third World Transitions*, War-Torn Societies Project, Geneva: United Nations Research Institute for Social Development, 1996.

Painter, R., "Property Rights of Returning Displaced Persons: The Guatemalan Experience," *Harvard Human Rights Journal*, Vol. 9, Spring 1996.

Pottier, J., "Relief and Repatriation: Views by Rwandan Refugees, Lessons for Humanitarian Aid Workers," *African Affairs*, Vol. 95, No. 380, 1996.

Roberts, S. and Williams, J., *After the Guns Fall Silent: The Enduring Legacy of Landmines*, Washington, DC: Vietnam Veterans of America Foundation, 1995.

Schear, J., "Bosnia's Post-Dayton Traumas," *Foreign Policy*, No. 104, 1996.

Waters, T., "The Coming Rwandan Demographic Crisis: or Why Current Repatriation Policies Will Not Solve Tanzania's (or Zaire's) Refugee Problems," *Journal of Humanitarian Assistance*, Web site www.sps.cam.ac.uk.

Watson, C., *The Flight, Exile and Return of Chadian Refugees*, Geneva: United Nations Research Institute for Social Development, 1996.

UNHCR and IPA (International Peace Academy), *Healing the Wounds: Refugees, Reconstruction and Reconciliation*, Geneva and New York, 1996.

Zieck, M., *UNHCR and Voluntary Repatriation: A Legal Analysis*, University of Amsterdam doctoral thesis, Amsterdam, 1997.

The Asylum Dilemma

Amnesty International, *Cell Culture: The Detention and Imprisonment of Asylum Seekers in the United Kingdom*, London, 1997.

Anderson, E., "The Role of Asylum States in Promoting Safe and Peaceful Repatriation under the Dayton Agreements," *European Journal of International Law*, Vol. 7, No. 2, 1996.

Byrne, R. and Shacknove, A., "The Safe Country Notion in European Asylum Law," *Harvard Human Rights Journal*, Vol. 9, Spring 1996.

Carlier, J.-Y. and Vanheule, D (eds.), *Europe and Refugees: A Challenge?*, The Hague: Kluwer, 1997.

Carlier, J.-Y. et al. (eds.), *Who Is a Refugee? A Comparative Case Law Study*, The Hague: Kluwer, 1997.

Cohen, R., *The Cambridge Survey of World Migration*, Cambridge: Cambridge University Press, 1995.

Daoust, I. and Folkelius, K., "UNHCR Symposium on Gender-Based Persecution," *International Journal of Refugee Law*, Vol. 8, No. 1/2, 1996.

Diaz-Briquets, S. and Perez-Lopez, J., "Refugee Remittances: Conceptual Issues and the Cuban and Nicaraguan Experiences," *International Migration Review*, Vol. 31, No. 2, 1997.

ECRE (European Council on Refugees and Exiles), *Safe Third Countries: Myths and Realities*, London, 1996.

Human Rights Watch, "Crime or Simply Punishment? Racist Attacks by Moscow Law Enforcement Authorities," Report No. D712, New York, 1995.

International Migration Review, Special Issue on Ethics, Migration and Global Stewardship, Vol. 30, No. 1, 1996.

IOM (International Organization for Migration), *The Baltic Route: The Trafficking of Migrants through Lithuania*, Geneva, 1997.

Joly, D., *Haven or Hell? Asylum Policies and Refugees in Europe*, London: Macmillan, 1996.

Marshall, B., *British and German Refugee Policies in the European Context*, London: Royal Institute of International Affairs, 1996.

McDowell, C., *A Tamil Diaspora: Sri Lankan Migration, Settlement and Politics in Switzerland*, Providence: Berghan Books, 1997.

Newland, K., *U.S. Refugee Policy: Dilemmas and Directions*, Washington, DC: Carnegie Endowment for International Peace, 1995.

Papademetriou, D. and Hamilton, K., *Converging Paths: French, Italian and British Responses to Immigration*, Washington, DC: Carnegie Endowment for International Peace, 1996.

Plaut, W., *Asylum: A Moral Dilemma*, Westport: Praeger, 1995.

Preeg, E., *The Haitian Dilemma: A Case Study in Demographics, Development and U.S. Foreign Policy*, Boulder, C.O.: Westview Press, 1996.

Raoul Wallenberg Institute, *Temporary Protection: Problems and Prospects*, Report No. 22, Lund, 1996.

Simmons, A. (ed), *International Migration, Refugee Flows and Human Rights in North America: The Impact of Free Trade and Restructuring*, New York: Center for Migration Studies, 1995.

Teitelbaum, M. and Weiner, M. (eds.), *Threatened Peoples, Threatened Borders: World Migration and US Policy*, New York: W.W. Norton, 1995.

Weiner, M. and Munz, M., "Migrants, Refugees and Foreign Policy: Prevention and Intervention Strategies," *Third World Quarterly*, Vol. 18, No. 1, 1997.

Zucker, N. and Zucker, N., *Desperate Crossings: Seeking Refuge in America*, Armonk, N.Y.: M.E. Sharpe, 1996.

Periodicals

In Defense of the Alien, published annually by the Center for Migration Studies, New York.

International Journal of Refugee Law, published quarterly by Oxford University Press.

International Migration Review, published quarterly by the Center for Migration Studies, New York.

International Review of the Red Cross, published six times a year by the International Committee of the Red Cross.

Journal of Refugee Studies, published quarterly by Oxford University Press.

Refugee Survey Quarterly, published quarterly by Oxford University Press.

World Disaster Report, published annually by the International Federation of Red Cross and Red Crescent Societies.

World Refugee Survey, published annually by the U.S. Committee for Refugees, Washington, DC.

Selected Web Sites

United Nations Sites

UNHCR: http://www.unhcr.ch
UNHCR Refworld: http://www.unhcr.ch/refworld/refworld.htm
United Nations: http://www.un.org
UN Centre for Human Rights: http://www.unhchr.ch
UN ReliefWeb: http://www.reliefweb.int/

Other Sites

Amnesty International: http://www.amnesty.org/
European Council on Refugees and Exiles: http://www.poptel.org.uk/ein/ecre/
Human Rights Watch: http://www.hrw.org
Institute for Global Communications: http://www.igc.org/igc/
InterAction: http://www.interaction.org/
International Committee of the Red Cross: http://www.icrc.org/
International Crisis Group: http://www.intl-crisis-group.org/
International Federation of Red Cross and Red Crescent Societies: http://www.ifrc.org/

Journal of Humanitarian Assistance: http://www-jha.sps.cam.ac.uk
Lawyers Committee for Human Rights: http://www.lchr.org/
Migration and ethnic relations: http://www.ercomer.org/wwwvl/
Open Society Institute, Forced Migration Projects: http://www.soros.org/fmp2/html
Oxford Refugee Studies Programme: http://www.users.ox.ac.uk/~rspnet/
Palestinian refugees: http://www.Palestine-net.com/palestine.html

Refworld: UNHCR's CD-ROM

Refworld is a reference tool designed to meet the information needs of everyone who has an interest in the problem of forced displacement: governments, international organizations, voluntary agencies, academic institutions and lawyers. This CD-ROM is a collection of full-text databases that is updated twice a year, providing easy access to the most comprehensive and reliable refugee information available, drawn from the most current and reliable sources.

The information available on *Refworld* includes: data on conditions in refugees' countries of origin; national legislation and case law; international treaties and documents on human rights and refugee law; UN General Assembly and Security Council documents; official UNHCR documents; refugee statistics; and the catalogue of UNHCR's Centre for Documentation and Research.

Refworld is updated on a six-monthly basis and is available on an annual subscription basis for $250. Additional subscriptions can be ordered at a reduced rate of $125 per year. For more information and a demonstration disc allowing five hours of free access, contact *Refworld*, UNHCR Centre for Documentation and Research, CP2500, CH-1211 Geneva 2, Switzerland. Fax: (41–22) 739–8488; e-mail: cdr@ unchr.ch.

Philip Johnston

The key to shaping effective relief responses to disasters and conflicts is understanding how current relief situations are vastly different from those encountered in years past. Recent and dramatic changes in geopolitics and the environmental realities of today dictate a need to change relief work. Major changes are necessary in how relief work is coordinated and how the mandate for intervention is crafted and delivered.

The experiences of humanitarian organizations are helpful in understanding the reality of relief operations today. CARE, the Cooperative for Assistance and Relief Everywhere, one of the largest development and relief organizations, first began sending relief in form of "CARE packages" in 1946 to Europeans who had been left destitute by World War II. The founders of CARE felt deeply about the need to demonstrate a moral and humanitarian commitment to helping those who required help. CARE's dramatic growth as an organization reflected the desire of Westerners to participate in reaching out to others. CARE packages became a popular symbol of those who cared for those in need, and created goodwill toward the United States, earning the lifelong appreciation of millions who had been helped by these efforts.

After assisting the victims of World War II, CARE shifted to undertaking development work and responding to emergencies in the developing world. The organization responded to earthquakes, typhoons and large cross-border civilian movements in civil wars. Often, these were transient emergencies, lasting only a few months.[1] The task was to come in, help feed and provide basic health care to the affected and help them get back on their feet. Then CARE would leave, and people would get on with their lives.

Today such tragedies are exacerbated by several trends that have emerged over recent years and are redefining relief work. To being with, some emergencies are now long-term, and many are man-made. CARE is now immersed in several situations involving long-term droughts and long-drawn-out civil wars. In certain countries drought is becoming endemic because of the progressive degradation of arable land. Northwestern Sudan is an example where emergencies are likely to be continuous. The land has continually been degraded, and its capability to produce enough to feed families or sustain cattle is questionable. The long, heinous and ruinous war in Mozambique is another example of a manmade emergency lasting many years, in which provision of emergency assistance has been continuous.

The same services are still needed—namely, food and health care. In addition, though, safe drinking water is an increasing concern. Water has been a major relief commodity during the Cambodian refugee crisis in Thailand since the early 1980s. At one point in Ethiopia more than 400,000 gallons of water per day were being transported to refugee Somalis who were victims of the war and drought. It was a phenomenally expensive undertaking. CARE spends several million dollars a year on transporting water in Ethiopia alone.

Even if the current conflicts and disasters ended quickly, there is one big difference between today's relief situations and those of the past. In most of the countries affected today, the basic elements of a quality life were tenuous or nonexistent prior to the emergency. More often than not, the conditions of human life have no tolerance for deterioration, and an emergency crowds people out of the narrow margins of life they live on. Farmers in Ethiopia, Somalia, Bangladesh, Mozambique, Cambodia, Haiti or any one of a dozen other countries are living so close to the edge that a dramatic political or climatic shift is enough to change their lives permanently for the worse. Overpopulation and lack of access to quality land are doing more than anything else to undermine the ability of people to feed themselves. Typically, the poorest farmers live on the most marginal land and have the highest birthrates. The poor farmer has learned to survive by intensively working this marginal land and by having plenty of children, who will help out now and will provide a safety net when the farmer is too old to work. The farmer is caught in a no-win situation. The land does not produce enough food for him to save any in reserve. If war or drought disrupts the planting cycle, the family goes hungry, and once the crop cycle fails, the farmer resorts to selling major assets, such as cattle, just to survive. This scenario has been played out in Ethiopia, Sudan, Somalia, Mozambique and many other of the least-developed countries.

Conflicts and disasters force people to move from their homelands; usually they do not return for many years. The combination of civil war, drought and mass movements of whole communities creates disasters beyond the scope of any one humanitarian agency's ability to alleviate. As a result, relief responses must increasingly stress collaboration among the entire world humanitarian community.

Another major trend of the past several years affecting relief work is the increase in "economic" refugees. Western countries, wary of being overwhelmed by new immigrants, are defining major refugee movements as economic, not political, flights. In 1992 the U.S. government took the extraordinary step of intercepting fleeing Haitians at sea so it could technically comply with United Nations refugee conventions by turning them away before they reached U.S. territory.[2] While the economic prospects for Haitians are not rosy, their refugee status cannot be judged summarily. The nearby shores of the United States are appealing to people whose per capita income is less than $400 per year. Yet the flow of Haitians dramatically increased after the coup that deposed Jean-Bertrand Aristide, and an estimated 200,000 people hid within Haiti, fearful of being persecuted because of their political beliefs.[3]

Germany is also concerned and is making efforts to alter its constitution to make settlement within its borders more difficult for economic immigrants. The political changes in Eastern Europe and the former Soviet Union have produced the largest number of European refugees since World War II. Many Russians, Romanians, Turks, Bulgarians and Soviet Jews see Germany as the economic promised land.[4]

The truth is that most disaster situations, whether climatic or political, produce economic refugees. People are fleeing a tenuous life and need money to rebuild their lives, whether back in their home or in another country. The most basic problem facing the world today is how to increase people's standard of living no matter where they live.

LONG-TERM RELIEF SITUATIONS

Unfortunately, a long list of countries could serve as examples illustrating the above points and highlighting why responses to emergencies need to reflect current realities. The list includes Sudan, Mozambique, Cambodia, Ethiopia, Afghanistan, Angola, Haiti, Somalia and a dozen other countries affected by conflicts that have political, environmental and social dimensions beyond the norm. Let us examine the first three of these.

Sudan

For more than 20 years, Sudan has been a major refugee-hosting and refugee-producing country.[5] An estimated 4.7 million Sudanese are displaced, or internal, refugees; of these, 1.8 million are living in and around Khartoum. Another 200,000 Sudanese are external refugees. Close to one fifth of the total population of the country is displaced. Add to this another 700,000 refugees from Ethiopia and there have been close to five million refugees within the country living in a temporary existence, without their own land and often without food, water or decent shelter from the harsh desert weather.

While a long and persistent drought is a major cause of the food shortage that threatens more than one third of the country, the severity of the crisis is man-made. The ongoing civil war between the Muslim, mostly Arab north and the Christian, animist, and mostly African south has severely exacerbated the problem. As in Northern Ireland, the issues dividing the opposing groups are based on religious differences. Even when food aid is flowing, each side diverts or holds food or seeds from those of a different race or religious persuasion. A succession of openly corrupt and cynical military governments has purposely avoided confronting the humanitarian crisis and has so alienated the few countries and nongovernmental organizations willing to care about the crisis that the people of Sudan are almost without anyone to help them.

If the crisis in Sudan were to end today, if the government suddenly reformed itself, if peace between the north and south were achieved, and if relief efforts were again begun in earnest, it is still likely that the crisis would go on for years. Almost every Sudanese family has been affected, and the country suffers from a trauma that will not easily go away. The environmental degradation from the drought, war and neglect is so severe that it will take years of sustained development efforts to help the Sudanese people rebuild their country and their lives.

Mozambique

Mozambique has been locked into a civil war that totally disrupted its fragile infrastructure. The opposition group, Renamo, effectively disrupted the country's agricultural and economic system. Renamo opposed the South Africa-supported holders of power. This war produced 1.5 million external and 2 million internal refugees.[6]

Terrible droughts are aggravating an already tragic situation. Food production and distribution have been so disrupted by the war that only 5 percent of the arable land within the country is under cultivation.[7] Many Mozambicans are suffering from malnutrition, and starvation is evident.

The war crimes of Renamo have been well documented elsewhere.[8] The organization's widespread kidnapping of children and forcing them to shoot neighbors and family members are reminiscent of Khmer Rouge tactics. The atrocities may have irreparably ripped the moral fabric of the country.

If the crisis were to end today, if Renamo suddenly discovered a political agenda beyond terror, and if people were allowed to return to their homes, it would take years to get the country back to sustained economic growth. While Mozambique does have a government interested in democratic freedoms and protecting basic human rights, the country has been so devastated and the effects of the drought are so severe that it will take tons of short-term and long-term assistance to feed, shelter and empower the population to take care of itself.

Cambodia

Cambodia illustrates that the dilemma of long-term, persistent relief work is not confined to the African continent. The case of Cambodia is well known. The holocaust perpetuated by the Khmer Rouge led to a quarter of the population being killed. The resultant invasion by the Vietnamese stopped the killing fields but led to a long, protracted civil war and the seemingly permanent displacement of hundreds of thousands of Cambodians.

The removal of land mines, the rebuilding of an infrastructure designed to support life, and the reeducation of a population traumatized and devastated by the holocaust will take several years. Cambodia still experiences more loss of life and mutilation from mines than any other country. Millions of mines still exist.

COMMON CHARACTERISTICS

What do these examples have in common? First, each has a government or an insurgent movement that does not recognize internationally accepted rules of behavior, including those governing humanitarian assistance. The governments of certain East African countries, as well as the Khmer Rouge of Cambodia and Renamo of Mozambique, have denied aid to those not in their group and have sought to gain or retain power through illegitimate means.

Second, large proportions of the populations in each of the countries have been uprooted and disempowered. In each of the countries mentioned, between one fifth and one fourth of the population have been internally or externally displaced, and large numbers of people have been killed outright. In past wars most victims were combatants. Today most victims are civilians, largely women and children.

Third, each country, with the possible exception of Cambodia, has a fragile environment that has been altered to an extent that complicates long-term development prospects. Often the land has been so neglected or degraded that food production cannot be maintained at levels needed to feed the refugee and host populations. Additional burdens are felt because of high birthrates. The proportion of people who lack food security is high, increasing the need for both short-term and long-term food aid.

Fourth, these populations lack the kinds of skills needed to rebuild their societies. Engineers, managers, midwives and others needed to provide the basic human needs of food, water, organization and health care are not available. Often these types of professionals were killed or were the first to flee. Some problematic factors inhibit the ability of humanitarian organizations to respond to the current relief situations. The biggest problem is lack of money. The fact that relief efforts are long-term and affect millions instead of thousands of people means costs are high. The office of the United Nations High Commissioner for Refugees has been overwhelmed by the demand for its services as the worldwide refugee population has doubled since 1980. Unfortunately, its budget has not risen accordingly, and many countries are in arrears. Donations to CARE, from the American public in particular, are not keeping pace with the growing demand. An important part of this shortfall is that Western people are experiencing "burnout" with regard to providing emergency assistance. They have seen too many disasters that do not have easy solutions.

United States foreign aid priorities are changing, too. In the 1970s, humanitarian aid focused on helping the neediest of the needy. In the 1980s, U.S. humanitarian aid was increasingly used as an extension of short-term foreign-policy objectives.[9] In the early 1990s, there was a shift to providing aid where it was most likely to "have an impact."[10] Eastern Europe and the former Soviet republics received large increases in aid, while African countries saw decreases or stagnant levels.

The proliferation of brutal demagogues hostile to their own people and a world community unable to secure unfettered relief help to explain why so many situations defy solution. In addition, various Western nations have different criteria for providing aid when host governments are at odds with their own people, as is the case, for example, in Sudan, Ethiopia, Somalia and the former Yugoslavia. The Scandinavian countries seem to be more tolerant than the United States; they will continue to work with governments the United States has "given up on." As a result, Sudan, with close to five million refugees, has only a handful of humanitarian agencies remaining in that country. This has reduced important commodity lifelines and links to the world media capable of mobilizing efforts to help displaced Sudanese and other refugees.

POSITIVE DEVELOPMENTS

On a more positive note, in some ways the humanitarian community is better prepared to deal with the realities of relief work than it used to be. A great deal has been learned about how to provide efficient relief. The capability to respond faster and get more aid to more people is available. Success in mitigating disasters in Turkey with the Kurds and in Bangladesh helped reduce the numbers of those who died and suffered. The world can be proud of those efforts.

In addition, the partnerships between the military and nongovernmental organizations in Turkey, Bangladesh and Kenya have been truly enlightening. The military establishments have done a good job of providing the logistical capacity NGOs lacked. Envisioning a role for the military in relief work is a major breakthrough that could provide dramatic improvements in the ability of the humanitarian community to respond.

The realization that relief work has to have a developmental focus has also been a big plus. Almost every disaster response now has a training component for refugees or involves more integrated coordination with host country agencies. These efforts help build longer-lasting capacity in host countries and empower refugees in otherwise helpless situations.

Another major positive development is that a number of drawn-out relief situations are starting to see some movement toward resolution. Ethiopia, Angola and Cambodia are a few of the situations that could not be solved in the 1980s but now appear headed toward settlement. This list has been expanded by Rwanda and Bosnia in the 1990s. Progress in reducing the violence is being achieved in these countries, but progress is slow.

HUMANITARIAN INTERVENTION

Most of the disaster situations mentioned above have one other important factor in common. In retrospect, it is clear that some outside humanitarian intervention should have taken place to stop the violations of human rights occurring within the borders of each country. Even though this type of intervention is fraught with political land mines, it is clear that until recently, the world lacked the political will to prevent atrocities and violations of people's rights, even though we knew what was happening.[11]

The end of the Cold War has begun to strengthen the UN's ability to thrust humanitarian assistance into countries where sovereign governments are violating basic human rights of their population. Widespread violations of human rights and the deliberate endangerment of vast numbers of people can no longer be tolerated. Despotic rulers have got to be consistently put on notice to clean up their act. The end of the Cold War allows definitions of what is acceptable, based not on ideological terms but on internationally recognized humanitarian principles.

There is a great need to continue to build political institutions that make it impossible for demagogues and despots to have any legitimacy. The United Nations has made incredible strides in this direction during the past few years. The evolving concept of humanitarian intervention is gaining hold in the UN. Several years ago, UN Secretary-General Pérez de Cuéllar set the tone when he publicly reminded those violating human rights that they could not hide behind the veil of sovereignty. He observed that "the Universal Declaration of Human Rights has universal applicability. It is now accepted in practice that infringements, wherever they may be, are of common concern."[12] The world needs that kind of forceful leadership on an ongoing basis. The UN can lead the way in actively promoting the principle that throughout the world, all people, no matter which sovereign nation they reside in, are protected by an agreed-upon set of rights. All nations should be strongly persuaded to sign the Human Rights Convention and Protocol. The UN has taken some years to act, but it appears ready to take on the difficult role of mitigating human-rights disasters.

A major part of ensuring that despots do not feel free to violate people's human rights is the multilateral ability to intercede with humanitarian aid even without the approval of the local government. While nonforcible methods of humanitarian intervention must first be fully explored and exhausted, there will be times when bold action will be needed to adequately protect populations suffering human rights abuses. We have had enough mass killings to learn the lessons of Ukraine, Nazi Europe, Cambodia, Ethiopia and other clearly heinous examples of man's inhumanity toward man. Iraq, the former Yugoslavia and Somalia have drawn or are now drawing enough attention to warrant such a response from the United Nations. We need to develop this capacity further so we can collectively respond forcefully and quickly when it is clearly warranted.

There is enough evidence in the case of Somalia that the UN was not prepared to act in a situation with no government in charge. The new reality of relief is that the world must be prepared to provide humanitarian assistance to those caught in the middle of tribal or other internal struggles. The UN might have delayed too long to save the hundreds of thousands of Somalis trapped in this war.

FOOD AID

A major component of all relief responses will continue to be food aid. More and more food (and nutritious food) will have to be provided. Short-term food aid has always been part of the humanitarian repertoire. Serious long-term food aid will have to be part of the response, as well. In essence, long-term food aid has been provided, but it has been always framed in successive short-term food aid contracts. Short-term survival food, such as provided by the World Food Program, is not enough in a long-term situation. The relief situations today require long-term commitments of nutritionally balanced foodstuffs. While this kind of food aid costs more to provide, it is vital to keeping people alert and healthy enough to take a major role in helping themselves. Money spent initially on nutritionally healthy diets will be saved in reduced health care costs later on.

Other challenges include providing long-term food aid in a manner that does not undermine the ability of the people to produce their own food; storing, securing and transporting food to remote locations; and redoubling efforts to research new high-yielding varieties of crops that can be indigenously grown without harmful impacts on the environment.

INVOLVEMENT OF U.S. CITIZENS

Developing a collective political will to stand up to and defeat those who perpetuate human-rights violations must include actively involving the American public in relief and development organizations. It is important to show them how these situations directly affect the quality of life in the United States. Citizens have to see how being more active in world politics is advantageous. We have to do a better job of promoting the concept of interdependency, especially as it pertains to development, environmental degradation and battling human-rights abuses. We need to provide study groups, task forces and other vehicles to help organize a political movement that reenergizes the American public and adds meaning to development and emergency relief issues.

U.S. citizens can play a key role in building the capacity of NGOs. First, they can respond with financial support, not just to emergencies, but also to the long-term fight to end the kind of poverty that makes disasters in the developing world so devastating. Second, they can advocate continued government spending on Third-World relief and development by contacting their local representatives and expressing their support of the work that NGOs are trying to do.

FINAL THOUGHTS

The complexity and large-scale nature of current relief situations necessitates responses that are multidimensional and well coordinated. There is a need to begin planning for potential disasters before they occur. There may be a need to intervene in countries to neutralize internal threats precipitating large-scale migrations.

While there are environmental and technical hurdles to overcome, the most difficult task is marshaling the political will to create governance systems that are "rights-protective." We need to be vigilant in creating systems that make protection of human rights a central element of their mission. We need actively to help all citizens of every nation understand that they are part of one world with certain inalienable rights, such as adequate nutrition and security. The rights mandated at the 1990 World Summit for Children were a good start. The rights must be extended to all people, and the UN must take an active role in ensuring that nations afford these rights to all citizens. Creating rights-protective regimes will not eliminate disasters and conflicts, and will not drive CARE out of business (although we would all be glad not to be needed), but it will ease the difficult task of ensuring that people do not go hungry and that they live full and productive lives.

15 THE MÉDECINS SANS FRONTIÈRES EXPERIENCE

Joelle Tanguy

The 1971 creation of Médecins Sans Frontières (often called MSF or, in the United States, Doctors Without Borders) brought about a small revolution in the world of humanitarianism. The purpose of this chapter is to record how that revolution came about and how it continues today, more than a quarter-century later.

HOW MSF BEGAN

It was the commiseration of two groups of frustrated international relief doctors that sparked the genesis of MSF. Independently, both groups had reached the same conclusion: that deference to the will of individual nations obstructed efforts to provide medical relief quickly and effectively.

The first group of doctors had become recognized for its work in Biafra, a region of Nigeria torn apart by a brutal civil war, where it operated from 1968 to 1970 on behalf of the French Red Cross. The second group had become known for having volunteered in 1970 to treat the victims of a tidal wave in eastern Pakistan (now Bangladesh). Independently, these groups discovered—the first during a war, the second during the aftermath of a natural disaster—the shortcomings of international aid as it was then configured. This configuration provided too little medical assistance and was too deferential to international law to be effective in crisis situations. MSF was founded on December 20, 1971, when these two groups joined forces. By forming MSF, this core group of doctors intended to change the way humanitarian aid was delivered by providing more medical assistance more rapidly and by being less deterred by national borders at times of crisis.

RED CROSS ROOTS

MSF's creation was actually the culmination of a trend initiated ten years earlier by the International Committee of the Red Cross (ICRC), a trend that was in itself a response to the work of Red Cross societies. During the early part of the twentieth century, humanitarian emergency aid was provided primarily by the Red Cross movement. But the effectiveness of its actions has been compromised by slow transport facilities and cumbersome administrative and diplomatic formalities.

In times of war, the ICRC intervened. Its main role was to make sure that the belligerent nations complied with the Geneva Conventions providing for the protection of and assistance to prisoners and civilians in time of war. Until the beginning of the 1960s, the Geneva-based ICRC carried out its duties without sending medical units to battle sites.

The ICRC was not encouraged to send out medical units because most conflicts in the past century involved either industrialized nations opposing each other or industrialized nations opposing their colonies. In both types of conflict, medical care was provided by the military of the countries involved. In the first type of conflict, most victims were soldiers. The armies facing each other were medically well equipped: each had its own medical unit to treat its own wounded. Military doctors were assisted by nurses and stretcher bearers from the Red Cross sections of only their own countries. In the second type of conflict, the colonial powers used the principle of noninterference to outlaw any foreign medical assistance to nationalist guerrillas. Here, too, war medicine was limited to military medicine.

It took the multiplication of civil wars in the developing world after the decolonization era (Katanga in 1960, Yemen in 1962, Biafra in 1967) to prompt the ICRC to add medical assistance to its roster of help. These new conflicts were much harder on the civilian population than earlier wars because, for example, of food blockades, and because guerrilla and counterguerrilla strategies caused massive flows of refugees and internally displaced persons under very precarious circumstances. Most of these conflicts tore apart countries already lacking doctors and therefore limited in their capability to deal with the public-health problems with which they were abruptly confronted through the confluence of underdevelopment and war.

The Consequences of Biafra

The ICRC began its emergency medical efforts by sending out a few doctors, whom it hired temporarily for renewable three-month terms. These doctors were recruited by the national Red Cross societies. During the summer of 1968, the ICRC offered the French Red Cross (FRC) the opportunity to run its own independent medical mission in Biafra. The FRC accepted readily, particularly since its acceptance enabled the French government to support the Biafra secession without too much compromise.

From September 1968 until January 1970, under extremely dangerous circumstances, the FRC managed to send some 50 doctors to Biafra. These doctors were driven by a mixture of compassion, religious conviction and a desire to use their professional skills to save as many lives as possible. Among them were the future founders of MSF, including Bernard Kouchner, who later became France's first Minister of Humanitarian Affairs.

For many, the conflict over Biafra meant the discovery of the "Third World," of a little-known conflict and of the inability of humanitarian action to solve crises of enormous proportions. The Biafran War, which ended in 1970 with the Nigerian government's victory after the death of one million people, clearly revealed the shortcomings of the Red Cross in responding to emergencies. Some of the future founders of MSF opposed ICRC regulations that forbade the Red Cross staff from making public statements about human-rights violations and genocide. Furthermore, ICRC was not entitled to intervene in a country without the approval of the country's authorities. It had to accept the sovereignty of any state that accepted its assistance; thus ICRC personnel had to take a reserved attitude toward the events they witnessed during a mission.

Several FRC doctors defied this prohibition by organizing a "committee against the Biafran genocide" as soon as they were back in France— less to make the public aware of the plight of the Biafran population than to denounce the political sources of this conflict, which were too often hidden by the newspapers covering the war. The committee argued that medical action should not be turned into a blind and dumb instrument. These French doctors also criticized the Red Cross intervention techniques as being obsolete.

This activity attracted a group of approximately 50 people who were persuaded that conflicts such as Biafra would happen again and needed to be anticipated. Thus the Biafra veterans began meeting once a month to share and refresh their memories. In 1970 they organized the Groupe d'Intervention Médical et Chirurgical d'Urgence (Emergency Medical and Surgical Intervention Group, or GIMCU), in the hope of setting up an independent association specializing in providing medical emergency assistance free from the administrative and legal constraints facing the ICRC.

At the same time, another group of doctors was organized in France at the initiative of the medical journal *Tonus*. In 1970 *Tonus*'s editor, Raymond Borel, spoke on television about the distress of the Bangladesh tidal-wave victims and the lack of French doctors at the site of the disaster. On November 23, 1970, he published an appeal in the columns of his journal to establish an association: Secours Médical Français (French Medical Relief, or SMF).

Doctors responded to Borel's call to action for many reasons: a bad conscience in the wake of the disturbing television images; the feeling that France, because of its history, had a duty to cooperate with decolonized countries; or simply the desire to get away from routine medicine and benign pathologies in order to practice presumably more useful medicine under more stimulating conditions. On December 20, 1971, MSF was born from the merger of GIMCU and SMF.

THE "FRENCH DOCTORS" MOVEMENT

It is no accident that MSF was set up at this time and in France, a country preoccupied with its colonial past. MSF's creation further coincided with the democratization of air transport and information, with the era of electronics and satellites, and with the increasing perception of the world as a global village. These factors in combination made it possible to intervene increasingly rapidly at disaster sites. The instantaneous visibility of disasters and conflicts on television made it less and less acceptable either to do nothing or to offer only a confused effort at emergency assistance.

From its inception, MSF hoped to benefit from the experience of its "Biafran" firebrands and the infrastructures (offices and secretariat) of its *Tonus* group. But the first steps were difficult. From 1971 to 1976, MSF was more like a pool of doctors at the disposal of large development aid organizations than a truly independent medical emergency organization. Its budget was limited to a few hundred thousand francs, and its missions, with a few exceptions—such as in Nicaragua after the 1972 earthquake and Honduras after the 1974 hurricane—were not independent. For lack of resources and experience, these early and limited interventions were highly ineffective. In Nicaragua, for example, American assistance arrived well ahead of MSF.

MSF: THE FIRST DECADE

MSF remained a very small organization in the 1970s for several reasons. First, it consisted exclusively of volunteers, each of whom was employed outside MSF. In the circles of established international organizations, the MSF volunteers were considered amateurs, tourists or "medical hippies." Second, MSF's members refused to ask for charity from the public or to "sell" humanitarian services like a commercial product, a policy that was not conducive to growth.

MSF flourished for the first time from 1976 to 1979. A 1976 war mission in Lebanon in a Shi'ite neighborhood encircled by Christian militia and a free advertising campaign offered in 1977 by an advertising agency gave MSF an identity as an organization that dealt with dangerous emergencies and its first public recognition. MSF was of interest not only in France but also in the United States because the American press reported on the courage of the French doctors in Lebanon.

But despite its interventions during a widely reported war and the fruits of an advertising campaign, in 1978 there remained a large gap between the association's reputation in France and its actual impact. And despite its strong showing in the media, the organization's existence was more symbolic than operational. It sent out only a few dozen doctors per year.

The Refugee Camp Factor

The formidable growth of MSF after 1978 was fueled by one factor: the multiplication of refugee camps at the end of the 1970s. This single phenomenon defined for MSF its main fields of intervention. While the global refugee population remained stable between 1970 and 1976, it doubled between 1976 and 1979, from 2.7 million to 5.7 million. It doubled once again between 1979 and 1982, settling at eleven million persons until 1985.

This increase was due to the sharp growth in the number of conflicts in the southern hemisphere after 1975. These conflicts were caused largely by the reemergence, after the decolonization era, of old national antagonisms and ethnic rivalries, as well as the fact that the East-West confrontation had moved out of Europe.

At the same time, the Soviet Union began to increase its influence in several developing countries, profiting from 1975 onward from the U.S. withdrawal after the Vietnam defeat and the instability brought about in southern and eastern Africa because of the Portuguese decolonization and the fall of the Ethiopian ruler. The Soviet expansion fueled a number of conflicts in Angola and Mozambique between pro-Soviet regimes and counterrevolutionary guerrillas, as well as in the African Horn. There, Somalia and Ethiopia began to fight in 1977 over the control of the Ogaden region, an Ethiopian territory inhabited mostly by Somalis. In addition, the 1975 communist takeover of Indochina led to the exodus of hundreds of thousands of boat people and other refugees to Thailand, Malaysia and Indonesia. Meanwhile, ethnic and religious minorities in Eritrea and Lebanon began or continued civil wars to obtain their independence or more power. Millions of people were packed in camps along the borders of these warring countries, often under very poor sanitary conditions. Although the United Nations High Commissioner for Refugees (UNHCR) assumed responsibility for the refugees and built and supplied camps, it had tremendous difficulty finding medical personnel willing to work in these areas.

MSF saw the increasing number of refugee settlements in the world as a fertile field of action. In contrast to the UNHCR, MSF did not lack doctors. In the second half of the 1960s, the French job market was flooded by doctors from the baby-boom generation who did not have to repay their student loans (as they did in the United States) and who often had had their first taste of the Third World during their military service. Many general practitioners of this generation were experiencing an identity crisis. Faced in their daily practice with benign pathologies that did not interest them and unsolvable problems that they could only refer to specialists, many of them were tempted to practice what they saw as a "more authentic" form of medicine in the developing world.

From 1976 to 1979, MSF sprang to the aid of Angolan refugees in the former Zaire; Somali refugees in Djibouti; Saharan refugees in Algeria and Eritrea; and, above all, Vietnamese, Cambodian and Laotian refugees in Thailand. Initially MSF offered modest help to the American humanitarian organizations that had already been on the scene for more than a year (particularly the International Rescue Committee and World Vision). Yet the French doctors sometimes questioned the motivations of the organizations for which they were working, suspecting them of acting as much for political objectives (anticommunism) and religious reasons (proselytizing) as for humanitarian goals.

During this period, MSF gradually expanded its operations in Thailand, slowly replacing the American organizations, which began to withdraw from the refugee camps as the memory of the Vietnam War began to fade. In December 1979, MSF also sent 100 doctors and nurses to the Cambodian border.

The Tensions of Growth

The multiplication of its missions in refugee camps at the end of the 1970s forced MSF to adopt a more professional approach, which meant, for example, paying a coordinator in Bangkok and providing small stipends for doctors sent out for six-month periods. This trend, far from being welcomed by every MSF member, began to divide those who longed for the days of purely voluntary emergency medicine (including the veterans of Biafra) from the new generation of doctors wanting to serve for longer terms in refugee camps and to provide more demanding medical services. In 1979 these long-submerged tensions led to a split within MSF.

Until 1977 Bernard Kouchner had been the organization's undisputed leader. But his power was challenged in 1978 by the new generation of refugee camp doctors and by his most brilliant disciple, Claude Malhuret. The baby boomers, Malhuret's generation, were more numerous than Kouchner's followers, and they were also more pragmatic. Malhuret and his generation were concerned about the technical insufficiency of MSF interventions in refugee camps. Foremost among technical problems were logistical difficulties, including communications between Paris and the field and delivery of medical supplies. As advocates of short, independent, voluntary missions, the older generation were afraid that MSF would be turned into a bureaucracy if it addressed these problems.

The second disagreement between the two groups focused on MSF's media posture. Despite some of its founders' opposition to the Red Cross's policy of silence, until 1977 the MSF charter forbade its members to talk about what they had witnessed during their missions. The policy of silence was intended as a strong symbol of political neutrality as well as a strategic posture to ensure its ability to perform "border-free" operations, since it was thought that no state would accept the presence of overly garrulous doctors on its territory.

Many factors combined to create widespread agreement in French society in the late 1970s on the primacy of human rights. Some examples include the revelations of abuses and oppression in the Soviet Union by Russian dissident author Alexander Solzhenitsyn; growing awareness of severe oppression by dictatorships in Latin America such as Chile and Uruguay; and the 1977 award of the Nobel Peace Prize to Amnesty International. After 1978, some members of MSF spoke to the press in the belief that testimony in MSF's name would shake the public from indifference.

When Bernard Kouchner chartered a ship to rescue Vietnamese refugees in the Chinese Sea, he triggered the crisis that led to the 1979 split. Two hundred thousand boat people had fled communist Vietnam since 1975. Those who survived assaults by pirates and storms (only half) went to Thailand, Indonesia or Malaysia. In 1978, the capacity of these three countries became saturated by the sudden arrival of massive numbers of refugees. To put a spectacular end to international indifference to its problem, Malaysia decided on November 15 to close its Hai Kong coast to a drifting coaster carrying 2,564 Vietnamese refugees. The maneuver succeeded and, along with reports of the intolerable sanitary and hygienic conditions on the vessel, it aroused the indignation of the world press and international public opinion. On November 22, a group of French intellectuals, moved by the Hai Kong tragedy, founded the Ship for Vietnam committee, whose purpose was to charter a vessel to receive refugees off the Vietnamese coast and to transport them to a host country.

The committee soon asked MSF to take medical responsibility for the refugees received on the ship, which MSF agreed to do. But several MSF members accused Bernard Kouchner of playing too active a role in the operation without consulting others. Although they did not underestimate the media and symbolic interest of this initiative, both for the refugees and MSF, Claude Malhuret and MSF cofounder Xavier Emmanuelli nevertheless disputed its technical legitimacy: they considered a single ship insufficient to receive the host of refugees whom its presence encouraged to flee.

The correctness of this criticism prompted MSF to withdraw from the operation and was confirmed by the new objective the committee assigned the ship, L'Île de Lumière (Island of Light), in April 1979. The vessel was no longer destined to receive boat people in the Chinese Sea, but was to become a hospital ship designed to treat the 40,000 Vietnamese refugees on Poulo Boudong island. This controversy led to the final split between the majority of MSF founders (except Xavier Emmanuelli and Raymond Borel) and the new generation in power. In 1979 Bernard Kouchner left MSF to found Médecins du Monde, or Doctors of the World.

SURVIVAL AND GROWTH

From 1979 to 1986, the scope of MSF's activities grew at a galloping pace. This growth also led to its internationalization in the early 1980s. The MSF movement, while born in France, was enriched by the organization of Belgian and Swiss sections in 1981, a Dutch section in 1983 and Spanish and Luxembourgian sections in 1985. Between 1986 and 1995, this expansion continued with the creation of supporting sections in Australia, Austria, Canada, Denmark, Germany, Greece, Hong Kong, Italy, Japan, Norway, Sweden, the United States and the United Kingdom.

After serious competitive tensions arose among the various national sections during the 1980s, the increasing globalization of the world in which the organization works during the 1990s has brought about the recognition of the need for greater cooperation and cohesiveness. Today many emergency missions are undertaken by international teams drawn from the various sections. Directors of the sections meet regularly to decide on main lines and strategy. In 1990 both an international council and an international secretariat were created to facilitate coordination among all MSF sections.

Both the growth of the original section in France and the creation of new sections was partly due to a favorable international context in the beginning of the 1980s and to successful technical and strategic choices made by the organization. For the three leaders of the French section following Bernard Kouchner's departure, Claude Malhuret, Francis Charhon and Rony Brauman, the challenge was to convince their more skeptical colleagues of the need for structural change. Those changes included adoption of logistics and medical departments, a salaried administrative system and the organization of marketing activities.

In particular, they reasoned, the association needed substantial and dependable financial resources to guarantee its independence. Although the French section of MSF roughly tripled its income between 1979 and 1980 (from $1.5 to $4.3 million), its financial structure remained extremely fragile, depending mainly on the international economic situation—that is, they relied on isolated and spontaneous donations from institutions or private individuals who were prompted to donate by media representations of various disasters (for example the influx of refugees in Thailand, the Soviet invasion of Afghanistan, the famine in Uganda, the Polish siege and the Lebanese war). This financing method clearly had its limits, and in 1982, MSF began to introduce direct-mail fund-raising techniques based on the success of these methods in American presidential elections. These techniques, at the time unknown in France, for the first time gave MSF a regular income, making it less dependent on political changes and institutional donors.

The growth of private fund-raising has ensured MSF's independence from any single donor or government, and the organization has set clear policy that at least half of all funds raised must come from private sources. Despite its French origins, the organization has shied away from French government funding, which today represents less than half of one percent of the total budget. Some of the key institutional and government funders are the European Community Humanitarian Office (ECHO), United Nations High Commissioner for Refugees, the United States Office of Foreign Disaster Assistance, and Belgian, Dutch, Norwegian and other governments.

GROWING PROFESSIONALISM

Buffered by growing financial resources, MSF's interventions improved in effectiveness through an in-depth overhaul of its technical structures. First, to encourage participation and the stability of its pool of trained volunteers and staff, MSF began to pay salaries to the staff doctors working in the headquarters and a travel allowance and a stipend of about $700 per month to the doctors working in the field on longer-term missions. Second, the staff at the headquarters was expanded as technical units grew. Third, recruitment efforts were organized to include more screening and improved orientation training; in the early 1980s the number of doctors and nurses sent out increased considerably, to up to 600 departures per year. Today the organization dispatches approximately 2,500 volunteers to medical projects each year.

MSF has developed a standardized recruitment process designed to match qualified health care professionals with appropriate projects and to train them to undertake their medical missions under conditions that might be unfamiliar to them. The organization seeks general practitioners; specialists such as surgeons, anesthesiologists, obstetrician-gynecologists and ophthalmologists; registered nurses; midwives; and public-health and nutrition experts. Candidates submit a written application detailing medical training, professional experience (especially expertise with tropical medicine), foreign language ability and availability and flexibility. Applicants are then interviewed by MSF recruiters, who evaluate the candidates' motivation and ability to function and live with an MSF team. Once selected, candidates are placed on a recruitment reserve list.

The process of training volunteers is an essential component of MSF's commitment to the quality of its missions. MSF runs 52 weeks of courses per year targeted at volunteers at various levels of experience and expertise. Many volunteers take a preparatory course before their first mission that addresses specific health care issues as well as the contexts in which missions are conducted. Advanced courses in epidemiology, nutrition, immunization, and water and sanitation management are also available, as are courses in logistics coordination and management of missions.

THE LOGISTICS REVOLUTION

The expansion of MSF's logistical capacity marked an important step forward. By 1981, logistical problems had grown to the point of paralyzing medical activity in the field. From the refugee camps in Thailand and

Somalia, where supplies had to be provided for volunteer units of up to 40 persons, came the awareness that nonmedical activities were needed to ensure the effective provision of medical services. The first full-time logistics manager, Jacques Pinel, was appointed in Paris and was assisted by several experts in the field. Over time, he and his colleagues created the system of rapid response and support for which MSF has gained much recognition.

This logistics revolution had three central components: communications, transportation and the preparation of emergency kits for immediate response. Communications advances gave rise to the establishment of radio links between headquarters and the field. Now satellite transmission dishes arrive in the field with staff so that they will not be without access to their home section and to the outside world. Transportation logistics were developed in collaboration with the organization Avions Sans Frontières, or Aviation Without Borders, creating priority transport capability. For the ground, MSF bought cars and began to coordinate more efficiently its staff travel arrangements.

Finally, the logistics experts worked with medical experts to develop a sophisticated inventory of medical and field supplies. Because MSF faces the challenge of responding quickly to emergencies while adapting each response to specific and dramatically different situations (often unknown before an exploratory team is dispatched), there was a need to develop a series of medical and logistical kits that could be combined to meet any crisis.

As a result, MSF has developed ready-to-dispatch kits containing the hundreds of medical and nonmedical supplies that are necessary to accomplish specific tasks but are so time-consuming to gather from scratch. Upon evaluating conditions and needs in the face of an emergency, MSF personnel determine the types and quantity of kits to be deployed from a ready selection of some 50 kits that includes a basic medical kit, an emergency health kit, a vaccination kit and a surgical kit. Kits are composed of modules, or groups of basic supplies such as bandages, that can be restocked as needed during operation at a field location. Since the kits are stocked in advance, all materials in them have been selected and tested and are ready for use; and the cost, weight and size of specific kits are known. By using standard kits in combination, supplemented as needed by additional modules, MSF is able to adapt quickly to serve new or changing situations.

The size and completeness of the kits sometimes surprise observers who are unfamiliar with MSF. For example, to furnish medical assistance to a displaced population of 30,000 persons in an isolated area, MSF might elect to deploy three emergency health kits capable of serving 10,000 persons each for a period of three months, as well as various kits providing energy sources, all-terrain vehicles, office supplies, satellite communications equipment and other equipment and tools. Each emergency health kit would include modules of medicines, selected in accordance with MSF's medical protocols, and other basic medical supplies, such as bandages, rubber gloves, thermometers and syringes. Then, if an MSF exploratory team were to identify the risk of, say, a cholera epidemic in the population, MSF would be prepared to deploy immediately an additional kit containing the medicines and supplies necessary to combat cholera. During the cholera epidemic that swept seven countries of eastern and central Africa during the winter of 1997 and 1998, teams were able to set up cholera treatment centers to treat hundreds of patients within 48 hours of the first signs of the epidemic.

The progress made by MSF with the development of kits enabled it within the space of ten days in the spring of 1991 to send 75 airplanes loaded with some 2,500 tons of equipment to help the hundreds of thousands of Kurdish refugees who had fled Iraq. This progress also increased the effectiveness of MSF's interventions after certain natural disasters. After the earthquakes in Nicaragua, Algeria and Mexico, MSF's emergency units had arrived too late at the disaster sites. Therefore, after the 1986 earthquake in El Salvador and the 1988 earthquake in Armenia, MSF elected not to provide direct medical care to victims but rather to operate in the background by treating nonurgent conditions to allow local hospitals the space for truly serious cases, and by building shelters, drinking-water reservoirs and sanitary facilities to replace those destroyed by the disaster. The development of emergency kits has enabled MSF more often to provide lifesaving aid at the scene of a disaster before it is too late. Following the 1998 earthquake in northeastern Afghanistan, which reportedly killed 5,000 people, MSF was the first organization on the scene, arriving in the hardest hit city of Rostaq within two days of the disaster to provide critical care and to evacuate the most serious cases to the MSF-run hospital in nearby Taloquan.

THE MOVE TOWARD EFFICIENCY

If the period from 1979 until 1986 was for MSF marked by growing visibility without a similar increase in efficiency, the reverse occurred from 1986 to 1992, when the organization dramatically increased its capacity to intervene in emergencies, yet experienced a drop-off in media attention. The Ethiopian mission during the famine of 1984 was a turning point in the growing awareness of the organization's technical weaknesses. Concern about this situation coincided with the arrival of a generation of doctors who were less politically oriented and more technologically minded than the previous generation. These doctors expected to have more technical resources at their disposal.

In response to these concerns, MSF set about standardizing its procedures and protocols, beginning by drafting guidelines to be used in the most common emergency relief situations. Approximately 40 books of guidelines exist, covering basic medical practice as well as specialties such as surgery and ophthalmology. In addition, MSF has developed specialized expertise in nutrition and vaccination and has set up water and sanitation units. The latter development was important because medical teams in refugee camps must always deal with sanitary problems (well purification, construction of latrines, waste-water discharge) to prevent typhus or cholera epidemics.

Over the years MSF has helped to create several affiliated organizations that are devoted to pursuing specific areas of research in the field of emergency medicine and relief. In 1986 in Paris, MSF created Epicentre, a group of epidemiologists charged with epidemiological research and evaluation of the work of MSF and other aid organizations. In 1984 in Belgium, MSF members founded the Agence Européenne pour le Developpement et la Santé (European Agency for Health and Development, or AEDES), which consults on emergency project management, food security and other public health matters. In 1992 in Holland, HealthNet International was founded with the support of MSF to support the redevelopment of health and social services in the aftermath of a crisis.

A FRESH APPROACH TO HUMANITARIAN AID

From 1979 to 1986, wars and refugee camps became more than ever the preserve of MSF. The conflicts that started at the end of the 1970s were followed by wars in Chad and Uganda and the war between Iran and Iraq. The end of the decade was marked by the largest communist expansion in the history of the developing world—the Vietnamese invasion of Cambodia and the Soviet invasion of Afghanistan. In the early 1980s the United States decided to react to the Soviet advance. Ronald Reagan, then the U.S. President, led a crusade against communism, supporting several counterrevolutionary guerrilla movements. Regional conflicts, the center of the U.S.-Soviet struggle, continued and compounded the problem of refugees along the borders of warring nations. During this period, MSF intervened in some of the regions where the East-West antagonism was at its worst: Central America, southern Africa, the Horn of Africa, the Middle East and Southeast Asia.

As it continued its interventions, MSF strengthened its position as an original player on the international scene, thanks to its novel concept of humanitarian action. Guiding its action were three principles: the right of access to victims, the need for monitoring of aid, and the protection of humanitarian workers. To enforce these principles, MSF was willing to violate the two intangible principles imposed on ICRC workers: respect for national borders, and the duty to remain silent. MSF began to speak out against violations of these three ethics (in Cambodia, Afghanistan and Ethiopia) and to conduct clandestine missions when its presence was not officially welcomed (in Afghanistan, Kurdistan, El Salvador and Eritrea).

In Afghanistan, where MSF intervened clandestinely just a few months after the Soviet invasion, the organization undertook one of the most dangerous assignments in its history. Here, more than in any other country or conflict, MSF made incarnate the right of all victims to be treated. MSF's stance in Afghanistan set it apart from American relief organizations and the ICRC. For ten years, together with the teams of other French organizations, the 550 MSF doctors and nurses who replaced each other on Afghan territory were the only foreign humanitarians assisting the population on the side of the Afghan resistance fighters. Because of its rarity, the medical assistance offered by MSF gave the Afghans valuable psychological and political support. The foreign doctors were their link with the West to make the international community aware of their struggle, especially from the fall of 1981 onward, when the Red Army began to bomb the hospitals in which MSF was working. At the time, MSF denounced the Soviet acts and encouraged journalists to visit Afghanistan.

THE CHOICE TO SPEAK OUT

In Ethiopia, MSF continued its outspoken attitude, achieving a precise objective. In the spring of 1984, the organization began to send medical units to this country to help fight the famine. At the end of that year, the Ethiopian government began to move the northern population victimized by the drought to fertile regions in the south. When MSF assisted with the first transfer, it saw no reason for criticism. After all, what was more logical than to move people from arid regions to fertile ones? The violence observed at times by MSF members was viewed as an isolated problem rather than deliberate policy. To continue their humanitarian work, the doctors decided to remain silent.

The transfers became more authoritarian in early 1985, and the violence more frequent. MSF members witnessed roundups of hospitalized persons, noticing that no efforts were made to keep families together. Many persons died in transfer. The areas in which those being transferred were settled were frequently without adequate facilities or assistance, and the Ethiopian authorities had established food quotas in Addis Ababa. Furthermore, the transfers diverted many resources from the MSF rescue operations.

By autumn of 1984 it became clear that there was a political and ideological motivation behind the transfers, carried out with the twofold aim of weakening the guerrilla movements in the north (in Eritrea and Tigre) by removing their grassroots supporters and of putting these populations in villages in order to bring them ideologically in line with government policy. Under this scheme, humanitarian aid was used to attract villagers and blackmail them into going along with the program. After lodging many fruitless protests with the Ethiopian authorities, MSF decided in November 1985 that, regardless of the consequences to its ability to remain in the country, the organization could no longer remain silent. If it did so, MSF could appear to be condoning the brutality of these transfers, already responsible for more deaths than the famine (100,000 victims, according to MSF reports).

The presence of a host of aid organizations in Ethiopia made it less difficult for MSF to denounce the transfer practices in public and enabled MSF to take the risk of expulsion. A few days after officially requesting the discontinuance of the transfers, MSF was expelled from Ethiopia. MSF immediately briefed the media on the diversion of aid used to oppress instead of help. A few days after MSF's expulsion, the EEC and the United States decided to make further aid conditional on the discontinuance of these forced population transfers. Thus pressured, the Ethiopian government announced in early 1986 that it would cease its resettlement programs.

Despite a commitment to speak out in the face of massive human rights abuses, the leaders of MSF have limited their public declarations. The process of bearing witness, however, occurs on an ongoing basis with the intention of improving conditions for populations in danger. MSF field volunteers participate in witnessing by serving as an international presence in crisis areas and by raising public awareness about the populations they serve. In extreme situations, the witness process extends to openly criticizing or denouncing breaches of international conventions. This is a last resort used when MSF volunteers witness mass violations of human rights, including forced displacement of populations, forced return of refugees, genocide, crimes against humanity and war crimes.

MSF IN THE UNITED STATES

In 1990, MSF was introduced in the United States, where it is known as Doctors Without Borders. With its headquarters in New York City and an additional office in Los Angeles, its purpose is to raise funds for relief projects conducted in the field by MSF, to recruit American medical and nonmedical professionals to volunteer in the field, and to increase public awareness of populations in danger.

As a nonprofit charitable organization, MSF in the United States focuses its fund-raising activities on contributions from individuals, foundations, corporations and U.S. institutions. Since its founding, the U.S. organization has attracted 160,000 individual donors, who in 1997 provided $8.4 million to support projects ranging from aid to Rwandan refugees to the treatment of Kashin-Beck syndrome ("big-bone disease") in Tibet. These private funds strengthen the international organization's capacity to develop projects with full independence from government influences. The establishment of a U.S. section has also enriched the organization's pool of relief workers; in 1997, nearly 100 American volunteers participated in field projects. The U.S. organization also negotiates U.S. government funding for emergency and refugee operations for the international MSF network. Finally, the U.S. organization has been a focal point in MSF advocacy efforts with the United Nations, the U.S. government and other relief organizations. In recent years, MSF was on several occasions invited by Congress to testify on current humanitarian issues such as the 1994 genocide in Rwanda and subsequent refugee flight, the land mine crisis in Afghanistan and the 1996 and 1997 refugee crisis in Congo (former Zaire). In 1997, MSF joined several other organizations in a historic presentation to the UN Security Council on the refugee crisis in Africa's Great Lakes region.

CHALLENGES OF THE 1990S

With a yearly budget of about $250 million and 2,500 volunteer departures to the field each year, Médecins Sans Frontières has become one of the world's leading private medical emergency assistance organizations. Much of MSF's recognition derives from its missions in Afghanistan, Ethiopia, Iraqi Kurdistan, Somalia, Rwanda and Congo (former Zaire), which were widely reported in the media.

Although MSF's work is conducted in many of the same places today as in past decades, the activity has changed considerably in keeping with the changing global environment. While many countries such as Angola,

Thailand and Afghanistan are still dealing with the effects of large population displacements, the issue has been complicated by changes in the status applied to refugees and by the repatriation—both voluntary and forced—of several populations to their original countries. Although refugees remain an important focus for MSF (particularly in Africa's Great Lakes region), the organization is increasingly facing the challenge of new health care crises. Those challenges include the reemergence of once-controlled diseases such as sleeping sickness and tuberculosis; the emergence of new epidemics and especially the AIDS epidemic; lack of access to health care for excluded populations; failing health systems in the former Soviet Union; and the need for medical assistance in MSF headquarters' own backyards. At the same time, MSF and other aid organizations are facing previously unknown difficulties in maintaining a presence and ensuring the safety of its volunteers in the face of warring parties that neither recognize the neutrality of, nor protect, humanitarian aid workers.

Although the total number of registered refugees was reduced in the 1990s, MSF encountered a crisis of tremendous dimensions when one million people crossed into the Democratic Republic of Congo (former Zaire) from Rwanda in the aftermath of the 1994 Rwandan genocide. The crisis continued to escalate when a cholera epidemic broke out in the refugee camps of eastern Congo, prompting the largest intervention in MSF's history. Over the next three years, ongoing ethnic tension in the region and the failure of the international community to take action led to more violence, particularly when the camps were attacked in 1996, sending hundreds of thousands of refugees back into Rwanda and Burundi and farther into Congo. Those refugees who did not return to their home countries faced massacres, starvation and disease. Military forces blocked aid and manipulated relief workers, using their presence as bait to attract and eliminate refugees more easily. MSF teams, blocked in their effort to reach and assist the refugees, spoke out against these abuses and, along with three other humanitarian agencies, MSF was invited for the first time directly to address the UN Security Council on this issue.

The most significant geographic novelty of this period has been MSF's recognition of humanitarian needs in Europe. With the collapse of communism in Eastern Europe, MSF began to participate in the effort to restore the public-health systems in Romania, Bulgaria and a number of republics of the former USSR. The deterioration of the Soviet Union has posed a particular challenge even to MSF's most seasoned volunteers. These medical professionals were used to working in countries with little health care infrastructure and few doctors, but they were not accustomed to working in countries where infrastructures and doctors existed but in which the public-health structures did not function adequately. The rise of epidemics in the former Soviet bloc forced MSF quickly to develop new expertise, and in the mid-1990s, the organization launched an AIDS-prevention project in Moscow, a tuberculosis treatment project in Siberia, a massive polio vaccination campaign in Albania and a variety of public-health programs in Uzbekistan, to name just a few projects.

With continued economic uncertainty in Western Europe, MSF has turned its attention to the steadily increasing number of people who for a variety of reasons are not adequately served by their public-health systems. In such countries as Belgium, France and Spain, MSF has undertaken projects addressing those societies' most vulnerable populations, including drug addicts, people with AIDS, immigrants and asylum seekers, and other underserved communities.

The rapidly moving political and economic events of the post-Cold-War period have increased the complexity of the environment in which MSF works and have forced the organization, at times, to balance the needs of civilians against the negative consequences of aid and the growing dangers to humanitarian workers.

On October 19, 1991, MSF sent a humanitarian convoy to evacuate casualties from the besieged Croatian city of Vukovar. Several previous rescue attempts had failed, and the convoy was allowed to proceed only after protracted negotiations with the Yugoslav Army and the Croatian authorities. The twelve-vehicle convoy successfully evacuated an estimated 109 wounded soldiers and civilians. As it headed out of the city, however, one of the trucks struck a mine and two MSF nurses sustained serious injuries. Concern for the safety of volunteers placed MSF in the difficult position of having to rule out any attempts to rescue the remaining wounded in Vukovar's hospital.

This incident occurred despite the strictly humanitarian nature of the operation and despite assurances of safe passage from both sides of the conflict. Worldwide conflicts in which the impartial provision of humanitarian aid is less and less respected are becoming more common. In 1989 a missile destroyed an Avions Sans Frontières airplane in Sudan, killing two MSF members on board. In 1990 an MSF logistics expert was assassinated in Afghanistan, and in 1997, an MSF doctor was murdered in Somalia. The organization has faced kidnappings in Ingushetia and Sierra Leone. MSF has also faced serious safety problems in Iraq, the former Yugoslavia, Liberia, Chechnya, Rwanda and Congo (former Zaire).

Experiences in the 1990s have also taught MSF important lessons about working alongside military-humanitarian operations. The first such operation took place in Kurdistan, where a largely U.S.-led military force provided the logistics for a massive delivery of aid materials. While the latter experience taught the value of what military logistical capacity could add to an emergency aid operation, MSF's experience in Somalia, where peacekeepers became embroiled in the escalation of violence to the point of attacking civilians they had come to help, showed the pitfalls of such collaboration. Following the Somalia debacle, the United States in particular has been less quick to act, and MSF has voiced concern that too often peacekeeping operations make it their job to bring humanitarian aid, such as food distribution, while protection of civilians from attack is forgotten.

At the end of the twentieth century, the world has begun to resemble a global village connected by fax, phone and Internet, where what is said and done in a remote part of Africa can appear simultaneously on television in New York. In previous eras, lack of action could have legitimately been blamed on ignorance. Today, in the face of so much information, it would be easy to assume an accompanying increase in interest and sympathy. Yet it continues to be difficult to arouse this sympathy toward people who are still seen as far away and unfamiliar. The globalization of media will not solve this problem, and it will be the role of humanitarian agencies to keep these issues in the forefront of public awareness.

For MSF, greater awareness should lead to a greater sense of responsibility. That sense of responsibility has driven the organization to embrace the values of independence and impartiality and the ethic of volunteerism, and to seek and confront the greatest challenges in our midst. As MSF enters the twenty-first century, the pursuit of these values in a drastically changing world environment will continue to guide the organization's mission and work.

NOTE

An earlier version of this chapter, by Rony Brauman, was published in the first edition of *A Framework for Survival*.

Aengus Finucane

I was parish priest of Uli, Nigeria, in 1968. It was there, more than 30 years ago, during the Biafra/Nigeria civil war, that I had my first experience in the delivery of humanitarian aid and health services under conflict conditions. The eastern region of Nigeria had seceded as Biafra and the federal Nigerian government was sparing no effort to reintegrate the oil-rich breakaway region. Uli, a rural townland deep in Biafra, became the epicenter of a massive relief operation. The road just outside my parish residence was widened to make an airstrip. All flying was at night, and the planes had to run the gauntlet of the federal Nigerian forces. With vastly superior firepower, they were steadily squeezing and reducing Biafran-held territory. Uli Airport found a place on the world map. By October 1968 it had become the busiest airport in Africa. On some nights it handled as many as 50 planes. My parish church became a feeding center. Sermons were exhortations to eat mice, cockroaches and cassava leaves. Parish duties gave way to airport duties.

In the final months of the Biafra/Nigeria conflict in late 1969, I was based in Libreville, Gabon. From there I was organizing the airlift of relief supplies to Uli for Concern, a newly formed Irish relief organization. Having unloaded their relief cargoes at Uli, the returning planes brought thousands of near-dead children to be cared for by nongovernmental organizations (NGOs) in camps set up for them in neighboring countries.

More than 20 years later, in August 1992, I flew into Baidoa, a famine-stricken town of 60,000 people in Somalia. I was on board a cargo plane carrying sixteen tons of supplies for a Concern relief team. In Somalia, on the opposite side of Africa from Biafra, another chapter of misery, tragedy and famine was unfolding. Prior to this famine, Baidoa had been as little known to the outside world as Uli had been before the Biafra conflict. In August 1992, television, radio and print media in Baidoa catapulted the town into the center of the world stage. In the days I was there, the satellite dishes and elaborate equipment of two television groups beamed the misery and dying of Baidoa into living rooms around the world.

During the time of that visit to Baidoa, an average of 200 deaths were recorded daily. On one day, trucks collected 176 corpses for burial. These were the bodies of people with no friends to bury them. Most often the near-dead buried their dead in shallow graves. The population swelled as more and more starving people were drawn to the town. In the first ten days of September 1992, the trucks collected 2,353 bodies from the streets of Baidoa and 70 percent of them were children. By September 16, the grim tally had reached 3,520.

NGO ORIGINS AND GROWTH

Uli to Baidoa; Biafra to Somalia; 1968 to 1992. A huge proliferation and wide diversification of NGOs took place during these years. It is little short of obscene that two such gruesome landmarks as Uli and Baidoa stand as the parameters for this personal record of relief work.

There were NGOs before Biafra. But NGOs in the sense we know them today—as accepted players with a major role in the transfer of resources from rich to poor countries—became a prominent force on the multinational Third-World-aid stage only in the 1970s and 1980s. The whole concept of Third-World development through the transfer of resources from richer to poorer countries belongs to the postcolonial era of the second half of this century. The international Third-World NGOs we now know are, in a few instances, a development of older organizations. For example, Save the Children, U.K., has roots going back to 1919 and a shattered post-World-War-I Europe. Oxfam was formed in England in 1943 to help children in Belgium and Greece during World War II. CARE was formed in the United States to send relief parcels to post-World-War-II Europe.

Early NGOs were driven by a Western and Christian philosophy of caring for the needy. Church-founded or "confessional NGOs" developed only from the 1950s onward. Their core constituency consists of their church membership. Although they run parallel to church structures, they are usually at great pains to keep their development and relief work separate from their religious or evangelistic work. They make considerable efforts to ensure that their work is targeted on the most needy, regardless of their religious affiliation, and in ways calculated to benefit the population in general.

The past 30 years have also seen the emergence of many nonaligned NGOs on the international stage. While the majority are nondenominational and secular, they are still inspired by the same Western philosophy of caring that motivated the earlier NGOs.

There are countless nonprofit organizations and groups that are nongovernmental, which quite justifiably describe themselves as NGOs. This paper, however, is concerned only with international NGOs that have as their sole or prime purpose the righting of the imbalance between rich and poor countries by the transfer of resources. Some of these NGOs deal exclusively with children, or with crisis interventions, or health or agriculture. Some NGOs confine their efforts to fund-raising or the mobilization of resources such as pharmaceuticals and hospital supplies for developing countries. Others concentrate on development education or lobbying on behalf of developing countries.

As we approach the millennium, lines between the forms of activity pursued by NGOs are becoming increasingly blurred. The greater complexity of needs sometimes pushes organizations toward specialization and the development of high levels of expertise. Some other organizations, pressured to maintain or increase levels of funding, are pushed toward diversification in order to offer a wider range of choices to funders.

There is a major distinction between organizations that directly manage and implement projects in developing countries and organizations that confine themselves to raising funds or mobilizing resources for transfer to operational partners. Voluntary organizations frequently come under pressure from supporters to address domestic needs.

THE EFFECT OF BIAFRA ON NGOS

Third-World NGOs came into their own during the involvement in Biafra. Biafra created a new level of awareness in the West of Third-World famine and disaster. It was the first major disaster that was brought into the living rooms of the world by television, which, with its visual immediacy, challenged indifference to faraway suffering.

The Biafrans fought a good propaganda war. They engaged Mark Press, a Geneva-based public relations firm, to present their case to the world. The Biafrans used the sufferings of their people to great effect to disturb the world conscience. In Biafra, the many NGOs involved learned the usefulness of the media, a lesson that has stood them in good stead in winning support for their work ever since. The response to Biafra demonstrated that people do care; obtaining support is a question of getting the message to them. Since Biafra, NGOs have been very conscious of their responsibility to inform the world of disasters and suffering so that the problems may be addressed.

The "confessional" NGOs were the most active in Biafra. The Protestant organizations were grouped under the World Council of Churches (WCC), and the Catholic NGOs were grouped under Caritas. Together they formed a strong and influential operational body, Joint Church Aid (JCA), which was also substantially funded by the American Jewish Committee. It was an unprecedented example of cooperation between world religious bodies. Dozens of private agencies from 20 countries grouped together under the JCA banner. JCA funded and ran a huge airlift to beleaguered Biafra—a lifeline that linked into the extensive church networks on the ground and became a highly effective distribution system for the supplies being airlifted to the country by the international NGOs and other donors. In Western countries, NGOs that were not themselves operational joined Joint Church Aid or supported the relief efforts by donating to JCA.

New NGOs were formed in response to the needs in Biafra. Concern and Médicins Sans Frontières are two such organizations. Others, such as Canair Relief, were operational during the crisis, then disbanded. In the mid-1980s, Band Aid made a similar appearance in the response to famine needs in Ethiopia and Sudan, and then disbanded. After the Biafran crisis, Concern debated disbanding. However, the Bangladesh crisis of 1971 decided the question in favor of continuing.

The new and extraordinary role of NGOs in Biafra proved that there was indeed a niche and a role for NGOs on the international stage. In Biafra, NGOs discovered that they had particular strengths in emergency situations, and ever since they have played a prominent role in virtually every disaster relief operation in the intervening years. NGOs have become a great deal more professional and sophisticated. Many of the organizations that are now operational in disaster relief situations have become particularly effective in delivering health services and humanitarian assistance.

The biggest change in NGOs during the past 30 years has been an increase in size. Several grew into multimillion-dollar operations. Even some of the smaller ones most frequently active in conflict and disaster situations now have annual budgets of 40 to 50 million dollars. It is difficult to operate on a small budget in disaster situations. In some of the major disaster situations of the 1990s, among them Liberia, Somalia, Rwanda and Zaire, government services scarcely functioned. When governments break down, UN agencies, which usually operate through governments, are severely hampered. In such situations, NGOs that have not developed their own backup systems are also left adrift.

Idealism and humanitarianism were undoubtedly the forces that gave birth to many of the international NGOs. In the case of the "confessional" NGOs, religious motivation was added. Many organizations had charismatic founder members. Growth in scale inevitably meant organizations became less personalized. Although the general public still looks on the operatives in the NGOs as ill paid or even unpaid, and highly idealistic, most people might be somewhat shocked if they saw the salary and operating budgets of major, and even smaller, NGOs. While most NGOs are very cost-conscious, they are repeatedly confronted with the "pay peanuts and get monkeys" dilemma—to get the kind of high-level, professionally qualified personnel necessary to handle the complexities of large organizations costs money. Being entrusted with huge resources by the public and by governments and institutions imposes great responsibilities.

In Biafra, NGOs were effective and highly successful largely because there was an extensive network of professional, committed personnel already in place. No disaster, especially no disaster in a conflict situation, has since enjoyed that luxury. In Somalia, 25 years later, there were virtually no ready-made feed-in points with which NGOs could connect. Among the operational agencies, those with their own backup systems stood by far the best chance of doing extensive and effective work. It was distressing to see NGOs abounding in goodwill floundering because of lack of support systems. Again, at Goma in Zaire, during the mass exodus from Rwanda in 1994, a number of smaller NGOs had great operational difficulties because of the lack of independent support systems.

The JCA airlift into Biafra has never been fully recognized for what it was. Recalling it now helps put the belated and pathetic efforts to get assistance to Somalia in perspective. Many of the JCA planes carried fifteen tons per flight to Uli, and it was a major disappointment if each plane did not manage two flights each night. And they were operating by night under constant threat of federal Nigerian fire. At the height of the conflict, JCA handed out 376 tons of relief supplies in a single night at Uli. Although there was a cease-fire in Somalia in 1992 and Baidoa has a very good airstrip, two large U.S. air force planes were each making one trip a day from Mombasa to Baidoa and each carrying but nine tons of supplies.

Where there is a will, there is a way. There was a will in Biafra. Twenty-five years later, there wasn't a will in Somalia until very late in the game, and even then it was lukewarm for too long. One can only be cynical about the uncoordinated efforts of the superpowers in Somalia. In the years since Biafra, we had launched satellites into space, put people on the moon, and made all manner of technological advances. At the end of July 1992, there were 25 million metric tons of cereal in European intervention stores alone. Given these facts, how did the world community cope with the shame of watching hundreds of thousands of people die of starvation? It was not that we did not know.

There is an ever-present danger that NGOs may become overconfident because of their undoubted success in small undertakings. They often overstretch themselves, but they *should* stretch themselves. They can also annoy other actors on the stage by raising strident voices and finger-pointing, by exaggerating their own expertise and capabilities, by seeming to lay claim to a monopoly on caring. Such actions can build up unreal expectations. Often because of their own frustration and inability to deliver, bigger actors have lured NGOs out of their depth. The NGOs can be like small fishing trawlers tempted into deep waters to service large factory ships. Usually they respond with alacrity. When the factory ships fail to function, the smaller vessels are in dire trouble.

NGOs are but one actor, and usually a relatively small one, on the international aid stage. This should be borne in mind especially in conflict situations. They must function with an awareness of and with respect for bilateral, or government, donors, multilateral donors, host governments and, where they are present, local NGOs. Whether in conflict, disaster or long-term work situations, NGOs should respect local institutions, culture and customs. Far too often, many NGO personnel display a staggering lack of sensitivity and respect for their host environment.

GOVERNMENT-TO-GOVERNMENT AID

During the last 30 years there has been a growing disillusionment among donor governments with regard to recipient Third-World partner governments. Unreal expectations have been replaced with often bitter recriminations. In reviewing government-to-government or bilateral aid it should be borne in mind that seldom was such aid purely altruistic. Most bilateral aid is in large part motivated by self-interest and by political, commercial and strategic considerations. The former Prime Minister of Great Britain, Margaret Thatcher, was noted for putting things bluntly; she stated very simply that "British aid must foster British trade."

Through the 1980s and into the mid-nineties, bilateral donors, as already noted, channeled increasing amounts of aid through international NGOs. This was sometimes resented by Third-World governments.

They resented being bypassed and seemingly not trusted. I noted such reactions when dealing with officials in Ethiopia, Sudan and Bangladesh.

In 1993 the government of newly independent Eritrea took a strong stand against the involvement of international NGOs, and of UN agencies, in the delivery of aid. The Eritreans were the ones who most strongly voiced feelings increasingly shared by other Third-World governments. They were prepared to accept the consequent reduction in aid flows. This more independent line is gaining strength in the late nineties in the emerging African political bloc made up of Eritrea, Ethiopia, Uganda and Rwanda. This bloc enjoys the sympathies of Tanzania, Zambia, Zimbabwe and Burundi.

The sometimes startling growth in size of the international NGOs in the 1980s and 1990s is largely attributable to the partnership with donor governments in the transfer of aid. The growth in size too often entailed an erosion of ethos, which went hand in hand with the replacement of committed volunteerism and low-paid service by the costly professionalism that the more complex organizations required. More fundamentally, increased government funding of NGO work entails a lessening of the independence of the NGOs. This is, of course, particularly likely if an NGO becomes heavily dependent on a single government source. NGOs must be careful not to become the tools or simply the contractors of donor governments. At the same time, NGOs are committed to exploiting to the fullest all resource possibilities on behalf of their clients, and government resources offer the greatest possibility. Availing oneself of government resources to the fullest while retaining independence and remaining true to the ethos can be very difficult.

The scale of fund-raising necessary to maintain the larger NGOs has fostered many well-oiled NGO publicity and lobbying machines. Sadly, the growth and increased efficiency on the public relations and fund-raising side of the NGOs has too often not been matched by a proportionate improved performance, and has been accompanied by some sacrificing of independence. Bigger is by no means necessarily better.

Lobbying is a vitally important role that some NGOs specialize in and all NGOs exercise at times. For a year, while Somalia drifted ever faster toward anarchy, the country was not on the world agenda. Individual NGOs and NGO networks, which now exist in considerable numbers, worked hard to publicize Somalia's plight. Media personnel were encouraged to visit Somalia and were facilitated in every way. Once interest is nurtured to a certain point, it snowballs, feeding on itself.

Politicians and governments were lobbied at the same time as the public. As the wave of public concern for Somalia grew, so too did politician's awareness. Many, somewhat belatedly, showed an interest. In major disasters and conflict situations, the intervention of governments is critical in addressing the large-scale needs. Involving governments is a role NGOs can play. NGOs can blaze an action trail on the ground, but their resources, even when augmented by bilateral and multilateral inputs, cannot cope with disasters on a grand scale. The sooner governments become openly interested, the better.

Since the mid-nineties donor governments have shown preference for local or national organizations over international NGOs as operational partners in the distribution of aid. International donors, notably Britain, the United States and the European Union, have strengthened their field offices in tandem with this policy shift. International NGOs that had expanded through the eighties on the strength of government funding have sometimes found themselves with spare capacity. Some have retrenched. Many have seriously reviewed their strategies. Increasingly they, like the bilateral donors, are entering into partnerships with local or national groups in their countries of operation. While governments in the somewhat more stable developing countries can lay down stringent conditions for the aid donors, and aid donors can find seemingly suitable operational partners in these countries, there are many poor countries that cannot afford this stance where local partners are not available.

In most developing countries, when a major disaster strikes or there is a major population upheaval because of conflict, it is unlikely that services adequate in peacetime will be able to cope. The scope and need for international NGOs in these circumstances continues to be enormous. At such times recipient governments are open to offers of assistance, and their bilateral donors are glad to support international NGOs. Somalia was a recent example of this and was followed by Angola, Rwanda, Zaire; in 1998, North Korea and Burundi opened their borders to international NGOs.

The experience of Concern in the Rwandan and central African upheaval from 1994 serves to illustrate much of the foregoing. Concern responded to the mass exodus of refugees from Rwanda after the 1994 genocide and became operational in Tanzania, Zaire and Burundi. None of these countries had the capacity to deal unaided with the sudden inflow of hundreds of thousands of refugees. The genocide and the conflict had also shattered the coping capacity within Rwanda. The new Rwandan government guardedly welcomed international NGO involvement, and Concern established an operation in Rwanda that rapidly expanded through 1997, especially as masses of refugees returned. Rwanda, a member of the new and more independent political bloc that I mentioned earlier, and having Eritrean advisors working with its government, has exerted increasing controls on international NGOs. Donor governments, too, have been encouraging more local participation. For example, in dealing with a 1998 funding application, USAID/OFDA have stressed the importance of local capacity building. While the Concern involvement is still critical in Rwanda, it is decreasing. At the same time, in 1998, the Concern role in Burundi is increasing as crisis again mounts in that country.

BILATERALS IN SOMALIA

The slowness of governments in responding to nonstrategic tragedies was illustrated in Somalia. In August 1992, Ireland's David Andrews became the first foreign minister to visit famine-ravished Somalia. He went at the invitation of NGOs and was shocked into action by what he saw. He immediately contacted all European Community foreign ministers and the UN. The British, the Dutch and the Germans responded immediately with increased aid. The U.S. initiative followed shortly thereafter. Also at this time Boutros Boutros-Ghali, Secretary-General of the United Nations, ruffled many feathers by accusing the world community of neglecting the poor man's plight in Africa while paying great attention to the rich man's war in former Yugoslavia.

Some governments, notably the British, had been supportive of NGOs before, but it was only when other governments became openly involved that things began to move. For many, however, it was too late. It should be remembered that the tragedy of Somalia was enacted against the backdrop of world leaders gathered in Rio de Janeiro for the United Nations World Environmental Conference. The international chorus singing about a better world order in Rio was sadly out of tune with and seemingly unaware of the suffering in Somalia.

Funding relationships between donor governments and NGOs are highly important and useful to both parties in the delivery of services in disasters. Acting through NGOs enables donor governments to follow their consciences in transferring resources, even if they have grave reservations about the local government and do not wish to support it. They can bypass (to an extent) governments of which they disapprove and reach the "deserving poor."

For all kinds of reasons, governments may be less generous to some recipient countries than to others. There can be very definite political discrimination in the distribution of aid. This was particularly so during the Cold War. Ethiopia and Cambodia were ruled out by many Western countries for development aid. Now, with stress on the human-rights record of the recipient country, Sudan is very prominent on the negative listing. This criterion is, however, applied rather selectively. The tyrant Siad Barre was supported in Somalia for strategic reasons. If a clean human-rights record were made an essential criterion for receiving aid, there would be a very short recipient list.

Humanitarian aid, however, is treated differently from so-called development aid by donors. There are vastly less self-interest and fewer hidden political agendas attached. Donor governments may channel such aid through NGOs to movements they do not officially recognize as having legal status while they continue to recognize the de facto government. Eritrea and Tigre within Mengistu's Ethiopia are good examples of this.

THE MULTILATERAL ORGANIZATIONS

Despite their shortcomings, the multilaterals, especially the UN specialized agencies and the EC, are close and supportive forces for the NGOs in Third-World activities. In normal operating circumstances they are geared to longer-term work, and they can be slow off the mark in disaster situations. Many field offices become comfortable and complacent. Like many others—bilaterals and NGOs included—they are loath to move from development to relief or emergency work.

There are two dangers in analyzing the performance of any of the actors on the stage in disaster situations. One is to flail out and condemn the people on the ground doing the work, which is a bit like shooting the messenger. The other danger is of closing ranks and covering up—sweeping the death statistics under the carpet. An agency's operations are only as good as they are allowed to be by those who direct them. Operatives of UN agencies tend to be smothered by bureaucratic requirements; their flexibility is stifled; they cannot indulge the kind of gut reactions that are necessary to save lives in disasters.

NGOs too, in growing and handling very large budgets, can become very high-handed and excessively bureaucratic. As they grow, they tend to lose their flexibility and spontaneity. They become more and more like the multilateral and bilateral agencies that they criticize. They should learn from what happened to the bigger actors in Somalia. A permanent UN coordinating agency with the muscle to be effective is certainly needed. This body should include teams that can be deployed to disaster situations.

One of the greatest tragedies of disaster situations is the lack of experienced workers. The sight of a new generation sadly reinventing the wheel is common when disasters strike.

LOCAL RELIEF STRUCTURES

Normally, national and local government must be the principal actors in disaster situations. There are exceptions such as Somalia, where there was literally no government through 1992. In most disaster situations there is some developed services structure. While some such structures are quite sophisticated, in most countries in the Third World, health and humanitarian services are altogether inadequate even in normal times. There is no way they can cope alone with the massively expanded demands that arise in a major disaster. Neither is it likely that they will have the capacity to utilize quickly and effectively the resources handed over to them. Local governments are very unlikely to accept this reality. They are generally, and understandably, slow to admit to any weakness.

Host governments should be respected. Unfortunately there may come a point at which, for humanitarian reasons, government and government regulations should be circumvented. It is important to consider the role of local NGOs that are funded by international donors. There has been a proliferation of nongovernmental organizations in developing countries because of the development of foreign aid during the last 20 to 30 years. These organizations depend for their existence on being part of the delivery of international aid within their own countries. For the most part, unlike the international NGOs, they do not raise funds by soliciting donations for their work within their own countries.

Many international NGOs have devoted considerable effort to fostering the growth of local NGOs. Quite often the local NGOs were set up as partners linked to the principal. This has particularly been the case with confessional NGOs. Parent churches that had earlier developed local counterpart churches have formed development sections for the transfer of material aid to developing countries. They have supported local churches in developing parallel recipient aid sections.

Besides the confessional NGOs linked to churches, purely secular NGOs dependent on international funding have emerged. Large amounts of international aid, sometimes amounting to millions of dollars annually, have been channeled through them. Some of these NGOs are highly sophisticated and operate on a grand scale. However, as with the international NGOs, they are vulnerable to the hazards of growth.

Many developing countries afford a poor climate for the development of local NGOs, especially for NGOs with international linkages. Few developing countries have real democratic governments. Many are under military rule or are governed by a one-party system. NGOs are unlikely to enjoy a great deal of freedom. There is a desperate desire on the part of some international NGOs, shared by theorists and increasingly by major funders, to demonstrate a high level of local NGO participation in the delivery of aid. The international development literature portrays a very inflated image of local NGOs. The freedom of speech and action that is enjoyed by NGOs in Western democracies is presumed to obtain in developing countries; however, freedom of action and association is very limited in many Third-World countries. The local NGOs that can maintain strong international links stand the best chance of surviving. The reality is that there is no great body of independent and genuinely local NGOs in the Third World. They will undoubtedly play an ever-greater role in long-term development. However, they are unlikely to be major players in disaster and conflict situations in the foreseeable future.

The development of national NGOs in the developing countries will have a major bearing on the future role of the international NGOs. They will still have a role, but a lessening one within the more stable and democratic developing countries. The local NGOs, as the preferred partners of donor governments and being more acceptable to their own governments, will assume an ever greater role on the international aid stage in these countries. Very many developing countries, especially in Africa, do not provide the environment for the development of strong local NGOs. In these countries there will, for many years to come, be room for a very significant international NGO input in development as well as at times of natural disasters.

In times of conflict, of major population upheavals and refugee movements, the international donor community will for the foreseeable future continue to depend on the international NGOs to provide much of the last link in the chain of response. The private donors in Western countries are the most likely to continue to entrust their giving to the international NGOs. The personalized response of caring individuals to world poverty and disaster needs will continue to seek a channel other than official government channels. The international NGOs will also continue to be a conduit for some of the official aid from their own countries.

In a world where 1.3 billion people survive on the equivalent of less than a dollar a day, where nearly a billion are illiterate, some 840 million go hungry or face food insecurity and nearly a third of the people in the least-developed countries—most of them in sub-Saharan Africa—are not expected to survive to the age of 40, the need for NGOs is greater than ever. They are adapting and adjusting to circumstances. This they must continue to do. They must not question their relevance.

From Cyclones to Sustainable Development

Fazle H. Abed

INTRODUCTION

Bangladesh celebrated the silver jubilee of its independence in 1996. Unfortunately, political independence has not had the desired effect on the development of its impoverished population. Table 17.1 gives selected development indicators for Bangladesh compared to the South Asian region, developing countries and the developed countries. It is apparent that much remains to be done to improve the condition of the people of the country.

Yet Bangladesh has made impressive progress in some important sectors. Infant mortality has been reduced. The total fertility rate has declined from more than six per woman in the 1970s to about three in the mid-1990s, with a spectacular increase in contraceptive prevalence rate to nearly 50 percent. The immunization coverage has moved up to about 70 percent from 2 percent in the mid-1980s. As the South Asian Human Development Report concludes, "what is creditable is that this progress has been achieved despite a series of devastating floods, devastating cyclones and unprecedented tidal waves."[1]

Bangladesh does not appear very often in international news coverage. But when it does, it usually captures world headlines because of some environmental or natural disaster. In reporting the stories of tragedy, human misery and suffering that befall our country, the media do not always tell the whole story. We hardly ever come across reports of the many successes that take place in Bangladesh, or of the indomitable courage and resoluteness that its people show in facing difficult odds. While international NGOs can offer vital assistance during humanitarian crises, the primary obligation must fall on a nation's own people. Many do

Table 17.1: Selected Development Indicators: Bangladesh Compared to Others

Development Indicators	Bangladesh	South Asia	Developing Countries	Developed Countries
Life expectancy (years)	56	61	62	74
Adult literacy (% 15+)	37	48	69	98
Years of schooling	2.0	2.4	3.9	n/a
Under-five mortality rate	117	120	101	18
GNP per capita (US$)	220	309	970	16,394
Real GDP per capita (PPP$)	1,290	1,370	2,696	15,136
Expenditure on education (as percentage of GNP)	2.3	3.4	3.9	5.4
Expenditure on health (as percentage of GNP)	1.4	1.4	2.0	n/a
Military expenditure (as percentage of GDP)	1.5	3.8	4.4	3.1
Military/social spending ratio	41	72	60	33

Source: Haq, 1998.

not appreciate the role of local NGOs because the world media usually focus on tales of charity performed by their own citizens. This provides an unbalanced picture. This chapter shows how a nongovernmental organization deals with the sudden violent disaster caused by cyclones that strike our coastal areas, and offers an account of how a large segment of the Bangladeshi people is fighting a deliberate battle to improve the condition of their lives.

COPING WITH CYCLONES

The Bay of Bengal is a natural breeding place for tropical cyclones. Of all the earth's tropical cyclones, 10 percent are formed here. The bay's geography—its tropical location, the shape of the landmass that forms Bangladesh, the Himalayas lying to the north, and the funnel-shaped coastline touching the bay—makes it susceptible to such disasters. On average, five tropical storms are formed every year in the bay; half of them turn into cyclones, and at least one cyclone every two years gathers strength and takes a path that strikes Bangladesh.

The land that is now called Bangladesh has historically been prey to cyclones. The first recorded cyclone hit a village in Chittagong during the sixteenth century, killing a large number of people and destroying all the buildings except a temple.[2] The cyclone of June 1775 destroyed all but five buildings in a Chittagong town. A description of a cyclone in 1876 is available from the account of a British civil servant:

31st October was a night of the full moon. Sea level was naturally higher than usual high tide levels. Severe wind was blowing from 10 PM to 3 AM and it prevented the normal discharge of Meghna river into the bay. By 8 AM on 1st November the wind grew fiercer and hit the coastal area of Chittagong, Feni, Laxmipur, Bhola, Patuakhali, Barisal, Jhalakati and Khulna Districts. The accompanying tidal surge ranged from 18.29 to 9.14 meters in various places. It hit Chittagong with a surge 3.66 meters high. 12,000 people died in Chittagong due to this cyclone. An epidemic that followed the tidal bore killed 14,778 persons. In other affected areas 100,000 people died of the cyclone and the tidal surge, and the subsequent epidemics took a toll of 200,000 people. In Chittagong area alone more than 60,000 boats and ships were sunk, battered or destroyed by the cyclone.[3]

Over a 30-year period (1965 to and 1991), 35 severe cyclones hit the coastal belt of Bangladesh. The 1970 cyclone in which 500,000 people perished was the most disastrous in terms of human losses. But much was learned from that terrible event.

The Cyclone of April 1991

On the night of April 29 to 30, 1991, the coastal areas of Bangladesh were struck by a severe cyclone accompanied by a tidal surge from the bay of Bengal. Nearly 5 million people in 8 of 64 districts were affected. In terms of human losses, this cyclone was the worst since the cyclone of 1970. According to government estimates, more than 130,000 people perished, and property worth $2.4 billion, equivalent to the national annual development expenditures for two years, was destroyed.

Although the wind speed and the height of the tidal surge were similar in the cyclones of 1970 and 1991, the latter one caused far fewer casualties. Several reasons may explain this. Following the cyclones of the early 1960s, the government constructed a number of concrete buildings to serve as cyclone shelters. A total of 60 double-story coastal community centers and 40 single-story subcoastal community centers were constructed. This was clearly not enough, and the structures were not appropriately placed. Although the number of shelters available was insignificant compared to the need, they saved many lives. One study of the 1991 cyclone estimated that at least 20 percent more deaths would have occurred if these shelters had not been constructed.[4]

The cyclone warning system in Bangladesh had also undergone tremendous development since the cyclone of 1970. A tropical depression is first detected from the satellite network, and this information is then forwarded to the meteorological department, which tracks the cyclone and issues regular bulletins on its location and wind speed, and the areas it is likely to strike. These bulletins are circulated through the press, radio and television, and repeated frequently.[5]

The Bangladesh Red Crescent Society (BRCS) has more than 20,000 village-based volunteers, all located in coastal areas, who transmit the danger warnings to volunteers through its network of district and subdistrict control offices. The volunteers, in turn, alert people through megaphones and house-to-house contact, and encourage them to proceed to nearby shelters (if available) or safe places.

Finally, embankments have been constructed in most areas along the coastline to resist the initial thrust of the cyclone. Though the 1991 cyclone destroyed the embankments in many places, they were able to weaken the initial onslaught.

The nation rallied to provide succor and relief to the survivors. There were no major postcyclone disasters such as epidemics, disease or food shortages. In contrast to the situation of previous cyclones, related deaths occurred only during the storm and the surge, not in the postcyclone period. In most earlier cyclones, more people died in the aftermath from diseases than because of the actual impact of the cyclone.

The government response was obviously indispensable and was bolstered by primary and bilateral international aid. But the focus of this chapter is on the capacity of individual citizens to form private voluntary organizations and, thereby, control their destiny. The major local NGO is the Bangladesh Rural Advancement Committee (BRAC). The basic facts about BRAC can be seen in Table 17.2.

The NGO Response

The large NGO community maintained its tradition of quickly responding to a disaster situation. BRAC's response is one such example. After receiving the news from a radio broadcast that the coastal area was hit by a cyclone, BRAC went to Chittagong. Several teams of BRAC workers were already in the area for an immunization program, and we mobilized them for relief work. A central relief control office was set up in Chittagong with a senior director of BRAC as its coordinator. We provided relief to nearly 200,000 cyclone-affected people. The rehabilitation phase concentrated on the continued supply of food, clothing, medical and housing assistance, as well as creating jobs to rehabilitate the people in their own environment and situation. In one of the subdistricts, with a population of 100,000, BRAC later initiated a long-term development project for the poor that included education, health, institution-building

Table 17.2: Some Basic Facts about BRAC (December 1997)

Full-time staff	18,000
Part-time functionaries	34,000
Participants in credit program	2.2 million (95% women)
Amount of loans disbursed to the poor	US$ 500 million
Repayment rate	98%
Amount saved by the poor	US$40 million
Villages with BRAC programs	50,000
Total primary schools run by BRAC	34,000
Total pupils enrolled in primary school	1.2 million (70% girls)
Participants in health programs	25 million
Total BRAC budget (annual)	US$108 million
Number of districts with BRAC programs	64 (out of 64)

and poverty alleviation. This project also included constructing sixteen concrete structures that would be used as schools during normal times and as shelters during a cyclone.

NGOs did not stop at providing relief and rehabilitation services. Researchers were commissioned to study the epidemiology of cyclone deaths, people's perceptions about the warning system, the effectiveness of the cyclone shelters and the nutrition impact and morbidity effects of the cyclone.[6]

It was not only BRAC that was involved in this task. Almost all national-level NGOs participated, and coordination was provided by the Association of Development Agencies in Bangladesh, the central coordinating body of NGOs in the country. The coastal area was new to many of these organizations. NGO staff who had been working in the area provided orientation to their new colleagues.

The Bureau of NGO Affairs, a government body designated to oversee NGO interest in the government, was effective in facilitating emergency relief operations of the NGOs. Waiving its usual requirements, the Bureau allowed NGOs to work without receiving prior permission from the government.

The Aftereffects

The above discussion shows how Bangladesh faced the 1991 cyclone—a massive disaster by any proportion. Contrary to popular expectations, there was hardly any postcyclone disaster. There were no postcyclone deaths from epidemic or food shortage. The government and NGOs, with logistical support from within and outside the country, transported the required amount of foodstuffs to the affected areas. The distribution system was much better organized than before and very well coordinated. There were no reports of any major misappropriation of relief goods. Studies on postcyclone morbidity found little evidence of any major epidemics. The prevalence of diarrhea in children during the third week of June (the cyclone struck on April 29 to 30, 1991) was 10 percent, an expected figure for that time of year.[7]

Observations on the use of oral rehydration therapy (ORT) in the field were much more encouraging than survey reports in nonemergency situations. People's knowledge of ORT undoubtedly contributed to lower diarrhea mortality levels in the postcyclone period.

In Bangladesh more than 90 percent of the population have access to tube-well water. The cyclone and the tidal surge contaminated and damaged most of the tube wells. Because of the efforts made by the government, NGOs and the people, the tube wells were ready for use within a few days. Use of tube well water for drinking and washing utensils, in fact, increased during the postcyclone period. Children and women were seen walking long distances with pots to fetch water from tube wells not damaged by the cyclone. An international team studying the postcyclone water and sanitation sector was impressed by the functioning of the tube-well program and found that the tube-well water was free from coliforms.[4]

The reason Bangladesh managed so well can be traced to a number of developments, but a major one was the growth of the NGO sector. With their base at the grassroots level, enhanced management capacities, ability to act quickly and improved credibility among donors, local NGOs have proven to be an important and effective force. The slow but important efforts to strengthen the economic base of the rural poor by NGOs such as Grameen Bank and BRAC have resulted in the improved capacity of individual households to cope with natural disasters. The expansion of irrigation facilities led to increased agricultural production throughout the year. The diversification of the rural employment sector has created employment opportunities for the poor in nonfarm sectors. Poorer households are now better prepared to face and cope with a disaster situation.[9–11]

COPING WITH DIARRHEA: BRAC'S ORT PROGRAM

As in most other developing countries, diarrhea is an important cause of mortality and morbidity in Bangladesh.[12] It is a major factor in the low nutritional level of the population. Among children under five years of age, nearly a third of all deaths are due to this disease. Bangladesh is, incidentally, the country where oral rehydration therapy (ORT) was developed and perfected in the late 1960s. Little attempt was made, however, until the early 1980s to make this wonder therapy, which one medical journal called the most significant medical advance of this century, widely available to the people. BRAC identified diarrhea as a major health problem right from the start. Field-testing of ORT had shown its potential; also, work with ORT among Bangladeshi refugees in the Calcutta area during the 1971 Liberation War had shown what ORT could do in epidemic situations. All these considerations led BRAC to embark on a nationwide ORT program. The decision to undertake this large-scale program forced BRAC to choose carefully between distributing oral rehydration salt (ORS) packets and teaching mothers how to mix and use a homemade solution. Research at BRAC and International Centre for Diarrhoeal Disease Research, Bangladesh (ICDDR,B) had found that a pinch of salt and a fistful of unrefined sugar mixed in half a liter of water produced a solution with most of the qualities of the packets. BRAC had found that it was possible to teach village women how to make the solution and at the same time teach them a short, seven-point message about diarrhea prevention and treatment. Furthermore, BRAC felt strongly that even if sufficient quantities of ORS could be produced, packaged and marketed, poor people, particularly in remote areas, would not have either physical or economic access to it. Thus BRAC decided that its nationwide effort would focus on teaching mothers to make the solution it had developed. In the early months of 1979, BRAC started to work with 30,000 families at Sulla, the organization's first field project site. This became the testing ground for effective teaching methods and for working out the management and logistics necessary to scale up the program and maintain quality control. In early 1980, BRAC launched its nationwide effort to teach oral rehydration therapy to every women of the thirteen million village households in the country.

Backed by an experienced group of managers and a well-developed management information system, teams of female workers trained by BRAC went house to house, teaching village women how to make the solution properly and how to give it to their children. The teaching method and materials were carefully structured and based on an intelligent use of local belief systems; the teachers were recruited from villages in the same regions of the country where they worked. Under an incentive salary plan, they were paid according to the quality of their teaching. Monitoring teams followed them into villages two weeks later, interviewing a random sample of 5 percent of village women to find out how well they had understood and learned the messages, and collecting samples of solutions mixed by the women, which they sent to laboratories for testing of the electrolyte contents. A worker's pay was determined by how correctly the sampled mothers could prepare the solution and the number of messages they could recall spontaneously from the basic seven. Supervision of the teachers as they moved from village to village was strict but supportive. Teaching materials and training were modified and improved constantly. One month after the first 50,000 mothers had been trained, surveys found that although more than 90 percent displayed adequate message retention and mixing skills, the oral rehydration solution was used in only 5 percent of diarrheal episodes. Analysis of the situation revealed a major deficiency in the implementation strategy: the program had focused on women alone, but since men were important decision-makers in the family, it was difficult for the women to administer ORT without the concurrence of their husbands, their fathers or other men in the family. Accordingly, the program was modified to include male teachers whose job was to hold meetings and seminars with men in mosques, marketplaces and schools. The inclusion of men in the target group very quickly increased ORS use to 20 percent.

Anthropological research studies revealed further problems. In some parts of rural Bangladesh, people recognized four types of diarrhea, for which they had different names and treatments. Only one of these types— a severe, watery diarrhea—was known to the women by the word "diarrhea." Since the classification into four types had been unknown to the oral rehydration workers (ORWs), in the initial teaching they had used the Bangladeshi equivalent of the term "diarrhea." As a result, the mothers thought the solution was for that type only. In the early stages of the program, ORS was being used for 52 percent of that type of diarrhea, but not for the other types. This discovery led to a change in terminology and a major change in the seven points to remember.[13]

In November 1990, a decade after the nationwide ORT teaching effort began, BRAC completed teaching the therapy to the last of the thirteen million village households. ORT is now an accepted part of the treatment of diarrhea throughout the country; in fact, it is now becoming a part of the country's folk culture. A recent study of eleven- to twelve-year-old children's knowledge of important life skills found that 70 percent of participants knew how to prepare oral rehydration solution. Most of these children had not been born or had been very young at the time their mothers were taught about ORT by BRAC. Manifestation of BRAC's enduring work is also reflected regularly in the work of cartoonists or column writers in newspapers.

This ORT program provided several important lessons for Bangladesh, for BRAC, for donors and for health professionals. The program exploded the myth that poor village women cannot be taught basic health messages. It also dispelled the perception that NGOs are capable of only small, localized activities of little consequence nationally. Furthermore, it dispelled any notions that health programs are necessarily less effective if implemented on a large scale. It taught BRAC managers to think nationally and inspired confidence to "go to scale" in other programs. Finally, the program confirmed the potential of women workers to convey useful health information and change health behavior.

DEMYSTIFYING THE TREATMENT OF TUBERCULOSIS

Tuberculosis (TB) remains a global public health problem. The major challenge of any TB control program is case-finding and compliance of treatment. The treatment is rather long (six to twelve months) and as such, the compliance is low. Recognizing the depth of the problem, both in terms of disease prevalence and treatment challenges, BRAC began a community-based tuberculosis control program in 1984. A national survey carried out in 1987 and 1988 found 0.87 percent sputum-positive cases in the population fifteen years old and over; men were infected twice as often as women, and the problem was more acute in urban areas (see Table 17.3).

Although the national government, with assistance from the World Bank and bilateral aid, is responsible for treatment programs, tuberculosis diagnosis and control is politically a low-priority program. It is in this area that BRAC focuses its attention.

The core of BRAC poverty-alleviation programs at the village level is the women's groups, with membership from the poorest households. In each group a woman is trained as a community health worker who treats

Table 17.3: Tuberculosis in Adults Fifteen Years and Over As Determined by the National Prevalence Survey on Tuberculosis in Bangladesh (1987–1988)

Population Groups	Percent Sputum-Positive
Total	0.87
Male	1.08
Female	0.60
Rural	0.80
Urban	1.61

selected common illnesses in the village. She does not receive any salary but receives a small markup on the sale of selected essential drugs. As a member of the village organization, she also receives loans for gainful income-generating activities. These are mostly illiterate women with an average age of about 35 years. Each worker covers about 200 households and is supervised by BRAC field staff. BRAC also trained these women in TB treatment. They distribute information about tuberculosis to the community, follow up individuals with chronic cough of four weeks' duration or longer, and collect two early-morning sputum samples. These samples are examined microscopically for acid-fast bacilli (AFB) in a local BRAC laboratory. The national program also assists in quality control of diagnostic procedures. Positive patients are contacted by their community health worker and asked to register for treatment.

Patients willing to participate are asked to pay a deposit of 200 *taka* (about US$5), equivalent to about five days' wages, and sign a written agreement as an incentive to complete the full course of treatment. Drugs are provided free to BRAC by the National Tuberculosis Control Program and at no cost to the patients. At the end of treatment, 100 *taka* is returned to the patient and the rest is given to the community health worker for her work. If the patient is too poor to pay the deposit, his or her village organization or other community members will usually pay. The community health worker receives 25 *taka* for each new or relapsed positive patient whom she identifies. If the patient does not complete the treatment course, the whole deposit in forfeited; the community health worker gets her share of the deposit, but the remainder is retained by BRAC.

The first phase of the BRAC tuberculosis program covered 220,000 people. Results from the pilot program, which used a standard twelve-month treatment regimen, suggested that about two thirds of patients completed the full course. Eighty-one percent completed the full twelve-month course, and in 85 percent of these patients, the sputum became AFB-negative by the start of the third month (see Table 17.4). Another program studied all patients on an eight-month regimen; more than 85 percent of new cases and 90 percent of relapsed patients were AFB-negative and were deemed to be cured at the end of the eight-month regimen (see Table 17.5).

POVERTY ALLEVIATION: A HOLISTIC APPROACH

The twin objectives of BRAC are poverty alleviation and empowerment of the poor. BRAC works particularly with the women from poorer families whose lives are dominated by extreme poverty, illiteracy, disease and

Table 17.4: Treatment Outcomes for AFB-positive Patients Treated with Twelve-Month Regimen (Phase Two)

Outcome	Number of Cases (n = 3,497)
Cured/completed*	2,833 (81.0)
Died	336 (9.6)
Failed treatment	51 (1.6)
Defaulted	109 (2.1)
Migrated/referred/transferred	168 (4.8)

* Cured—negative sputum at month 13; samples not available at month 13 for 402 patients who were, therefore, classified as completed.
Source: Chowdhury et al., 1997.

malnutrition. Poverty is looked at in a holistic sense. Poverty is not only a lack of income or employment but a complex syndrome that is manifested in many different ways. BRAC works for the development of institutions of the poor, conscientization and awareness building, savings mobilization, children's education, health, gender equity, training and so on. Central to all these is an "enabling environment" in which the poor can participate in their own development and are able to perform to their fullest potentials. All of BRAC's efforts are geared to creating such an environment.

The Process of Social Mobilization

The process of social mobilization in a village starts with the identification of the poor belonging to BRAC's defined target group.

Table 17.5: Treatment Outcomes for AFB-positive Patients Treated with Eight-Month Regimen (Phase Three)

	Number of cases (n = 1741)		
Outcome	New (n = 1,525)	Retreatment (n = 216)	Total (n = 1,741)
Cured	2,301 (85.3)	195 (90.3)	1,496 (85.9)
Completed	1 (0.1)	2 (0.9)	3 (0.3)
Died	226 (8.2)	3 (3.2)	133 (7.6)
Failure	43 (2.8)	8 (3.7)	51 (2.9)
Defaulted	36 (2.4)	4 (1.9)	40 (2.3)
Migrated/referred/ transferred	23 (1.2)	–	18 (1.0)

Source: Chowdhury et al., 1997.

An institution of the poor, called a village organization or VO, is formed as soon as an adequate number of individuals show definite interest. Two activities start simultaneously: a conscientization program, and compulsory savings. Through the conscientization program, the women are made aware of the society around them. They analyze the reasons for the existing exploitative socioeconomic and political system and what they could do to change it in their favor. A formal course on Human Rights and Legal Education (HRLE) is provided to the members. Under savings, the members participate in compulsory saving of at least 2 *taka* per week. Savings is considered by BRAC and group members as an old-age security.

Within a month of formation, VO members are allowed to apply for loans from BRAC. Three types of credit are disbursed. The members may request credit for any (a) traditional activity such as rural trading, transport (boat and rickshaw) and rice processing, or (b) nontraditional (for women) activity such as a grocery store or a rural restaurant, or a technology-based activity such as high-yielding varieties (HYV) of poultry, sericulture or mechanized irrigation; they can also request for (c) housing loans. While the interest on a housing loan is 10 percent, it is 15 percent for the other types. The repayment rate is 98 percent. Consciousness on the part of the members, peer-group pressure and BRAC staff supervision are the important reasons for this impressive outcome.

BRAC also provides skill-training to VO members. An important feature of the poverty-alleviation activities is that they try to link the poor women with the market. For example, in the case of the poultry program, BRAC starts with providing training to women on how to rear HYV chickens. Loans are given for operating low-cost hatcheries to supply day-old chicks to other village women. The women then rear these until they start laying eggs. The eggs are then sold to the hatchery as well as to consumers. One of the major problems of poultry rearing in Bangladesh is high mortality of the birds. The government livestock department keeps stocks of vaccines, but these are little used. What BRAC has done in this backward and forward linkage is to train a VO member on how to vaccinate poultry and link her to the local livestock department of the government that supplies vaccines. The woman receives the vaccine and then inoculates chickens in her own village for a small fee. This way the woman increases her own income and, at the same time, ensures survival of her neighbors' chickens. Similar backward and forward linkages have also been successfully established for other programs such as sericulture, in which case BRAC also has been able to establish a marketing outlet for the producers through a chain of stores called Aarong.

SALIENT FEATURES OF BRAC PROGRAMS

Promotion of Women in the Development Process

BRAC has been promoting a new culture in the development field with women in the forefront of all activities. Most of the recipients of credit are women; 70 percent of students and 80 percent of the teachers of non-financial enterprises (NFPE) schools are female; and health and poultry workers are also all women. Breaking the barriers of a predominantly conservative traditional Muslim society, BRAC has even succeeded in training female workers to use motorbikes in performing their duties. Women are running rural restaurants, vaccinating chicks, treating patients, doing carpentry or teaching and studying in schools, traditionally all activities falling in the male domain.

Infusion of Technology

The fullest potential of microcredit to improve the lives of the poor on a sustainable basis has been offset by a lack of concomitant promotion of technology. Much of such credit has been used for traditional activities, and not enough has been done to include technology along with it. The profit made from traditional activities is not always substantial—not enough to generate an investible surplus. In the case of BRAC, 70 percent of its credit portfolio is occupied by traditional activities. The need for technological infusion is recognized, and BRAC has been making concerted efforts toward this. The Rural Enterprise Project has been working since the mid-1980s to innovate and test possible areas of technology use in BRAC-sponsored income-generating activities of the poor. Examples in this respect are: HYV bird, vaccination, hatchery and chick-rearing units in poultry, artificial insemination in livestock, deep tube-well irrigation in crop production, improved varieties of mulberry trees, quality production of cocoons and modern reeling facilities. About 30 percent of the existing credit portfolio is on these kinds of technology-oriented/intensive activities.

Scaling Up

Small is beautiful but big is necessary. The seeds of change that have been sown need to be multiplied to universalize the benefits and also for the sake of greater impact and sustainability. The following explains why BRAC continued to exist after completion of its initial relief objectives:

> When BRAC was started in 1972 we thought that it would probably be needed for two to three years, by which time the national government

would consolidate and take control of the situation and the people would start benefitting from independence. But as time passed, such a contention appeared to be premature. After 16 years, we feel that we have not yet outlived our utility and need to do more and more.[16]

The notion that NGOs should restrict themselves to small-scale pilot projects and leave it to the government to replicate their more successful experiments is challenged by BRAC. Each project, whether government or NGO, has its own style of implementation, and the pilot projects draw heavily on the organization's own culture and strategies. Replication is best done by the organization concerned, given that it has the necessary capability, resources and willingness to do it. BRAC believes that its successful experiments can best be replicated by itself.

Links with the Public Sector and Other NGOs

BRAC works closely with the government. How the poultry program of BRAC is linked with the public sector has already been discussed above. BRAC also works with the government in health and has been providing assistance in social mobilization for the Expanded Program on Immunization (EPI) and the family planning programs.

BRAC also works closely with other NGOs. In education, BRAC assists more than 230 small local NGOs in running nonformal primary schools for children. It also worked with eight other medium-sized NGOs in developing their management information systems (MIS). BRAC believes in pluralism and maintains that all organizations, small or large, must have the right and freedom to work for the good of the poor according to their own philosophy and strategy.

Part III

SOLUTIONS AND FUTURE OPTIONS

In this final section, four international humanitarian workers look to the future, offering new approaches based on lessons learned, often from their own past failures. In Chapter 18, Kevin M. Cahill considers the growing realization that humanitarian assistance is not a field for amateurs; it is both obvious and essential that all who presume to offer help in crises first demonstrate evidence of their qualification by study of an accepted basic training course. Shepard Forman addresses the critical need to develop a more stable financial base for international aid efforts in Chapter 19. Larry Minear illuminates some of the difficulties in achieving effective coordination in Chapter 20. Finally, in Chapter 21, former United States Secretary of State Cyrus Vance invites a new generation to join in the struggle in the ever-evolving field of international humanitarian affairs.

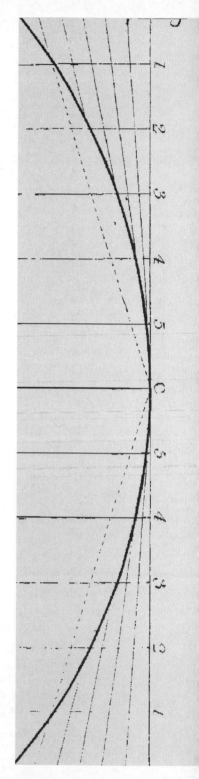

TRAINING FOR HUMANITARIAN ASSISTANCE

18

Kevin M. Cahill, M.D.

International humanitarian-assistance work is a professional discipline influenced, appropriately, as are the professions of medicine or nursing, by the loftiest ideals of civilized society. To help one's fellow man by alleviating hunger and pain, giving succor to the starving and homeless, uniting destroyed families and recreating destroyed societies is the noble goal of humanitarian assistance. But the sheer scope and extent of the human calamities that follow conflicts and disasters make most individual efforts in such situations touching but ineffectual. Unless humanitarian assistance is carefully planned, coordinated and delivered, with understanding and sensitivity, it often produces more harm and pain to individual victims and fragile communities; it also endangers and frustrates the very donors who wish to help.

One of the fundamental reasons for so much failure in the attempt to do good is a lack of training in the fundamentals of humanitarian assistance. Goodwill, or the desire to share in human tragedy, is simply not an adequate foundation. If timely and effective help is to be delivered, all participants in these great recurrent global dramas must develop a common language, and this depends on a universally accepted basic standard of training.

Assistance workers must understand how complex humanitarian crises develop, and what the potential roles and required skills are, when, as strangers, they become involved in traumatized communities where the normal supportive services of society have collapsed and entire populations have become vulnerable dependents. Those who presume to offer help in such situations, who accept the privilege of providing lifesaving aid, must be taught to appreciate the early-warning signs of impending disasters so that prevention as well as reaction becomes part of their approach. They must learn from previous catastrophes how to devise the most efficient and rapid response for each challenge; no two humanitarian crises are identical, and one must be flexible in developing an operational plan.

There are basic tenets, however, common to all disaster relief efforts, and these must be learned or we will continue to repeat the errors of the past. One must learn to be vigilant against the known dangers of inappropriate aid, to preserve, even in the midst of chaos, an equanimity, a humility and respect that are the hallmarks of true professionals in every discipline. Humanitarian workers must learn to develop—and utilize— accurate tools to measure the extent of needs and to evaluate the efficacy of aid programs. Humanitarian-assistance workers must also learn to use a new, universally accepted vocabulary so they can coordinate their efforts with other international agencies and especially with local authorities and leaders. They must properly plan programs so they can eventually extricate themselves and their support without adding insult to existing injury.

Many factors mandate a change in the way humanitarian-assistance workers should be trained. International relief efforts are now "big business" with profound diplomatic, military, political and economic implications. In 1996, $7 billion was spent on humanitarian assistance. Yet there were no accepted training programs to certify the multiple actors in this critical discipline.

The International Diploma in Humanitarian Assistance (IDHA) is a product of the loss of innocence that followed the Somalia debacle in the early 1990s. It reflects a new and profound appreciation of the dangers aid workers face and can create. My interest in the levels of training offered by different agencies was sharpened when I was asked to care for a young woman who had just been raped in Somalia in 1992. She had been sent into anarchy, armed with a pleasant two-day orientation program, and was led to believe that, somehow, if she caressed the starving babies, the problems of Somalia would be solved. No one told her that when societies collapse, people rob and murder—and rape. As I looked further I discovered that even the largest international aid organizations offered mostly in-house courses of differing durations and quality. None offered a university diploma that could become part of a person's educational resumé, a very useful credential as one moves on, changing jobs. The International Diploma in Humanitarian Assistance offered by the Center for International Health and Cooperation (CIHC) and Hunter College at the City University of New York, in partnership with the Royal College of Surgeons in Ireland, fills that essential need.

Young volunteers, as well as seasoned professionals, now frequently move from local voluntary organizations to national governmental agencies, to the international divisions of the United Nations, and back and forth. This movement of skills and personnel between organizations is both desirable and inevitable. While each organization, understandably, has its own unique ideology, agenda, goals and limitations, the movement of personnel promotes cross-fertilization and should be encouraged.

However, this very movement of personnel makes it imperative that there be a common foundation—an acceptable basic minimum standard of training. Maybe there was a time when two-day orientation courses for humanitarian volunteers were sufficient, but that surely is no longer true. There is a role for year-long master's degree training courses for the committed professional, but such programs are hardly suitable for preparing large numbers of people urgently needed to serve in humanitarian crises, particularly in conflicts and disasters. Just as one would not consider sending a soldier into battle without a period of basic military training—without instruction in the use of weapons and the essential structure of a combat corps—so also one must provide—and should insist upon—an adequate level of preparedness before permitting any involvement in complex humanitarian emergencies.

The Center for International Health and Cooperation (CIHC) has developed a widely accepted curriculum that offers the necessary practical, thorough grounding in the fundamentals required for international humanitarian assistance. The International Diploma in Humanitarian Assistance course was developed after extensive consultation with colleagues from leading agencies involved in humanitarian assistance—the United Nations, the International Federation of the Red Cross and the International Committee of the Red Cross, governmental and nongovernmental voluntary organizations, and university analysts.

An indispensable ingredient in making the IDHA program unique was the involvement of academia. It was critical that prestigious universities acknowledge practical humanitarian assistance training as a legitimate scholarly discipline worthy of an international diploma. Even the best in-house courses in the best organizations could not confer a university diploma, one that could be utilized in formal resumés and curriculum vitae by humanitarian workers seeking positions throughout their careers. The recognition by major universities demonstrates that the IDHA training syllabus satisfies accepted international standards. A careful, thoughtful curriculum, based on solid field experience as well as academic analyses and research studies, should now replace the vague, emotion-laden ideological approach that characterized so many previous programs.

Humanitarian crises seem to cry out for an immediate response. The affected communities have obvious basic needs that must be met. The vulnerability of internally displaced persons is often greater than that of cross-border refugees, particularly if the local government is hostile to the displaced. The acute emergency frequently becomes a chronic situation and thus requires a response that is capable of evolving from lifesaving aid to rehabilitation and development.

Humanitarian crises can often be predicted and may be preventable or their impact minimized with appropriate foresight and planning. Social, cultural, political and economic forces influence crises, and one must be taught to define these and other critical factors, such as the local levels of health education and existing social service traditions. Health concerns in humanitarian crisis situations are not limited to the control of communicable diseases, the provision of food and water, the treatment of malnutrition and other medical and surgical problems. One must also be aware of the severe psychological stresses that follow torture, rape and displacement from the security of family and neighborhood. Thus a course designed to prepare for an appropriate "humanitarian response" must have its foundation in a multidisciplinary approach involving and integrating personnel from a variety of backgrounds, including health, logistics, management, engineering, agriculture, communications, education, conflict resolution, advocacy, international law, economics, politics and diplomacy.

The IDHA course is purposefully intensive. It was constructed to mimic a humanitarian crisis, with long days of hard work and a forced intimacy of shared meals and dormitory accommodations. Twelve hours a day, six days a week for a full month, candidates participate in seminars and meetings, absorbing the thoughts and experiences of an expert faculty. All faculty in the IDHA programs have had extensive field experience in conflicts or disasters. Theory must be welded with experience if one is to train people for real crises. A remarkable cadre of men and women who have lived through the hells of Somalia and Rwanda, of Liberia, Bosnia and Chechnya joined in teaching the initial courses.

In complex humanitarian emergencies it is often difficult to identify any single paramount feature; transport, housing, sanitation and security are as essential, for example, in a health program as are the more easily understood efforts toward diagnosis, immunization and therapy. Throughout, the IDHA course fosters an appreciation of the myriad facets in a humanitarian crises. The program enables those who intend to provide help to do so with respect for the basic rights and dignity of those affected by such crises. The course and the diploma promote cooperation and dialogue among the critical triad—the international, governmental and nongovernmental agencies—on which international humanitarian assistance depends.

The IDHA program is rooted in an academic structure that can establish and maintain standards, support research, evaluate interventions and identify examples of good practice. By learning the hard lessons of a painful past, one will be better equipped, it is hoped, to develop new methods by which humanitarian crises may be anticipated and even prevented. The evolving discipline of humanitarian assistance must develop an essential institutional memory that should allow operating agencies to avoid the most egregious failures and errors of earlier programs.

The curriculum approaches humanitarian assistance by devoting the first week to disaster preparedness, identifying those economic and political forces that make nations vulnerable to collapse. The second week considers the emergency response. The third week is spent defining the steps necessary to rehabilitate fractured societies. In the fourth week, candidates reflect on exit strategies and, where possible, on how to assure the critical transition from emergency relief to local development. Finally, the candidates are challenged by various forms of assessment to satisfy academic criteria for a university diploma.

Throughout the course there is an emphasis on specificity—on exact definitions, methods of quantification and assessment, exact measurement of effectiveness—for without these tools only words and emotions prevail. It is easy to stress the need for training, but it is equally essential to recognize the obstacles to learning, the inherent prejudices of institutions and individuals even in times of great humanitarian need. Lectures and seminars on politics—or lack of political will—on basic human rights, ethical issues and codes of conduct are integral parts of the humanitarian puzzle, and they must be addressed and debated in an academic experience. Regardless of the candidate's background or aspirations, the IDHA curriculum prepares humanitarian-assistance workers to understand how political, climatic and agricultural forces influence a crisis, and how logistics and supplies are essential elements in every undertaking.

It is of little benefit partially to immunize a vulnerable population against a deadly disease. Adequate supplies, appropriate and thorough planning and efficient application are obviously a better approach than feeble, haphazard attempts to quell a crisis. Throughout the course, there is an emphasis on those most affected in humanitarian crises—on children, too often the victims of preventable disease, too often lost or orphaned, frequently traumatized by seeing the violent deaths of family, even being forced themselves into conflict. Lecturers train the IDHA candidates in how best to help reunite families lost in a massive flood of refugees and how to help victims come to terms with the stress of national or clan collapse, personal injury and family loss.

The curriculum is embracive, recognizing, for example, the important role and limitations of the military during a humanitarian crisis. There is a continuous effort to promote coordination among the multiple actors that influence a humanitarian crisis. Individuals and organizations, each with their own viewpoints, interests and even selfish agendas, must be encouraged or even forced to cooperate if overwhelming problems are ever to be resolved. The problem of how to assure funding for humanitarian efforts, how to eliminate the wasteful and demeaning "begging bowl" approach for each crisis and how to divide a finite fiscal pie so that all parts of the humanitarian triad can continue to contribute are essential topics for discussion. The role of the media—for good or for ill—is also studied. In Rwanda and the former Yugoslavia, for example, the perverse use of the radio helped promote and even justify horrible genocidal acts. Yet without media attention—the "CNN factor"—international leaders can and do conveniently ignore obvious famine and oppression.

The IDHA course content (see Appendix I) indicates the complexity of international charity. The syllabus reflects a profound appreciation of the dangers aid workers face and can create, if they are poorly prepared for the multiple challenges they will inevitably face. The IDHA program is designed for international assistance in a new millennium, one based on the lessons of earlier interventions—the failures as well as the successes.

UNDERWRITING HUMANITARIAN ASSISTANCE

Mobilizing Resources for Effective Action

Shepard Forman

INTRODUCTION

The hopes and aspirations for international cooperation that marked the end of the Cold War had their most exuberant expression in the industrialized countries' ambitious approach to humanitarian intervention. Confronted with an unprecedented number of internal conflicts and media images of mass suffering, the Security Council charged the United Nations with more than a dozen new missions between 1987 and 1996. Conceived largely as peacekeeping operations, these interventions nonetheless took on the requirements and drama of humanitarian assistance as genocide, mass migrations and starvation took their toll on millions of people.

The costs of these interventions by and large has been borne by a small number of industrialized countries, principally the United States and European Community members. Yet, despite their generosity in responding to humanitarian crises, little has been done to translate the moral imperative of humanitarian assistance into an effectively organized international response. In fact, as the following pages will argue, the current modes of resource mobilization, including methods of fund-raising and the timing and distribution of funds, actually exacerbate problems of equity and efficiency in the delivery of humanitarian assistance.

It should not be surprising that the sudden onrush of humanitarian assistance in complex emergencies would reveal a host of unanticipated problems. A large number of diverse actors—donor governments, intergovernmental agencies, international and local NGOs, local authorities, warring parties and the victims themselves—placed demands and expectations on a new humanitarian enterprise that was in many ways making it up as it went along. Even venerable institutions with long and admirable track records, such as the United Nations High Commissioner for Refugees, the International Committee of the Red Cross, CARE and Save the Children, saw their mandates extended, their capacities taxed and their best intentions put to the severest tests. A plethora of political, ethical and practical problems arose that seemed to call into question the essence of the humanitarian imperative itself. Little wonder that the very countries which established peacemaking and peacekeeping as the buzzwords of the decade began themselves to pull back and question the basic assumptions of humanitarian assistance. Ambivalence replaced ambition as the driving force of this experiment with post-Cold-War intervention in domestic crises. Funding levels inevitably declined, placing core humanitarian response capabilities seriously at risk.

The "crises within the crisis" that have characterized humanitarian assistance over the past decade have spawned a remarkable number of reexaminations of the humanitarian enterprise. Some, as in the case of the United Nations, take the form of institutional reform and reorganization; others occasion deep introspection regarding the role of humanitarian workers and their organizations. A number actually question the basic value of interventions, which are said possibly to prolong the conflicts and suffering they were intended to abate. In response, a sizable academic investment is seeking to extract lessons from a fairly complete catalog of case studies of humanitarian interventions over the past decade. Intergovernmental and nongovernmental organizations are working to develop new standards of fund-raising and accountability and appropriate structures for collaboration. Each of these efforts contributes to the redesign of a more effective humanitarian enterprise, and merits careful attention. Central to that redesign, however, is a careful analysis of the role that resource mobilization has played in both the successes and difficulties of humanitarian assistance.

This chapter begins with an analysis of the overall financial situation facing the humanitarian enterprise, with a primary focus on complex emergencies. It examines the way in which the timing and distribution of funding, as well as aggregate amounts, adversely affect the delivery of services in the field. It makes several proposals intended to strengthen capacity and performance in a more integrated humanitarian system, improve the quality of services and contain overall costs. These proposals include advanced funding to ensure the readiness of humanitarian agencies; expansion of the donor base through some regional burden-sharing; and creation of regional and local cadres of humanitarian workers.

The first of these proposals calls for an up-front investment in preparedness measures such as standby capacity, needs assessment and contingency planning, and early response. The second and third proposals, namely regional burden-sharing and local and regional staffing, would appear to have merit in their own right but also make sense strategically in developing an argument for advanced funding. In brief, the current major donors are more likely to commit support for international humanitarian organizations if they can expect some level of burden-sharing in the regions in which crises occur. In turn, the establishment of regional and local cadres of humanitarian workers will reinforce the incentive for regional governments to share in some of the costs.

Taken together, these proposals would dramatically reform the way humanitarian assistance is currently conceived and organized. As the following pages will argue, a package of financing reforms is needed to stabilize and depoliticize the humanitarian response, make it more efficient and ultimately improve services. At root is a belief that the moral imperative that has driven humanitarian assistance in the past needs to be complemented by an effectiveness imperative, lest the political will to engage in humanitarian crises be further eroded in the current donor community. In brief, I am suggesting that a public service model of preparedness replace the present political and altruistic modalities, thereby ensuring that effective response mechanisms are in place when they are next needed.

CURRENT FUNDING PATTERNS

The unprecedented surge in armed conflict within states that followed the end of the Cold War resulted in a dramatic increase in the number of people in need of humanitarian assistance. In 1996, more than 40 million people were dependent on humanitarian aid, an increase of 60 percent since the mid-1980s.[1] Their suffering became a common sight on television newscasts, often stimulating demands for assistance among the citizens of donor countries in the West. Triggered in part by this so-called CNN effect, levels of spending on humanitarian assistance increased dramatically during this same period. The proportion of official development assistance (ODA) that the industrialized countries spent on emergency aid quintupled since the early 1980s. Between 1990 and 1996, more than $30 billion was spent on humanitarian assistance, with more than 80 percent coming from OECD governments.[2] Annual aggregate funding levels peaked at around $7 billion in 1994, and recently leveled off at a little more than $3 billion per year.

While this recent decline in humanitarian assistance may reflect a declining number of ongoing emergencies, current funding levels still may not represent sufficient resources to meet current needs. Without systematic and transparent need and impact assessments, it is difficult to determine whether existing levels of aggregate expenditure are in fact adequate. Unfortunately, government funding tends to arrive following the onslaught of a crisis, when political support has peaked, rather than in its incipient stages, when comprehensive need assessments should be carried out. Moreover, national interest criteria usually guide donor government decisions and seriously compromise the equitable distribution of humanitarian assistance across crises, rendering it insufficient in many cases. In any event, there is a strong sense of resource constraint among the community of aid providers.[3]

The intergovernmental agencies and United Nations departments most active in humanitarian relief—the United Nations High Commissioner for Refugees (UNHCR), the World Food Program (WFP), the United Nations Children's Fund (UNICEF), the World Health Organization (WHO), the United Nations Development Program (UNDP), the International Organization for Migration (IOM) and the United Nations Department for Humanitarian Affairs (DHA) [now the Office for the Coordination of Humanitarian Affairs (OCHA)]—often have to struggle to obtain funds from governments whose national interest priorities usually determine where and for what purposes assistance will be provided. For their part, the private voluntary agencies that implement the majority of humanitarian aid find themselves increasingly dependent on earmarked government funds for their emergency response efforts and spend increased staff time and financial resources raising donations from the public for their general support activities. Furthermore, governmental efforts to encourage private voluntary agencies to play a primary role in the provision of humanitarian assistance have encouraged a proliferation of NGOs that now compete openly with each other for funds.

Mobilizing the financial resources needed for an effective humanitarian response has become a costly ordeal for both the intergovernmental and nongovernmental organizations delivering the aid and even for the donor governments themselves. Bilateral donors continue to confront specific funding requests by UN agencies and NGOs and general funding appeals by individual UN agencies and the Red Cross Movement. Other financing mechanisms include emergency funds maintained by most UN agencies,[4] the Red Cross Movement and the larger international NGOs; allocations from the Central Emergency Revolving Fund (CERF) administered by DHA; and public appeals by NGOs, either individually or in consortia. In addition, donors occasionally respond directly, providing resources through donor agency emergency teams, civil defense teams, or military contingents in a humanitarian delivery or support role. While these multiple channels may provide several potential funding windows, they also create ambiguities in the system and often lead to inefficiencies in planning, coordinating and implementing humanitarian responses in the field.

The percentage of financial resources derived from each of these mechanisms is difficult to determine.[5] Donor governments provide the bulk of the financial support—nearly 85 percent in 1996 (see Figure 19.1 for funding breakdown). Rough estimates suggest that the United Nations Inter-Agency Humanitarian Assistance Consolidated Appeals Process (the CAP) accounts for about half of donor government contributions; direct donor responses to general funding appeals or requests from humanitarian agencies comprise slightly less.[6] Financial support from nongovernment sources (corporations, foundations and the general public) appears to be less than one sixth of total global funding.[7]

UN General Assembly Resolution 46/182, adopted by member states in 1991, sought to rationalize the system of fund-raising and coordination of relief efforts through the creation of the Department of Humanitarian Affairs and the office of the Emergency Relief Coordinator, the CAP, the Inter-Agency Standing Committee and the Central Emergency Revolving Fund (see Jan Eliasson's chapter in this volume for a description of the tasks of each of these organs). Unfortunately, these efforts have only

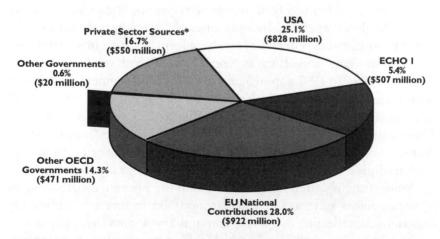

Figure 19.1: Global Funding for Humanitarian Assistance by Source, 1996
Total $3.2 billion

* See Note 8.

partially succeeded in resolving the complex problems of coordination and competition that result when multiple and diverse agencies seek to raise large amounts of money rapidly in response to complex emergencies.

SHORTCOMINGS OF CURRENT ARRANGEMENTS

The CAP has been a useful device for aggregating demand, but it has been unable to mobilize sufficient resources to meet global humanitarian needs. In 1997, only 62.2 percent of the Consolidated Appeals were met, down from 69.2 percent in 1996, 72.7 percent in 1995 and 75.8 percent in 1994 (see Table 19.1). Admittedly, the CAP accounts for only one half of donor contributions, and there is some question regarding the degree to which the "requirements" stipulated in the appeals accurately reflect actual needs on the ground.[8] Still, there is general agreement that its data provide, as one major donor suggested, a "good proxy for the trends in donor response to emergency humanitarian needs."[9] As such, they suggest that aggregate spending has become increasingly insufficient to meet overall needs.

Funding shortfalls are particularly acute in cases of "forgotten emergencies." Somalia, for example, has received less than 40 percent of its CAP requirements for each of the last three years. Afghanistan, which received 52.6 percent of its CAP requirements in 1995 to 1996, received only 33.3 percent in 1997. Similarly, Sudan, Angola and Iraq hovered at or below the 50 percent mark in each of the last three years. While there may be many explanations for the uneven distribution of humanitarian assistance, patterns of funding tend to represent clear political choices on the part of the donor agencies. Indeed, some observers have noted that the current humanitarian system may involve a form of triage, in which strategically "important" areas (such as North Korea, which received 79.2 percent of its 1996 to 1997 appeals) or widely publicized emergencies (such as the Great Lakes region, which received 88.2 percent of its 1995 to 1997 appeals) are well funded, while other emergencies are largely ignored. The dominance of such political calculi undermines the "humanitarian" character of these efforts and, in too many cases, leaves humanitarian organizations without the resources necessary to carry out their missions.

Donor funding preferences also result in uneven distribution of resources across sectors. In particular, nonfood sectors are consistently underfunded, reflecting the perception of many donors that such sectors are of a lesser priority. The World Health Organization, for example, received less than 15 percent of its CAP requirements for more than half of the emergencies in 1997; in several emergencies (Liberia, Sierra Leone

Table 19.1: Percent of Consolidated Appeals Covered, 1994 to 1997

Affected Country or Region	Percent of Requirements Covered for Appeals Launched in 1994	Percent of Requirements Covered for Appeals Launched in 1995	Percent of Requirements Covered for Appeals Launched in 1996	Percent of Requirements Covered for Appeals Launched in 1997
Afghanistan	59.8%	52.6%	–	33.3%
Albania	–	–	–	56.4%
Angola	83.2%	45.9%	56.6%	52.0%
Burundi	62.2%	–	–	–
Caucasus	62.5%	60.3%	35.2%	62.4%
Chechnya	–	90.0%	90.5%	48.7%
D.P.R. Korea	–	–	78.8%	84.3%
Eastern Zaire	–	–	69.3%	–
Former Yugoslavia	92.5%	89.5%	68.6%	67.9%
Great Lakes Region	–	91.7%	86.1%	84.4%
Haiti	55.5%	–	–	–
Iraq	32.1%	50.8%	57.4%	–
Kenya	57.1%	–	–	–
Lebanon	–	–	100.0%	–
Liberia	–	74.4%	–	36.4%
Mozambique	62.2%	–	–	–
Republic of Congo (Brazzaville)	–	–	–	7.9%
Republic of Yemen	15.7%	–	–	–
Rwanda/Subregion	95.5%	–	–	–
Sierra Leone	–	52.7%	67.2%	41.6%
Somalia	–	30.3%	(38.6%*)	38.6%
Sudan	81.3%	50.1%	51.4%	40.4%
Tajikistan	63.3%	77.2%	(92.6%**)	92.6%
TOTALS	**75.8%**	**72.7%**	**69.2%**	**62.2%**

* Somalia appeal covered 10/96–12/97.
** Tajikistan appeal covered 12/96–8/97.
Data from DHA's Financial Tracking Database, available on the Internet at http://www.reliefweb.int/fts/fintrack.html (visited 5/28/98).

and the Caucasus), WHO received *none* of its stipulated requirements.[10] This tendency of donors to fund only certain types of activities hinders the humanitarian agencies' efforts to strengthen the integrated programming approach of the CAP and compromises the effectiveness of the overall multisectoral humanitarian program.

The crisis-driven nature of donors' responses may also result in higher costs over the long run. Donor governments (and private sector contributors) are reluctant to respond with major commitments until compelled to do so by media coverage of tens of thousands of lives in immediate

Table 19.2: Requirements, Funding, and Shortfalls for Humanitarian Emergencies, 1997

Affected Country or Region	Implementation Period	UN Consolidated Inter-Agency Appeals Requirements (U.S. Dollars)	Funding (U.S. Dollars)	Carryover Funds (U.S. Dollars)	Total Funds Available (Contributions & Carryover Funds, in U.S. Dollars)	Shortfall* (in U.S. Dollars)	Percent of 1996 Requirements Covered
Afghanistan	1/97–12/97	133,009,192	44,297,886	0	44,297,886	88,711,306	33.3%
Albania	4/97–6/97	10,332,522	5,831,391	0	5,831,391	4,501,131	56.4%
Angola	1/97–12/97	198,735,512	103,246,953	0	103,246,953	100,872,975	52.0%
Caucasus	6/96–5/97	91,291,109	52,981,411	9,278,970	62,260,381	34,280,082	62.4%
Chechnya	1/97–12/97	11,853,100	2,976,816	2,800,000	5,776,816	6,076,284	48.7%
D.P.R. Korea	4/97–3/98	184,393,998	158,465,967	0	158,465,967	28,865,287	84.3%
Former Yugoslavia	1/97–12/97	443,813,734	217,105,896	91,644,011	308,749,907	142,463,827	67.9%
Great Lakes Region	1/97–12/97	313,054,253	205,948,983	73,676,089	279,625,072	48,729,181	84.4%
Liberia	1/97–12/97	31,235,149	11,359,872	0	11,359,872	19,875,277	36.4%
Republic of the Congo (Brazzaville)	11/97–1/98	17,730,595	1,394,682	0	1,394,682	16,335,913	7.9%
Sierra Leone	3/97–2/98	57,415,103	23,878,455	0	23,878,455	33,539,089	41.6%
Somalia	10/96–12/97	100,558,830	20,063,199	21,371,790	41,434,989	61,755,255	38.6%
Sudan	1/97–12/97	120,800,500	48,799,282	0	48,799,282	72,001,218	40.4%
Tajikistan	12/96–8/97	33,044,037	24,073,725	0	24,073,725	2,431,919	92.6%
TOTALS		1,747,267,634	920,424,518	198,770,860	1,119,195,378	660,438,744	62.2%

* A surplus in one commodity or for a particular agency does not offset a shortfall in another; DHA has adjusted shortfall estimates to reflect actual remaining needs.

Data from the UN Department of Humanitarian Affairs' Financial Tracking Database, available on the internet at http://www.reliefweb.int/fts/index.html.

danger. This can cause the humanitarian imperative to converge with a fund-raising imperative, causing agencies to rush into the field (where funding is made available) and often encouraging them to remain there at the expense of a careful assessment of their "comparative advantage" to act in certain crises and not in others. Often, agencies have been forced to defer possible early-stage mitigating activities and to react to emergencies at a later stage when the complexities of the disaster have expanded exponentially. While hard numbers are not available, it is generally accepted that the human costs are considerably higher at these later stages and that the impact of each aid dollar is much lower.

The short-term nature of donor commitments carries additional costs. Most of the major donor aid agencies will consider only three- or six-month project proposals. These short-term commitments make it difficult for humanitarian organizations to maintain adequate levels of funding beyond a few months. Humanitarian providers are often forced to borrow funds for field operations from other budget lines, anticipating restoration through later payments by donors. With small reserves in constant need of replenishment, humanitarian providers often face cash-flow problems and sometimes deficit spending.[11] These financial pressures shorten the providers' operational vision, leading them to plan and budget only for short-term projects. The added burden of continually turning out new proposals and concomitant reporting requirements not only requires staff time and resources that might be better utilized in service delivery but also heightens competitiveness among provider agencies. Crisis-driven funding of this sort, therefore, may well waste resources. It certainly inhibits planning and undermines the effectiveness of programs. Moreover, under these arrangements, donors find it difficult to track the impact of successive appeals or to hold providers accountable for expenditures under specific grants.

Financial dependence on donors with short-term funding horizons also restricts the capacity of humanitarian agencies to set priorities and implement programs that they deem appropriate to needs in the field. As suggested earlier, donors' decisions to fund only certain programs can severely limit the range of choices provider agencies face. In cases in which donors designate a lead agency as the primary channel for their funding, NGOs may find themselves reacting as contractees subject to the lead agency's agenda rather than as partners in the design and implementation of a shared humanitarian response.[12]

Unfortunately, neither the CAP nor the designation of lead agencies has fostered the effective donor coordination they were designed to promote. Lack of real consultation in donor funding decisions creates confusion and inefficiencies in the humanitarian response. In Rwanda, for example, UNHCR asked donor governments to provide "service packages" in an effort to ensure that all sectors were sufficiently covered. Because these efforts were not adequately coordinated among donors, however, certain vital sectors, such as sanitation provision, received little donor support, while higher-profile activities, such as the establishment of cholera treatment centers and centers for unaccompanied children, received disproportionately more funding.[13]

Uncoordinated needs assessments exacerbate this problem. In fact, the Consolidated Appeals Process has been criticized as being little more than the aggregation of multiple "shopping lists" compiled from the various provider agencies. In at least one instance, inadequate or nonexistent donor coordination may have even contributed to short-term excess. From July to September 1994, at the height of media coverage and public awareness of the Rwandan emergency, the funding "tap was turned on" so dramatically that many agency personnel recall that it was possible "to do anything."[14] Better coordination and more systematic and transparent needs assessments could have resulted in a more appropriate and sustainable allocation of resources. Accomplishing these, however, would have required up-front resources designated precisely for that purpose.

The fact that virtually all humanitarian activities, with the exception of modest core costs of some of the UN specialized agencies, are financed through voluntary contributions increases the unpredictability of revenues. Voluntary contributions are typically tied to the donors' annual budgetary processes and are subject to political will. Furthermore, because current financing arrangements are crisis-driven, many organizations have difficulties covering their nonemergency operational support costs, including those associated with personnel recruitment, training, development and management; public education and associated appeals; financial management; and administration.[15]

While greater coordination of efforts, including a clearer division of labor, together with administrative and management reforms undoubtedly would help to reduce fixed institutional costs, some provision for reasonable overhead charges is necessary if the remarkable strength and resiliency of the humanitarian agencies is to be preserved.[16] Rather than promoting a healthy division of labor among agencies that should be collaborating to ensure that an effective humanitarian response is in place, current patterns of financing create an unhealthy competition among service providers for scarce funds needed to underwrite their operations. In order to attract donor funding, agencies often vie for visibility through the media, profiling themselves in campaigns designed to raise public awareness of an emergency and their own funding requirements. When successful, this phenomenon can create an ironic feedback loop: as donors respond, the increased funding attracts even more humanitarian organizations to the field. Well-publicized emergencies like the one in Rwanda in 1994 can become overcrowded with relief agencies, creating "the impression of a bazaar" and a "battle of logos and T-shirts."[17] The constant competition for funding may skew the humanitarian imperative and hinder coordination among humanitarian agencies.

IN SEARCH OF SOLUTIONS

To address these financing dilemmas and related problems of logistics and coordination, the Center on International Cooperation at New York University convened a meeting on "Resources for Humanitarian Assistance" on September 11 and 12, 1997, at the Pocantico Conference Center, in New York state. The meeting brought together 23 senior staff from UN agencies, NGOs, donor governments and other experts in the field for two days of intense working sessions focusing on several critical topics in humanitarian assistance.[18] Participants at the meeting argued strongly that improvements in the timing, predictability and flexibility of financing mechanisms would greatly strengthen the humanitarian response. They also believed that cost savings could be obtained through effective investment in a well-organized humanitarian preparedness system, including on-the-ground material standby and logistical arrangements, rapid deployment capacity and staffing. They further recommended more concerted efforts at coordination among donor agencies as well as between service providers' headquarters and field staffs. In particular, three ideas emerged from the Pocantico meeting that the center is now developing into a set of proposals. If accepted, these could substantially alter the way in which humanitarian assistance is now structured and financed.

Proposal 1. Up-front, un-earmarked funds would enhance significantly agencies' response capacities, thereby helping to mitigate the worst effects of crises, save lives and lower long-term costs.
Current modes of short-term, tightly earmarked and crisis-driven financing impede the capacity of humanitarian organizations to plan ahead, provide early and potentially mitigating interventions and fund programs that might have longer-term, postcrisis benefits. Noting that the uncertain funding for humanitarian assistance makes organizational planning extremely difficult, meeting participants argued strenuously for more

predictable and flexible financing to ensure that the core competencies of humanitarian provider agencies could be maintained.

In order to respond efficiently and well to emerging crises, humanitarian agencies need to maintain their readiness. As Larry Minear notes in Chapter 20 of this volume, "The world does not have the luxury of gearing up from scratch for each new emergency." In real terms, this means having sufficient standby capacity in the form of experienced personnel, as well as adequate material stocks and the means to deploy them; the ability of agencies to conduct carefully coordinated assessments of needs in the field and undertake their own contingency planning; and the wherewithal to intervene early in a crisis when their actions can help mitigate rapid degeneration. Current patterns of crisis-driven funding deny them these capacities.

Some level of predictable, un-earmarked, up-front funding is necessary to ensure preparedness in the face of unexpected emergencies.[19] One might well ask what incentive there would be to governments, already reluctant to provide overhead, to advance funds to provider agencies. The answer lies in part in the logic of the argument: to wit, up-front funding will ensure readiness; permit early intervention that helps mitigate the crisis, thereby resulting in long-term cost savings; and enable providers to make more deliberate decisions about entry and exit rather than rush to a crisis and remain there because it contains the font of resources they need for survival.

Convincing governments that the economic calculus makes sense even in the face of strong domestic political constraints will be a formidable task. Most government agencies are reluctant to provide headquarters' costs because they believe their publics prefer to see funds going directly to field operations. Others worry about the accountability of agencies. Both of these obstacles should be surmountable. Since annual budgets for humanitarian assistance are set in advance, and donors know on average what they are likely to spend over a period of time, it should be possible for political leaders to make the case for advance funding if indeed it were to prove more cost-effective and provide better services over time. Moreover, better accountability could result from organizations' ability to make more deliberate decisions about the appropriateness and timing of their activities, moving from "reflex to reflection," in the words of Smith and Weiss.[20]

To demonstrate the efficacy of this argument, the center was urged by participants at the Pocantico meeting to undertake a study of the response capacities of several agencies and their impacts on the quality of field operations and ultimate costs. The study, now under way in collaboration with the UNHCR, Oxfam-U.K. and the International Rescue Committee,[21] is examining: (1) those tasks (and related costs) that are essential to maintain sufficient standby capacity, to enable careful needs assessments and thoughtful contingency planning and to facilitate early interventions; (2) their time sensitivity; and (3) the percentage of overall emergency response budgets they represent. This inquiry should permit us to make a reasonable calculation of the percentage of up-front funding that would be needed by each organization to maintain its core competency at a certain level of readiness. To further make the point, the study is examining with participating agencies actual cases in which the availability of up-front funding made a substantial difference and those in which the lack of resources impeded an early response with demonstrable costs to victims and to the agencies and their donors.

Whether these advance funds are best provided bilaterally or through a CERF-like mechanism would have to be determined. While the former is more likely to satisfy the predilection of donors to fund organizations headquartered in their own countries, the latter—if governance arrangements were properly worked out—would help to free humanitarian aid from some of its political fetters and make allocation of resources more equitable across crises. It could also permit more coordination in the maintenance and deployment of material stocks and provide a mechanism for competitive bidding among agencies. In this way it would substitute a real market mechanism for the current bazaarlike arrangements in the distribution of humanitarian aid.

Proposal 2. Regional burden-sharing will be an essential component of resource mobilization in the future. In addition to helping even out gaps in funding for particular emergencies, it would encourage the current major donors to maintain their commitments to the international humanitarian infrastructure, while ensuring that those most closely affected by crises participate directly in their resolution.

Even at its peak in 1994, humanitarian assistance constituted a very small portion of spending in the world economy, representing only 0.03 percent of world GDP, or less than 1 percent of world defense expenditure for the same year. On a per capita expenditure basis, humanitarian assistance also proved remarkably inexpensive, amounting on average to less than $100 per person in need in 1996.[22] Most importantly, had the humanitarian response not been forthcoming, loss of human life would have been much greater.

Notwithstanding, overall levels of funding for humanitarian emergencies would appear not to be adequate if judged either by the percentage of consolidated appeals actually met or the distribution of funds across crises, sectors and, possibly, agencies. Moreover, the percentage of realized CAP appeals has declined from 75.8 percent in 1994 to 72.7 percent in 1995, 69.2 percent in 1996 and only 62.2 percent in 1997. The fluctuating percentages of appeals met for specific agencies from year to year, even considering changing needs in emergency situations, at best complicate actual response and planning and at worst threaten the organizational well-being of the agencies themselves. Most important, the needs of many victims are not being met at all.

As noted earlier, the OECD countries provide some 80 percent of the financing for humanitarian assistance. Some $5.5 billion, or 92 percent of the $6 billion in total reported donor funding for humanitarian assistance in the 1995 to 1996 biennium, came from ten donor countries (more than 50 percent of it from the European Community and the U.S. alone). Another 7 percent was received from an additional ten countries, including Australia, Italy, Switzerland, France, Belgium, Finland, Spain and Austria. Some 36 countries accounted for the remaining 1 percent, leaving more than 129 UN member states as noncontributors. Of those countries providing humanitarian assistance in 1995 and 1996, fewer than 20 exceeded $10 million in contributions per annum.

Unless there is a shift in the political will of current major donors, it seems unlikely that we can expect increases in their current allocations for humanitarian activities or a reallocation of funds from their other areas of international expenditure. New donors will have to be identified if the present downward trend in meeting humanitarian requirements is to be reversed. While a few additional donor candidates might be found among those nondonor countries with growing GDPs and which rank high in the UNDP human development index, a more comprehensive strategy for responding to emergency crises will probably required.

One possible means to extend the donor base would be to regionalize part of the appeals and response process. There is growing evidence in Africa, Asia and Latin America that regional and subregional groupings are opting to resolve their own problems and seeking ways to control their own economic and political destinies. Led by regional powers or in various coalitions, subregional and continental leaders are asserting their desires to settle regional and local conflicts, often through their own trade associations and economic blocs. Regional analyses of emergency situations and their real and potential economic costs, along with an assessment of current (and projected) GDPs and economic growth strategies could demonstrate particular points of convergence between regional or subregional interest, capacity and expressions of responsibility.

Evidence suggests that regional economic communities and development banks can marshal some of the resources needed to respond to emergencies that threaten human lives, political stability and economic growth. Precedents for the creation of such regional response mechanisms exist. In 1974, the African Development Bank, then wholly African in its membership, established a Special Relief Fund to deal with droughts and other natural disasters with earned dividends that member states agreed to forego. A Special Emergency Assistance Fund, earmarked for the same purpose, was created in 1985. As of 1993, it had received combined contributions of $50 million.[23] Also in 1993, the Organization of African Unity established a Peace Fund for conflict-management-related activities.[24] The Fund for Emergency Programs and Common Services was established with $50 million in 1976 within the Caribbean Development Bank. The Islamic Development Bank utilizes interest earned on its assets for humanitarian aid within the Islamic community. ASEAN members have agreed to a collective regional response to humanitarian crises but as of this date had yet to create the mechanism or provide the capital for it.

These experiences suggest that the institutional capacity exists to mobilize funds regionally. Moreover, a number of countries that have enjoyed real growth in the last few years[25] might be willing and able to contribute financially to the resolution of humanitarian crises that threaten to undercut emerging public- and private-sector investor interest in their regions. The risk, of course, is that current donors might seek to absolve themselves of responsibility by devolving it entirely on local and regional actors. Furthermore, structures would need to be in place to ensure that humanitarian assistance is not used as a cover for local hegemonic actions (although that is hardly an intraregional risk alone). Finally, there would need to be some attention paid to a possible dilution of universal humanitarian standards into a variety of regional and ethnic response models that further erode current availability and quality of services.

These are formidable problems, but it should be possible to devise a formula whereby secure funding for international humanitarian organizations would be provided by the ten to twenty major donors, while a more inclusive burden-sharing system for responding to humanitarian emergencies is developed regionally or subregionally. The newfound vitality of subregional organizations might make them the logical starting place to explore whether a framework could be created for an authentic partnership between local and global actors who until now have been left to play out mutually unsatisfactory roles of donors and recipients.

Proposal 3. The humanitarian enterprise would be greatly strengthened by a more systematic use of local and regional response capabilities. This could be accomplished by training standby cadres of civil servants and other professionals who could be seconded by their employers for humanitarian relief efforts.

Human capital is a prerequisite of a successful humanitarian response. The talented and dedicated staffs of intergovernmental and voluntary agencies carry out extremely difficult missions, often at considerable risk to themselves. Many organizations, however, report that finding experienced staff to deploy to unfamiliar and unstable field locations is one of their biggest challenges. Moreover, unpredictability in the frequency and magnitude of humanitarian crises creates ongoing human resource management problems for NGOs and UN agencies, which are forced to expand and contract their recruitment and training efforts quickly, often without advance planning. UNHCR, for example, has contracted its staff by 33 percent since its peak operations in 1994. Whether this represents a momentary lull in the number of crises or is part of a more generalized "downsizing" of intergovernmental organizations, it presents a serious challenge to the UN system and NGOs alike: how to maintain adequate staff capacity during slack periods between crises.

Recruitment and training of qualified aid providers are particularly acute problems in emergency situations, which demand skilled and knowledgeable personnel. Crisis workers are often recruited in a hasty, ad hoc manner for overseas assignments in remote, unfamiliar places to implement complex programs for which they lack adequate experience. They are typically young and mobile individuals whose resourcefulness only partially compensates for their lack of field preparation. They often have scant knowledge of local politics, economic conditions and cultures and generally lack the language skills needed to communicate directly with the people whom they are there to serve.[26] More important, while some international presence is often desirable, there is a growing sense that expatriate aid workers displace local human resources that could be employed both to mitigate crises in their acute phase and to promote longer-term peace-building and developmental goals. [27]

Current personnel preparedness arrangements are largely dependent on a set of reserve rosters maintained for recruiting purposes. Although many NGOs utilize their own reserve rosters for their staffing needs, several of the intergovernmental organizations rely on standby arrangements with NGOs. The self-selecting nature of these rosters and the adequacy of screening and accrediting practices have raised questions about quality control in the recruitment process. Ironically, these same criticisms have limited the use of regionally based rosters that have been developed to facilitate the hiring of local staff.[28]

There is a growing sense in the humanitarian community that the use of local professionals in senior operations positions can greatly enhance the emergency response. Yet while many organizations employ large numbers of local staff,[29] they serve mainly in support functions and there is a clear preference for employing Westerners in senior policy and management positions.[30] These preferences may be based in legitimate concerns for security, fiduciary responsibility and political neutrality. Nonetheless, the dominance of Westerners is problematic on a number of fronts—politically and ethically, as well as in terms of efficiency and comparative costs. In particular, the relatively rapid turnover of Western recruits, many of whom are available for one to six months, adds to the extremely high costs of field personnel.[31] At the same time, local staff bring special skills and strengths to senior positions, including a greater understanding of the particular political and cultural context in which they are operating. Moreover, building local capacity in the civil sector also contributes directly to postemergency reconstruction goals and more sustainable solutions.[32]

One possible approach to this set of problems would be the establishment of regional and local cadres of civil servants and other professionals who could be seconded by their employers for emergencies within their regions. A set of regionally based, standardized training programs could add to and aggregate available skills and talents into an effective standby response capability. Issues of security and equity would need to be addressed. For example, some contend that local staff would be more vulnerable to political pressure and physical threat than international humanitarian workers, although—as recent events have sadly shown—the immunity from harm once attached to Western status no longer seems to apply. Moreover, it is high time to correct the asymmetrical system that exists in the field, with local staff enjoying less authority, smaller salaries and fewer privileges than their Western counterparts.

Many intergovernmental and nongovernmental agencies recognize the value of training and development programs for both senior management and new recruits. Anticipating high levels of staff burnout and turnover, however, and with donor emphasis on actual provision of goods and services in the field, these agencies invest relatively few resources in improving worker skills. Some intergovernmental and agency training programs exist, but they are by and large tailored to individual agency needs, philosophies and operating styles. Moreover, even when inclusive of local staff, they are designed largely to enhance individual competencies in particular functional areas.

A standardized training program, flexible enough to incorporate attention to local conditions, could serve several purposes. It could help to prepare standby cadres of humanitarian workers in the field and reinforce the current set of underfinanced individual agency training programs. It could, further, provide the basis for certification of humanitarian workers, thereby resolving some of the riskier aspects of current recruitment practices. Making a proposal of this kind practicable, however, would require development of a demand-driven curriculum that would be acceptable to both employing agencies and local users. It also would require a more cooperative system of standby arrangements among agencies and special agreements with seconding institutions.

With will and financing, an experimental program along these lines should not be hard to implement. A number of existing efforts, including national-level disaster relief programs, could provide the building blocks. Internationally, training modules for UN and other personnel working in complex emergencies have now been developed by the new UN Staff College in Turin, Italy. An International Diploma in Humanitarian Assistance, offered by the Center for International Health and Cooperation, provides the basis for a certification program. NORAFRIC, the Norwegian effort to create a standby force of 50 African nationals for professional service with UN agencies for emergency operations in Africa, already suggests a model for broader replication. The UN's Disaster Management Training Program might provide an initial starting point for a broader effort of the kind outlined here.

Applying this model more widely could help to create a standby capacity of trained, accredited professionals who could be called up on short notice for mission assignments. Such an arrangement would mitigate existing problems of rapid recruitment of often inexperienced and untrained personnel, help to contain costs and contribute to sustainable practices throughout the regions. It would create a sense of local ownership and reinforce local responsibility. There would appear to be sufficient redundancy in the staffs of government agencies worldwide to allow such a program to work. Additionally, the skills and experience acquired by their staffs could bring a host of benefits to the seconding institution.

CONCLUSION

The shortfalls and predicaments that exist in the current pattern of financing of emergency humanitarian assistance are amenable to correction.

Three related proposals that would substitute the current voluntaristic modalities with a public service model for ensuring the provision of essential services have been advanced. These proposals call upon the current major donors to underwrite the international infrastructure required for an effective humanitarian response, and subregional and regional actors to assume some responsibility for cost sharing when crises occur in their regions. The third proposal urges that the humanitarian workforce be realigned to incorporate regional and local cadres of humanitarian workers at all levels of the emergency response.

These proposals, if adopted, would dramatically restructure the way in which humanitarian assistance is now conceived and organized. They would establish an international division of labor based in several partnerships, between major donors and regional governments and institutions, between intergovernmental and nongovernmental organizations, and between international and local NGOs. They would empower local actors and direct their attentions to preventive action as preferential to a far more costly crisis-driven response. Internationally, they would result in increased specialization among public and private agencies, each exercising its particular comparative advantage as part of a systemwide determination of essential core competencies. Overall, they would result in a more efficient and effective delivery system with increased emphasis on cost-effectiveness and impact.

Clearly, a realignment of this magnitude will not be easy to accomplish. It will require extraordinary political will on the part of current donors and a new sense of purpose and responsibility among regional actors, intergovernmental agencies and international NGOs. There may be enough in the way of incentives for most of these stakeholders, however, to encourage them to try. The community of humanitarian providers has learned a great deal from the successes and failures of recent times. The dawn of the new century provides just the right opportunity for them to redefine their goals and cooperate for the realization of these goals.

20 LEARNING THE LESSONS OF COORDINATION

Larry Minear

Coordination of humanitarian activities involves the systematic utilization of policy instruments to provide effective assistance and protection to vulnerable populations. Such instruments include strategic planning, gathering data and managing information, mobilizing resources and assuring accountability, orchestrating field activities, negotiating a framework of access with the resident political authorities, and providing leadership to the overall international effort.[1]

Everyone puts a premium on coordination. Donors insist upon it as an investment in the cost-effectiveness of their resources. Political authorities on the receiving end, already hard-pressed in major crises, look to their international 1ocutors for coherent programs and complain when a multiplicity of actors requires individual attention. Humanitarian organizations themselves have an interest in concerted action and fear media exposés of interagency competition. The public has had enough experience with humanitarian circuses to expect the worst and are all too ready to have their worst fears confirmed.

Yet while devotees at the shrine of coordination are legion, coordination is as little understood as it is avidly sought alter. There is widespread awareness of the presence of myriad humanitarian organizations—be they UN agencies, governmental aid ministries, private relief groups or the International Committee of the Red Cross (ICRC)—on the scene of major international emergencies. Yet there is little understanding of why the effective orchestration of their activities proves so difficult.

Moreover, many of today's complex emergencies—unlike natural disasters or the Cold War challenges of assisting refugees fleeing beyond their countries or origin—involve a newly complex array of actors. On the local scene, there are not only recognized governments but also insurgent groups—not to say criminal elements—to be reckoned with. On the international scene, actors include not only aid workers and human-rights advocates but peacekeeping forces and international civil servants, often with police, security and other administrative functions in conflict zones. Coordination, a challenge of monumental proportions within the humanitarian sphere, becomes even more daunting when this wider array of actors, some of them committed to use humanitarian efforts for their own purposes, is factored in.

In an effort to illuminate some of the difficulties of achieving effective coordination in the complex emergencies of the post-Cold-War period, this chapter begins with a review of experience in the Great Lakes region (Section I), examining both those problems of coordination among humanitarian organizations and those at the interface with political actors. It then turns to experiences in other major recent crises, which confirm the recurring difficulty of putting humanitarian principles into practice (Section II). It then assesses progress in making the necessary reforms in humanitarian policies and procedures (Section III), finding that while numerous changes have been introduced, the underlying problems identified remain largely unresolved. It links resistance to institutional change with four characteristics of the culture of humanitarian organizations: their tendency to approach every crisis as unique, their action-oriented nature, their defensiveness to criticism and their lack of accountability (Section IV). The chapter concludes with a discussion of an agenda for future action (Section V).

I. THE GREAT LAKES EXPERIENCE

The experience in responding to the crisis in the Great Lakes region is a logical starting point, both because the experience has proved so searing and because the associated lessons-learning process has been unusually carefully tracked. Among the evaluations at hand are the 1996 five-volume multidonor evaluation of the Rwanda response,[2] a review of follow-up action to the evaluation as of a year later[3] and an independent study commissioned by the United Nation's Interagency Steering Committee (IASC) in 1997.[4] These and other studies identity coordination among humanitarian organizations and at the political interface as the two critical areas of weakness in the international response to the genocide in April 1994, the uprooting of Rwandans that followed, the festering problems that led to the creation of the Democratic Republic of the Congo, and the continuing crisis of insecurity, human need, and human rights abuse throughout the Great Lakes region.

The IASC study links the weakness of the UN's humanitarian response to the lack of clear and decisive authority to exercise coordination. "The simple reality is that within the diverse UN family, no element has adequate authority to command, coerce or compel any other element to do anything."[5] Describing the prevailing situation as "coordination-light," it picks up on a recurrent theme of earlier studies on Rwanda and elsewhere: that a more assertive model of coordination is necessary for activities to be effective. A 1994 UN Rwanda review distinguishes among coordination by command, by consensus and by default, and concludes that humanitarian coordination in complex emergencies generally relies on coordination by consensus or default.[6] Advocating that the UN's coordinating nexus, the Department of Humanitarian Affairs (DHA), "must tighten its managerial and institutional grip on the coordination of complex emergencies," the study concludes that: "the donors (and the general public) cannot forever claim that the UN is ineffective in coordinating emergencies while at the same time refusing to give it the means and the resources to do so."[7]

Weaknesses in the area of coordination in the Great Lakes have also played themselves out at the more operational level in the lack of a balanced deployment of resources and programs. The Multidonor Study contrasted the nonresponse to the genocide in April 1994 with the outpouring of assistance following the mass displacement later in the year. The existence of a continuing problem is confirmed by the IASC study, which noted that the consolidated appeal process does not function as an instrument of UN systemwide strategic planning and observed that protection activities were underfunded while "hundreds of millions of dollars were relatively easily obtained for moving large volumes of relief supplies."[8]

Once again, however, the failure to act upon lessons identified earlier has returned to haunt the system. The 1994 DHA study noted that: "DHA's credibility would be well served by a limited dose of coordination by command, both in terms of some un-earmarked funds, which could be obtained through CERF [the Central Emergency Revolving Fund] or another mechanism, and in terms of leadership and authority on the ground."[9] In early 1998, however, the system appears no closer to acting on that recommendation than when it was tabled.

The various studies of the Great Lakes also identify recurring difficulties at the interface between humanitarian organizations and political actors, both international and local. The multidonor study, while citing numerous problems among humanitarian organizations, saves its most blistering critique of international political actors for acts of omission and commission. It was they who misread the signs of approaching genocide and reduced rather than strengthened the ranks of the UN peacekeeping force once the bloodshed had begun in earnest. It was they who responded to an underlying political crisis in exclusively humanitarian terms and sent mixed signals to political and military actors in the region.

Lack of political coherence is indeed a recurring constraint on effective humanitarian action. This was underscored at a February 1998 Symposium on the Relationship between Humanitarian Action and Political Military Action, organized by the Belgian Ministry of Foreign Affairs in cooperation with the International Committee of the Red Cross. One of the symposium's three working groups identified the absence of coherence among political institutions—donor governments, UN member states, Security Council members, international and regional intergovernmental bodies, and the UN's political department—as a more serious constraint on consistent and effective humanitarian action than problems among aid agencies themselves. In fact, the reality of coordination by default between and among political actors works against the creation of a policy framework within which humanitarian action in complex emergencies can succeed.

Problems of political coherence at the international level are compounded by local political actors. As the IASC study notes, coordination "is a function of interaction between elements of the UN system and those political and military actors that are legally, morally and materially responsible for the welfare of affected populations, i.e., national government local governments, armies, and in some instances, rebel authorities.[10] In the Great Lakes, such political-military actors represented a threat even to the most effectively coordinated humanitarian efforts. They were best dealt with when consistency existed at the international political level, enabling special representatives of the Secretary-General to negotiate access in selected settings. "Elsewhere, especially in Rwanda, where donor nations and the UN system's agenda often were not in harmony, envoys did little to create humanitarian space, or to pressure for consent to humanitarian action."[11]

By all accounts, the lessons of the Great Lakes are clear: coordination-light is inadequate to the formidable challenge of orchestrating effective humanitarian action in complex emergencies, and the absence of political coherence has deprived aid agencies of the indispensable framework for humanitarian action. Various remedies have been suggested: for example, the consolidation of such aid activities into a single agency and the provision of more assertive and consistent political direction. Later sections of the paper suggest why these recommendations have not been acted upon.

II. OTHER RECENT EXPERIENCES

From the experience in other post-Cold-War conflicts, confirming that of the Great Lakes, emerge several recurring problems that confront and frustrate humanitarian action. From Somalia to Chechnya, from Liberia to Karabakh, the United Nations has not found effective ways of dealing on humanitarian concerns with nonstate actors—and with state actors under duress from insurgents. UN humanitarian agencies, with governing bodies composed of sovereign states and themselves integral parts of a world organization made up of such states, have exhibited well-documented structural difficulties in discharging their mandates to carry out needs assessments, provide assistance and protection to civilians, and monitor their programs in government- and rebel-controlled areas alike.

Problems in the Sudan are illustrative.[12] In 1989, Operation Lifeline Sudan (OLS), breaking new ground, negotiated humanitarian access with the warring parties—only to see such access eroded by the belligerents and by its own decision to shift OLS's administrative base from New York to Khartoum. A 1990 OLS case study noted the importance of "coordinating activities from a location removed from each party in a civil war."[13] Decisions about situating relief administration in places such as Monrovia, Luanda and Zagreb have subsequently created similar problems in carrying out nonpolitical functions on highly politicized terrain. The UN has been no more effective in needs assessment in Chechnya and Nagorno-Karabakh than in the run-up to OLS. As for on-the-ground presence, UN aid agencies have been excluded from those two settings altogether.

Despite its failure to address the generic problem of carrying out humanitarian functions in situations of contested sovereignty, the United Nations system continues to position itself as the focal point for coordination, a position accepted by donor governments and other member states. But there are, however, alternatives. James Ingram, a foreign executive director of the UN World Food Program (WFP), has expressed his considered judgment that there is "no reason" why a coordinated international response to future complex emergencies "should be built around the United Nations" and a variety of reasons why it should not. He recommends the ICRC or a new organization situated outside the UN system.[14]

If the UN is indeed to remain at the center of the world's aid efforts in contested settings, steps could and should be taken to clarify that humanitarian action by UN organizations does not confer sovereignty upon those with whom access is negotiated. Such an understanding allowed UNICEF to take the lead in negotiating the terms of OLS with insurgents and the UN-recognized authorities alike. Why should such an understanding not be written into the mandates of other UN aid organizations (WFP's governing body has moved in that direction) or, alternatively, become the rationale for creating a new UN relief dedicated to complex emergency response?

Post-Cold-War conflicts have raised serious questions not only about the nature of humanitarian principles but also about how these may best be preserved in practice. In fact, the post-Cold-War period can be read as a time of testing established principles in the cauldron of internal armed conflicts. The experience in the former Yugoslavia highlights the extent to which, confronted with the same challenges of the denial of humanitarian access, the UN and the ICRC responded in different fashions. The ICRC took a principled stand, negotiating the access provided under international humanitarian law with the belligerents and being prepared to suspend operations if a party reneged on its obligations. The UN took a more pragmatic approach, ceding the belligerents greater authority over its activities and accepting greater political conditionality in the process.[15]

Which approach works better, in what circumstances, for what reasons, and for how long? The IASC study makes the intriguing observation that strategic planning and coordination "worked best when grounded in specific tenets of international humanitarian law."[16] It is difficult to say whether this conclusion might be writ large over post-Cold-War experience to date. However, it would be useful to explore whether there is a positive correlation between principled action and successful humanitarian action.

The UN system and its stakeholders have yet to address a related problem in the area of principle and practice, flagged in several earlier studies. At issue is the extent to which the effectiveness of humanitarian activities and the security of aid personnel may be jeopardized by association with other more political elements of the UN system. The IASC study identifies difficulties created for aid actors by the political framework of international action within which they function. "Humanitarians in the UN system, and their NGO partners," it observes, "have borne the brunt of anti-UN, anti-humanitarian sentiments from beyond that for which they are responsible."[17]

Such difficulties are not unprecedented, although the extent to which the effectiveness, not to say the principles, of humanitarian action is compromised is often understated by political policy-makers and even by officials at aid headquarters. In the former Yugoslavia, for example, the association of UN aid officials with UN peacekeeping activities and with economic sanctions created a certain "schizophrenia" within the UN and complicated the performance of their humanitarian mission.[18] While such problems at the peacekeeping interface may have eased in recent years, the reason probably lies not in the improved management of the inherent tensions but rather in a reduction of the number of peacekeeping operations themselves.

The United Nations system has an uneven track record in identifying lessons such as these and, once they are identified, in instituting the changes deemed necessary. Among the useful steps taken to date has been an exercise by the IASC, begun in 1994 and completed in 1996, to examine tensions between humanitarian principles and other activities of the UN system.[19] OCHA's current review of the mandates of individual humanitarian organizations may provide a useful point of departure for a formulation of options in this area. As indicated in the discussion to follow, however, the structural nature of such problems has made them unusually difficult to resolve.

III. THE LEARNING CURVE

Scholarly analysis has yet to examine in any detail the dynamics of institutional change within humanitarian institutions. Numerous studies of corporate and public sector institutions remain largely without analog in the humanitarian sector. Yet aid agencies are subject to the same forces that are producing change elsewhere, however idiosyncratic the dynamic among humanitarian organizations may be. These forces include new technology, changing roles of governments and nonstate actors, disparities between resources availability and demands, greater media scrutiny, a more informed public, growing competition in the marketplace and a newly global environment.[20]

Once again, the Great Lakes experience, better documented than most, is a logical starting point for examining the impact of the learning process, and evaluations of it, on institutional behavior. From the Great Lakes studies mentioned earlier, augmented by experience from other settings, emerge the main outlines of a laconic learning curve.

The multidonor study of Rwanda provides an instructive example of the importance of evaluation exercises—but also of their limited ability, in and of themselves, to produce institutional change. The initiative was launched in November 1994 by a steering committee of some 37 institutions: governmental, intergovernmental and NGO. The study enlisted 52 consultants who in March 1996 produced a five-volume work. With direct costs alone of some $2 million, the evaluation reviewed issues related to aid programs that in the April to December 1994 period had cost $1.4 billion.

If this "mother of all evaluations" was unprecedented in scope and detail, so too was a follow-up initiative that urged and monitored implementation of its recommendations. The Joint Evaluation Follow-Up Monitoring and Facilitation Network (JEFF) was forced in May 1996 by eleven individuals from the original study, and founded by concerned donors. A preliminary JEFF report, released in February 1997, was followed by a final report in June 1997, after which the JEFF group disbanded.[21]

Of the 64 recommendations in the multidonor study, the JEFF study found that, based on submissions from 19 of the 37 members of the original evaluation's steering committee, about two thirds had received some positive action during the initial fifteen months. Of course, some of the 64 were more important than others, and as it turned out, the more critical recommendations had received the least responsive treatment. *Ignored altogether* were the most overarching, such as the recommendation to foster policy coherence in the UN Security Council, General Assembly and UN Secretariat and the recommendation to encourage effective prevention and early suppression of genocide. *Reviewed but rebuffed* were recommendations to institute coordination-by-command arrangements in the aid sector and to set up an independent watchdog to keep international institutions' feet to the fire. *Acted upon to one degree or another* were recommendations that involved the least radical options on coordination and accountability, the commissioning of four additional studies and—most encouraging—a number of measures to strengthen international human-rights machinery. At several points, the JEFF survey found fuller implementation outside the UN system than within.

The impact of the multidonor study points to a larger conclusion, one corroborated by other evaluations and evaluators: that the role played by formal evaluations in institutional change is modest at best. Indeed, "evaluation x" rarely causes "change y," although a given study may contribute to subsequent reforms. While such a conclusion "may come as a disappointment to policy researchers and to foundation officers and others who underwrite their work, rarely does the impetus for change come only or even primarily from an assessment, whether by outsiders or insiders."[22] The JEFF review did find, however, that the multidonor study probably accelerated changes already under discussion, facilitating and supporting the process of lessons-learning and policy dialogue within and among institutions.[23]

That said, failure to implement some of the specific changes that had been recommended contributed to the recurrence of the identified problems in the ensuing years. The lack of attention to refugee camp security and the empowerment of the *génocidaires* led to the unraveling of the situation described in detail by the 1998 IASC study. Festering discontent in 1996 and 1997 confirmed the urgency of specific recommendations to remove barriers to repatriation. There was an occasional encouraging note: for example, the JEFF study found that several "immediate and urgent" measures recommended for Burundi had indeed been put into place, recalling the progress acknowledged by the IASC study in fashioning and implementing a common humanitarian policy.[24]

Nevertheless, the follow-up study on the multidonor initiative concluded on a bleak note: "the case of Burundi must lead us to conclude that, one year on, a great deal has *not* changed, despite all the debate and meetings described above."[25] In fact, reflecting the passage of time between February and June 1997, the final JEFF commentary expressed even more keen disappointment than had the preliminary review at the absence of action on many key fronts.

A 1996 study of the Rwanda crisis by the UN Department of Peacekeeping Operations makes for some interesting comparisons. In reviewing how the international response could have been improved, DPKO's terms of reference are far more circumscribed. "It is important not to search for idealistic solutions," the study states, "but rather to remain within the constraints of the reality of the United Nations system today."[26] Yet the 43 "lessons learned" are decidedly critical of the response mounted. Seven are related to coordination and exhibit little patience for coordination-light. Lesson 11, in tact, urges that "The United Nations overall presence in a country should reflect a unified, cohesive structure. The SRSG [Special Representative of the UN Secretary-General] should be recognized institutionally as the head of the United Nations family in the mission area."

What of the broader lessons-learning process beyond the Great Lakes? Unfortunately, no counterpart to the JEFF review exists surveying actions to implement recommendations in other evaluation studies or to address problems identified. Yet it is possible to retrace some illustrative steps taken, whether in response to evaluation studies or, more likely, to the cumulative pressure for change.

Foremost among macro-level changes was passage in late 1991 by the General Assembly of Resolution 46/182, opening additional humanitarian space in situations of contested sovereignty. "Humanitarian assistance should be provided with the consent of the affected country," the resolution stated, "and in principle on the basis of an appeal by the affected country."[27] The expanded space was staked out through a carefully negotiated text that spoke of "consent" rather than request, of "country" rather than government, "in principle" rather than in every particular instance, and based on an "appeal" rather than a formal application.

Passed in the wake of the first major post-Cold-War humanitarian response, and reflecting donor government concern about the disarray of the relief effort on behalf of the Kurds, the resolution also created the position of Emergency Relief Coordinator. In early 1992 the Secretary-General established the Department of Humanitarian Affairs. While the relaxation of sovereignty drew more immediate attention, the orchestration of humanitarian efforts would prove the more consuming challenge. As the situation has evolved, both the relaxation of sovereignty and the effort of DHA to ensure greater coordination have proved by and large serious disappointments in their practical consequences for a more responsive and effective international humanitarian regime.

Other changes of major proportion and potential include the heightened involvement of the Economic and Social Council (ECOSOC) in the humanitarian sphere. The decade has seen greater engagement by ECOSOC (and its sub-working groups), which has required of the IASC and its member agencies in-depth reviews of their capacities to respond to emergencies. Preparation of the requisite reports has provided a focus for IASC discussion on such issues as coordination and resource mobilization. Again, however, the results to date have disappointed. The ECOSOC review of humanitarian action scheduled for mid-1997, which was expected to bring a new rigor to the process, was upstaged by the UN reform discussions, then at a critical juncture.

Also of significance at the interagency level has been the establishment in 1997 by the Secretary-General of executive working groups designed to achieve greater policy coherence and interaction in the political, peace-keeping, humanitarian, human rights and development dimensions of the UN system's response to crises. The inclusion of the High Commissioner for Human Rights on the Executive Committee on Humanitarian Affairs (ECHA)—and, for that matter, now on the IASC as well—reflects the implementation of lessons distilled from a variety of conflicts regarding the centrality of human-rights issues, and is a departure from 46/182. An ECHA working group tasked with recommending steps for implementing the reform package made a number of useful suggestions. However, no significant expansion of coordination authority is in sight, and confusion remains regarding the division of labor between ECHA and the IASC.

Reform has been achieved in the ground rules governing the withdrawal of UN staff from insecure situations. Responding to situations earlier in the decade, when the withdrawal of UN staff from places such as Somalia left the system without essential information about the deteriorating plight of the civilian population, the UN Secretariat has drawn up and implemented new ground rules that allow essential humanitarian personnel to remain in place, after less critical UN staff have been withdrawn. NGOs, too, have taken steps to inform their decisions and equip personnel on matters related to the security of staff and programs.[28] Progress has also been made in formulating ground rules for the use of military and civilian assets in responding to major humanitarian crises.

At the intergovernmental level outside the UN system, the OECD's Development Assistance Committee has devoted attention to the impact of conflict on development activities. A task force formed in 1995 has produced a set of guidelines on conflict, peace and development cooperation, which were embraced in a policy statement in May 1997 by development ministers and others. The statement pledges to: "Work with colleagues within our governments to ensure that all our policies—including in the areas of security, policy and economic relations, human rights, environment and development co-operation—are coherent in fostering structural stability and the prevention of violent conflict." The statement raises the possibility of "an independent co-ordinating authority to monitor donors' adherence to agreed principles."[29] The DAC Expert Group on Evaluation is also involved in major efforts in the lessons-learning area.

Beyond interagency and intergovernmental arenas, there have been other changes of potentially major proportions in individual agencies and governments. In late 1996, the World Bank approved a new policy on postconflict reconstruction, followed by a decision to establish a new department to orchestrate expanded operational involvement. UNICEF has promoted successful adoption of a Convention on the Rights of the Child and has backstopped a detailed study on the impact of armed conflict on children, which has subsequently been endorsed by the General Assembly and has contributed to a more rights-based philosophy of programming.[30]

The World Health Organization has reviewed its role in complex emergencies, noting structural and administrative inadequacies and recommending that the agency "should not normally take a direct role in service delivery or procurement and delivery of supplies."[31] The ICRC is about to implement recommendations flowing from its multiyear Avenir project. The Netherlands' government has positioned its humanitarian assistance activities within its conflict resolution unit in an attempt to capitalize on the expected synergies. Such changes often reflect individual lessons-learning studies, some of them confidential, others available to the public.

As the focus shifts to the more programmatic and procedural level, there is a proliferation of developments to report. One example is provided by the recent Report of the Tripartite Lessons Learned Study of the Great Lakes.[32] The report highlights what it considers "the importance of the achievements of the three agencies ... in developing the new formal and informal modalities of operational coordination and joint action." At the same time, it acknowledges that even such improvements "often could do little to harmonize agency operations" in the face of personality clashes, interagency competition and other "natural" tendencies of the emergency system. The study's 28 recommendations offer an agenda for further progress.[33]

In view of the multiplicity of arenas, actions and studies involved, it is difficult to establish with any precision the significance of the changes achieved to date, to say nothing of the extent to which they have resulted from lessons-learning processes. The evidence suggests, however, that the observations in the various Rwanda studies and their follow-up represent a microcosm of the larger picture of institutional change in the post-Cold War.

That is, while the mechanisms and mechanics of the humanitarian apparatus have been adjusted, the more systemic problems remain to be addressed. Reforms to date have been largely technical, procedural, logistical and administrative in nature. These include memoranda classifying relationships among humanitarian agencies of the UN system, guidelines for the utilization of military and civil defense assets, and rosters for personnel with particular expertise available for rapid deployment. In other words, the easiest changes have been made. Still to be addressed are the weak structures of humanitarian coordination and the knotty political and humanitarian tensions underlying the intergovernmental system itself. Taking stock of the situation in 1995, one study concluded that "the United Nations has made surprisingly few fundamental changes of an institutional or a policy nature."[34] Three years later, a similar verdict would be equally justified, and more alarming.

IV. CULTURAL IMPEDIMENTS TO LEARNING

The fact that more significant changes have not been forthcoming, despite profound changes in the external environment, reflects a number of constraints in the institutional cultures of humanitarian organizations. Four are examined here.

The first is *the tendency to approach every crisis as unique.* Sooner or later in most discussions of humanitarian crises, someone observes that Zaire is not Cambodia, Somalia is not Bosnia, Sierra Leone is not El Salvador. The point, while not exactly profound, is legitimate. Complex emergencies being complex, a one-size-fits-all response is inappropriate. The idiosyncratic dynamics of individual conflicts need to be taken into account in charting effective international responses. In a more fundamental sense, however, no crisis is unique:

> Each crisis pits the same institutions (the United Nations, governments, NGOs) against the same [interlocutors] (government and insurgent groups, civilian and military host officials) in a continuing effort to find solutions to recurring problems (the obstruction of humanitarian access, the manipulation of relief, inequitable economic relationships, the absence of viable and accountable local structures). As long as every crisis is perceived as wholly without precedent or parallel, there will be little scope for institutional learning."[35]

In fact, overemphasis on the idiosyncratic reinvents the wheel and leaves earlier lessons unlearned. The manipulation of belligerent and criminal elements of the refugee camps in eastern Zaire in 1994 was a rerun of problems unaddressed in Cambodian refugee camps along the Thai border years before. The rebuffs in Sierra Leone in 1997 and 1998 were not the first time that humanitarian agencies had been barred from fulfilling their mandates in insurgent regions. Yet, as noted above, little has been done to address the structural political constraints inhibiting the discharge of the UN's humanitarian responsibilities, whether in Khmer Rouge-held territory in Cambodia, SPLA-controlled southern Sudan, sovereignty-asserting Nagorno-Karabakh or perilous Chechnya.

The second constraint to learning is *the action-oriented nature of the humanitarian ethos.* Much has been written about the hyperactive pace of the relief enterprise, born of the need to respond to rapid-onset crises. In the heat of a crisis, humanitarian agencies and staff can hardly be expected to pause and reflect. The reality that "crisis x" is often followed by "crisis y" and "crisis z"—if not accompanied by them—may shift such reflection more permanently to the back burner. As a result, copies of the multi-donor Rwanda study and others like it remain intact in their cellophane wrappers.

There is an underlying tension, if not contradiction, between the can-do spirit of concern for suffering humankind and the discriminating calculations needed for effective functioning in today's internal armed conflicts. Only in recent years have the agencies taken specific steps to facilitate reflection on their mandates, strategies, modus operandi and results. In fact, after some progress in approaching humanitarian activities with greater deliberation, the pendulum may be swinging in the opposite direction. Some NGO practitioners are now concerned that overdue attention to the broader political, military and social context in which humanitarian interventions are set is beginning to serve as a rationalization for inaction rather than a prelude to more strategic intervention.

The third cultural deterrent to learning is a certain *defensiveness toward criticism*. Dismissive treatment by the Secretary-General's spokesperson of the multidonor study surely impeded serious review of that very detailed and thoughtful examination of the UN response to the Rwanda crisis. Her comment to the press at a time when the report was still embargoed—"we will not continue to take such criticisms lying down"—was interpreted by those preparing to launch the findings and recommendations as "an attempt to undermine the report and unbalance media coverage of the launch."[36] The implicit message to UN officials was that the changes proposed were unneeded and, in the view of senior management, did not deserve serious consideration.

While institutions dependent upon public support are understandably reluctant to wash their dirty linen in public or to see others hang out their laundry, there are various signs of the emergence of a more self-critical breed of humanitarianism. Agencies that only a decade or two ago rebuffed efforts to examine the implications of the prevailing East-West political framework for humanitarian action are now much more prepared to consider the political dimensions of their work. Assessments themselves have become a cottage industry, with think tanks, universities, research groups and consultants cranking out more material than can be digested, much less acted upon. A recent compilation of peacekeeping studies published during the first seven years of the post-Cold-War period tallied 2,200 titles in English alone. That number doubtless dwarfs the recent upsurge in policy reviews of humanitarian activities, whose numbers, as suggested by the ALNAP inventory, are nonetheless numerous.[37]

The swing of the pendulum from a dearth of thoughtful material to an abundance of it is welcome and overdue. Yet the latter extreme may be as unhelpful to the process of learning and change as was the former. Even the proliferation of so-called lessons-learned units is not in and of itself a sign of progress. Since serious learning requires institutional change, such units might better be called "lessons-learning" or "lessons-identified" units and viewed as means to an end rather than ends in themselves.

In any event, both DHA/OCHA and the Department of Peacekeeping Operations (DPKO) now have such bodies. They review the same crises, although from different perspectives, with different methodologies and without much consultation. Each has mounted half a dozen major studies in the past several years. DPKO's unit, which applies a standard set of questions and an established and highly iterative process to each review, is well staffed and securely situated within its parent department. That arrangement has concomitant advantages, such as access to information and engagement of professional colleagues, as well as disadvantages, including more circumscribed terms of reference and less independence. DPKO's studies appear not to have attracted much comment either in-house or beyond.

The DHA (now OCHA) unit is smaller and less adequately provided for within the regular budget of its parent office. Reaching beyond its own staff to engage outside researchers in its studies, its approach is generally less constrained by institutional politics and more wide-ranging and independent in nature. While individual UN agencies have their own internal lessons-learning processes, DHA reviews have sparked interest across the broader humanitarian community and attracted a wide following in academic and policy circles.

Certainly the spirit of the times requires asking tough questions and subjecting policies and programs to rigorous scrutiny. One thoughtful critic has recently observed that in recent years, the agenda may have shifted "from a debate regarding how to reform the humanitarian system, to the question of whether it is worthy of reform at all."[38] As long as reasonably satisfactory answers emerge, however, tough questions may be a vehicle for rekindling respect for the humanitarian impulse and principles. The court-martial of several Canadian peacekeepers for mistreating Somali captives did not lead the Canadian public to demand, or the Ottawa authorities to initiate, reduced national involvement in international crises. Canada has indeed reaffirmed and continued its tradition of engagement. That said, many humanitarian institutions remain more wary of criticism than open to it.

The fourth constraint on lessons learning is *the prevailing lack of accountability.* The lessons-learning process is undercut by "the culture of impunity": that is, the failure to hold actors responsible for their actions. As noted earlier, donor governments often send mixed signals to UN agencies and fail to demand appropriate accountability from their operational nongovernmental organization (NGO) partners. UN agencies point the finger at governments rather than taking responsibility for variables they themselves control. (Adapting the figure used in the IASC Great Lakes study, the UN, while neither king nor rook, it is nevertheless more than pawn.)

NGOs rationalize dubious levels of professionalism through appeals to their good intentions and voluntary ethos. Armchair generals criticize peacekeeping operations from desks in parliament without having slept in the UN barracks in Srebrenica or gone on patrol in Abkhazia. Conflict specialists pontificate about peace-building without having set foot on an ethnic fault line. Researchers do not take time to read what others write or assume responsibility for their own recommendations.

A recent study on improving the UN's management of economic sanctions—commissioned by the IASC, utilizing independent researchers arranged by DHA and underwritten in part by the agencies—provides both a fascinating insight into confused accountabilities and a good example of constructive post-Cold-War change.[39] The study noted that humanitarian organizations are asked by governments to offset the "unintended consequences" of sanctions on vulnerable groups living under targeted regimes, consequences that in reality can be foreseen and are often indeed intended. Aid actors are then faulted for failing to relieve suffering, in part because of the unwieldy system by which governments simultaneously exempt and control humanitarian shipments. Governments themselves, monitoring humanitarian items closely as a threat to the integrity of sanctions, turn a blind eye to illicit imports. The Security Council's Sanctions Committees take decisions of major humanitarian import behind closed doors, well protected from public scrutiny.

For their part, UN aid organizations lack clear policy on how to function in countries under sanctions, yet are reluctant to seek clarification for fear that stakeholder governments will tie their hands further. Among and within NGOs, themselves lacking policy in this highly political area, there is a high degree of opinionation by individual staff, often reflecting the particular responsibilities of given staff in the organization and their personal views. The blurring of who among those involved in sanctions is accountable to whom for what reflects the lack of coherence and transparency in the sanctions scene.

The issue of sanctions illustrates two dimensions of the problem of accountability. The first is the lack of clear policy and lines of authority by which actions of individuals and institutions may be judged. Should a UN aid official be chastised for expressing critical views about the impacts of sanctions on vulnerable groups when his or her organization lacks clear policy about how it will function when sanctions have been imposed? Should an aid organization be faulted for not delivering relief supplies effectively? Is a diplomat who votes to impose sanctions responsible for the pain they cause civilians? More often than not, accountability is something expected of someone else. Everybody—but also nobody—is ultimately responsible in the shell game.

The second dimension concerns the multiple points of accountability. NGOs are responsible to their boards of directors and the constituents who elect them, to donor governments and/or multilateral organizations from whom they receive resources, to partner organizations in crisis countries with whom they collaborate, and to beneficiaries on whose behalf they mount programs. Indeed, aid organizations attach great importance to their obligations to beneficiaries, although the prevailing measurement of accountability are largely Western in orientation and character and quantitative in nature.

But change is taking place. The sanctions study was the outcome of efforts within the interagency body and by individual agencies over a period of several years to address difficulties in Iraq, Haiti, the former Yugoslavia, Burundi, and Sierra Leone.[40] Following through on the study, which proposed a methodology and indicators for preassessing and monitoring sanctions impacts, the IASC formed an interagency technical group and also sent a first-ever communiqué to the Security Council articulating its concerns on the humanitarian impacts of economic sanctions.[41] During the years 1996 to 1998, DHA/OCHA also carried out and/or coordinated sanctions missions to the Sudan, Burundi and Sierra Leone. Such steps hold promise for addressing underlying as well as procedural problems experienced by the humanitarian community and for enhancing accountability.

Accountability is currently being enhanced in other ways as well. NGOs have taken steps to promote a voluntary code of conduct and to establish certain minimum essential thresholds in key programming sectors. The Sphere Project seeks to improve not only the quality of humanitarian response but also "the accountability of humanitarian agencies to beneficiaries, members and supporters." Some donor agencies are now making a given NGO's endorsement of the code a condition for receiving grants and contracts.

Yet since accountability also involves issues at the interface with political-military actors, it needs to be approached on various fronts in concert. There is little value in holding aid organizations accountable for problems encountered in reaching people inside Afghanistan, for example, when small-arms trade, acquiesced to or engaged in by governments, is at the heart of the problem. Accountability is not just a one-way street.

IV. AN AGENDA FOR THE FUTURE

Learning from mistakes ... requires more than a compilation of experiences. A condition for learning lessons and improving our performance is an environment that is favorable for frank criticism, both from inside the organization and from outside researchers.

—Jan Pronk, Netherlands Minister of Development Cooperation,
Statement to the Second Committee, UN General Assembly,
October 14, 1996.

Constraints to learning such as those identified here, however deeply rooted in the culture of humanitarian institutions, are not beyond remedy. Correcting the tendency to approach every crisis as unique will require development of greater institutional memory and greater attention to comparative analysis of similarities as well as differences among major humanitarian crises. Institutional implications include providing greater support for in-house evaluation capacity and more consistent and creative use of the results of outside studies.

The action orientation of humanitarian institutions is not likely to change significantly. However, it can and should be balanced by a more reflective approach to the challenges confronted. The idea is not that the agencies should become, Hamlet-like, "sicklied over with the pale hue of thought," but rather that their activities should be impelled and informed by more savviness about political, military and social realities on the ground.

Defensiveness to criticism will not metamorphose overnight into more openness to change. The constraints run far deeper than will be remedied by placing a "suggestion box" outside the chief executive's office. Yet ways may be found to institutionalize incentives for constructive criticism and promote a culture receptive to thoughtful critiques of current policy and suggestions of alternatives. The studies reviewed confirm an indispensable role for outside researchers in keeping the system honest, although the data reviewed suggest that evaluations, external and internal alike, have at best limited impact on institutional change.

The prevailing lack of accountability is perhaps the most difficult constraint to address, since it reflects confusion in the prevailing approach to coordination-by-consensus. The shell game described earlier, in which no single individual or institution is held accountable for international humanitarian interventions, undermines effective action. Accountability requires clear lines of authority, which in turn means clear-cut delineation of responsibility, political no less than humanitarian.

The future agenda for lessons-learning cannot be tackled in isolation from the issues of coordination and the present lackluster learning curve.

That is, learning the lessons of the early post-Cold-War period and of future crises will require a more sober view of institutional resistance to change and a more strategic approach to creating and managing opportunities for reform. Such an approach might infuse the unglamorous day-to-day work of coordination with greater purpose and energy. It would inject greater rigor into interagency coordination efforts such as those of the Inter-Agency Standing Committee. It would place a higher premium on achieving effective coordination in the countries in crises themselves.

It is clear that donors have an indispensable role to play in supporting the processes of lessons-learning and institutional change within the agencies. The impression currently abounds that many governments are not interested in serious reforms in aid policies and activities, since these would require greater political coherence in their relations with individual UN agencies and with the UN system as a whole. They are viewed, as is the 46/182 resolution, to be mandating greater coordination while frustrating efforts to achieve it.

Yet government initiative is reflected in some of the creative initiatives in recent years, such as the multidonor evaluation of Rwanda and follow-up JEFF initiative. While some governments have resisted the recommended humanitarian safeguards in economic sanctions, others have rallied behind them. Is it not high time for governments to put most of their funding into common funds for programs in a given country and, as some are already doing, fund only those agencies that subscribe to the NGO Code of Conduct?

The present moment is opportune for taking stock of the lessons learned and to be learned, and for vetting a strategy for institutional change. A widespread sense of disillusionment with the humanitarian enterprise prevails among insiders and outsiders alike. There is new leadership at the United Nations in the offices of the Secretary-General, the Emergency Relief Coordinator, the High Commissioner for Human Rights and elsewhere. Various proposals are on the table, including the creation of an independent watchdog entity to promote greater accountability. It is time for humanitarian interests to come together to develop a consensus on a strategy for tackling these critical issues. The process of formulating and implementing such a strategy will itself require effective coordination.

MEETING THE CHALLENGES OF THE NEW MILLENIUM

Cyrus Vance

As we entered the 1990s, scores of people began offering definitions of what has been called a "new world order." A number of them seem to have in mind only enhanced collective military security. For my part, I am convinced that a "new world order" cannot be confined to questions of military security, nor can it be based on notions of the United States as world arbiter. In that spirit, and recognizing that the world situation impels us to look for solutions that might have been previously impossible, let me offer a few suggestions.

I propose them as challenges for us to rise to as we move through space and time to keep our date with the millennial year 2000. A new world order for the twenty-first century, I believe, should be structured along the general lines of the 1991 Stockholm Initiative to meet the following six imperatives:

- International peace and security;
- Sustainable economic development;
- Curbing uncontrolled population growth and environmental degradation;
- Providing adequate global health care;
- Fostering democracy and human rights;
- Strengthening key international institutions.

INTERNATIONAL PEACE AND SECURITY

The first and primary imperative of a new world order must be the maintenance of peace and security on both a global and a regional scale. Although the Cold War may be over, we need to look no further than the nightly television news to recognize that national, ethnic, religious and other conflicts—both across and inside national borders—continue to pose grave threats to peace and security.

The disintegration of Yugoslavia into bitter civil war tragically demonstrates how real and destructive these conflicts can be. The dissolution of the former Soviet Union contains serious flash points—some of which have already led to conflict. Other potential flash points also exist in Eastern and Central Europe. Nor is ethnic and religious conflict limited to Europe. We must never forget, nor can the world ignore, similar violence in Somali, Rwanda, Liberia and other parts of Africa, Central Asia and the Indian subcontinent. In short, the end of the Cold War has by no means brought an end to violence and conflict on our planet.

Beyond maintaining appropriate military capabilities, we should begin our search for peace and greater security by strengthening the mandate and the capabilities of the institution that has the widest and potentially most effective reach—the United Nations.

The UN's collective security potential was demonstrated during the Gulf crisis. After Iraq's invasion of Kuwait, nations working within the UN framework impressively and effectively applied an unprecedented policy of embargo, containment and enforcement. And when the war ended, there was no choice but to turn increasingly to the United Nations to provide long-term stability and humanitarian aid.

Yet, with new thinking in mind, imagine for a moment what might have been possible had the UN at the time of the Gulf War possessed the capability to head off Iraq's aggression.

In this connection, Prime Minister Ingvar Carlsson's Stockholm Initiative recommends the establishment of a global emergency system within the United Nations. This proposal has been reinforced by then UN Secretary-General Boutros Boutros-Ghali in *An Agenda for Peace.*

Under this proposal, which I support, UN political offices would be established inter alia in key locations, such as Iraq/Kuwait and South Korea/North Korea, to provide early warning of potential aggression and thus, it is hoped, deter potential conflict. But that alone would be inadequate. The UN also needs its own collective security forces—by which I mean earmarked forces that would be available on the call of the Security Council—to intervene when the Security Council so determines.

To make the global emergency system effective, the Secretary-General should be granted greater leeway to deploy the organization's diplomatic, monitoring and dispute-resolution capabilities whenever requested by a member state.

A UN with such capacity and authority could have posted buffer forces on the Iraq-Kuwait border, could have facilitated early peaceful discussion of the two countries' border disputes and could have signaled clearly that Iraqi aggression would almost certainly trigger a collective response by the world community.

But the United Nations cannot be everywhere. To keep the peace, we also need to modernize regional security arrangements, particularly in volatile areas like the Middle East, the Horn of Africa and South Asia, where no effective regional institutions now exist.

The Conference on Security and Cooperation in Europe—known as CSCE—has facilitated to a degree the post-Cold-War thaw that is taking place in Central and parts of Eastern Europe. The North Atlantic Treaty Organization was the Western shield that kept a fragile situation stable until a thaw could take place. But it was CSCE, through treaties and confidence-building measures, that helped the former Soviet Union and Central and Eastern European countries to begin to work their way to democracy and free-market economies. But much more remains to be done.

As the Middle East peace process moves painstakingly forward, the CSCE model should be considered. Obviously, on one level, the meetings now under way are discussing Arab-Israeli relations and the issue of a Palestinian homeland. On another level, affected nations both inside and outside the region are beginning to tackle a broader range of issues, including regional security arrangements, human rights, environmental degradation, refugees, economic cooperation and restraints on the development and transfer of all kinds of weapons.

As to the last of these, there is a crying need to rid the Middle East of all weapons of mass destruction and methods of their delivery as soon as possible. The radical limitation of conventional arms exports to the Middle East must also be addressed as a matter of top priority.

In the United States we regard it as quite normal that we should be beginning to reduce strategic weapons and other military expenditures and reallocate the resources to domestic priorities. Yet in the Middle East and much of the rest of the world, arms sales continue minimally abated. Unfortunately, the United States and other arms-exporting nations persist in viewing such transfers as commercial opportunities rather than potential threats to regional and, as we have seen, our own security. We urgently need a convention limiting the sale of conventional arms, especially in the Middle East.

SUSTAINABLE ECONOMIC DEVELOPMENT

Correspondingly, peace and development will be served if a prospective new world order includes a recommitment to international economic cooperation and increased development assistance.

Both the United States and other countries have had bouts of protectionist flu as economic pressures and changing world trading patterns have endangered the previous worldwide consensus on access to goods and money. President Kennedy, when he signed the historic Trade Expansion Act of 1962, remarked that "a rising tide lifts all boats." The premise remains true, but sadly, its support is less widespread than one would hope.

The General Agreement on Tariffs and Trade (GATT) needs to be reinforced, not weakened, as seems to be the drift today. When the International Monetary Fund (IMF) and the World Bank were created at Bretton Woods, the GATT was seen as the global trade organization that could accommodate the interests of both developed and developing countries, while holding back the protectionist and mercantilist forces that were so destructive in the past. But protectionist forces now seem, unfortunately, to be gaining strength, rather than waning.

The GATT, World Bank, IMF and UNCTAD—the UN Conference on Trade and Development—all are important global institutions. They are complemented by regional trade and financial entities such as the European Community; the Asian, African and Latin American development banks; and the European Bank for Reconstruction and Development.

Regional groups have taken on new life. That is good. But it would be tragic for all of us if this were to end up dividing the world into European, Asian and North American economic blocs pitted against each other, while leaving the world's poor nations on the outside looking in. Have-not nations cannot prosper absent a free and open international economic and financial environment. But such an environment alone will not ensure sustained growth. No viable new world order can be based on a trickle-down theory.

We must not forget, however, that the history of the past 50 years has shown us a number of surprising economic success stories. The development process, once begun, takes on a dynamic momentum that carries it forward at a self-sustaining rate. Certain interrelated factors can be identified as reasons for success:

- Investments in human capital through better education, health care, population planning and training;
- Investments in infrastructure and industry that have the long-term prospect of bringing success in international markets;
- Development of domestic agricultural production, distribution and processing.

By the same token, we have learned that grandiose projects such as dams, superhighways, steel mills and modern airport complexes often do not make sense *unless* they are part of sound, overall plans for sustainable economic development.

We must face the dual realities that slow growth in both developed and developing nations illustrates a downside of interdependence, namely, that slow growth in each diminishes demands for products of the other. Similarly, we must also recognize that debt service continues to consume a major share of developing-country resources. Even resource-rich but heavily indebted potential powerhouses such as Brazil will do well in the next decade not to lose ground. And it is evident that these issues are severely aggravated by problems of population, environment and refugees.

The common thread that links these complex intersecting factors is evident: no nation can resolve all its own problems without the help of other nations. *Common action and common security are essential.* We have learned from hard experiences that multilateral global action is the only way we can achieve widespread sustainable economic growth and expanding investment.

The United Nations estimates that one billion people—one fifth of the world population—now live in extreme poverty. Yet the World Bank estimates that with sufficient investment, this number could be reduced by almost half by the end of the decade. Such an effort would require that all nations commit themselves to simple and discrete targets. The worldwide cost of meeting key social development targets is estimated at $20 billion annually—the cost of sustaining the Persian Gulf War for two weeks. It is all a question of priorities: Do we care enough to make a similar investment in the future of humanity?

The long-cited target for development assistance is that each industrialized country provide seven tenths of 1 percent of its GNP to international development. With slow world growth, this will be hard to achieve. As we know, a heavily indebted developing world will be hard-pressed to borrow enough money to generate enough wealth internally *unless* direct assistance is forthcoming and spent wisely. This is a reality we cannot avoid.

CONFRONTING CRITICAL GLOBAL ISSUES

There are three commanding, sensitive and closely interrelated issues that both rich and poor must confront if a successful new world order is to emerge. I am talking, of course, about population, environment and health care. A fourth critical issue, the adequacy of global and local food supplies, is largely dependent upon the interactions of these three variables and the constructive interdependence of nations outlined above.

Population

As to population, as nations develop, birthrates invariably recede—another reason why promoting economic development is in our long-term interest. Nonetheless, long-standing religious and social pressures will continue to make it difficult to curb population growth to the extent necessary to relieve pressures on both human health and the global environment.

It is sobering to realize that if current projections hold, the 1990s will produce the largest generation yet born—with some 1.5 billion children entering an already crowded world.

Population growth, by definition, tends to reduce standards of living except in nations that enjoy remarkable economic growth. Population growth also adds to environmental pressure—most directly, in areas where new deserts are created as forests are destroyed to provide land for cultivation. Such growth encourages exploitation of children, migrants and others in the workplace. It pits neighboring countries against each other as they feel each other's population pressures.

It will take political courage, but leaders of both developed and developing nations must commit themselves to population planning programs as an integral part of their plans for economic development. A good place to start would be for the United States to renew its funding of the UN Fund for Population Activities.

Environment

In contrast to population, the related issue of the environment is on everyone's mind. But the question remains: Are we willing to invest the political and financial capital required to both restore and protect the health of the planet?

In the rush to development, humanity has already done irreversible damage to the planet. And both developed and developing countries are to blame. More than half of Africa's arable land is at risk of becoming desert. One third of Asia's and one fifth of Latin America's land are in the same state. We learn daily of the environmental catastrophe that exists in the former Soviet Union and in much of Eastern and Central Europe. We are aware, however, that further damage can be checked and some of the prior damage reversed, if we muster the political will to act.

Various ideas for future progress are already in place. Debt-for-environment swaps permit host countries to receive debt relief in return for protecting vital environmental resources. The Global Environmental Facility, created by the UN and the World Bank, has helped to raise public consciousness and offer practical alternatives. There is an emerging international consensus that environmental impact assessments should be built into economic development plans at both national and international levels.

Issues of global warming and ozone depletion, already high on the international agenda, must not be shunned or postponed simply because they are politically difficult. To come to grips with these challenges, the nations of the northern hemisphere alone will need to reduce emissions of carbon dioxide from the combustion of oil, coal and other fossil fuels by perhaps 50 percent in the next 25 years or so. And we must eliminate the use of chlorofluorocarbons—or CFCs—and halons on a far more rapid and comprehensive scale than we have so far committed ourselves to.

The scope of the problem is illustrated by the stark fact that if just four industrializing countries—India, Brazil, China and Indochina—were to increase their use of CFCs and halons up to the limit now *permitted* under the 1987 Montreal Protocol, the annual release of CFCs would *increase* by 40 percent rather than diminish.

Unfortunately, the 1992 UN Conference on Environment and Development was more a rhetorical than a substantive success, in no small part hampered by the reactionary position of the United States. Yet the conference did provide an important beginning for change, much as the Helsinki Conference on Human Rights did some years ago. The industrialized countries must take the hard choices of environmental protection if they are to have any hope of persuading the poorer nations to join in.

Providing Adequate Global Health Care

Any new world order must also include provision for adequate global health care. Dazzling accounts of organ transplantation and manipulation of the human genome fill our newspapers and periodicals. Yet, despite giant strides in medical research and development, the global delivery of adequate health care is lagging woefully behind ever-increasing demand. Complaints of failing health care systems are voiced daily around the world. In many countries we hear predictions that health care is rapidly becoming the number-one problem and that many of us, laypersons and doctors alike, are failing to meet our human responsibilities and the challenges at hand.

The facts are clear. In the United States we continue to face such long-standing problems as heart disease and cancer. In addition, newer scourges, such as AIDS and widespread international drug abuse, beset us. And new challenges, such as providing maximum functioning and independence to rapidly expanding *elderly* populations, test our skills and political will. On the other side of the coin, difficulties in delivering adequate medical care to expanding *infant* populations, especially those in our own inner cities, continue to hobble us. We have yet to demonstrate maintenance of effort in the long haul.

However, it is in the developing nations of the world where health statistics document the growing disparity between the haves and have-nots, a gulf that divides the world of North from South as effectively as the East-West separation of the Cold War years. Throughout the tropics, schistosomiasis, river blindness, pneumonia and dysentery continue to cripple and kill. We have shown that great strides forward are possible: childhood immunizations, oral rehydration therapy for diarrhea, the conquest of smallpox—but unfortunately, we can balance tales of success with numerous failures.

Infant mortality and life-expectancy rates in the developing world must be analyzed not merely as cold numbers in columns; they represent the tragic waste of human lives, dreams and potential in countries that can ill afford such a constant loss. AIDS is decimating whole areas of central Africa, disproportionately destroying the young, educated, urban hope of that continent. In some areas more than 30 percent of the entire population is infected with the fatal human immunodeficiency virus. There has been a resurgence of ancient scourges, with drug-resistant tuberculosis and malaria, as well as cholera, once again reaching epidemic proportions in Africa, Asia and Latin America. Eradication and control schemes are paralyzed by lack of funds and an inadequate cadre of skilled health workers.

And let no one think that these problems will be long confined to the developing nations of the world; infectious diseases simply do not recognize political borders, and the speed and frequency of air travel have broken the old quarantine barriers against contagious transmission. We also confront the vexing issuing of skyrocketing medical costs and the fact that those who suffer most are located not only in the developing countries but also among the poor, including the working poor, in the United States. There can be no doubt that providing decent and humane medical assistance, particularly to the less fortunate, will be a most pressing issue in any new world order. For all these reasons, we must take the necessary actions to close the existing gap. But what should we do?

Recognizing the importance and complexity of these issues, let me, as a layperson, offer a few suggestions. First, we must put increased emphasis on exploring the linkages among health care, population and environment. On population, I make three suggestions:

- Strengthen biomedical research on human reproduction;
- Strengthen psychosocial research on human reproduction;
- Foster incorporation of family planning into health services, especially in the field of primary care.

One vehicle for the achievement of all these objectives would be to broaden and invigorate the Human Reproduction Program of the World Health Organization.

Second, as to environment, absent careful control of the way in which growth takes place, there are often negative environmental repercussions that adversely affect human health. Examples include lead poisoning, asbestosis, inadequate sanitation, and the direct and indirect threats to health posed by poorly planned, overcrowded urban environments. There are also potential dangers to health from larger environmental problems, such as damage to the ozone layer, toxic wastes and the incalculable long-term consequences of damage to the ecosystems of the world's great oceans.

Unfortunately, at the UN Conference on Environment and Development, there was not a clear and strong call for significantly increased health-related research backed by concrete proposals for international collaboration. It goes without saying that assuring adequate funding is also essential.

Third, as to health care systems, I believe the international community must increasingly share experience and information on the comparative advantages and disadvantages of various systems, with a view to containing health care costs without compromising access to, and the quality of, medical care. Health care is a fundamental human need, and access to it is a fundamental human right. It must not be a privilege of the elite. Therefore, ways of providing access without generating unacceptable costs must be reexamined intensively and put into place.

In our own country excellent health care is often available—to those who can pay for it. However, more than 30 million Americans have no medical insurance coverage whatsoever. This means that they do not receive care, they take their chances with charity care, or they exhaust their very meager savings.

Further, for many years health care costs in the United States have risen at a rate more than twice that of general inflation, and neither the private nor the public sector can allow this to continue. Retired people are losing their benefits, working people are making do with reduced benefits, and many small-business employers offer no health insurance coverage. The American public-policy community presently is trying to find answers; but all the alternatives are crushingly expensive, and both the White House and Congress are deadlocked on what to do.

Most Western nations seem dissatisfied with their own systems, and many poor nations have no effective system at all. Each nation seems to stumble, by trial and error, through a succession of failures and shortfalls until it adopts a system that in the end is still not satisfactory. This will not do. The world community can and must demonstrate the political will necessary to develop effective systems, at acceptable costs, and with accessible services distributed equitably within societies.

Finally, further to the point that adequate health care is both a fundamental need and a human right, I suggest that doctors could be more active in addressing issues of health promotion and disease prevention as they relate to the wider national and world communities. If we are to contribute effectively to the urgent health needs of poor nations, we cannot merely transfer our elaborate, curative medical technology. It is an inappropriate system in many other lands and distracts from the basic public health needs of most developing countries. We must learn to put greater emphasis on sanitation and nutrition, safe water supplies, and basic education and vaccination programs, projects that may not be as dramatic as disaster relief efforts but hold the only hope for long-term improvement.

Governor Dean of Vermont, himself a physician, has emphasized that doctors' analytical skills and knowledge are badly needed in public life. He is not talking about the understandable need for doctors to organize to protect themselves against matters such as possible malpractice actions. Rather, he is talking about the need for doctors to take a more active role in the public processes concerned with satisfying the basic right of each individual to receive adequate health care. As we all know, good health not only affects the well-being of those who are fortunate enough to enjoy it; it also generates expanded productivity and enhanced economic growth and stability.

Finally, it should be noted that health and humanitarian assistance can be an effective tool in preventive diplomacy, not only providing immediate lifesaving help but offering a common ground that can sometimes open the difficult doors to political negotiation. There is much sustained work to be done by both medical personnel and laypersons in addressing a wide range of serious health-related problems. To do so will require a level of cooperation among different sectors of society rarely achieved.

FOSTERING DEMOCRACY AND HUMAN RIGHTS

There is yet another issue that all too often is ignored. It is the erroneous belief that the internal affairs of other nations are not a proper subject for state-to-state discourse, and that internal events in other countries, such as human rights violations, are not our concern. I strongly disagree. Although our options may at times be limited in dealing with such questions, we should never stop trying to apply diplomatic, economic and political pressures that will help the human family continue its passage toward a more open, more democratic and freer life.

Those countries that have attempted to create economic development in a totalitarian framework have found it does not work. The human spirit, liberated, is capable of productivity and achievement undreamed of under the deadening hand of conformist control, just as we have seen that economic and social policy steps contribute to development—the establishment of constitutional government, the rule of law, accountability of government officials, openness and respect for human rights.

Moreover, I believe that, just as the United Nations should establish early-warning mechanisms to foresee and, if possible, forestall military conflict between nations, the UN must continue to expand and strengthen its machinery for monitoring and bringing pressure to bear on violations of political and human rights. As I mentioned above, the tragic ethnic conflicts that devastated Yugoslavia and parts of the former Soviet Union and are still rife among other countries—Somalia, Rwanda, the Congo—are at core egregious violations of human rights.

The tide of history is not running in the wrong direction. Although some events are currently beyond our control, the tide still flows toward openness and freedom of the individual—concepts that lie at the heart of many religious and ethical traditions around the world.

STRENGTHENING KEY INTERNATIONAL INSTITUTIONS

In the 1940s, the international community held historic summits in San Francisco and Bretton Woods that helped establish a basis for a more enlightened world order. The Stockholm Initiative, to which I referred earlier, proposes that a comparable world summit on global governance be called to address the unprecedented challenges and opportunities that confront us today.

Such a global summit, which would have to be very carefully prepared through a process of consultation and negotiation among the participants, would, I suspect, lead not only the United States but most nations to the realization that it is incumbent on us to modernize institutions of cooperation—and to create new or modified instructions where needed. Much has been done to modernize, streamline and strengthen the United Nations to meet the tasks that face it. There must be ongoing efforts to broaden the UN's mandate at the Security Council level, strengthen the authority of the Secretary-General and continue to improve and stabilize the UN financial system.

I have suggested several structural changes that could be steps on the road to greater international peace and security, to shared and sustainable economic development, to curbing uncontrolled population growth and environmental degradation, to providing adequate global health care, to fostering democracy and human rights, and to creating a world order in which both law and justice become the norm, rather than the exception.

As we rush toward our date with the millennium, now less than a year away, we have, I believe, an unparalleled chance to define that future. Let us seize the moment.

CONCLUSION

Kevin M. Cahill, M.D.

There are no final answers; there cannot be in our finite and imperfect state. In public health all the old challenges remain, and new diseases seem constantly to emerge. The explosion of drug-resistant tuberculosis is a classic result of public complacency about an old but resurgent infectious plague; new viruses and environmental changes continue to challenge our capacity to adapt and respond. So, too, in the endless search for world peace, statesmen realize that one cannot afford simply to accept failure, to adhere impotently to outmoded approaches. None should be surprised that our noble goals prove elusive, and we must constantly adapt if we are to survive. Samuel Beckett, in typical fashion, summarized the long struggle of life simply: "Try again, Fail again, Fail better."

The chapters in this book clearly demonstrate that those who have devoted their lives to alleviating human suffering in the midst of conflicts and crises around the world are hardly pessimists. They are discovering how intimately entwined are pursuits that once were seen as separate and even competitive. In complex humanitarian crises, those delivering food, shelter or health now share their burdens and opportunities with political, military and diplomatic colleagues. All now appreciate the unique acceptability humanitarian efforts earn, and such efforts are increasingly recognized as one of the most valuable foundations in rebuilding traumatized societies.

Profound differences of philosophy and method, the accidents of history and geography, the divisions of time and civilization, are all present in the chapters, and they are real. But far more impressive are the human bonds, the mutual interests and the shared dedication to the relief of suffering and the prevention of needless cruelty and death in conflicts. For perhaps the first time, leaders in diplomacy and humanitarian assistance understand that they are not trains running on separate tracks but cars joined together in common cause. They understand that health, human rights and disaster relief must be moved from the periphery into the center ring of foreign policy and never again considered merely as matters of transient emotional interest.

Just as mass communications have transported distant tragedies into the center of the world's consciousness and conscience, so too can we no longer blot out the knowledge of terrible human-rights violations. We cannot escape epidemics that sweep across continents and attack the rich as well as the poor. We are inextricably linked on this earth to the fates of all innocent victims of oppression. Whether we like it or not, we cannot avoid this transcendental fact: we are, and must be, involved in the suffering of others.

And that surely is my basis for hope. I am convinced that by cooperating in efforts to heal the wounds of war and eliminate the causes of widespread violence, we can construct a new framework to support society's endless search for peace and devise new approaches that are more promising than the military and political alliances that have dominated international relations through so many troubled years.

APPENDIX

The International Diploma in Humanitarian Assistance
CIHC/CUNY in Partnership with RCSI
February 1999

PROJECT AND ACADEMIC DIRECTORS

Kevin M. Cahill, M.D., President and Director, CIHC; Professor and Chairman, Department of International Health, RCSI; Clinical Professor of Tropical Medicine, New York University
David Caputo, Ph.D., President, Hunter College, City University of New York

PROJECT COORDINATOR

Larry Hollingworth, Humanitarian Coordinator, CIHC

GENEVA COURSE COORDINATION

Joachim Kreysler, Academic Advisor to IFRC
Sylvie Gelin, Course Administrator, IFRC

TUTORS

Deborah Harris, (Administrative Tutor), Director of Continuing Education, CUNY
Larry Hollingworth, Chief, Humanitarian Assistance Projects, CIHC
Michel Veuthey, ICRC
Joachim Kreysler, Academic Advisor to IFRC
Tim O'Dempsey, M.D., Senior Lecturer, Department of International Health, RCSI
Cecilia Vasquez, Resident Tutor

FACULTY

K. Annan, The Secretary-General of the United Nations
J. Benjamin, Senior Advisor and Anthropologist, IRC
B. Bierens deHaan, Health Coordinator, ICRC
J. Black, Director, Information Systems Department, International Federation of Red Cross and Red Crescent Societies

R. Boland, Professor, Thunderbuilt University

B. Boutros-Ghali, Director CIHC, Former Secretary-General, United Nations

G. H. Brundtland, WHO, Director-General, Former Prime Minister of Norway

H. H. Bruun, HE, Danish Ambassador to Switzerland

L. Buttenheim, Senior Political Advisor to the UN Director-General, Geneva

F. Burkle, Director, Center of Excellence, University of Hawaii

N. Buzard, Project Director, Sphere

M. Carballo, Director, International Organization, Migration and Health

K. M. Cahill, M.D. ,President, CIHC; Professor and Chairman, Department of International Health, RCSI

D. Caputo, President, Hunter College, City University of New York

L. Clarke, Department of Humanitarian Affairs

R. Conti, Head of Unit, Water and Habitat, ICRC

R. Coupland, Health Coordinator, War Surgery, ICRC

M. Crahan, Professor of Political Science, Hunter College, CUNY

R. Davis, NBC Television Anchor Man

S. Deely, Senior Officer, Disaster Policy Department, International Federation RC/RC

Y. Etienne, Head, Training Unit, ICRC

J. Eliasson, Director CIHC, Secretary of State, Foreign Affairs, Sweden

P. Emes, Head, Recruitment and Human Resources Planning Service, International Federation RC/RC

S. Forman, Director, Center on International Cooperation

H. Gilles, Dean Emeritus, Liverpool School of Tropical Medicine

A. Golaz, Medical Epidemiologist, CDC

P. Grossrieder, Director-General, ICRC

D. Halliday, Former Under-Secretary-General UN; Former Humanitarian Coordinator, UN; Iraq

R. Hauser, World Food Program

D. Heyman, Executive Director, Communicable Diseases, WHO

C. Higgins, Field Coordination Support Unit, Disaster Response Branch, OCHA

J. Hocke, Former UN High Commissioner for Refugees

L. Hollingworth, Chief, Humanitarian Assistance Projects, CIHC

K. Janowski, Spokesman for UNHCR

N. Karlsberg, Chief Emergency Section, UNICEF

V. Keyes II. Kittani, Former President, UN General Assembly: SG's Special Representative in Somalia

J. Kreysler, Senior Relief Officer, Relief Health Service, DROC, International Federation RC/RC

I. Lazzarini, Head of Europe Sector, Central Tracing Agency and Protection Division, ICRC, Geneva

A. Loretti, Team Coordinator Al, Development Activities, WHO

W. Lyerly, Group Leader of Emerging Threats and Crisis Response Unit, USAID

H. Masterson, Head, Training Support Service, International Federation RC/RC

K. Madi, Project Officer, Emergency Division, UNICEF

F. May, Trainer, ICRC

S. Male, UNHCR

S. Viera di Mello, UN Under-Secretary-General for Humanitarian Affairs

G. Moose, HE, American Ambassador to Switzerland

J. Muhlebach, Head of National Staff Unit, ICRC

R. Nancholas, Director, Europe Department, DROC, International Federation RC/RC

E. Noji, Senior Medical Officer, HINAB Coordinator, WHO

T. O'Dempsey, M.D., Senior Lecturer, Department of International Health, RCSI

O. Otunnu, UN Special Representative for Children in Armed Conflict

D. Owen, M.D., Director CIHC, Former U.K. Foreign Minister and EU Representative to the former Yugoslavia

S. Petersen, UN Deputy High Commission for Refugees

V. Petrovski, Director-General of UN office, Geneva

T. Planting, Field Security, Coordination Officer, DROC, International Federation RC/RC

B. Ramcharan, UN Deputy High Commission

G. Rodier, WHO

J. P. Revel, Senior Relief Health Officer, Relief Health Service, DROC, International Federation RC/RC

A. Redmond, Professor of Accident and Emergency, Keele University, U.K.

M. Robinson, Commissioner for Human Rights

J. Roy, Senior Officer, International Federation RC/RC

R. Russbach, M.D., President, Geneva Foundation

M. Al Sadar, Histopathologist

F. Savage, Medical Officer, Department of Child and Adolescent Health and Development, WHO

J. L. Siblot, WFP

H. Siem, Special Advisor of WHO Director-General in Moscow

N. Stockton, Director, Oxfam

P. Tarrnoff, Director, CIHC, Former President, Council on Foreign Relations

E. Ter Horst, Special Representative of Secretary-General in El Salvador and Haiti

R. Towle, Senior Legal Advisor, UNHCR

C. Vance, Director, CIHC, Former U.S. Secretary of State

C. Vasquez, Resident Tutor

M. Veuthey, Doctor of Law, Legal Advisor, 50th Anniversary of the Geneva Conventions, ICRC

M. Wahlström, Under-Secretary-General, Disaster Relief Operations Coordination, DROC, International Federation RC/RC

J. Watt, Relief Officer, Relief Service, DROC, International Federation RC/RC

G. Weber, Secretary-General, International Federation RC/RC

A. Whitley, Special Assistant to Secretary-General, UNCTAD

R. Wilkinson, Editor, *Refugee Magazine*, UNHCR

P. Wijmans, Advisor, Sphere

J. Ziegler

Bossey Centre Staff

Ecumenical Council of Churches

OCHA

UN Human Rights Centre

Plus academic staff from CUNY and representatives of NGO and UN and international agencies.

INTRODUCTION—COURSE CURRICULUM/TIMETABLE

Six-Day Week Daily Timetable Plan

Session i	1 hr.	8.30–9.30
Session ii	1 hr.	9.30–10.30
Break	15 min.	
Session iii	1.5 hr.	10.45–12.15
Lunch /Library	1 hr. 45 min.	
Session iv	1.5 hr.	14.00–15.30
Break	15 min.	
Session v	1.5 hr.	15.45–17.15
Break	30 min.	
Session vi	2.5 hr.	17.45–20.00

Examination: Continuous assessment; Written assessment; Assessment of syndicate teamwork and individual presentation skills; Viva
Language: English
Location: Residence: Chateau de Bossey, Czigny, Switzerland
Note: This timetable may be subject to unavoidable changes.

WEEK I: SETTING THE AGENDA AND DISASTER PREPAREDNESS

Sunday, January 31

	16.00–18.00	Registration	
	18.00–19.00	Introduction to course	K. M. Cahill
			J. Kreysler
			L. Hollingworth
			T. O'Dempsey
	19.30–21.00	Personal introductions, social	Students/faculty

Monday, February 1

Session i	09.00–09.20	Welcome to IDHA	K. M. Cahill
			I. Kittani
			G. Weber
			P. Grossrider
	09.20–09.30	Introduction (video)	K. Annan
	09.30–10.00	The need for training and obstacles to learning	K. M. Cahill
Session ii	10.00–11.00	Humanitarian assistance: a historic perspective	P. Grossrider
Session iii	11.20–12.20	Humanitarian assistance: a current international perspective	M. Wahlström
Session iv	13.45–14.30	Humanitarian assistance: a personal perspective	H. Bruun
Session v	14.30–15.15	Humanitarian assistance: a UN perspective	N. Karlsberg
Session vi	15.45–16.30	Creating humanitarian crises	D. Halliday
Session vii	16.30–17.00	Discussion	

Session viii	17.30–19.30	Identifying the roles and agendas of stakeholders: the UN, international agencies, multilateral, bilateral, NGO	L. Hollingworth J. Ziegler J. Kreysler M. Veuthey

Tuesday, February 2   **Emergencies in context information and communication**

Session i	08.30–10.00	Communication, information technology and the international network	J. Black, IFRC
Session ii	10.30–12.15		W. Lyerly
	12.15–14.00	Introduction to library, computer facilities and IDHA website.	Bossey Centre Staff
Session iii	14.00–17.00	Political and economic analysis of emergency situations: the need for specificity	University of Geneva
Session iv	17.30–19.00	Presentations by representative participants of their organizations	L. Hollingworth J. Kreysler M. Veuthey W. Lyerly
Session v	19.00–20.00	Discussion: Who is the "right person" for work in humanitarian assistance and what are their expectations?	R. Boland J. Kreysler C. Vasques W. Lyerly Allocate Syndicates

Wednesday, February 3   **Disaster preparedness: early warning indicators**

Session i, ii	08.30–10.30	Political and economic social and population trends environmental and agricultural	M. King J. Kreysler M. Veuthey
Session iii	10.45–12.15	Trends in nutrition and patterns of disease	F. Savage
Session iv	4.00–15.30	Comparing natural disasters and conflicts	B. Lyerly
Session v	15.45–17.15	Effecting a rapid response	L. Hollingworth J. Kreysler
Session vi	17.45–20.00	Debate (see topic list)	

Thursday, February 4   **Problems facing refugees and internally displaced: an overview**

Session i	08.30–09.30	Social, cultural and psychological	B. Bierens de Haan
Session ii	09.30–10.30	Political and economic	A. Loretti/ M. Carballo
Session iii	10.45–11.45	Children in conflict	K. Madi
Session iv	11.45–12.15	Key differences between refugees and internally displaced	M. Veuthey
Sessions v, vi	14.00–17.30	International law in relation to refugees/ internally displaced. Asylum seeking	M. Veuthey
		Legal status and rights/privileges of international aid workers	R. Towle
Session vi	18.00–19.00	Defending the worldwide right to asylum	R. Towle

Friday, February 5   **Planning for emergencies: management and logistics**

Session i	08.30–09.30	Planning for an acute emergency I	J. Watt
Session ii	09.30–10.30	Planning for an acute emergency II	J. Watt
Session iii	10.45–12.15	Mobilizing resources for humanitarian assistance	L. Clarke
Session iv	14.00–16.30	Logistical considerations	R. Hauser
Session v	16.30–17.15	Practical demonstration re refugee needs	Y. Etienne
Session vi	17.45–20.00	Debate (see topic list)	

Saturday, February 6

Sessions i–iii	08.30–12.15	Ethical issues and code of conduct UN Human Rights Centre	M. Veuthey
Session ii	14.00–17.15	Specialist options (a) Politics, economics, diplomacy (b) Law	A. Whitley

WEEK 2: THE EMERGENCY RESPONSE

Monday, February 8   **Basic physical needs**

Session i	08.30–09.00	Introduction to environmental health in emergencies	R. Conti
Session ii	09.00–10.30	Site planning, shelter, clothing	P. Wijmans N. Buzard
Session iii	10.45–12.15	Water and sanitation	R. Conti
Session iv	14.00–15.30	Meeting nutritional needs of the vulnerable	F. Savage
Session v	15.45–17.15	Food seeking Local and external food providers and suppliers Fuel and cooking Food constraints Food for work Food for training ACC/SCN	R. Hauser
Session vi	17.45–20.00	Funding humanitarian assistance	S. Forman

Tuesday, February 9   **Methods of needs assessment and monitoring in emergencies**

		Workshop	
Sessions i–v	08.30– 17.15	Topics for discussion include: Population size, structure and dynamics. Rapid population assessment. Selection and measurement of key indicators Information systems and monitoring Surveys: relevance and appropriate methodology	E. Noji (organizer)
Session vi	17.45– 20.00	Land mines	R. Coupland

Wednesday, February 10   **Health I: control of communicable diseases**

Session i	08.30–09.30	Introduction	D. Heyman
Sessions ii–iii	09.30–12.15	Priority diseases: Measles Diarrhoeal diseases Acute respiratory infections	D. Heyman H. Siem A. Loretti

| Sessions iv–vi 14.00–17.15 | Other communicable diseases of potential importance in refugee settings | |
| Session vii | 17.45–20.00 | Discussion |

Thursday, February 11   Health II: health program

Session i	08.30–09.30	Medical and laboratory supplies	CDC
		Essential drugs	B. Berkholder
			A. Golaz
Session ii	09.30–10.30	Immunization programs	A. Golaz
Session iii	10.45–12.15	Reproductive health	M. King
Session iv	14.00–15.30	Physical trauma and rehabilitation	R. Russbach
			A. Redmond ICRC
Session v	15.45–17.15	Syndicate exercise: Epidemics in Goma and Ngara: What went right, what went wrong?	J. Kreysler
Session vi	17.45–20.00	Syndicate presentations	

Friday, February 12   Crisis as it affects the individual: The Individual in the context of the community

Session i	08.30–09.30	Psychological problems affecting victims of conflict	B. Bierens de Haan
			J. P Revel, IFRC
Session ii	09.30–10.30	Gender issues: the changing roles of women and men in situations of conflict and displacement	J. Benjamin
Session iii	10.45–11.45	Rape as a weapon of war	M. Carballo
	11.45–12.45	Torture	M. Al Sadar
Session iv	14.00–15.30	Tracing and reuniting families	I. Lazzarini
Session v	15.45–17.15	Individual case histories	T. O'Dempsey (syndicate work)
Session vi	17.45–20.00	How can we best achieve appropriate representation and participation of host communities and services? Scenario workshop	CDC Team J. Roy

Saturday, February 13   Malnutrition

| Session i | 08.30–10.00 | Nutritional surveys and surveillance feeding programs and follow-up | J. Kreysler |
| Session ii | 10.00–12.15 | Clinical aspects and management | T. O'Dempsey |

Sunday, February 14   Clinical problems   T. O'Dempsey

WEEK 3:   THE EVOLUTION TOWARD RESOLUTION

Monday, February 15   Working with communities and establishing basic services

Session i	08.30–09.30	Working with local services and communities Cultural aspects	F. May
Session ii	09.30–10.30	Basic community services and structures	R. Nancholas
Session iii	10.45–12.15	Human resources within the community	H. Masterson P. Emes

Employment and training

Session iv	14.00–15.30	Management, administration and salaries	H. Masterson
			P. Emes
			J. Muhlebach
Session v	15.45–17.15	Refugee rights	UNHCR
Session vi	17.45–20.00	Debate	

Tuesday, February 16   Quality assurance and accountability

Sessions i–ii	08.30–10.30	Project proposals	
Sessions iii–v	10.45–17.15	Accountability and minimum standards	N. Stockton
		Sphere	
		Quality assurance	
		in humanitarian assistance	
		The Sphere Project	
Session vi	17.45–20.00	Syndicate presentations	J. Kreysler
		Critique on Sphere	N. Buzard

Wednesday, February 17   Conflict and conflict resolution:
repatriation, reintegration and rehabilitation

Sessions i–ii	08.30–10.30	Conflict and conflict resolution	E. Ter Horst
		in refugee/displaced communities	
Session iii	10.45–12.15	The role of the church	M. Crahan
		in the peace process	
Sessions iv–v	14.00–15.30	Postconflict rehabilitation	S. Deeley
		Demobilization	
Session vi	15.45–17.15	Lessons learned and future predictions	J. Hocke
			F. Burkle
Session vii	17.45–20.00	Developing an institutional memory	E. Noji
		of humanitarian crises	

Thursday, February, 18   The Military response: security

			T. Planting
			(organizer)
			L. Hollingworth

Friday, February 19   UN Day: dealing with a disaster

		Workshop	L. Buttenheim
			(organizer)
Session i	08.30–09.30		S. Jessen Petersen
			I. Kittani
Session ii	09.30–10.30		E. Ter Horst
			J. Hocke
Session iii	10.45–12.15		
Session iv	14.00–15.30		
Session v	15.45–17.15		
Session vi	17.45–20.00	Discussion	

Saturday, February 20   Human rights

Sessions i–ii	08.30–10:30	Human rights	B. Ramcharan
		Human Rights Centre	
Session iii	10.45–12.15	National security and human rights	M. Crahan
			M. Veuthey
Session iv	14.00–17.15	Human rights issues	I. Levine
			M. Crahan
			M. Veuthey

WEEK 4: REESTABLISHING STRUCTURE AND FUNCTION: THE MEDIA CASE STUDIES

Monday, February 22		**Managing the transition to sustainable development: exit strategies**	
		Preventive Diplomacy	
Session i	8.30–12.15	Defining the objectives	S. Jessen Petersen
Sessions ii–iii		Macroeconomic stabilization	E. Ter Horst
		"Check lists" for sustainability	
Session iv	14.00–15.30	Exit strategies in humanitarian assistance programs	J. Kreysler
		Syndicate exercise	
Session v	15.45–17.15	International aid workers and personal health	K. M. Cahill
Session vi	17.45–20.00	An American's experience in assistance	G. Moose

Tuesday, February 23		**The media and humanitarian crises**	A. Whitley
		Preventive diplomcy	R. Wilkinson
			K. Janowski
Session i	08.30–09.30	Humanitarian assistance as news: images, values and impact	
Session ii	09.30–10.30	The power of the press	
Session iii	10.45–12.15	The images of crisis	G. Peress
Sessions iv–v	14.00–17.15	The role of TV and radio	
Session vi	18.00–20.00	Round table with Geneva press	

Wednesday, February 24			
	08:30–10.30	Written assessment	
	11:00–12.15	Case studies	J. Kreysler
			H. Gilles
		Film: *The Second Civil War*	

Thursday, February 25		**Case studies**	
	18.00–21.00	Case presentation	J. Kreysler
			H. Gilles

Friday, February 26			
	08.30–12.30	Oral	K. M. Cahill
			D. Caputo
			Y. Etienne
			M. Wahlstrom
	14.00–17.30	CIHC directors roundtable: humanitarian action and politics	K. M. Cahill
			D. Owen
			P. Tarnoff
			J. Eliasson
			B. Boutros-Ghali
			C. Vance
	18.00–19.00	Graduation ceremony	K. M. Cahill
			D. Caputo
			B. Boutros-Ghali

Saturday, February 27			
	10.00–12.00	Course evaluation and feedback	

DISCUSSION TOPICS/SEMINAR TITLES

1. Humanitarian assistance: the price of international political complacency and inertia?
2. Is the international community obliged to respond to each and every crisis?
3. Is the assistance of the logistics of the military the most suitable solution to a crisis?
4. Is the military logistic machine the best response to a humanitarian crisis?
5. The local impact of refugee communities.
6. The aftermath of ethnic conflict: justice or revenge?
7. Is asylum seeking a lost cause?
8. Advocacy: the role of international agencies and NGOs.
9. Can the international community negotiate with key players if they have "blood on their hands"?
10. Measuring household food security in emergency situations.
11. Child soldiers: What will the long-term impact be on development?
12. Is an integrated multidisciplinary response an impossible ideal?
13. Building a collective institutional memory.
14. Independent research and evaluation in acute and chronic crises.
15. Is Bosnia getting more than its fair share?
16. What is the UN? World parliament, meeting place? What and where do you want it to be?
17. Regional problems. Regional solutions?
18. Central Africa. What would have happened if the world had done nothing?
19. Harmonization of refugee procedures and legislation.
20. Competition or cooperation: How can aid organizations optimize their effectiveness?
21. Forced repatriation: How do we respond? How should we respond? How can we respond?
22. The UN and its agencies: mechanisms of accountability. Are there any? Do they function?
23. How are funds raised for humanitarian assistance projects?
24. Should refugees be kept in camps?
25. Professional registration in emergency situations.
26. Humanitarian assistance through partnership with host governments and services.
27. How can we optimize opportunities for training of staff in countries afflicted by humanitarian crises?
28. Misappropriation and misuse of donor funds and resources.
29. Problems posed by borders in provision of humanitarian assistance.
30. The role of humanitarian assistance in establishing peace and reconciliation.
31. Humanitarian assistance in situations of conflict: relief for victims or sustenance for perpetrators?
32. Humanitarian assistance: Always positive?
33. Do we have the capacity to control emerging infectious diseases?

NOTES

CHAPTER I

1. U.S. Committee for Refugees. *World Refugee Survey* 1997 (Washington, DC, July 1997).
2. UNHCR Web page, May 1998.
3. M. J. Toole and R. J. Waldman. "Prevention of Excess Mortality in Refugee and Displaced Populations in Developing Countries." *Journal of the American Medical Association* 1990; 263: 3296–3302.
4. Centers for Disease Control and Prevention. "Famine-Affected, Refugee and Displaced Populations: Recommendations for Public Health Issues." *Morbidity and Mortality Weekly Report* 1992; 41: RR–13.
5. Goma Epidemiology Group. "Public Health Impact of Rwandan Refugee Crisis: What Happened in Goma, Zaire, in July 1994?" *Lancet* 1995₁ 345: 339–344.
6. Centers for Disease Control and Prevention. "Public Health Consequences of Acute Displacement of Iraqi Citizens—March–May 1991." *Morbidity and Mortality Weekly Report,* 1991; 40: 443–446.
7. C. Paquet and M. van Soest. "Mortality and Malnutrition among Rwandan Refugees in Zaire. *Lancet.* 1994; 344: 823–24.
8. UNHCR. "Ruhinga Refugee Camps." Unpublished interim report by CDC medical epidemiologists. July 13, 1992. Cox's Bazaar, Bangladesh.
9. M. J. Toole, R. W. Steketee, R. J. Waldman, P. Nieburg. "Measles Prevention and Control in Emergency Setting." *Bulletin of the World Health Organization* 1989; 67: 381–388.
10. M. J. Toole and R. J. Waldman. "The Public Health Aspects of Complex Emergencies and Refugee Situations." *Annual Review of Public Health* 1997; 18: 283–312.
11. M. J. Toole et al. "Micronutrient Deficiency Diseases in Refugee Populations." *Lancet* 1992; 333;1214–1216.
12. Médecins Sans Frontières, *Nutrition Guidelines* (Paris, 1995).
13. Office of the High Commissioner for Refugees, *Water Manual for Refugee Situations* (Geneva, 1992).
14. M. J. Toole, S. Galson, W. Brady. "Are War and Public Health Compatible?" *Lancet* 1993; 341: 935–938.

CHAPTER 2

1. Kevin M. Cahill, M.D., *Famine* (New York: Orbis Press, 1982).
2. ———. *Health on the Horn of Africa* (London: Spottiswoode Ballantine, 1969).

3. ———. *Somalia: A Perspective* (Albany: State University of New York Press, 1980).

4. J. Erdrishinghe. "Infections in the Malnourished: With Special Reference to Malaria," *Ann. of Tropical Pediatrics* 6 (1986), p. 233.

CHAPTER 3

1. Masefield, G. B. *Food and Nutrition Procedures in Times of Disaster.* Rome: Food and Agriculture Organization of the UN, 1967.

2. Kent, R. C. *Anatomy of Disaster Relief: The International Network in Action.* London: Pinter Publishers, 1987.

3. Ingram, J. "Food and Disaster Relief: Issues of Management and Policy." *Disasters* 1988; 12: 12–18.

4. Borton, J. and Shoham, J. "Experiences of Non-Governmental Organisations in the Targeting of Emergency Food Aid." *Disasters* 13;1989: 77–93.

5. Eldridge, C. "Thought for Food: Suggestions for a Systematised Approach to Emergency Food Distribution Operations." *Disasters* 13;1989: 135–152.

6. The International Committee of the Red Cross. *The Geneva Conventions of August 12, 1949.* Geneva, Switzerland: ICRC Publications, 1969.

7. International Committee of the Red Cross. *Protocols Additional to the Geneva Conventions of 12 August 1949.* Geneva, Switzerland: ICRC Publications, 1977.

8. International Committee of the Red Cross. "Rules of International Humanitarian Law Governing the Conduct of Hostilities in Non-International Conflicts and Declaration on the Rules of International Humanitarian Law Governing the Conduct of Hostilities in Non-International Conflicts." *International Review of the Red Cross* No. 278; September–October 1990: 383–409.

9. Aldrich, G. H. "Compliance with International Humanitarian Law." *International Review of the Red Cross* No. 282; May–June 1991: 294–312.

10. Boothman, I. M. "A Historical Survey of the Incidence of Drought in Northern Somalia." In: I. M. Lewis, ed., *Abaar: The Somali Drought.* London: International African Institute, 1975.

11. Amnesty International. *Somalia: Report on an Amnesty International Visit and Current Human Rights Concerns.* New York: Amnesty International, U.S.A., 1990.

12. Ungar, S. J. "Africa: The Military Money Drain." *Bulletin of the Atomic Scientists* September 1985: 31–34.

13. Personal and privileged communication with representative of UN agencies in Nairobi, February 17, 1992.

14. de Waal, A. and Leaning, J. *Somalia: No Mercy in Mogadishu. The Human Cost of the Conflict and the Struggle for Relief.* Boston and New York: Physicians for Human Rights and Africa Watch. March, 1992.

15. Kunder, J. "Somalia—Civil Strife." Situation Report No. 7. Office of U.S. Foreign Disaster Assistance. Washington, DC: Agency for International Development, January 30, 1992, p. 3.

16. International Committee of the Red Cross. Emergency Plan of Action: Somalia. March 5, 1992. As cited in de Waal and Leaning, *No Mercy in Mogadishu.*

17. Bongaarts, J. and Cain, M. "Demographic Responses to Famine." Working Paper 77. Center for Policy Studies. New York: Population Council, November, 1981.

18. International Committee of the Red Cross. "Somalia: Global Approach the Only Means of Averting Famine." *Bulletin* March, 1992.

19. Perlez, J. "U.S. Says Airlifts Fail Somali Needy." *New York Times* July 31, 1992, A9.

20. Perlez, J. "Officials Say Somali Famine Is Even Worse Than Feared." *New York Times* September 6, 1992, A1.

21. Personal and privileged communication with representative of the ICRC in Somalia, February 16, 1992.

22. Sandoz, Y. "'Droit' or 'Devoir d'Ingerence' and the Right to Assistance: The Issues Involved." *International Review of the Red Cross* No. 288, May–June 1992: 215–227.

23. Perlez, J. "No Easy Fix for Somalia." *New York Times*, September 7, 1992, A1, A5.

24. Engelberg S. "U.N. Official Pleads for Help for Beseiged Bosnians." *New York Times* August 18, 1992, A3.

25. Estimate attributed to Gen. Lewis MacKenzie, in charge of UN forces at Sarajevo, in Apple R. W. Jr., "Baker Aide Says War Crimes Inquiry into Bosnian Camps." *New York Times* August 6, 1992, A1, A9.

26. Estimate attributed to Lt. Gen. Barry R. McCaffrey, in Gordon, M. R. "60,000 Needed for Bosnia, a U.S. General Estimates." *New York Times* August 12, 1992, A8.

27. Perlez, J. "Food Relief Grows but So Do Somalia's Dead." *New York Times* July 19, 1992, A1, A8.

28. Perlez, J. "UN Observer Unit to Go to Somalia." *New York Times*, July 20, 1992, A3.

29. Faison, S. "U.N. Head Proposes Expanded Effort for Somali Relief." *New York Times* July 25, 1992, A1, A4.

30. Tyler, P. "UN Chief's Dispute with Council Boils Over." *New York Times* August 3, 1992, A1, A9.

31. Natsios, A. S. "Humanitarian Relief Intervention in Somalia: The Economics of Chaos." In: Clarke, W. and Herbst, J., eds. *Learning from Somalia: The Lessons of Armed Humanitarian Intervention.*" Boulder, CO: Westview Press, 1997: 77–98.

32. Perlez, J. "No Easy Fix for Somalia." *New York Times* September 7, 1992, A1, A5.

33. Woods, J. L. "U.S. Government Decisionmaking Processes during Humanitarian Operations in Somalia." In: Clarke, W. and Herbst, J., eds. *Learning from Somalia*, 151–172.

34. International Federation of Red Cross and Red Crescent Societies. *World Disasters Report 1997*. Geneva: IFRC, 1997: 68–78.

35. Refugee Policy Group. *Lives Lost, Lives Saved: Excess Mortality and the Impact of Health Interventions in the Somalia Emergency*. Washington, DC: RPG, November 1994.

36. Omaar, R. and de Waal, A. *Somalia Operation Restore Hope: A Preliminary Assessment.* London: African Rights, May 1993.

37. Stevenson, J. "Hope Restored in Somalia?" *Foreign Policy* No. 90, Spring 1993: 138–154.

38. Toole, M. J. "Military Role in Humanitarian Relief in Somalia. *Lancet* 1993; 342: 190–91.

39. Lorch, D. "Last of the U.S. Troops Leave Somalia." *New York Times* March 26, 1994: 1,2.

40. Prendergast, J. *Crisis Response: Humanitarian Band-Aids in Sudan and Somalia*. London: Pluto Press with Center of Concern, 1997: 139–152.

41. Blumenthal, S. "Why Are We in Somalia? Letter from Washington." *The New Yorker* October 25, 1993: 48–60.

42. Clarke, W. "U.S. Military Planning for Complex Humanitarian Emergencies: The Troubled Planning Environment." Draft paper for conference on civil-military relations in complex humanitarian crises. Kennedy School of Government and Marshall Legacy. March 13–15, 1998, Cambridge, MA.

43. Lewis, P. UN Set to Debate Peacemaking Role. *New York Times* September 6, 1992, 7.

44. Putzel, M. "U.S. Preparing Units to Help UN in Bosnia." *Boston Globe* July 1, 1992, 1,12.

CHAPTER 4

This chapter incorporates materials from Diana Quick, "Refugee Women at Risk," *Freedom Review*, Vol. 26, No. 5, New York, 1995.

1. Human Rights Watch, *Shattered Lives: Sexual Violence during the Rwandan Genocide and its Aftermath* (New York, Human Rights Watch, September, 1996), pp. 56–58.

2. "Refugees, Feminine Plural," *Refugees*, No. 100/II, UNHCR, 1995, p. 3.
3. "Rebuilding a Future Together: II," United Nations High Commissioner for Refugees (Geneva, 1997).
4. Human Rights Watch, *Shattered Lives*, p. 19.
5. Susan Forbes Martin, *Return and Reintegration: The Experiences of Refugee and Displaced Women*, Refugee Policy Group (September 1992).
6. Women's Commission for Refugee Women and Children, "Project to Advance Refugee Women's Participation and Protection: Year End Report" (New York, 1997)
7. United Nations High Commissioner for Refugees, "Review of the Implementation and Impact of UNHCR's Policy on Refugee Women," 1993; 29, 111.
8. Women's Commission for Refugee Women and Children, "Project to Advance Refugee Women's Participation and Protection.
9. Roberta Cohen, *Refugee and Internally Displaced Women: A Development Perspective* (Washington: Brookings Institution–Refugee Policy Group Project on Internal Displacement, 1995), p. 17.
10. Women's Commission for Refugee Women and Children, "The Children's War: Towards Peace in Sierra Leone" (New York, 1997).
11. Colville, Rupert "The Difficulty of Educating Leyla," *Refugees*, United Nations High Commissioner for Refugees II—1995, p. 24.
12. Women's Commission for Refugee Women and Children (New York, June 1994).
13. "AIDS Brings Another Scourge to War-Devastated Rwanda," *New York Times* (May 28, 1998).
14. *Ibid.*
15. Shana Swiss, M.D., Joan E. Giller, M.A., *Journal of American Medical Association*, "Rape as a Crime of War: A Medical Perspective," Vol. 270, No. 5 (August 4, 1993).
16. Shana Swiss, M.D., Journal of American Medical Association, "*Violence Against Women During the Liberian Civil Conflict*," Vol. 279, No. 8 (February 25, 1998).
17. Women's Commission for Refugee Women and Children, "Tanzania Report" (August 1995).
18. Sydia Nduna and Lorelei Goodyear, International Rescue Committee, New York, "Pain Too Deep for Tears: Assessing the Prevalence of Sexual and Gender Violence Among Burundian Refugees in Tanzania" (September 1997).
19. *Ibid.*
20. "Policy on Refugee Women," United Nations High Commissioner for Refugees (Geneva, 1990).
21. "UNHCR Guidelines on the Protection of Refugee Women," United Nations High Commissioner for Refugees (Geneva, 1991).
22. "Sexual Violence Against Refugees: Guidelines on Prevention and Response," United Nations High Commissioner for Refugees (Geneva, 1995).
23. "People Oriented Planning: A Practical Training Tool for Refugee Workers," United Nations High Commissioner for Refugees (Geneva, 1993).
24. The Convention on the Elimination of All Forms of Discrimination Against Women (CEDAW), an international bill of rights for women, has been ratified by more than 154 countries.

CHAPTER 5

1. UNICEF ICDC, *Children and Violence*, p. 3.
2. Compiled from Bellamy, p. 13, and Otunnu p. 7.
3. Women's Commission for Refugee Women and Children, p. 2.
4. *Op. cit.*, p. 21.
5. Boothby et al., "The UNHCR response to the Machel Study," in *Children and Youth*, Refugee Participation Network Issue 24, p. 14–15.

6. Schenkenberg van Mierop, ed. "Protection of Civilians in Conflict," in Médecins Sans Frontières, p. 2.
7. Colletta et al., p. (v).
8. Hammarberg, p. 2.
9. See WHO—executive summary and chapters 1 and 2.
10. See Landers, the principal resource for this section, for a detailed discussion of the issue.
11. See Kunder and UNHCR, the principal resources for this section, for a full review of the issue.
12. WHO, p. 1.
13. Kunder, p. 21.
14. Kunder, p. 20.
15. See discussion in Kadjar-Hamouda, pp. 3–4.
16. Women's Commssion, *op. cit.*, p. 13.
17. See World Vision Staff Working Paper No. 23 for a detailed discussion of the issue.
18. Doris Schopper, Preface, p. viii, in Médecins Sans Frontières.
19. Hammarberg, p. 1.
20. Otunnu, p. 3.
21. Quoted with some editorial adaptations from Levine, *Promoting Humanitarian Principles*.
22. Subject of a discussion between the author and Dr. Magne Raundalen, Norwegian child psychologist, Algiers, July 1998.
23. See Levine, *Protecting Children in Emergencies*, the principal resource for this section.
24. See Hamilton, which is acknowledged as an excellent source for this section, for its incisive critique of IHL, the Convention on the Rights of the Child and their adequacy for children in armed conflict.
25. Namely, the right to life, dignity and freedom, protection from torture and humiliating treatment, unjust imprisonment or being taken hostage.
26. UNICEF, *First Call for Children*, p. 65.
27. Quoted from United Nations General Assembly, *Impact of Armed Conflict on Children*, paras. 209 and 210, p. 60.
28. Quoted from Levine, *op. cit.* ., p. 2.
29. Quoted from Ressler et al., p. 119.
30. Quoted from Ratner, p. 66.
31. Coalition to Stop the Use of Child Soldiers, p. 7.
32. *Op. cit.*, p. 8.
33. United Nations *op. cit.*, quoted from paras. 220, 230 and 234, pp. 62, 65 and 66.
34. Levine, *Promoting Humanitarian Principles*, p. 14.
35. Quoted from Vittachi, p. 10.
36. *Op. cit.*, p. 1.
37. *Op. cit.*, p. 22 and chapter 2, pp. 15–31.
38. Cohn, pp. 3–5.
39. See Ombudsman for Children for a review of the role of the Ombudsman in Norway.
40. Ratner, pp. 76–77.
41. Peter Hansen quoted in Bellamy, p. 33.
42. *Op. cit.*, p. 28.
43. World Bank, p. 6.
44. Australian National Committee on Violence, quoted in UNICEF ICDC, *Children in Violence*, p. 3.
45. Quoted from North-South Institute, p. 2.
46. Adapted from Bellamy, p. 40.

CHAPTER 6

1. R. E. Morgan and G. Mutalik, "Bringing International Health Back Home," Policy Paper for the 19th Annual Conference on the National Council for International Health (Washington, DC: National Council for International Health, 1992).
2. *Directory of U.S. International Health Organizations, 1992* (Washington, DC: National Council for International Health).
3. Kathleen N. Lohr, Neal A. Vanselow, and Don E. Detmer, Eds., *The Nation's Physician Workforce: Options for Balancing Supply and Requirements.* (Washington, DC: National Academy Press, 1996).
4. A. Mejia, H. Pizurki, E. Royston, eds., *Foreign Medical Graduates: The Case of the United States* (Lexington, Mass.: Lexington Books, 1980); H.A. Ronaghy, K. Cahill, and T.D. Baker, "Physician Migration in the United States: One Country's Transfusion is Another Country's Hemorrhage," *JAMA* 227 (1974): 538–42; World Bank. Health Sector Policy Paper, 2d ed. (Washington, DC: World Bank, 1980).
5. J. Crofton, "Tobacco: World Action on the Pandemic" (editorial), *British Journal of Addiction* 84 (1989): 1397–1400.
6. M. Silverman, P.R. Lee, and M. Lydecker, "The Drugging of the Third World," *International Journal of Health Services* 12 (1982): 585–95.
7. T. D. Baker, C. Weisman, and E. Piwoz, "U.S. Physicians in International Health," *JAMA* 251 (1984): 502–4.
8. Ibid.; T. D. Baker, C. Weisman, and E. Piwoz, "United States Health Professionals in International Health Work," *American Journal of Public Health* 74 (1984): 438–41.
9. P. H. Grundy and P. B. Budetti, "The Distribution and Supply of Cuban Medical Personnel in Third World Countries," *American Journal of Public Health* 70 (1980): 717–9.
10. Baker et al., "United States Health Professionals," p. 349.
11. R. E. Pust, "U.S. Abundance of Physicians and International Health," *JAMA 252* (1984): 385–88.
12. S. P. Asper, "Report on the Survey of International Activities of U.S. Health Professions Schools," *Academic Medicine* 64 (1989, supplement): S33–36; S.P. Asper and W.W. Steele, eds., *1988 Directory of International Programs and Projects of U.S. Schools of Medicine, Dentistry, Pharmacy and Public Health* (Philadelphia, Pa.: Educational Commission for Foreign Medical Graduates, 1988).
13. S. P. Aspen, "Report on the Survey of International Activities of U.S. Health Professions Schools," *Academic Medicine* 64 (1989): 533–36. S. P. Aspen, W. W. Steele, eds., *1988 Directory of International Programs and Projects of U.S. Schools of Medicine, Dentistry, Pharmacy, and Public Health* (Philadelphia: ECFMG, 1988).
14. D. A. Kindig and G. L. Lythcott, "A Proposal: Share Our Doctors Abroad," *The New Physician* 10 (September 1984).
15. V. W. Sidel, "International Health: A World View for Medical Students," *Einstein Quarterly Journal of Biology and Medicine* 3 (1985): 50–51.
16. J. Javits, R. Schweiker, and M. Humphrey, SB–3103—International Health Act of 1978, 95th Congress, 2nd session.
17. J. E. Banta, Statement before the Labor and Human Resources Subcommittee on Health and Scientific Research, United States Senate. Washington, DC, July 2, 1980.
18. AMSA International Health Task Force, *International Health Electives for Medical Students,* 5th ed. (St. Louis, Mo.: St. Louis University School of Medicine, 1989); *Faculty Contacts and Curricular Information on International Health at U.S. Medical Schools* (Reston, VA: American Medical Student Association, 1987). Also note C. Krogh and R. Pust, *International Health: A Manual for Advisers and Students* (Kansas City, MO: Society of Teachers of Family Medicine, 1990); L. Barthauer, *International Health Funding Guide* (Reston, VA: American Medical Association, 1990).
19. *The International Partnership Program in Community-Based Medical Education* (Reston, VA: American Medical Student Association, 1992).

20. M. Barry and F. J. Bia, "Departments of Medicine and International Health," *American Journal of Medicine* 80 (1984): 1019–21.

21. *International Dimensions: News on Activities and Opportunities in International Medicine* (Chapel Hill, NC: University of North Carolina School of Medicine, Office of International Affairs, June–July 1992).

22. B. Unland, R. Waterman, W. Wiese, et al., "Learning from a Rural Physician Program in China," *Academic Medicine* 67 (1992): 307–309.

23. R. S. Northrup, "Preparing Students for Overseas Electives," *Academic Medicine* 66 (1991): 92.

24. J. E. Heck and D. Wedemeyer, "A Survey of American Medical Schools to Assess their Preparation of Students for Overseas Practice," *Academic Medicine* 66 (1991): 78–81.

25. R. E. Pust and S. P. Moher, "A Core Curriculum for International Health: Evaluating Ten Years' Experience at the University of Arizona," *Academic Medicine* 67(1992): 90–94.

26. *Proceedings of the International Health Medical Education Consortium (IHMEC), Washington, DC* June 22–23, 1991 (Rochester, NY: IHMEC, University of Rochester Medical Center, 1991).

27. R. S. Northrup, "Preparing Students for Overseas Electives," p.92.

28. S. L. Kark, *The Practice of Community-Oriented Primary Health Care* (New York: Appleton-Century Crofts, 1981).

29. H. J. Geiger, "Community Health Centers as an Instrument of Social Change," in V. W. Sidel and R. Sidel, eds., *Reforming Medicine* (New York: Pantheon, 1984).

30. "U.S. Agencies Utilizing U.S. Physicians Abroad," *JAMA* 263 (1991): 3237–45.

31. R. G. Pierloni, W. H. Waddell, and E. Suter, "The Interinstitutional Development of an International Health Course," *Journal of Medical Education* 54 (1979): 75–80.

32. Educational Commission for Foreign Medical Graduates. "Strategies for Developing Innovative Programs in International Medical Education." Proceedings of the 1988 International Invitational Conference. *Academic Medicine* 64 (1989) supplement.

33. E. M. Einterz, "Getting Doctors to the Third World" (editorial), *Post-graduate Medicine* 79 (1986): 15–22.

CHAPTER 7

1. The normal state of human relations, between communities and within a single community, is peace. Humanitarian law does not contradict this rule but confirms it; this is borne out by the Preamble to Additional Protocol I of 1977, in particular the first, second and fourth preambular paragraphs thereof.

2. William Broyles Jr., *Brothers in Arms: A Journey from War to Peace* (New York: Knopf, 1986):

> To transform ordinary men into warriors requires that they give up a piece of their civilized selves, that they develop the ability to see other men and women as abstractions, as enemies to be killed. That powerful idea is easy to learn and hard to forget. But the idea of the enemy, so fundamental in the heat of war, is always temporary. Wars end. No enemy is an enemy forever. We have made our peace with the British, the Germans, the Japanese; we have brought the North and the South of our own Civil War together. We will be reconciled with the Vietnamese. As my former enemies said, the past is the past. We all did our duty, most of us honorably. Life goes on. The war is over.

3. The principle of the limitation of armed violence is reflected, in contemporary written law, in the Saint-Petersburg Declaration of 1868, as well as in Article 22 of The Hague Regulations of 1907, which stipulates that: "The right of belligerents to adopt means of injuring the enemy is not unlimited." This text is taken up again, slightly reworded, in Paragraph 1 of Article 35 ("Basic Rules") of Protocol I of 1977: "In any

armed conflict, the right of the Parties to the conflict to choose methods or means of warfare is not unlimited. "

4. See Paul Kennedy, *Preparing for the Twenty-First Century* (New York: Random House, 1993), p. 130:

> In this larger and more integrated sense, "national" security becomes increasingly inseparable from "international" security, and both assume a much broader definition; in place of the narrower military concept there is emerging a larger definition which can encompass a whole spectrum of challenges, old and new. Indeed, we may eventually come to agree that a threat to national security means anything on the globe which challenges a people's health, economic well-being, social stability, and political peace.

5. The principle of humanity, the cornerstone of humanitarian law, has frequently been set against military necessity. Here we uncover two essential factors of humanitarian law which are, however, not necessarily contradictory. Humanity and military effectiveness are often complementary; and the best approach is indeed to highlight the mutual military, political and economic benefit of recognizing the enemy—civil or combatant—as a human being with the same dignity as oneself.

6. Sadako Ogata, United Nations High Commissioner for Refugees, at the Conference "Internal Conflicts: the Role of Humanitarian Action," organized by Webster University, Geneva, April 2, 1998.

7. Zbigniew Brzezinski, *Out of Control: Global Turmoil on the Eve of the Twenty-First Century* (New York: Scribners, 1993), p. xv. See also: *Preventing Deadly Conflict: The Final Report of the Carnegie Commission on Preventing Deadly Conflict* (New York: December 1997), p. 257, and Bernard Lown, "Clearing the Debris. (The Atomic Age at 50)," *Technology Review* (August 18, 1995):

> The bestialities unleashed in Bosnia, Rwanda, and Chechnya provide evidence, if such be needed, that barbarism is just below the integument in all human societies, whatever their purported moral values or avowed religious persuasions. In the words of an Auschwitz survivor, the psychotherapist Victor Frankl: "Since Auschwitz we know what man is capable of. And since Hiroshima we know what is at stake. "

8. Erich Fromm, *You Shall Be As Gods* (New York: Holt, Rinehart and Winston, 1966). Cf. also this statement by the American Rabbi, Marc Tannenbaum: "You must first learn to love yourself before you're able to love your neighbor. Frequently, hatred of the other emerges out of people who don't love themselves" (quoted by *Christopher News Notes*, New York, No. 267). Confucius writes in the *Analects* (15, 23): "If there is one maxim which ought to be acted upon throughout one's life, surely it is the maxim of loving kindness. Do not do unto others what you would not have them do unto you." Christ says: "In everything do to others as you would have them do to you" (Matthew 7: 12). In Islam, the Sunnah proclaims: "No one is a believer until he desires for his brother that which he desires for himself." These quotes and others in John Catoir, *World Religions: Belief Behind Today's Headlines* (New York: The Christophers, 1989).

9. See the excellent collection of essays published in French and English by UNESCO, in collaboration with the ICRC and the Henry-Dunant Institute, under the title *International Dimensions of Humanitarian Law* (Paris, 1986).

10. Buddhism contains two fundamental principles, *maitri* (friendliness, benevolence) and *karuna* (mercy, compassion) closely related to the principle of humanity.

11. For Hinduism, numerous rules on the kind treatment to be granted to the vanquished are found in the *Mahabharata* (XII, 3487, 3488, 3489, 3782, 8235), which also prescribes loyalty in combat (XII, 3541–42, 3544–51, 57–60, 64, 3580, 3659, 3675, 3677). See also the famous Laws of Manu, VII, 90–93 (*The Laws of Manu*, Oxford, 1886).

12. On Taoism, see Lao Tsu, *Tao Te Ching*, and in particular No. 68 ("a good winner is not vengeful") and No. 38: "When Tao is lost, there is goodness; when goodness is lost, there is kindness; when kindness is lost, there is justice; when justice is lost, there is

ritual") (Lao Tsu, *Tao Te Ching*. A new translation by Gia-Fu and Jane English, New York: Random House/Vintage Books, 1972).

13. On Bushido, see Sumio Adachi, " Traditional Asian Approaches: A Japanese View," *Australian Yearbook of International Law*, Vol. 9, 1985, pp. 158–167, and, by the same author, "The Asian Concept," in: *International Dimensions of Humanitarian Law* (Paris: UNESCO, 1986), pp. 13–19, which also considers Buddhism.

14. On Judaism, see Erich Fromm's work quoted above in Note 8, which contains a commentary, among other things, on the Book of Leviticus, revealing the restrictive interpretations confining the notion of neighbor solely to other members of the Jewish community, and the broader interpretations extending the definition to all human beings. Fromm also also quotes other passages from the Old Testament on the injunctions handed down to the Israelites for humanitarian treatment of their vanquished enemies.

15. On Christianity, Max Huber, *The Good Samaritan: Reflections on the Gospel and Work in the Red Cross* (Neuchâtel, 1943) (also translated into French; the German original was published under the title *Der barmherzige Samariter. Betrachtungen über Evangelium und Rotkreuzarbeit*, Zürich 1943). See also Joseph Joblin, *L'Eglise et la Guerre. Conscience, violence, pouvoir* (Paris, 1988), and in particular, for *jus in bello*, pp. 193 on; Alfred Vanderpol, *La doctrine scolastique du droit de la guerre* (Paris, 1919); Francisco de Vitoria, *Leçons sur les Indiens et le droit de la guerre* (Geneva, 1966); Ernest Nys (ed.), *De Indis et de jure belli relectiones* (Washington, 1917).

16. On Islam, see among others Marcel Boisard, *L'Humanisme de l'Islam* (Paris, 1979); Jean-Paul Charney, *L'Islam et la guerre, De la guerre juste à la révolution sainte* (Paris, 1986); the article published in the *International Review of the Red Cross* by M. K. Ereksoussi, "Le Coran et les conventions humanitaires" (November 1960); Hamed Sultan, "La conception islamique du droit international humanitaire dans les conflits armés," *Revue Egyptienne de Droit International*, Vol. 34, 1978 pp. 1–19; and Ghassan Maarouf Arnaout, *Asylum in the Arab-Islamic Countries* (Geneva: HCR/International Institute of Humanitarian Law, 1986).

17. On African customs, see Emmanuel Bello, *African Customary Humanitarian Law* (Geneva: ICRC, 1980); the articles by Yolande Diallo published in February and August 1976 in the *International Review of the Red Cross* under the title "Humanitarian Law and African Traditional Law. "

18. See Geoffrey Best, *Humanity in Warfare: The Modern History of the International Law of Armed Conflicts* (London: Weidenfeld and Nicholson, 1980), p. 400.

19. Another translation, available on the Web site http: //www. mtholyoke. edu/acad/ intrel/kant/kant1. htm:

    No State shall, during War, permit such Acts of Hostility which would make mutual Confidence in the subsequent Peace impossible: such are the employment of assassins *("percussores")*, poisoners *("venefici")*, breach of Capitulation, and Incitement to Treason *("perduellio")* in the opposing State.

20. For bilateral agreements, cf. Dieter Fleck, "Suspension of Hostilities," in: *Encyclopedia of Public International Law*, Vol. 4, 1982, pp. 239–240, who quotes S. D. Bailey, "Ceasefires, Truces and Armistices in the Practice of the U.N. Security Council," American Journal of International Law, Vol. 71, 1977, pp. 461–473. Bailey points out that the truces negotiated by the Security Council in 1948 between the Netherlands and Indonesia and in Kashmir between India and Pakistan included military, political and humanitarian clauses. See also Charles Rousseau, *Le droit des conflits armés* (Paris, 1983), p. 103, who quotes a few examples of special agreements between belligerents, otherwise known as cartels, on the exchange of prisoners: Cartel of May 12, 1813, between Great Britain and the United States, and the Dix-Hill Cartel, named after its two signatories, Generals J. A. Dix and D. H. Hill, concluded on July 22, 1862 between the American Federal Government and the Southern Confederates, the texts of which may be found in Howard S. Levie (ed.), "Documents on Prisoners of War,"

International Law Studies Vol. 60 (Newport, RI, U.S. Naval War College, 1979), pp. 18–22 and 34–36.

21. See Henry Dunant, *A Memory of Solferino* (Geneva: ICRC, 1939).
22. Geneva Convention for the Amelioration of the Condition of the Wounded and Sick in Armed Forces in the Field, August 12, 1949; Geneva Convention for the Amelioration of the Condition of the Wounded, Sick and Shipwrecked Members of the Armed Forces at Sea, August 12, 1949; Geneva Convention Relative to the Treatment of Prisoners of War, August 12, 1949; Geneva Convention Relative to the Protection of Civilian Persons in Time of War, August 12, 1949.
23. Protocol Additional to the Geneva Conventions of August 12, 1949, and relating to the Protection of Victims of International Armed Conflicts (Protocol I); Protocol Additional to the Geneva Conventions of August 12, 1949, and relating to the Protection of Victims of Non-International Armed Conflicts (Protocol II).
24. Convention on the Prohibition of Use, Stockpiling, Production and Transfer of Anti-personnel Mines and on their Destruction, signed at Ottawa on December 4, 1997.
25. The United Nations Convention on the Prohibition of Military or Any Other Hostile Use of Environmental Modification Techniques (ENMOD), adopted on December 10, 1976.
26. Convention on the Rights of the Child, adopted by Resolution 44/25 of the United Nations General Assembly on November 20, 1989.
27. See Jean Pictet, *Humanitarian Law and the Protection of War Victims* (Leiden, 1975).
28. This was the term used by the Diplomatic Conference on the Reaffirmation and Development of International Humanitarian Law Applicable in Armed Conflicts (CDDH), which met at Geneva from 1974 to 1977 to adopt the two Additional Protocols to the Conventions of 1949.
29. "Law of war" is the expression still most widely used today in military circles. Cf. Frederic De Mulinen, *Handbook on the Law of War for Armed Forces* (Geneva: ICRC, 1987.
30. "Law of Geneva" is sometimes used with the intention of stressing aspects relating to the protection of victims of war, as opposed to the regulation of conduct as regards methods and means of destruction between combatants, designated by the expression "law of The Hague. "
31. The Protocols of 1977 have to some extent merged the law of Geneva and the law of The Hague; this was merely the culmination of a trend that began when the rules of The Hague relating to the treatment of prisoners of war were incorporated and expanded upon in the Second Geneva Convention of 1929, and later the Third Convention of 1949; similarly, the Fourth Convention of 1949 incorporated most of The Hague Regulations of 1907 on military occupation. All this is of considerable significance: apart from the historical memory, it is the customary nature of the rules of The Hague (and hence of the provisions incorporated in 1949 and 1977) that should be emphasized.
32. This was the term used by the United Nations for almost ten years after the International Conference on Human Rights held in Tehran (April 22–May 13, 1968). Numerous resolutions of the United Nations General Assembly advocating further codification and describing how this was to be done were adopted under the heading of "Respect for human rights in armed conflicts," as well as reports by the Secretary-General of the United Nations (A/7720 in 1969, A/8052 in 1970, A/8370 in 1971, A/8781 in 1972, A/9123 in 1973, A/9669 in 1974, A/10195 in 1975).
33. Humanitarian law may be defined as the principles and rules restricting the use of violence in armed conflicts in order to spare the persons who are not (or are no longer) directly engaged in the hostilities (civilians, wounded and sick, shipwrecked, prisoners of war), and to limit the use of methods and means of warfare of such a nature as to cause superfluous injury (or excessive suffering, as in the case of dumdum bullets, or with gas warfare), or which could cause severe damage to the natural environment or betray an adversary's confidence in agreed-upon obligations ("perfidy").

34. The protection of cultural objects, essentially set out in the Convention of The Hague of May 14, 1954 for the Protection of Cultural Property in the Event of Armed Conflict, is reaffirmed in Article 53 ("Protection of cultural objects and places of worship") of Protocol 1 of 1977 and Article 16 of Protocol II. See Stanislaw Edward Nahlik, "Protection of Cultural Property in International Dimensions of Humanitarian Law," UNESCO and Henry-Dunant Institute (Paris/Geneva, 1988), pp. 203–215.

35. An article in each of the two Additional Protocols of 1977 is devoted to the protection of objects indispensible to the survival of the civilian population: Protocol I, Article 43; Protocol II, Article 14. The protection afforded to medical units, in particular civilian ones, was substantially extended by Protocol I (the main points being reaffirmed in Article 11 of Protocol II): Article 8 ("Terminology"), sub-paragraph e, defines "medical units"; Articles 12, 13 and 14 describe the protection afforded and its limits.

36. The prohibition of attacks on works and installations containing dangerous forces (dykes, dams, nuclear electrical generating stations) is also set out in the two Protocols of 1977: Protocol I, Article 56; Protocol II, Article 15.

37. The causing of widespread, long-term and severe damage to the natural environment, thereby prejudicing the health or survival of the population, is outlawed in Article 55 of Protocol I and in the United Nations Convention on the Prohibition of Military or Any Other Hostile Use of Environmental Modification Techniques of December 10, 1976. In this connection, see Geza Herczegh, "La protection de l'environnement naturel et le droit humanitaire," and Alexandre Kiss, "Les Protocoles additionels aux Conventions de Genève de 1977 et la protection des biens de l'environnement," in Christophe Swinarski (ed.), *Studies and Essays on International Humanitarian Law and Red Cross Principles* (Geneva: The Hague, 1984).

38. See Henri Meyrowitz, "Réflexions sur le fondement du droit de la guerre," in: Christophe Swinarski, *op. cit.*, pp. 419–431, and Michel Veuthey, "Le droit à la survie, fondement du droit international humanitaire," in: *Essais sur le concept de "Droit de Vivre" en mémoire de Yougindra Khushalani* (Brussels, 1988), pp. 233–249.

39. Denise Bindschedler-Robert, *A Reconsideration of the Law of Armed Conflicts: Report to the Conference on the Law of Armed Conflict* (Geneva: Carnegie Endowment, September 15–20, 1969), p. 61 (Conclusion).

40. Sam Keen, *Faces of the Enemy: Reflections on the Hostile Imagination. The Psychology of Enmity* (San Francisco: Harper and Row, 1986), p. 181.

41. International Court of Justice, Nicaragua Case, June 27, 1986, Vol. 114, para. 218. On this case, see: Rosemary Abi-Saab, "The 'General Principles' of Humanitarian Law According to the International Court of Justice," *International Review of the Red Cross*, July–August 1987, pp. 367–375.

42. See I. William Zartman (ed.), *Collapsed States. The Disintegration and Restoration of Legitimate Authority* (Boulder, CO: Lynne Rienner, 1995), p. 301.

43. See Robert Fox, "On the Age of Postmodern War. Beyond Clausewitz: The Long and Ragged Conflicts of the Coming Millenium," *Times Literary Supplement*, May 15, 1998.

44. As Martin van Crefeld puts it in *The Transformation of War* (New York: Free Press, 1991); "Once the legal monopoly of armed force, long claimed by the State, is wrestled out of its hands, existing distinctions between war and crime will break down."

45. Preparatory document drafted by the ICRC for the first periodical meeting on international humanitarian law, Geneva, January 19–23, 1998, Armed conflicts linked to the disintegration of State structures, mentioning Resolution 814, para. 13 (Somalia), Res. 788, para. 5 (Liberia).

46. Cornelio Sommaruga, "Humanitarian Challenges on the Threshold of the Twenty-First Century": Keynote address, 26th International Conference of the Red Cross and Red Crescent. See also: Elie Wiesel, quoted in Robert Jay Lifton and Eric Markusen, *The Genocidal Mentality: Nazi Holocaust and Nuclear Threat* (New York: Basic Books, 1990), p. 1: "Once upon a time it happened to my people, and now it happens to all

people. And suddenly I said to myself, maybe the whole world, strangely, has turned Jewish. Everybody lives now facing the unknown. We are all, in a way, helpless. "

47. United Nations Commission on Human Rights. Sub-Commission on Prevention of Discrimination and Protection of Minorities. Thirty-eighth session. Item 7 of the provisional agenda "Gross Violations of Human Rights and International Peace" E/CN.4/Sub.2/1985/11 (June 25, 1985) para. 18: " Genocide, the most extreme form of discimination and massive disregard of the right to life, recognized as a crime against humanity, was considered as a major threat to international peace and security."

48. Zbigniew Brzezinski, *Out of Control: Global Turmoil on the Eve of the Twenty-First Century* (New York: Charles Scribner's Sons, 1993), Chapter 1 ("The Century of Megadeath").

49. During the Spanish Civil War, the bombings of Madrid aimed at the civilian population from October to December 1936 were abandoned because they failed to have the expected effect of terror, thereby confirming what had already been observed during the Sino-Japanese war: far from weakening a people's morale, such operations, which are condemned by international law, inspire fierce hatred, bringing the will to resist to a climax (cf. E. Wanty, *L'Art de la guerre* (Verviers, 1967, Vol. II, p. 279). Similar conclusions have been drawn in official American reports as regards the bombing of Germany (United States Strategic Bombing Survey, Overall Report—European War, Washington, DC, USGPO, 1945, p. 109) and by the former German Minister of War, A. Speer, in his memoirs (*Au coeur du Troisième Reich*, Paris, 1971, p. 394 for the allied bombings on German towns and p. 399 for Germany's misguided policy of launching raids on British towns rather than concentrating on military objectives).

50. Article 17, Protocol II ("Prohibition of forced movement of civilians").

51. Ben Barber, "Feeding Refugees, or War? The Dilemma of Humanitarian Aid," *Foreign Affairs*, Vol. 76/No 4 (July/August 1997).

52. Adam Roberts, *Humanitarian Action in War. Aid, Protection and Impartiality in a Policy Vacuum* (Oxford: Oxford University Press, 1996), p. 96 (Adelphi Paper 305). As for Somalia, see the Security Council Resolution S/RES/794 (1992) of December 3, 1992, and especially paragraphs 4 and 5 and this preambular paragraph: "Determining that the magnitude of the human tragedy caused by the conflict in Somalia, further exacerbated by the obstacles being created to the distribution of humanitarian assistance, constitutes a threat to international peace and security." The report of the Secretary-General of the UN on "The causes of conflict and the promotion of durable peace and sustainable development in Africa" (S/1998/318), of April 13, 1998, highlights the importance of abiding by international humanitarian law in paragraphs 49 to 54.

53. "Se battre pour une vérité en veillant à ne pas la tuer des armes mêmes dont on la défend": (*Actuelles, III, Chroniques algériennes* [1939–1958], Paris, 1958), p. 24.

54. See the *International Review of the Red Cross*, December 1973, p. 641 ("The International Committee's Action in the Middle East").

55. James Reston Jr., *Sherman's March and Vietnam* (New York, 1984), evokes "General William Tecumseh Sherman's 'March to the Sea' when civilians and their communities were ravaged and, in the Civil War's aftermath, the festering bitterness of Reconstruction," adding that still today "in the south, the mere mention of Sherman elicits an instant emotional response." On the same conflict, the war of annihilation against the South, see also James M. McPherson, *Battle Cry of Freedom* (Oxford, 1988). Very relevant, even today, here is the statement by the Chairman of the Security Council on November 11, 1976 to the 1969th meeting (S/INF/32, p. 5), in which paragraph 3 reads:

> 3. To reaffirm that the Geneva Convention relative to the Protection of Civilian Persons in Time of War is applicable to the Arab territories occupied by Israel since 1967. Therefore, the occupying Power is called upon once again to comply strictly with the provisions of that Convention and to refrain from any measure that violates them. In this regard, the measures taken by Israel in the occupied Arab territories which alter

their demographic composition or geographical character, and in particular the establishment of settlements, are strongly deplored. Such measures, which have no legal
validity and cannot but prejudice the outcome of the efforts to achieve peace, constitute an obstacle to peace.

56. J. J. Stremlau, *The International Politics of the Nigerian Civil War, 1967–1970* (Princeton: Princeton University Press, 1977), p. 205.

57. See Mohamed Bedjaoui, *La Révolution algérienne et le droit* (Brussels 1961).

58. These efforts still continue and are also receiving the support of outside governments.
Also relevant here is Resolution 43/145 adopted by the United Nations General
Assembly ("Situation of human rights and fundamental freedoms in El Salvador"),
which contains a preambular paragraph recalling the applicability of Article 3 common to the Conventions of 1949 and Protocol II of 1977, and an operative paragraph
11 with the following wording:

> Requests the Government of El Salvador and the Frente Farabundo Marté para la
> Liberación Nacional—Frente Democrático Revolucionario, with a view to humaniz-
> ing the conflict, to continue ensuring that the agreements for the evacuation of the
> war-wounded and war-injured for medical attention will not be made contingent on
> further prisoner exchanges and negotiations.

59. Article 123 of the Third Geneva Convention and Article 140 of the Fourth Geneva
Convention create the obligation, in times of armed conflict, to set up an agency to
collect all the information it may obtain through official or private channels on prisoners of war and all other persons protected under international humanitarian law,
particularly the civilian population. See G. Djurovic, *The Central Agency of the International Committee of the Red Cross* (Geneva: ICRC, 1986).

60. Louis Joinet, Special Rapporteur to the Human Rights Commission, "Study on
Amnesty Laws and Their Role in the Safeguard and Promotion of Human Rights"
(E/CN. 4/Sub. 2/1984/15, para. 30).

61. Sylvie-Stoyanka Junod, *Commentary on the Protocol Additional to the Geneva Conventions
of August 12, 1949 and relating to the Protection of Victims of Non-International Armed
Conflicts (Protocol II)* (Geneva: ICRC, 1987), p. 1402, para. 4618.

62. Alfred M. de Zayas, who gives this example in his article "Amnesty Clause," in: *Encyclopedia of Public International Law*, Vol. 3, 1982, p. 15, also quotes Article 2 of the
Treaty of Utrecht of 1713, Article 2 of the Treaty of Aix-la-Chapelle of 1748, Article
2 of the Treaty of Paris of 1763, Article 2 of the Treaty of Westphalia of 1648, Article
16 of the Treaty of Paris of May 30, 1814, and the mutual amnesties concluded
between France and Algeria in the Evian Agreement of March 19, 1962.

63. Trial of Pakistani Prisoners of War, Order of December 15, 1973, ICJ Reports 1973,
p. 347.

64. See Paul Tavernier, "The Experience of the International Criminal Tribunals for the
Former Yugoslavia and for Rwanda," in the *International Review of the Red Cross*,
November 1, 1997, and Gerhard Erasmus and Nadine Fourie, "The International
Criminal Tribune for Rwanda: Are All Issues Addressed? How Does It Compare to
South Africa's Truth and Reconciliation Commission?" in the *International Review of
the Red Cross*, no. 321, pp. 705–715.

65. See the Web site of the NGO Coalition for an International Criminal Court: http:
//www. igc. apc. org/ tribunal/.

66. See Samuel Griffith, in his excellent translation of Sun Tzu, *The Art of War* (Oxford:
Oxford University Press, 1980): II. 19. Treat the captives well, and care for them. III.
1. Generally in war the best policy is to take a state intact; to ruin it is inferior to this.
III. 2. To capture the enemy's army is better than to destroy it; to take intact a battal-
ion, a company or a five-man squad is better than to destroy them.

67. Octavio Paz, *Tiempo Nublado, One Earth, Four or Five Worlds: Reflections on Contemporary History* (San Diego, CA: Harcourt Brace Jovanovich, 1985).

68. "La Compassion, Pilier de la Paix Mondiale," Lecture at the University of Geneva, August 31, 1983.

69. *Freedom in Exile: The Autobiography of the Dalai Lama* (Calcutta, 1992).

70. For instance, decisions by the International Monetary Fund, a typical "peace" organization, may have caused riots or even civil war in some Third-World countries.

71. See Resolution 8 ("Peace, International Humanitarian Law and Human Rights") of the Council of Delegates (Sevilla, November 25–27, 1997).

72. François Grünewald: "From Prevention to Rehabilitation: Action Before, During and After the Crisis: The Experience of the ICRC in Retrospect," article based on a study presented to the Colloquium: "Emergency—Rehabilitation—Development." Arche de la Fraternité, Paris, November 17, 1994 in the *International Review of the Red Cross*, No. 306, pp. 263–281.

73. Peter Fuchs, "Conflict and the Global Economy: Towards a New Sharing of Responsibility," address by Dr. Peter Fuchs, Director-General, International Committee of the Red Cross (ICRC) at the Hôtel Baur en Ville, Zurich, February 29, 1996.

74. See Article 1, Common to the four 1949 Geneva Conventions: "the High Contracting Parties undertake to respect and to ensure respect for this Convention in all circumstances. "

75. These ideals could be social, political and/or spiritual and should not divide but unite. As Bede Griffiths writes in *Return to the Center* (Springfield, IL: Tempelgate, 1977), p. 71: "I have to be a Hindu, a Buddhist, a Jain, a Parsee, a Sikh, a Muslim, and a Jew, as well as a Christian, if I am to know the Truth and to find the point of reconciliation in all religion." Hans Küng also considers that international peace presupposes peace between religions. See Hans Küng, *Projekt Weltethos* (München: Piper, 1990), p. 191 and Hans Küng (ed.), *Ja zum Weltethos: Perspektiven für den Such nach Orientierung*. (*Global Responsibility: In Search of a New World Ethic*) (München: Piper, 1995), and his statement on the "Declaration Towards a Global Ethic" on http://kvc.kit.nl/kvc /ukverslagükung.html as "a minimal basis consensus relating to binding values, irrevocable standards and moral attitudes, which can be affirmed by all religions despite their 'dogmatic' differences and can also be supported by non-believers."

   A better world order will ultimately only be created on the basis of

   • common visions, ideals, values, aims and criteria;
   • heightened global responsibility on the part of peoples and their leaders;
   • a new binding and uniting ethic for all humankind, including states and those in power, which embraces cultures and religions. No new world order without a new world ethic, a global ethic.

76. Quoted in Martin Luther King Jr., *Strength to Love* (Cleveland: North Light Books, 1963), p. 53. See also this quote by Martin Luther King:

   The chain reaction of evil—hate begetting hate, wars producing more wars—must be broken, or we shall be plunged into the dark abyss of annihilation. Far from being the pious injunction of an utopian dreamer, the command to love one's enemy is an absolute necessity for our survival.

CHAPTER 8

1. Although the Cold-War atmospherics have definitely been superseded, many of the concerns and encounters persist, particularly in the Asia/Pacific region: Korea is divided, China remains committed ideologically and structurally to an authoritarian form of state socialism, there is an unresolved revolutionary war in the Philippines and a not-fully-resolved territorial dispute between the former Soviet Union and Japan about the status of the Kuriles islands. Despite such considerations, for purposes of this chapter the post-Cold-War terminology seems appropriate. There is no longer any strategic conflict of global scope. Policy response at the United Nations, and elsewhere, is no longer blocked by the sort of rigid bipolarity that was characteristic of the era of superpower rivalry.

2. See "Intelligence Sources See Air Ban as Ineffective and 'Political,'" *The Guardian* (August 20, 1992).
3. "Report of the Secretary-General of the United Nations" (New York, 1991), p. 5.
4. "The Limits of Sovereignty," *UN Focus: Human Rights*, undated newsletter, page 1.
5. See articulation of this position in Thomas M. Franck's book on the World Court, *Judging the World Court* (New York: Priority Press, 1986), especially pp. 53–76.
6. The sort of shift toward liberalism noted and favored by Joseph Nye in "What New World Order?" *Foreign Affairs* 71 (1992): 83–96.
7. "U.S. Isolates Major over Iraq," *The Guardian* (August 20, 1992).
8. See John Vincent, *Nonintervention and International Order* (Princeton, NJ: Princeton University Press, 1974), especially pp. 64–141.
9. See W. Michael Reisman and Andrew Willard (eds.), *International Incidents: The Law That Counts in World Politics* (New Haven, CT: Yale University Press, 1988).
10. For convenient texts of these treaties see Burns H. Weston, Anthony D'Amato and Richard Falk (eds.) *Basic Documents in International Law and World Order*, 2nd rev. ed. (St. Paul, MN: West Publishing Co., 1990), pp. 147–180 and 230–252.
11. "Report of the Secretary-General," p. 11.
12. Richard Falk, *Explorations at the Edge of Time* (Philadelphia: Temple University Press, 1992).

CHAPTER 9

1. P. Dasgupta, *An Inquiry into Well-Being and Destitution* (Oxford: Clarendon Press, 1993).
2. P. Dasgupta, "Well-Being and the Extent of Its Realization in Poor Countries," *Economic Journal* 100 (1990).
3. J. Waldron, "What Do We know About the Causes of Sex Differences in Mortality? A Review of the Literature," *Population Bulletin of the United Nations* 18 (1985); and S. R. Johansson, "Welfare, Mortality and Gender: Continuity and Change in the Explanation of Male/Female Mortality Differences over Three Centuries," *Continuity and Change* 6 (1991).
4. R. Martorell et al., "Long-Term Consequences of Growth Retardation during Early Childhood" (Ithaca, NY: Cornell University, 1991).
5. R. Martorell et al., "Maternal Stature, Fertility and Infant Mortality," *Human Biology* 53 (1981).
6. F. Falkner and J. M. Tanner (eds.), *Human Growth 2: Postnatal Growth* (New York: Plenum Press, 1978).
7. L. J. Mata, "The Fight Against Diarrhoeal Diseases: The Case of Costa Rica," in: J. Vallin and A. D. Lopez (eds.), *Health Policy, Social Policy, and Mortality Prospects* (Paris: Institut National d'Etudes Demographiques, 1985).
8. World Bank, *World Development Report* (New York: Oxford University Press, 1992).
9. L. J. Mata, *The Children of Santa Maria Cauque: A Prospective Field Study of Health and Growth* (Cambridge, MA: MIT Press, 1978).
10. K. Hill and A. R. Pebley, "Child Mortality in the Developing World," *Population and Development Review* 15 (1989).
11. V. Fauveau et al., "The Contribution of Severe Malnutrition to Child Mortality in Rural Bangladesh: Implications for Targeting Nutritional Interventions," *Food and Nutrition Bulletin* 12 (1990).
12. M. K. Chowdhury et al., "Does Malnutrition Predispose to Diarrhoea during Childhood? Evidence from a Longitudinal Study in Matlab, Bangladesh," *European Journal of Clinical Nutrition* 44 (1990).
13. J. C. Waterlow (ed.), *Protein Energy Malnutrition* (London: Edward Arnold, 1992).
14. A. Briend, "Is Diarrhoea a Major Cause of Malnutrition among the Under-Fives in

Developing Countries? A Review of Available Evidence," *European Journal of Clinical Nutrition* 44 (1990).

15. Dasgupta, *Inquiry into Well-Being*.

16. A. Chavez and C. Martinez, "Behavioural Measurements of Activity in Children and Their Relation to Food Intake in a Poor Community," in: E. Pollitt and P. Amante (eds.), *Energy Intake and Activity* (New York: Alan R. Liss, 1984).

17. J. M. Meeks Gardner et al., "Dietary Intake and Observed Activity of Stunted and Non-stunted Children in Kingston, Jamaica. Part II: Observed Activity," *European Journal of Clinical Nutrition* 44 (1990).

18. A. Chavez and C. Martinez, "Consequences of Insufficient Nutrition in Child Character and Behaviour," in: D. A. Levitsky (ed.), *Malnutrition, Environment and Behavior* (Ithaca, NY: Cornell University Press, 1979); and Chavez and Martinez, "Behavioural Measurements of Activity. "

19. For references see Dasgupta, *Inquiry into Well-Being*, ch. 14.

20. M. Colombo and I. Lopez, "Evolution of Psychomotor Development in Severely Undernourished Infants Submitted to an Integral Rehabilitation," *Pediatrics Research* 14 (1980).

21. J. Dobbing, "Early Nutrition and Later Achievement," *Proceedings of the Nutrition Society* 49 (1990).

22. F. Falkner and J. M. Tanner (eds.), *Human Growth: A Comprehensive Treatise*, Vol. 3, 2nd ed. (New York: Plenum Press, 1986).

23. The study of the effect of malnutrition on mental development is shot through with difficulties of interpretation. See the chapter by S. M. Grantham-McGregor in Waterlow, *Protein Energy Malnutrition*.

24. G. B. Spurr and J. C. Reina, "Influence of Dietary Intervention on Artificially Increased Activity in Marginally Undernourished Colombian Boys," *European Journal of Clinical Nutrition* 42 (1988).

25. E. Pollit, *Malnutrition and Infection in the Classroom* (Paris: UNESCO, 1990).

26. Waterlow, *Protein Energy Malnutrition*.

27. World Health Organization, *Energy and Protein Requirements*, Technical Series, no. 724 (Geneva, 1985), p. 85.

28. *Ibid.*, pp. 87–89.

29. A. M. Prentice, "Variations in Maternal Intake, Birthweight and Breast Milk Output in the Gambia," in: H. Aebi and R. G. Whitehead (eds.), *Maternal Nutrition during Pregnancy and Lactation* (Bern, Switzerland: Hans Huber, 1980); A. M. Prentice et al., "Prenatal Dietary Supplementation of African Women and Birth Weight," *Lancet*, Vol. 1 (1983); and A. M. Prentice et al., "Dietary Supplementation of Lactating Gambian Women. II: Effect on Maternal Health, Nutritional Status and Biochemistry," *Human Nutrition: Clinical Nutrition*, Vol. 37C (1983).

30. L. S. Adair and E. Pollitt, "Seasonal Variation in Maternal Body Dimensions and Infant Birthweights," *American Journal of Physical Anthropology*, Vol. 62 (1983); and L. S. Adair, "Marginal Intake and Maternal Adaptation: The Case of Rural Taiwan," in Pollitt and Amante, *Energy Intake*.

31. D. P. Chandhuri, *Education, Innovation and Agricultural Development* (London: Croom Helm, 1979). See also I. Singh, *The Great Ascent: The Rural Poor in South Asia* (Baltimore: Johns Hopkins University Press, 1990).

32. For references see Dasgupta, *Inquiry into Well-Being*.

33. S. H. Cochrane, "Effects of Education and Urbanization on Fertility," in R. Bulatao and R. Lee (eds.), *Determinants of Fertility in Developing Countries*, Vol. 2 (New York: Academic Press, 1983).

34. Dasgupta, *Inquiry into Well-Being*.

35. A.K.M.A. Chowdhury, "Child Mortality in Bangladesh: Food Versus Health Care," *Food and Nutrition Bulletin* 10 (1988).

36. J. Bhagwati, "Education, Class Structure and Income Inequality," *World Development* 1 (1973).
37. Dasgupta, "Well-Being and the Extent of Its Realization. "
38. L. Summers, "The Most Influential Investment," *Scientific American* 267 (1992).
39. Dasgupta, "Well-Being and the Extent of Its Realization"; and P. Dasgupta and M. Weale, "On Measuring the Quality of Life," *World Development* 20 (1992).
40. Dasgupta, *Inquiry into Well-Being*.

CHAPTER 10

1. Report of the Independent Commission on International Humanitarian Issues, *Winning the Human Race?* (London: Zed Books, 1988).
2. F. Fenner, D. A. Henderson, I. Arati, Z. Yezek, and I. D. Lednyi, *Smallpox and Its Eradication* (Geneva: World Health Organization, 1988).
3. Report of the Independent Commission on International Development Issues, *North-South: A Programme for Survival* (London: Plan Books, 1980).
4. Report of the Carnegie Commission on Preventing Deadly Conflict, *Preventing Deadly Conflict: Final Report* (New York: Carnegie Corporation, 1997). Also available at http: //www. ccpdc.org.
5. Report of the Independent Commission on Disarmament and Security Issues, *Common Security: A Program for Disarmament* (London: Pan Books, 1982).

CHAPTER 11

1. Mary Robinson, *A Voice for Somalia* (Dublin: O'Brien Press, 1992), p. 33
2. 40th session of the United Nations General Assembly.
3. A Report for the Independent Commission on International Humanitarian Issues, *Famine—A Man-Made Disaster?* (London: Pan Books, 1985), p. 50.
4. Dawit Wolde Giorgis, *Red Tears: War, Famine and Revolution in Ethiopia* (Trenton, NJ: Red Sea Press, 1989), p. 152.
5. Report on the Third IDS Food Aid Seminar. p. 12.
6. D. W. Giorgis, *Red Tears*, p. 132
7. Graham Hancock, *Lord of Poverty* (Atlantic Monthly Press, 1989), p. 32.
8. *Ibid.*, p. 31
9. *Famine—A Man-Made Disaster?* p. 106.
10. D. W. Giorgis, *Red Tears*, p. 211
11. UN Association of the US. *Acts of Nature, Acts of Man: The Global Response to Natural Disaster* (UN Association of the U. S., 1977), p. 29.
12. *Famine—A Man-Made Disaster?* p. 102
13. D. W. Giorgis, *Red Tears*, p. 230
14. Walter Clarke and Jeffrey Herbst (eds.), *Learning from Somalia* (Westview Press, 1997), p. 217.
15. World Bank Paper, 1997. "A Framework for World Bank Involvement in Post-Conflict Reconstruction," Environmental and Social Policy Division, Executive Summary, para 17.
16. Larry Minear, *Humanitarianism Under Siege* (Red Sea Press, 1991), p. 57
17. *London Observer*, August 23, 1992
18. Michael Maren, *The Road to Hell* (Free Press, 1997), p. 240.
19. Jennifer S. Whitaker, *How Can Africa Survive?* (Harper and Row, 1988), p. 71.
20. *The Leadership Challenge for Improving the Economic and Special Situation in Africa* (Nigeria: Africa Leadership Forum, 1988), p. 73.
21. A Report for the Independent Commission on International Humanitarian Issues. *Refugees—Dynamics of Displacement* (Zed Books, 1986), p. 29.
22. Kurt Janson, *The Ethiopian Famine* (Zed Books, 1990), p. 23.

23. *Ibid.*, pp. 24–25.

24. *Ibid.*, p. 24.

25. David Smock and Chester Crocker, *African Conflict Resolution* (United States Institute of Peace Press, 1995), p. 2.

26. World Bank Paper 1997, "A Framework for World Bank Involvement," para. 6.

27. A Report for the Independent Commission on International Humanitarian Issues, *Refugees*, p. 127

28. *Ibid.*, p. 128

29. Boutros Boutros-Ghali, UN Secretary-General, "An Agenda for Peace," UN document. June, 1992.

30. World Bank Paper 1997, "A Framework for World Bank Involvement," para. 17.

31. Walter Clarke and Jeffrey Herbst (eds.), *Learning from Somalia*, p. 220.

32. M. Robinson, *A Voice for Somalia*, p. 70.

CHAPTER 14

1. Notable exceptions included the Bihar famine in 1966 and 1967 and the Pakistan/ Bangladesh crisis of the early 1970s. These crises, more typical of the relief situation today, foreshadowed the trends outlined below.

2. The State Department claimed the United States was technically in compliance with the 1951 United Nations Convention Relating to the Status of Refugees because it was sending the Haitians back to Haiti before they entered U.S. territory. The claim that U.S. Coast Guard cutters were intercepting boats because they were "unseaworthy" was quickly challenged by human rights organizations, but the Supreme Court upheld the legality of the interdiction.

3. *News from Americas Watch National Coalition for Haitian Refugees*, Vol. 4, No. 4, June 1992.

4. At the end of 1991, Germany harbored more than 250,000 refugees. During the first six months of 1992, Germany received an additional 125,000 refugees from Yugoslavia alone. In addition, a steady stream of 10,000 to 15,000 refugees from other countries sought asylum each month.

5. For number of refugees within the country, see U.S. Committee for Refugees, *World Refugee Survey 1992* (Washington, DC: American Council for Nationalities Service, 1992), pp. 52–53.

6. *Ibid.*, p. 47.

7. *Ibid.*

8. See Neil Boothby, "Living in the War Zone," in U.S. Committee for Refugees, *World Refugee Survey 1989 in Review* (Washington, DC: American Council for Nationalities Service, 1992), pp. 40–42; and Robert Gersony, *Summary of Mozambican Accounts of Principally Conflict-Related Experience in Mozambique* (Washington, DC: U.S. Department of State, 1988).

9. Larry Minear, "Civil Strife and Humanitarian Aid: A Bruising Decade," in U.S. Committee for Refugees, *World Refugee Survey 1989 in Review*, pp. 13–19.

10. Stuart Auerbach, "Developing Countries Get Short Shrift in Group of Seven Deliberations," *Washington Post*, July 8, 1992, p. A34.

11. See Michael J. Bayzler, "Reexamining the Doctrine of Humanitarian Intervention in Light of the Atrocities in Kampuchea and Ethiopia," *Stanford Journal of International Law*, Vol. 23, No. 2 (Summer 1987), pp. 547–619; and David Schaeffer, "Toward a Modern Doctrine of Humanitarian Intervention," *University of Toledo Law Review*, Vol. 23, No. 2 (1992), pp. 253–293.

12. Address to the United Nations Association of the United States, April 30, 1985, *UN Chronicle*, Vol. 22, No. 1 (1985), p. 23.

CHAPTER 17

1. Haq, M. *Human Development in South Asia*, Karachi: Oxford University Press, 1998.
2. Haq, M., "Relief in Full Swing," in H. Hossain et al. (eds.), *From Crisis to Development*, pp. 27–54.
3. *Ibid.*
4. Chowdhury, A. M. R. et al., "The Bangladesh Cyclone of 1991: Why So Many People Died," *Disasters*, 17; 291–304, 1993.
5. *Ibid.*
6. UNICEF Cyclone Review Team, "Health Effects of the 1991 Bangladesh Cyclone," *Disasters*, 17: 153–165, 1993.
7. *Ibid.*
8. *Ibid.*
9. Lovell, C. *Breaking the Cycle of Poverty*, Hartford: Kumarian Press, 1992.
10. Ahmed, M., et al., *Primary Education for All: Learning from the BRAC Experience*, Washington DC: Academy for Educational Development, 1994.
11. Chowdhury, A. M. R. and Cash, R. A, *A Simple Solution: Teaching Millions to treat Diarrhoea at Home*, Dhaka: University Press Limited, 1996.
12. Chowdhury, A. M. R., and Vaughan, J. P. "Perception of Diarrhoea and the Use of a Home Made ORS in Rural Bangladesh," *Journal of Diarrhoeal Diseases Research*, 6: 6–14, 1988.
13. *Ibid.*
14. World Health Organization. *Review of the National Tuberculosis Control Program of Bangladesh*, Dhaka, 1997.
15. Chowdhury, A. M. R., et al., "Control of Tuberculosis through Community Health Workers in Bangladesh," *Lancet*, 350: 169–172, 1997.
16. Abed, F. H. and Chowdhury, A. M. R. "The Role of NGOs in International Health," In: M. Reich and E. Marui (eds.), *International Cooperation for Health*, Dover, MA: Auburn House Publishing Company, 1989.

CHAPTER 19

I want to thank Rita Parhad for her comments and assistance in preparing this chapter. It draws heavily for data on an earlier draft paper, "Paying for Essentials: Mobilizing Resources for Humanitarian Assistance," which she coauthored and which can be found at http://www-jha. sps. cam. ac. uk/a/a404. htm. That paper was prepared as a background discussion document for a meeting on "Resources for Humanitarian Assistance," convened by the Center on International Cooperation at the Pocantico Conference Center in New York on September 11–12, 1997. I also would like to thank Douglas Stafford, Thomas Weiss and Randolph Kent for their excellent suggestions. Cesare Romano and Lorenzo Garbo provided valuable comments on earlier drafts.

1. According to former Under-Secretary-General Yasushi Akashi, head of the Department of Humanitarian Affairs and UN Emergency Relief Coordinator, about 42 million people worldwide were dependent on humanitarian assistance in 1995. See "Security Council Debate on Humanitarian Crises, Assembly Work on Improved UN Capability, Mark New Peacekeeping Era," *International Documents Review*, May 26, 1997, p. 1. See also *Global Humanitarian Emergencies, 1996* (New York: United States Mission to the United Nations, 1996); and *World Refugee Survey 1996* (U.S. Committee for Refugees, 1996).
2. According to the U.S. Mission to the United Nations, OECD countries provide about five sixths of global humanitarian aid. See *Global Humanitarian Emergencies, 1996* (New York: United States Mission to the United Nations, 1996), p. 23.
3. The widespread perception that dwindling resources for development assistance are being diverted to short-term emergency relief only exacerbates this sense of resource constraint. Many intergovernmental and nongovernmental development organiza-

tions such as CARE and Oxfam now devote a substantial proportion of their resources to emergency assistance, even though preventive intervention and longer-term development assistance are widely believed to be more cost-effective.

4. These include WFP's International Emergency Food Reserve, UNHCR's Emergency Response Fund, and UNICEF's Emergency Program Fund.

5. According to the Joint Evaluation of Emergency Assistance to Rwanda, the difficulty in determining a percentage breakdown from each mechanism is compounded by several practices: funds allocated for one activity are often used for another activity; funds allocated ahead of an appeal are sometimes subsequently counted against the appeal; and agencies sometimes make arrangements for borrowings and reimbursements at a local level. Joint Evaluation of Emergency Assistance to Rwanda, *The International Response to Conflict and Genocide: Lessons from the Rwanda Experience. Study 3: Humanitarian Aid and Effects*. (Odense: Steering Committee of the Joint Evaluation of Emergency Assistance to Rwanda, 1996), p. 111.

6. In 1996, donor governments provided $1.35 billion, or about 49 percent of total donor funding, through the CAP. Donors reported approximately $1.21 billion, or 44 percent of total donor funding, contributed to NGOs and intergovernmental organizations outside the CAP. The remaining 6–7 percent was delivered by donor governments themselves and through bilateral channels.

7. This estimate is based on data obtained from many of the major humanitarian agencies regarding the percentage of their resources derived from nongovernment sources. Variation in methodologies and definitions render this figure only a very rough approximation. These private donations are critical since they represent contributions to core costs of organizations or permit flexible responses in particular emergency situations.

8. The urgency and the rapidly changing dynamics of a complex emergency necessarily complicate needs assessments, and the desire for rapid donor response may encourage assessment teams to overstate requirements. It should be noted, however, that the Consolidated Appeals are based on a synthesis of information from DHA and humanitarian agencies, in consultation with donor representatives at the country level. Moreover, these appeals are updated frequently—and scaled down as necessary—to reflect changing needs and/or more accurate assessments as they become available.

9. *Global Humanitarian Emergencies*, 1996 (New York: United States Mission to the United Nations, 1996), p. 22.

10. Conversely, WFP usually receives well over 70 percent (and often close to 100 percent) of its stipulated requirements. See the *Financial Tracking Database for Complex Emergencies* (visited 05/04/98) at http: //www.reliefweb.int/fts/index.html.

11. Even the ICRC, one of the most financially stable of humanitarian organizations, has experienced cash-flow problems in recent years. Other organizations that have had annual expenditures exceeding annual income include UNHCR, Oxfam, Save the Children, the International Organization for Migration, and Concern.

12. For a comprehensive discussion of current tendencies to "contract out," see Thomas G. Weiss, *Beyond UN Subcontracting: Task Sharing with Regional Security Arrangements and Service-Providing NGOs* (New York: St. Martins Press, 1998).

13. *The International Response to Conflict and Genocide: Lessons from the Rwanda Experience. Study 3: Humanitarian Aid and Effects*, p. 72.

14. *Ibid.*, p. 117.

15. See Ian Smillie, "NGOs and Development Assistance: A Change in Mind-Set," in: Weiss, *op. cit.*, 190 ff., for a useful discussion of the costs of not providing sufficient overhead.

16. Practices on overhead charges differ widely. For example, lead agencies are reluctant to cover their "partners'" overheads. Not only does UNHCR deny overhead to their "contracting" partners, but it requires them to cost-share in the provision of services. USAID, on the other hand, negotiates a percentage for overhead charges with NGOs

that regularly receive contracts and grants from USAID; this percentage is then added automatically to all contracts and grants with that NGO. See also Larry Minear's article in this volume.

17. Richard Dowden, *The Independent* on Sunday, September 4, 1994, quoted in *The International Response to Conflict and Genocide: Lessons from the Rwanda Experience. Study 3: Humanitarian Aid and Effects*, p. 48.

18. A Meeting Report, including summary notes from the eight working sessions and the plenary discussions, is available on the Center's Web site at http: //www.nyu.edu/pages/cic.

19. USAID "service contracts" were intended to provide guarantees to selected provider agencies, but they serve simply as statements of intent and carry no cash payments to ensure that the providers will be ready when called upon.

20. Edwin M. Smith and Thomas G. Weiss, "UN Task-Sharing: Toward or Away from Global Governance," in Thomas G. Weiss, *op. cit.*, p. 234.

21. The study's results will be available on the Center's Web site at http: //www.nyu.edu/pages/cic.

22. This calculation is made on the basis of an estimated 40 million in need of humanitarian assistance and aggregate expenditures of $4 billion.

23. E. Philip English and Harris M. Mule, *The African Development Bank* (Boulder, CO: Lynne Rienner Publishers), 1996, p. 119.

24. On that occasion, Secretary-General Salem Ahmed Salem, said, "We now have a mechanism, a means which empowers us to act together in the search of solutions to our conflicts. What we need now is to believe in it, to strengthen it, to use it. We must share the burden." *Financial Times*, July 8, 1996. From 1993 to 1996, the fund received $11 million in contributions, nearly half from OAU member states.

25. Sub-Saharan Africa's GDP is estimated to have grown by 4 percent in 1995, a trend that seems to be continuing.

26. Participants at the Pocantico meeting suggested that older, more experienced individuals might be better able to manage stress and cope with bureaucratic frustrations. They also contend that more mature personnel show greater tolerance (rather than moral absolutism) in accepting imperfect means and ends.

27. See "Aid Groups Are Hands That Help In Bosnia," by Elizabeth Becker, *New York Times*, Sunday, April 17, 1998, p. 7.

28. For example, Africa Humanitarian Action, an Addis-Ababa-based NGO, maintains a roster of close to 1,000 entries of Africans available for rapid deployment across the continent.

29. For example, CARE, Concern, the ICRC and Médecins Sans Frontières report staffing figures of 80 to 95 percent local hires.

30. Except when UN personnel are seconded under special "mission replacement" arrangements, recruits are typically Westerners. Obviously, increasing the number of non-Western UN personnel in special field assignments would advance staff development and diversify the profile of humanitarian workers abroad. However, mission replacement often creates serious staffing difficulties at headquarters and does not guarantee that the most qualified people are in the field.

31. A comparison between local and expatriate staff costs suggests that expatriates may cost 10 to 40 times more than locals. This estimate is based on costs reported by one organization, without indication as to the type of work performed by expatriate and local staff (e.g., management versus support services). Francis Kpatindé, "Real Purchasing Power," *Refugees: The High Cost of Caring* (Geneva: The United Nations High Commissioner for Refugees, 1996), pp. 16–18.

32. See Alex de Waal, "Dangerous Precedents: Famine Relief in Somalia 1991–1993," *War and Hunger: Rethinking International Response to Complex Emergencies* (New Jersey: Zed Books, 1994), p. 151.

CHAPTER 20

This chapter is adapted from a paper commissioned by the United Nations Office for the Coordination of Humanitarian Affairs for a Seminar on Lessons Learned on Humanitarian Coordination held in Stockholm in April, 1998. The author codirects the Humanitarianism and War Project, an independent policy research initiative based at Brown University in Providence, Rhode Island, that is underwritten by funds from several dozen UN organizations, governments, NGOs, and foundations. Most of the Project's publications referenced in this study are available at its Web site, http://www.brown.edu/Departments/Watson_Institute/H_W.

1.   This definition is adapted from one used in an early case study by the Humanitarianism and War Project. Cf. Larry Minear, U. B. P. Chelliah, Jeff Crisp, John Mackinlay and Thomas G. Weiss, *United Nations Coordination of the International Humanitarian Response to the Gulf Crisis, 1990–1992* (Providence, RI: Watson Institute, 1992).

2.   Steering Committee of the Joint Evaluation of Emergency Assistance to Rwanda, *International Response to Conflict and Genocide: Lessons from the Rwanda Experience* (Copenhagen: 1996), five volumes.

3.   Joint Evaluation Follow-Up Monitoring and Facilitation Network, "The Joint Evaluation of Emergency Assistance to Rwanda: A Review of Follow-Up and Impact One Year After Publication," February 2, 1997; and "The Joint Evaluation of Emergency Assistance to Rwanda: A Review of Follow-Up and Impact Fifteen Months After Publication," June 12, 1997, *Journal of Humanitarian Assistance*.

4.   Sue Lautze, Bruce D. Jones and Mark Duffield, *Strategic Humanitarian Coordination in the Great Lakes Region, 1996–97: An Independent Assessment* (New York: IASC, March 15, 1998).

5.   Lautze et al., *op. cit.*, para. 118. (Note: citations refer to the draft report, dated January 10, 1998; the paragraph numbers have been deleted and the text itself may have been altered in the final report, which was not available at this writing.)

6.   Antonio Donini and Norah Niland, *Lessons Learned: A Report on the Coordination of Humanitarian Activities in Rwanda* (New York: UN Department of Humanitarian Affairs, November 1994), pp. 8–9. The typology was later applied to two other crises in Antonio Donini, *The Policies of Mercy: UN Coordination in Afghanistan, Mozambique, and Rwanda* (Providence, RI: Watson Institute, 1996).

7.   *Ibid.*, pp. 37–38.

8.   Lautze et al., *op. cit.*, para. 107.

9.   Donini and Niland, *op. cit.*, page 38.

10. Lautze et al., *op. cit.*, para. 7.

11. *Ibid.*, para. 274.

12. For an initial review of the issues, see Larry Minear, in collaboration with Tabyiegen A. Aboum, Eshetu Chole, Koste Manibe, Abdul Mohammed, Jennefer Sobstad and Thomas G. Weiss, *Humanitarianism Under Siege: A Critical Review of Operation Lifeline Sudan* (Trenton, NJ: Red Sea Press, 1991). For a detailed update of the situation, see Barbara Hendrie, Ataul Karim, Mark Duffield, Susanne Jaspars, Aldo Benini, Joanna Macrae, Mark Bradbury, Douglas Johnson and George Larbi. *Operation Lifeline Sudan: A Review* (no publisher or place of publication given; July 1996). For a review of the 1996 study, see Larry Minear, "Time to Pull the Plug on Operation Lifeline Sudan?" *Crosslines Global Report*, March/April 1997, pp. 59–60.

13. Larry Minear, Tabyiegen A. Aboum, Eshetu Chole, Koste Manibe, Abdul Mohammed, Jennefer Sebstad and Thomas G. Weiss, *A Review of Operation Lifeline Sudan: A Report to the Aid Agencies* (Providence, RI: Watson Institute, 1990), p. 44.

14. James Ingram, "The Future Architecture for International Humanitarian Assistance," in: Thomas G. Weiss and Larry Minear (eds.), *Humanitarianism Across Borders: Sustaining Civilians in Times of War* (Boulder CO and London: Lynne Rienner, 1993), p. 183.

15. For an elaboration of the comparison, see Minear et al., *Humanitarian Action in the*

Former Yugoslavia, op. cit., particularly "Dealing with Belligerents Who Defy International Humanitarian Law" (pp. 78–85). A description of the UN negotiation of humanitarian access to East Moister in August to September 1993, which involved agreeing to "a series of complex and unattractive collateral agreements," is provided by Cedric Thornberry in "Peacekeepers, Humanitarian Aid and Civil Conflicts," in Jim Whitman and David Pocock, eds., *After Rwanda: The Coordination of United Nations Humanitarian Assistance* (London: Macmillan, 1996), p. 238 ff.

16. Lautze et al., report dated March 15, 1998, p. 85.

17. Lautze et al., para. 79.

18. For an elaboration of the point, see Minear et al., *Humanitarian Actions in the Former Yugoslavia, op. cit.*, particularly "Protecting the Integrity of Humanitarian Action," pp. 92–102.

19. Inter-Agency Standing Committee, *Respect for Humanitarian Mandates in Conflict Situations* (New York: United Nations, 1996).

20. The innovations made and the changes introduced in humanitarian institutions in the post-Cold-War period are analyzed in Thomas G. Weiss and Larry Minear, *The Dynamics of Learning by Humanitarian Institutions after the Cold War: An Evolving Introduction to the Issues* (Providence, RI: Watson Institute, forthcoming), p. 4.

21. Joint Evaluation Follow-Up Monitoring and Facilitation Network, "The Joint Evaluation of Emergency Assistance to Rwanda: A Review of Follow-up and Impact One Year After Publication," February 2, 1997; and "The Joint Evaluation of Emergency Assistance to Rwanda: A Review of Follow-up and Impact Fifteen Months After Publication," June 12, 1997.

22. Weiss and Minear, *Dynamics, op. cit.*, p. 5.

23. It was not possible within the limited time and scope of the current paper to review the impact of evaluations by individual governments on their respective humanitarian and political processes. However, it is understood that recommendations made in individual studies have accelerated the process of institutional change.

24. Lautze et. al., *op. cit.*, para., 213.

25. JEFF, *op. cit.*, June 12, 1997, p. 70 [emphasis in original].

26. Department of Peacekeeping Operations, "Comprehensive Report on Lessons Learned from United Nations Assistance Mission for Rwanda (UNAMIR), October 1993–April 1996," *op. cit.*, para. 4, p. 2.

27. A/Res/46/182, December 17, 1991.

28. For example, an NGO training course, funded by USAID and mounted by InterAction, is described in *Monday Developments*, March 9, 1998 (Vol. 16, No. 4), pp. 1, 10–11.

29. Development Assistance Committee, *Conflict, Peace and Development Co-operation on the Threshold of the 21st Century* (Paris: OECD, 1998), pp. 8, 35.

30. UN General Assembly, "The Promotion and Protection of the Rights of Children: Impact of Armed Conflict on Children" (A/51/306, August 26, 1996).

31. WHO Division of Emergency and Humanitarian Action, "Summary Record, EHA Consultation with Donors and Collaborating Agencies on the Role of WHO in Complex Emergencies," March 3, 1997, p. 1.

32. "Draft Report of the Tripartite Lessons Learned Study of the Great Lakes Emergency Operation Since September 1996," prepared by UNICEF, the UN High Commissioner for Refugees and the UN World Food Program, March 1998.

33. Tripartite Study, *op. cit.*, paras. 8–9.

34. Larry Minear, "The Evolving Humanitarian Enterprise," in: Thomas G. Weiss, *The United Nations and Civil Wars* (Boulder, CO, and London: Lynne Rienner, 1995), pp. 89–106.

35. *Ibid.*, pp. 64–65.

36. JEFF, *op. cit.*, February 2, 1997, p. 9.

37. Cindy Collins and Thomas G. Weiss, *An Overview and Assessment of 1989–1996 Peace Operations Publications* (Providence, RI: Watson Institute, 1997). The ALNAP database now lists several hundred titles, although it limits its catalog to works more strictly defined as "evaluations."

38. Joanna Macrae, "The Death of Humanitarianism? An Anatomy of the Attack," paper prepared for a conference entitled, "The Emperor's New Clothes: The Collapse of Humanitarian Principles," Disasters Emergency Committee, London, February 4, 1998, p. 1.

39. Larry Minear, David Cortright, Julia Wagler, George A. Lopez and Thomas G. Weiss, *Toward More Humane and Effective Sanctions Management: Enhancing the Capacity of the United Nations System* (Providence, RI: Watson Institute, 1998).

40. For a description of the efforts by UNHCR to improve the functioning of the system, cf. Pirkko Kourula, "International Protection of Refugees and Sanctions: Humanizing the Blunt Instrument," in *International Journal of Refugee Law*, Vol. 9, No. 2, 1997, pp. 255–265.

41. Letter dated February 20, from the Secretary-General addressed to the President of the Security Council, S/1998/147.

ABOUT THE AUTHORS

Fazle H. Abed is the Founder and Executive Director of BRAC, the leading non-governmental development organization in Bangladesh. Dr. Abed has received numerous international awards, including the Ramon Magsaysay Award for Community Leadership, UNESCO Noma Prize for Literacy, Alan Shawn Feinstein World Hunger Award and Maurice Pate Award. He has also been a Visiting Scholar at the Harvard Institute for International Development.

H. E. Mr. Kofi Annan is Secretary-General of the United Nations. Previously, he served as UN Under-Secretary-General for Peacekeeping Operations, Assistant Secretary-General for Personnel, Controller and Special Representative to the former Yugoslavia.

Kevin M. Cahill, M.D., is the President of the Center for International Health and Cooperation. He also serves as Director of the Tropical Disease Center at Lenox Hill Hospital in New York, Professor and Chairman of the Department of International Health at the Royal College of Surgeons in Ireland and Clinical Professor of Tropical Medicine at New York University School of Medicine and is senior consultant to the United Nations Health Service and to numerous foreign governments.

Partha Dasgupta is Professor of Economics and Chairman of the Faculty of Economics and Politics at the University of Cambridge. Previously, he was Professor of Economics, Professor of Philosophy and Director of the Program in Ethics in Society at Stanford University. He has written extensively on the economics of destitution, economic demography and political philosophy. Professor Dasgupta is President of the Royal Economic Society and President of the European Economic Association.

Mary F. Diaz is the Executive Director of the Women's Commission for Refugee Women and Children, a nonprofit advocacy and education organization devoted to improving conditions for refugee communities around the world. She also chairs the UNICEF-NGO Working Group on Children in Armed Conflict and is a member of the Women's Foreign Policy Group. Prior to joining the Women's Commission, Ms. Diaz ran a refugee and immigration organization and managed various projects in the field of international education.

Jan Eliasson is Secretary of State for Foreign Affairs of Sweden. He was Sweden's Ambassador to the United Nations from 1988 to 1992 and served as the first UN Under-Secretary-General for Humanitarian Affairs. Ambassador Eliasson has mediated in the Iran-Iraq and Nagorno-Karabakh conflicts.

Richard Falk is Albert G. Milbank Professor of International Law and Practice at Princeton University. He is the author of *Human Rights and State Sovereignty, On Humane Governance: Toward a New Global Politics* and, most recently, *Law in an Emerging Global Village: A Post-Westphalian Perspective.*

Abdulrahim Abby Farah, a Director of the Center for International Health and Cooperation, served for twenty years as Under-Secretary-General and Senior Political Advisor on African Affairs in the United Nations. He also served as Somalia's Ambassador to Ethiopia and Permanent Representative to the United Nations.

Rev. Aengus Finucane, C.S.S.p., has worked for more than thirty years for the poorest, beginning in Biafra in 1968. Most of his career has been with Concern Worldwide, the Irish-based international relief and development agency that he helped found thirty years ago. He spent the last sixteen years as Chief Executive of the organization and is currently Honorary President of Concern Worldwide USA in New York.

Nigel Fisher is currently Visiting United Nations Fellow at the Canadian Centre for Foreign Policy Development in Ottawa and advises the Minister of Foreign Affairs on Canadian foreign policy regarding children affected by armed conflict. Prior to that, he served with UNICEF for more than twenty years in Africa, Asia and the Middle East, including in several countries affected by civil conflict. He was UNICEF's Special Representative in Rwanda in 1994 and 1995 and was Director of UNICEF's Office of Emergency Operations before his return to Canada in 1998.

Shepard Forman is Director of the Center on International Cooperation at New York University, a policy research institute devoted to the improved management and financing of the international public sector. He has taught anthropology and development studies at Indiana University, the University of Chicago and the University of Michigan and authored and edited three books and numerous articles based on his fieldwork in Brazil and East Timor. He was formerly Director of the Ford Foundation's Human Rights and Governance and International Affairs program.

H. Jack Geiger, M.D., MPH, Sc.D. (hon.), is the Arthur C. Logan Professor Emeritus of Community Medicine, City University of New York Medical School. Most of his career has been focused on the problems of health, poverty and human rights. He is a founding member and past President of Physicians for Human Rights and of Physicians for Social Responsibility and is the current President of the Committee for Health in Southern Africa.

Philip Johnston worked for CARE for thirty-four years, the last fifteen as its President. During late 1992 and early 1993, while on a leave of absence from CARE, Dr. Johnston was the United Nations Coordinator of Humanitarian Relief in Somalia.

Jennifer Leaning, M.D., S.M.H., is Senior Research Fellow at the Harvard Center for Population and Development Studies, Assistant Professor of Medicine, Harvard Medical School, and Attending Physician in the Department of Emergency Medicine, Brigham and Women's Hospital. She is lead editor of *Humanitarian Crises: The Medical and Public Health Response*, Editor-in-Chief of the journal *Medicine and Global Survival* and a member of the Board of Directors for Physicians for Human Rights.

Larry Minear directs the Humanitarian and War Project at the Thomas J. Watson Jr. Institute for International Studies, Brown University, Providence, Rhode Island. Prior to the inception of the Project in 1991, he headed the Office for Development Policy of Church World Service and Lutheran World Relief. He has written widely on humanitarian and development issues.

Sadako Ogata is the United Nations High Commissioner for Refugees. Prior to her appointment as Commissioner, Mrs. Ogata was Dean of the Faculty of Foreign Studies at Sophia University in Tokyo, the Representative of Japan on the United Nations Commission on Human Rights, and Chair of the Executive Board of UNICEF.

Lord David Owen, M.D., former Foreign Secretary of the United Kingdom, has also served in his government as a Member of Parliament, Minister of the Navy and Minister of Health. He helped to found the Social Democratic Party (SDP) and was its leader for almost a decade. He has been a member of the Independent Commission on Disarmament and Security Issues and the Independent Commission on International Humanitarian Issues.

Joelle Tanguy has worked with Doctors Without Borders since 1989 and has been Executive Director of Doctors Without Borders USA since 1994. She has led emergency and refugee operations for the organization in Uganda, eastern Zaire, Armenia, Somalia and Bosnia; consulted on funding projects; assisted in the development of MSF in Japan and Australia; and coauthored a number of publications in this field.

Michael J. Toole, M.D., is a medical epidemiologist and head of the International Health Unit at the Macfarlane Burnet Center in Melbourne, Australia. He has worked with OXFAM, MSF and the U.S. Centers for Disease Control in epidemics and war zones throughout Africa and Asia.

Cyrus Vance, former U.S. Secretary of State, has been a Personal Envoy of the Secretary-General of the United Nations. A naval officer in World War II, he later served as Secretary of the Army and as Deputy Secretary of Defense.

Michel Veuthey has been with the ICRC for thirty years (with the Legal Division, then Head of the Division of International Organizations, Assistant to the President and then Regional Delegate for Southern Africa). He has written articles and a book on International Humanitarian Law and has a Doctorate of Laws from Geneva University.

THE CENTER FOR INTERNATIONAL HEALTH AND COOPERATION

The Center for International Health and Cooperation was founded by a small group of physicians and diplomats who believe that health and other humanitarian endeavors sometimes provide the only common ground for initiating dialogue, understanding and cooperation among people and nations shattered by war, civil conflicts and ethnic violence. The center has devised a widely accepted diploma course to train workers for humanitarian crises (the International Diploma in Humanitarian Assistance), has sponsored symposia and published books, including *Silent Witnesses*; *A Framework for Survival: Health, Human Rights and Humanitarian Assistance in Conflicts and Disasters*; *A Directory of Somali Professionals*; and *Clearing the Fields: Solutions to the Landmine Crisis*, that reflect this philosophy. The center and its directors have been deeply involved in trying to alleviate the wounds of war in Somalia and the former Yugoslavia. A CIHC amputee center in northern Somalia developed a model program, one that would be replicated in other war zones where there is an urgent need for simple, rapid and inexpensive prostheses. In the former Yugoslavia, the CIHC has been active in prisoner and hostage release and in legal assistance for human and political rights violations and has facilitated discussions between combatants.

The center has been accorded full consultative status at the United Nations. In the United States it is a fully approved charitable agency.

DIRECTORS

Kevin M. Cahill (President)
Cyrus Vance
David Owen
Paul Hamlyn
Boutros Boutros-Ghali
Jan Eliasson
Peter Tarnoff
Daniel Boyer
Eoin O'Brien
Abdulrahim Abby Farah

INDEX

Abed, Fazle H., 187, 257–70
Abgal subclan, 34
accountability, 174–75
actors, array of, 298–316
Afghanistan, 50, 54, 239
African Charter on the Rights and
  Welfare of the Child, 80, 89
African Development Bank, 293
Africa Watch, 36
Agenda for Peace (Boutros-Ghali),
  47–48, 133–34, 193, 318
Agreement on Groundrules, Sudan
  People's Liberation Movement/
  Operation Sudan Lifeline, 82–85
Aidid, Mohammed, 34–37, 40, 43–44
AIDS: in Europe, 243; and girls,
  68–70; as global, 160–61; and nutri-
  tion, 144; among refugees, 19; in
  Rwanda, 53–54; and stability of
  states, 1–2
Algeria, 85
American Jewish Committee, 248
American Medical Association (AMA),
  106–7
American Medical Student
  Association (AMSA), 101–3
Amnesty International, 83, 98, 232
Andrews, David, 253
anemia, 146
Annan, Kofi, 156

appeals: consolidated, 192, 283–88,
  292; weighing of, 171–74
Aristide, Jean-Bertrand, 218
assessment, 170–71, 299–306, 308–9
Association of American Medical
  Colleges, 106
Association of Southeast Asian
  Nations, 155
Avions Sans Frontières, 236, 243

Bangladesh, 257–70
Bangladesh Rural Advancement
  Committee (BRAC), 260–70
Banta, J. E., 102
Barre, Siad, 5, 34, 254
Bhutanese Refugees Aiding Victims
  of Violence, 59
Biafra, 83–84, 226–29, 245–50
bilateral aid, 253–54, 282–84
Boissier, Pierre, 119
Borel, Raymond, 229
Bosnia: vs. Africa, 45–46, 162, 253;
  diplomacy on, 123–27, 143–35;
  NATO in, 157; rape in, 69, 81; UN
  in, 196, 202, 207–8, 303–4
Bosnian Women's Initiative (BWI),
  52, 58
Boutros-Ghali, Boutros, 8, 46–48,
  133–34, 184–85, 193, 253, 318
Brauman, Rony, 234